MARTIAL CULTURE, SILVER SCREEN

MARTIAL CULTURE SILVER SCREEN

War Movies and the Construction of American Identity

EDITED BY
MATTHEW CHRISTOPHER HULBERT
AND MATTHEW E. STANLEY

Louisiana State University Press ||| Baton Rouge

Published by Louisiana State University Press
www.lsupress.org

Copyright © 2020 by Louisiana State University Press
All rights reserved. Except in the case of brief quotations used in articles or reviews,
no part of this publication may be reproduced or transmitted in any format or by
any means without written permission of Louisiana State University Press.

DESIGNER: Michelle A. Neustrom
TYPEFACE: Whitman

Cover image courtesy stevecoleimages/iStock.com.

Cataloging-in-Publication Data are available from the Library of Congress.

ISBN 978-0-8071-7134-9 (cloth) — ISBN 978-0-8071-7472-2 (paperback) —
ISBN 978-0-8071-7470-8 (pdf) — ISBN 978-0-8071-7471-5 (epub)

CONTENTS

Introduction
American War Films—An Archive of Us Imagining Ourselves
MATTHEW CHRISTOPHER HULBERT AND MATTHEW E. STANLEY / 1

History, Sir, Will Tell Lies as Usual
Founders, Patriots, and the War for Independence on Film
KYLIE A. HULBERT / 21

Attacking Antebellum Slavery on Screen
Hollywood Portrayals of Militant Emancipation, 1937–2016
JASON PHILLIPS / 47

No, Will, He Just Died
The Abandonment of Triumphalism in Recent Civil War Films
BRIAN MATTHEW JORDAN / 65

The Indian Wars for the American West
Custer, Costner, and Colonialism
ANDREW R. GRAYBILL / 84

Manifest Mythology
Cinematic Distortions of Antebellum American
Imperialism and Manhood
JAMES HILL "TRAE" WELBORN III / 103

To End War and Bring Peace
World War I, Peace, and Antiwar Films
LIZ CLARKE / 142

Heroes and Superheroes
The Twenty-First-Century World War II Film
RICHARD N. GRIPPALDI AND ANDREW C. MCKEVITT / 160

The Forgotten War in American Film
The Evolving Portrayal of the Korean Conflict
DAVID KIERAN / 189

We Have Seen the Enemy and He Is Us
Hollywood, the Cold War, and Battling the Enemy Within
JESSICA M. CHAPMAN / 214

Survivors of Natural Disaster
American Identity in Vietnam War Films
MEREDITH H. LAIR / 233

Virtually There
The War on Terror
CALVIN FAGAN / 261

List of Contributors / 293

Index / 297

MARTIAL CULTURE, SILVER SCREEN

American War Films

An Archive of Us Imagining Ourselves

MATTHEW CHRISTOPHER HULBERT AND MATTHEW E. STANLEY

Act 1, Scene 1: The Opening

I t was the war that began during the pinnacle of Hollywood's golden age. Well-known directors like John Ford went to work as documentarians and photographers for the Office of Strategic Services. Some of the film industry's biggest stars, including Henry Fonda, Clark Gable, and Jimmy Stewart served in uniform—as did future leading men such as Charles Bronson, Paul Newman, Charlton Heston, Lee Marvin, and Audie Murphy. (Some Hollywood mainstays, such as Ward Bond, attempted to enlist but were rejected on genuine medical grounds; others, most notably Bond's close friend and frequent collaborator, John Wayne, used various deferments to avoid active duty.) Yet even as the Second World War raged in Europe and the Pacific—and even as so many marquee names had swapped make-up trailers and backlots for foxholes and cockpits—moviemakers in southern California were fast at work simulating the combat, exoticizing the locales, and dramatizing the home fronts in now-classic films such as *Foreign Correspondent* (1940), *49th Parallel* (1941), *Casablanca* (1942), *Destination Tokyo* (1943), *Sahara* (1943), *The Sullivans* (1944), and *The Best Years of Our Lives* (1946).[1]

Off-screen, beyond Sunset and celluloid, the real war proved the most lethal event in human history. The deterioration of military philosophy that historian Jay Winter calls "civilianization," combined with economic catastrophe among the world's most powerful nations, provided an opening for authoritarian ideologies. With economic liberalism in a death spiral, political liberalism retreated. The world's number of constitutionally elected governments shrunk by two-thirds between 1920 and 1944. Fascism filled much of the void. Appealing to their own artifacts of the past (a "return to national greatness"), these new anti-liberal and anti-communist regimes used older notions of national and ethnic identity to facilitate blood-and-soil nationalism, fundamentalist race theories, and genocide. The total war triggered by these developments combined fully industrialized killing technologies, the construction of the largest armies the world had ever known, and a blurring of the lines that had traditionally demarcated soldier from civilian in the Western world. Whether by bullet, bomb, disease, starvation, or pogrom, all told, the Second World War generated some 70,000,000 corpses.[2]

The blood spilled between 1939 and 1945 was not meted out equally, however. Such was particularly the case in Europe. Great Britain, the nation at war with Nazi Germany the longest, suffered approximately 450,000 combined soldier and civilian deaths. Meanwhile, roughly 75 percent of all United States servicemen and servicewomen killed during the war fell in the European Theater—a total of around 300,000 fatalities. The loss in human life for the other major Allied power, the Soviet Union, was so devastating as to render it incomparable. At least 27,000,000 Russian soldiers and civilians died waging the Nazi-Soviet war between June 1941 and May 1945. Roughly 60 percent of Russian families lost a member of their immediate family unit, or of what would become widely known as their "nuclear family" in postwar America.[3] Put another way, for every single American who died fighting the Germans, eighty Soviets died doing the same thing. Incredibly, 3 out of every 4 German soldiers killed in combat during the war were dispatched by a Russian.

There exists a broad consensus among historians regarding the primacy of the Eastern Front and the Soviet role. Even Western scholars agree that the Red Army was primarily responsible for victory over Hitler, with many asserting that the Soviets would have defeated the Nazis without either Anglo-American aid or military intervention.[4] Even British nationalist and staunch anti-communist Winston Churchill called the Red Army advance after Stalingrad "the greatest cause of Hitler's undoing . . . the guts of the German army largely torn out by Russian valour."[5] But objective history and collective memory seldom converge. Case in point: a 2015 YouGov poll, conducted in the United States and Western Europe, approximate to the seventieth anniversary of V-E Day, asked respondents which country had done the most to defeat Nazi Germany. Americans overwhelmingly cited their own role as the most critical to rolling back Nazi domination; in turn, no less surprisingly, the British believed they had contributed most to the Allied victory. Even though the Red Army waged the war's costliest campaigns, seized the most German territory, and vanquished the German capital in the war's final battle, in no country polled did the Soviet

Union top the list.[6] In fact, the narrative of US victory has grown exponentially since 1945, at least in parts of Western Europe. A 1945 poll revealed that 57 percent of the French public believed the USSR had contributed the most to Allied victory. By 2015, 15 percent believed that to be the case.

This is of course not to minimize the suffering or sacrifices of common Yanks and Tommies, only to scrutinize the cultural work done ostensibly on their behalf. In other words, why the striking gulf between history and memory with regard to the role that nations—not individual soldiers—played in surmounting the Third Reich? Answers run the gamut from Cold War geopolitics to generational factors to cultural orientation.[7] But the discrepancy also lies in the effectiveness of American institutions in constructing and perpetuating notions of US military supremacy, not during, but perhaps especially *since* the Second World War.

In Hollywood, this "*Saving Private Ryan* effect" is a result of cinematically expressed ideas and aesthetics within and beyond the World War II canon.[8] As Paul Fussell acknowledges, popular coverage of D-Day has been thorough, perhaps even disproportionately so.[9] In addition to altering and contorting historical significance, commemoration can sometimes supplant the event it seeks to commemorate. For instance, although US armies reached zero Nazi death camps (all of which lay east of Berlin), Western-liberated work camps and concentration camps have grown in popular memory in direct proportion to American involvement. Along with the most ignominious of Final Solution sites, Auschwitz-Birkenau (featured in *Sophie's Choice*, 1982; *Triumph of the Spirit*, 1989; *Schindler's List*, 1993; *The Grey Zone*, 2001; and in *Mr. Death*, a 1999 documentary chronicling the bizarre story of self-taught engineer-turned-Holocaust-denier Fred A. Leuchter Jr.), Western publics now know the names of concentration camps such as Belsen and Dachau above those of the major death facilities of Treblinka, Sobibór, Bełżec, Chełmno, and Majdanek not only because they were liberated by British and American forces, but also due to their representation in film media. Though not an extermination camp and not among the top fifteen Holocaust killing sites in terms of estimated deaths, Kaufering and its principal camp, Dachau, now a major tourist site, have been highlighted in Hollywood productions including *Band of Brothers* (2001) and *Shutter Island* (2010).[10]

Big-screen representations of wars often influence popular metanarratives in history and trends in collective remembrance well beyond the bounds of the specific conflict they depict. Filmic portraits of the blood-red tides of Normandy and the corpse-littered sands of Iwo Jima loom large in the Western imagination, clearly. Yet there is an undeniable tether—if an admittedly more oblique one—tying together mass perceptions of the past, the more generalized reach of American war movies, and American identity. The zombie allegories of George A. Romero shaped collective attitudes toward the Vietnam War at the same time the soldierly performances of George C. Scott wielded imagery of a "Good War" to recast perceptions of a "quagmire." Those representations were, consequently, reshaped by the rights to violence, heroic individualism, and national redemption of characters like John Rambo (Sylvester Stallone, *Rambo: First Blood, Part I*, 1982), James Braddock (Chuck Norris, *Missing in Action*, 1984), and even Alan "Dutch" Schaefer (Arnold Schwarzenegger, *Predator*, 1987). Thereby, far-reaching depictions of American wars involving patriotic and redemptive stories of reverence toward the nation—as well as counterthemes of military overreach, defeat, and imperial retreat—have all conditioned the way audiences perceive American violence, belligerency, and supremacy.

Act 2, Scene 1: The Idea

Martial Culture, Silver Screen explores this relationship between American wars, collective memory, and national identities forged in violence as it relates to cinema. As the long-established center and apogee of the motion picture industry, Hollywood has both created a unique relationship between Americans and the movies and spawned a disproportionate emphasis on American-centric histories and perspectives. In that context, this volume is especially concerned with how movies operate within what Eric Hobsbawm and Terence Ranger identify as the "invention of tradition": the establishment of social cohesion through collective identities; the legitimization of social institutions and hierarchies; and the socialization of people into particular positions, ranks, and contexts.[11] "Invented traditions" are created collective practices that lay claim to a historical basis by dipping selectively—and fictitiously—into the past in order to inculcate specific values and achieve particular functions in the present. However, this facade of continuity can be "disrupted" by revolutions, progressive movements, and shifting balances of social power, as well as by the delineations in pop culture and media wrought by such social changes.[12]

The nation-state, and concomitant national borders, national languages, and understandings of nationalism, are striking examples of "traditions" that have been "invented" in the modern world yet claim to be "natural" and eternal realities. The nation is also a mechanism through which such traditions are formulated and reproduced, constituting what Anthony D. Smith terms "the most compelling identity myth in the modern world."[13] The collective "sense of self" based on notions of shared history and spatial-political sovereignty, national identity is a cultural phenomenon that is essential to the functioning and legitimacy of the nation-state. Both producing and produced from dominant ideologies, and often based on oppositional postures toward different or antagonistic "others," national identity conditions people to self-understand in terms of nation-first, rather than according to class, religion, gender, race, language, or other social demarcations (though political nations may build on such commonalities). Crises, notably war, tend to heighten these centripetal impulses of "us" and "them," "we" and "they."[14] Likewise, national identity, such as that developed in France and elsewhere during the Age of Revolutions, emphasizes degrees of civic nationalism, in which national identity is governed by legally defined territory and those common belonging to the body politic therein. However, it might also underscore racial nationalism, in which national loyalty is determined primarily by racial, genetic, or ethnocultural features (the most infamous example being Nazi Germany). Because the United States has historically contained elements of both civic and racial nationalism, our interest is in national identity as a rather expansive concept, which may entail near-universal acceptance *or* be restricted to how more particular groups view themselves as the ultimate archetypes of the nation-state. Most critically, national identity relies on the creation, reception, and continuous reconstitution of a shared past.

Nowhere in American life is "invented" national identity disseminated more widely than through filmic representations of American men and women waging war. Ranging from colonial times to the Civil War to the World Wars to the War on Terror, depictions of these conflicts—of their causes, of the men and women who wage them, of the home front that undergirds (or betrays) them, of the enemy forces that must be vanquished in them, and of the modes of violence judged civil and uncivil within them—have been employed to wield immense social, cultural, political, and economic control in the relative present. Films, as well as television shows, popular texts, video games, and public art, cast and recast the American martial past. They frame ideological positions; create political communities and networks of celebration or grief; confirm victimhood or heroism; transmit and alleviate latent communal stains and neuroses; cement tradition and convention, or reject it. And all create and destroy myth, sometimes simultaneously. In other words, movies are powerful identity-forging apparatuses, portraying past wars and promoting the prevailing values that make current and future wars possible and sometimes even seemingly desirable.[15] In this way, collective memory narratives emanated from Hollywood are part and parcel of ideology, or the terrain of conscious and subconscious "systems of ideas" and practices that relate to configurations of power.[16] Specifically, these narratives form part of an established national militaristic ideology which, among other things, and through the manufacture of consent, is the intellective device that "persuades men and women to mistake each other from time to time for gods or vermin."[17]

Owing to such notions, this book is dedicated to laying bare how motion picture representations of warfare and memories of warfare have been used in the construction and evolution of national identity. These themes can and should be used for the broader purposes of investigating distinctive notions of exceptionalism, individualism, democracy, pluralism, militarism, capitalism, space, and expansionism. Per the "Good War" thesis, each contributor probes how Americans have understood and continue to understand themselves through ideas of "uniquely American warfare" and how they interact with the popular materials that foster those understandings in different times, places, political environments, and socioeconomic settings. In short, essayists have been tasked with analyzing how and why Americans use war movies to understand what it actually means to be American and, as a result, to establish who and what "belongs" within the American experience. Without exception, they have each accomplished that mission with colors flying high.

Act 2, Scene 2: The Book

Regarding the chronological structure of the book, the film-selection process, and an editorial promise: First, the essays will proceed in chronological order of conflict discussed, beginning with the American Revolution and ending with the slightly more amorphous War on Terror. Within the texts themselves, authors are free to discuss films from different eras in whatever order or in whatever comparative arrangement they deem most effective. (In short, this book is not organized by decades of film production.)

Second, our contributors had complete discretion in their respective filmographies. We did, however, encourage authors to grapple with recent productions, and quite a few of their essays offer inaugural analysis of certain films. In some cases, such as the American Revolution or the Korean War, fewer films made for less agonizing processes of selection. In others, like the Indian Wars, the World Wars, and Vietnam, logistical considerations (that is, the book could not be thousands of pages) necessitated old standards and favorites not receiving primary treatment. Pictures like *The Longest Day* (1962), *Midway* (1976), *Patton* (1970), *M.A.S.H.* (1970), *The Great Escape* (1963), *Seven Days in May* (1964), *She Wore a Yellow Ribbon* (1949), *Fort Apache* (1948), *The Steel Helmet* (1951), *Lawrence of Arabia* (1962), or *The African Queen* (1951) did not make the final cut.

Third, our essayists come from several different disciplines within the humanities—from film studies, cultural studies, and communications to history and American studies—and they hail from the United States, Canada, and Great Britain. They also all share in our belief that it would be something like a sin against the movie gods to produce a book on this topic solely for other academics. This is to say that we have assembled a diverse group of experts and tasked them with the steepest of stylistic and methodological climbs: penning incisive, analytical essays in the jargon-free prose and with the dynamic narratives needed to make them fully accessible to nonacademic readers. As editors, we have included a "manifesto" of sorts—immediately following the essay summaries below—for the dual purpose of defining terminology and providing our fundamental approaches to film, memory, and identity construction. While perhaps not of the greatest interest to nonacademic readers, we felt this to be a worthwhile tool for enabling further scholarly debate.

Act 2, Scene 3: The Previews

Kylie Hulbert's contribution outlines the two commemorative paradigms that dominate American memories of the Revolution of 1776: the everyman colonist-turned-killing-machine v. the pen-wielding Founders with lofty intellects and loftier principles. Combining well-known films like *The Patriot* (2000) and *1776* (1972) with lesser-known offerings such as *The Scarlet Coat* (1955), *The Devil's Disciple* (1959), and even the truly dreadful *Revolution* (1985), she offers up a dichotomous arrangement not unlike the elusive electron of a Higgs boson particle (which can be predicted or pinpointed, but never each at the same time); in simpler terms, Hulbert blueprints an arrangement in which Americans rely on both revolutionary traditions in cinema to make sense of the nation's "Big Bang"—but can never seem to reconcile nor utilize both versions simultaneously.

In his essay, Jason Phillips reconceptualizes the violent, abolitionist struggle that preceded the Civil War as not just the root cause of that mammoth conflict but as a war *unto itself*. He enlists a trio of pre-civil rights movement films featuring John Brown from the 1930s, 1940s, and 1950s—including the often-overlooked *Souls at Sea* (1937)—for comparison with modern depictions of violent antislavery activities in pictures like *Django Unchained* (2012) and the controversial *The Birth of a Nation* (2016). As Phillips ultimately argues, the ways in which many Americans justify violence as it relates to emancipation—whether in the form of white terrorism or a slave-led revolt—has not changed nearly as much as we might like to imagine.

With cutting-edge takes on *Free State of Jones* (2016) and *The Beguiled* (2017), among several other recent pictures, Brian Matthew Jordan plots a cultural trend borne of shifting historiographical boundaries: triumphal, reconciliatory renditions of the Civil War have almost entirely given way to darker and less politically gratifying interpretations of the conflict. And as Jordan reveals in his assessment of this gritty turn in Civil War cinema, the shift toward irregular violence, home-front destruction, emotional trauma, and political dissent have made it increasingly difficult for everyday Americans to employ the war—once famously labeled "our only 'felt' history, history lived in the national imagination" by Robert Penn Warren—in conceiving present notions of Americanness. Or, in short, the more realistic representations of the rebirth of the Union become, the less contemporary Americans *feel* its history.

Andrew Graybill's coverage of the Indian wars on film dissects the "original sin of American history": the violent dispossession of Native peoples. Beginning with classics from the golden era of the western genre like *They Died with Their Boots On* (1941) and *The Searchers* (1956) before pivoting to successive waves of revisionist pictures—*Soldier Blue* (1970) and *Little Big Man* (1970), then *Dances With Wolves* (1990) and *Hostiles* (2017)—Graybill chronicles how the story Americans most liked to tell about themselves in the first half of the twentieth century—a narrative of rugged, individualistic cowboys and pioneers, settling the frontier and fulfilling the Republic's destiny—went out of style. He contends that newer understandings of trauma and combat changed both the genre of the western war film *and* how Americans use them.

James Hill Welborn's essay resituates involvement in seemingly un-American (literally) or lesser-known conflicts—the Texas Revolution of the 1830s, the occupation of the western territories hijacked from Mexico in the 1840s, and the unsanctioned invasions of Latin America by southern filibusters in the 1850s—within the context of American imperialism, slavery, and manhood. In doing so, he produces a far less flattering composite of Manifest Destiny on the big screen. On one hand, Welborn's readings of *The Alamo* (2004), *Walker* (1987), and *Ravenous* (1990) force readers to confront how "the West" of Frederick Jackson Turner's thesis was actually acquired and, perhaps most importantly, *why* it was desired. On the other hand, his essay exposes why films pushing contemporary Americans to own those details tend to flop at the box office.

Despite a number of international classics—films like G. W. Pabsts's *Westfront 1918* (1930) and *Kameradschaft* (1931), or Raymond Bernard's *Wooden Crosses* (1932)—which deal incisively with matters of nationalism, ethnicity, and class conflict, it is no secret that World War I has been, and still is, a popular vehicle for Hollywood to deliver generic, and at times clumsy, antiwar messages. The popularity of that purpose notwithstanding, by comparing standards of the genre such as *All Quiet on the Western Front* (1930) and *Johnny Got His Gun* (1971) to the recent megahit *Wonder Woman* (2017), Liz Clarke points out just how frequently American World War I pictures are divorced, historically and contextually, from the "War to End All Wars" itself. Her essay excavates the origins of that cinematic tradition in the United States and asserts that World War I essentially became an important tool for remembering later, unpopular conflicts in American history—at the expense of its own nuanced legacy.

Richard Grippaldi and Andrew McKevitt chronicle how Hollywood gradually remade the ideal of a war hero to suit modernizing tastes. From *The Longest Day* (1962) to *Saving Private Ryan* (1998), consensus history of the "Good War" reigned supreme in American culture; ordinary men rose to the occasion, beat back the grasps of fascism, and restored democracy to the Western World. But with the rise of recent films like *Fury* (2014), *Hacksaw Ridge* (2016), *Captain America* (2011), and *Unbroken* (2014), Grippaldi and McKevitt reveal how audiences have come to expect the extraordinary or even supernatural from GIs—and how, in turn, villains had to evolve into bigger and badder foes than mere Nazis or sword-wielding Imperial officers. As a result, their essay illustrates how the "Good War" narrative struggles to retain credibility amid the darker themes of war on screen: PTSD, graphic death, lingering emotional trauma, collateral damage, racism on the home front.

As David Kieran underscores in his treatment of Korean War movies, sometimes the act of intentionally forgetting is equal to, if not more powerful than, the acts of remembering and commemorating. By assessing *Hold Back the Night* and *War Hunt* alongside Clint Eastwood's *Gran Torino*, he explains why Korea is the war Americans love to ignore (often refusing to even label it as a "war" in the first place). Kieran also blueprints how being trapped between World War II—the "Good War" fought by the "Greatest Generation"—and Vietnam—perhaps the least popular war in US history in terms of marketing spin—influenced how Americans could and would engage with the Korean War, its unsatisfying conclusion, and most notably with the South Korean allies it left in such a bad way at fighting's end.

Because the Cold War spanned decades, it is one of the very few American wars to have films about it produced as it actually unfolded. Thereby, in her essay on Cold War cinema, Jessica Chapman deals with both pictures made during the era itself—such as *I Was a Communist for the FBI* (1951), *The Manchurian Candidate* (1962), and *Dr. Strangelove* (1964)—and more recent attempts—*Good Night and Good Luck* (2005) and *Trumbo* (2015)—to critique the brand of paranoia-based patriotism pushed by the likes of Joseph McCarthy, Burt the Turtle, and Hedda Hopper. Chapman uses notions of "the enemy" to plot how American values changed radically between the 1950s and 1960s and the present; she ultimately underscores how the main threat perceived by Hollywood has evolved from a caricatured "communist menace" to those Americans who would persecute their fellow citizens for refusing to conform.

Unlike Korea, Vietnam has inspired in Americans an insatiable appetite for war movies—even if they don't know exactly how to make sense of them. As Meredith Lair's exploration of Hollywood's "'Nam" reveals, the conflict so often categorized as a military "quagmire" in the 1960s has remained equally problematic—if not altogether unusable—as an engine for identity-building from the 1980s to the present. And by linking genre classics such as *The Deer Hunter* (1978) and *Born on the Fourth of July* (1989) with newer features like *Tigerland* (2000) and *We Were Soldiers* (2002), she illuminates both how movies represent the war as a natural disaster and why the real-life disaster of Vietnam was, in fact, anything but natural.

The "War on Terror" marks a major departure from its martial predecessors: it lacks a cut-and-dry chronology; it unfolds on computer screens as much as on battlefields; the enemy is frequently a non-state actor; and its results are broadcast to viewers in real time, 24/7. Calvin Fagan's essay charts how new methods of waging war have led directly to changes in the representation of American servicemen and servicewomen on screen. By interpreting *Body of*

Lies (2008), *Syriana* (2005), *Good Kill* (2014), *In the Valley of Elah* (2007), and *Stop-Loss* (2008), he assesses how remote killing technologies alter perceptions of combat at the same time that confrontations with PTSD and suicide alter perceptions of those doing the fighting. In other words, Fagan illuminates the counterintuitive consequences of waging such a technologically advanced, yet seemingly endless, war.

Act 3, Scene 1: The Manifesto—On Film

To begin, movies *are not* history. As reflections of their architects, they broadcast, consciously or not, wider social ideas about politics, gender, race, class, and, perhaps above all, nation. Movies *are* vectors of apperception and escape— and by design, of deception. Their production involves curatorial choices. This is precisely where their power is derived: people manipulate images and images manipulate people. They manufacture versions of the past in order to entertain, to reclaim the past, to justify the present, or all of the above. As highly selective constructions, they intentionally distort time, distance, judgment, and consciousness. Filmic visualizations of memory-history (or, as Woodrow Wilson may or may not have famously quipped in 1915, as "history written with lightning") serve as proxies for society's contemporary fears and anxieties. Within that messaging, the movie-viewer relationship is typically unequal, built on power dynamics favoring producer over consumer. The moviegoer, like the individual, is "a ready-made subject," prone to receive, process, or internalize the concepts cast on screen.[18] As a result, the actors, sets, and plots from specific films become the stock faces and environs of our historical imaginations; moreover, they become the basis upon which audiences engage interpretations of the past to classify, order, and suggest rank, and even to "other."

Like symbols and monuments, films are not the Word of God. Crafting national stories involves not only producing and remembering, but also dismantling and forgetting. Suppression can be subconscious, even therapeutic, and part of a collective coping strategy, or what Primo Levi referred to as the "fossilized lie." This impulse to invent unanimity in order to conceal or absolve is by no means unique to America and its cinematic traditions. In fact, it has taken on discrete national forms: French *résistancialisme*, the "Great Patriotic War" in Russia, and the British idea of a "People's War."[19] In the United States, the so-called "Greatest Generation" and the myth of the "Good War" are constitutive of broader ideas about American exceptionalism.[20]

To be sure, war movies hold a special dynamism in the broader invention of national identity. The decision to use military force—to annihilate or be annihilated—is the gravest decision a society or its government can make. Nevertheless, sanguine citizens often sleepwalk into war because they are conditioned to do so. The "call to arms" and the rush to war eschew criticism and confer meaning, even (and perhaps especially) if that meaning is presented as a morally simplistic "good" versus "evil." This moral binary often confers a pass for audiences to not only internalize the lessons of on-screen brutality, but to *enjoy* it, as in the case of *Inglorious Basterds* (2009) when Sgt. Donny "The Bear Jew" Donowitz beats a Nazi sergeant to death with a baseball bat and proudly screams "Teddy fuckin' Williams knocks it out of the park! Fenway Park on its feet for Teddy fuckin' Ballgame! He went yardo on that one, out to fuckin' Lansdowne Street!"

War movies, then, add coherence; they provide purpose and security to what Mark Twain labeled "the killing of strangers against whom you feel no personal animosity." For as combat journalist Chris Hedges avows, war is "peddled by myth-makers—historians, war correspondents, film makers, novelists, and the state—all of whom endow it with qualities it often does possess: excitement, exoticism, power, chances to rise above our small stations in life and a bizarre and fantastic universe that has a grotesque and dark beauty."[21] This emphasis on the more seductive aspects of war—rather than victimhood, trauma, and arbitrary death—is part of an ideological mechanism that obscures questions of interests and renders the dissenter an apostate. As in the case of *The Green Berets* (1968), which used World War II and western genre tropes to condemn antiwar journalists and justify American military intervention in Southeast Asia, ideology is sometimes blatant, even farcical.[22]

In other instances, including *The Hanoi Hilton* (1987), which borrows from a 1940s and 1950s cinematic likeness of the "sadistic Asian," thereby equating imperial Japan with North Vietnam, and fascism with anticolonialism, ideology is expressed through suggestion, imagery, innuendo, and metaphor.[23] In either case, the most profound utility of war films is one of identifying external enemies and fostering unanimity amid vast internal differences, conflicts, or injustices. Westerns, for instance, rather than portrayals of the Civil War and its domestic discord, became the preferred war genre in part *because* they so easily lent themselves to the construction of national (and racial) "others," serving as a vindication of so-called American values (rugged individualism) and mission (foreign and economic policy) during the Cold War.[24]

But the function and net impact of cinema extends well beyond distortion, inculcation, and submission to authority. In greater variety and perhaps more subtle than Soviet cinema or fascist cinema (but perhaps not), Hollywood productions serve as repositories of varied beliefs, assumptions, impressions, values, and worldviews. If some films celebrate, validate, and transform killing and dying, others accentuate trauma, loss, and discontinuity. If popular movies have affirmed postwar American military predominance, buttressed the Cold War consensus at home, naturalized US political and economic institutions, and maintained the "normalcy" of a one-superpower world following the so-called "end of history," so too have they expressed counterclaims.

While many war movies served points of national (and particularly white and male) unification through "good" violence during the pronounced disunity of the Vietnam War, some were shaped by social changes from below, challenging that consensus either obliquely or through depictions of other conflicts (*The Wild Bunch,* 1969; *M.A.S.H.,* 1970; *Johnny Got His Gun,* 1971) or directly through allegory, irony, or counterhegemonic narratives (*Apocalypse Now,* 1979; *Full Metal Jacket,* 1987; *Hamburger Hill,* 1987; *Born on the Fourth of July,* 1989). As responses to societal shifts ranging from civil rights to the AIDS crisis, as well as the "needless" or "bad" wars of Vietnam and the War on Terror, such works emphasize the victimhood, nonlinearity, digression, and ambiguity of collective memory as it relates to US wars and interventions, America's global system of military bases and alliances, and the application of hard power.[25] Even at the conception of America's "Good War" bearing, popular filmmakers employed metaphor, mood, and aesthetic suggestion to question American innocence and intimate national sin, especially within the western and film noir genres.[26]

Act 3, Scene 2: The Manifesto—On Memory

Collective memory, like biological memory, is a retrieval process.[27] Individuals and societies reclaim, collect, organize, and preserve snippets of the past. But memory is a constructive process, too. In establishing the academic field of "collective memory," French sociologist Maurice Halbwachs, who viewed the past as "a social construction mainly, if not wholly, shaped by the concerns of the present," recognized the variations in how different groups salvage, arrange, and safeguard the past.[28] Appealing to emotion rather than intellect, collective memory is a commemorative alchemy that involves the construction of "memories" in order to forge common identity, often sanctifying the nation-state. But it is also a dialectical process in that it features the antithetical: responses to, and deconstructions of, prevailing narratives that thereby expose competing identities and interests.

As Halbwachs understood, all collective memory is generated within a social framework, and the ability to construct hegemonic narratives is both a salient byproduct of social power and the legitimation of that power.[29] Therein, memory as an outcome of social influence and the need for "imagined communities" to construct a past that sanctifies the nation-state is the primary reason, for example, that the overwhelming majority of all monuments in Washington, DC, are white male military figures.[30] When it comes to film, competing interpretations of the past—or recent debates over flags and monuments, for that matter—are often more than mere analytical disagreements; rather, they are age-old contests of social power, frequently enmeshed with justice struggles and rights revolutions. In what Geoffrey Perret calls "a country made by war," the memory of military conflict through cinema—and through popular culture generally—is an ever-present symbol and a constant, fluid benchmark for measuring social change in the present.[31]

While the relationship between movies, identity, and collective memory trends toward consensus and social "normalization," filmic representations of war may also defy the status quo. Alluding to vernacular memory and the Paris Commune in his masterwork, *The Age of Capital,* Eric Hobsbawm explained that the past is not important only in that it happened—or even for its achievements, no matter how considerable. In fact, the past is often *most* important in the myth that it generates and how everyday people overlay that myth onto their own lives and struggles.[32] Because filmmakers and audiences continuously reinterpret past representations or create new ones, challenging or displacing formerly dominant ones, the relationship of films to collective memory is fluid and perpetually contested.

In underscoring popular culture as a window into social change and identity, we, the editors, concur with Jim Cullen's conception of a "reusable past" in which, by attempting to reach large numbers of people (even if for profit or social supremacy), "the creators of popular cultural documents rely on vernacular words and ideas, even when they communicate in the most impersonal settings."[33] Employing common experiences and massified language to espouse counternarratives or to highlight subaltern realities—and often underscoring bottom-up conflict over top-down consensus—movies have the capacity to educate, build empathy, and foster solidarity.

Furthermore, we also agree that war movies and the identities they engender are part of what Theodor W. Adorno and Max Horkheimer call "the culture industry."[34] Whether espousing "official" or "vernacular" memories, filmmaking is part of a social reproduction of ideology, and that process is linked to movies as commodities.[35] All producers create for profit, clearly. And that profit depends on many factors, not least of which is the formula to entertain. But the deeper a studio's pocketbook—the further a filmmaker's reach—the greater potential a film has to "reproduce" its ideas. Although conditioned by the state through either legal regulation or various forms of coercion—HUAC merely made explicit Hollywood's role as an ideological apparatus and potential to condition behavior—American films are generally responsive to the profit motive. Cultural criticism is therefore typically muted, and it pays for art to either reinforce prevailing ideology or be open-ended, contradictory, and vague enough to appeal to—or at least not offend—the largest possible audience of consumers.[36]

Hollywood movies, and perhaps especially war movies, are predisposed to affirm assumptions about whiteness, masculinity, capitalism, and empire while marginalizing race, patriarchy, and class oppression. The result of mainstream movies tending to reflect a dominant ideology—or *the* dominant ideology—of the society in which they are produced is the legitimation of such ideas by presenting them as natural, obvious, and inevitable.[37] This replication of culture, and the hierarchies at play in its organization, speak to the central issue of not merely war films, but what and why a society remembers in the first place.

Act 3, Scene 3: The Manifesto—On Identity

Mass media *are* mass memory, and, for many Americans, such representations are interchangeable with "history." (In noting that "memory" and "history" are not the same thing, it is also worth clarifying that "history" and "the past" aren't synonymous, either: the former is an interpretation of the latter constructed by historians using various forms of primary evidence.) Thus, how publics "remember" the past collectively is critically important to how they formulate fundamental concepts of national identity, or, in this case, what it means to be American.

Martial Culture, Silver Screen surveys war movies because they offer a dynamic benchmark for how martial ideology and national identity interact with collective memory. Changing social realities alongside constant film production generate an equally constant flow of new analytical possibilities. This volume seeks to wed such analysis to recent and not-yet-fully explored film titles. In doing so, it provides an opportunity for scholars to both update the canon of historical writing to account for new evidence (films, politics, and society), and we also take a hard look at how historiography is either keeping up with or falling behind expressions of American memory-history in popular culture and mass media.

Films are a reliable and nearly universal way—arguably *the* most universal way—by which Americans have witnessed, processed, scrutinized, and attempted to reconcile the role of warfare in the American past. These films serve a dual propagandistic purpose: they tell us who we are in the present and how we got there. Better still, they help us keep track of the specific role played by violence in formulating our national sense of self. As a case study, take *Patton,* released in 1970, with the US military seemingly trapped in an unwinnable war in Vietnam and the antiwar movement rapidly gaining traction on the home front. Many Americans worried that the nation's martial legacy—a critical component of its ability to contain Soviet-style communism around the globe that had been forged by victories against Germany and Japan in the Second World War—was being irreparably damaged. In the film, General George Patton (played by George C. Scott) delivers the following monologue to his newly established army:

> Men, all this stuff you've heard about America not wanting to fight, wanting to stay out of the war, is a lot of horse dung. Americans traditionally love to fight. All real Americans love the sting of battle. When you were kids, you all admired the champion marble shooter, the fastest runner, big league ball players, the toughest boxers. Americans love a winner and will not tolerate a loser. Americans play to win all the time. I wouldn't give a hoot in hell for a man who lost and laughed. That's why Americans have never lost, and will never lose a war . . . because the very thought of losing is hateful to Americans.

The message was a clear and direct shot at the New Left and the burgeoning counterculture: *real* Americans don't protest wars; rather, they're inherently drawn to the fight. And real Americans certainly don't lose wars; instead, they unite and win them. The World War II generation had done it and cemented their position as champions—as *real* Americans. In this way, depictions of war on film even have the power to supersede the words and experiences of the men and women who really waged them; compared in a vacuum to the gravitas of Scott's speech, the dissenting ex-soldiers featured in *Winter Solider* (1972) and *Hearts and Minds* (1974), come across just as he proffered: as intolerable losers.

Far more recent documentaries about the Vietnam War have forced us to confront questions about the constructedness of patriotism, the fate of civil liberties in the age surveillance wars fought against non-state enemies on *our own* home front, and the broader implications of the American empire. Comic books and graphic novels, some written by preeminent scholars, rights leaders, and public intellectuals (Ari Kelman, John Lewis, and Ta-Nahisi Coates among them), continue to use superheroes, the supernatural, and the interpretive freedom provided by the inherent (but incorrect) assumption of many that such media are only for younger audiences, to speak both directly and indirectly to ongoing American conflicts and social divisions, both domestic and foreign.

Many new conflicts have been waged since 1970, and Hollywood depictions of American war-making from Jamestown to Fallujah are today interpreted and reinterpreted through the common (and presentist, at least for the moment) lenses of "endless" wars in the Middle East, the financial recession, and the "second Gilded Age," the ascendency of the first African American president, and through the presidency of Donald Trump. Indeed, most of the films discussed here both reflect and perpetuate what W. E. B. Du Bois termed the "propaganda of history." "It may be inspiring," Du Bois reminded, "but it is certainly not the truth."[38] Yet films, pop culture, and collective memory *do* channel truth. In reality, what the "false myth" of popular culture *does do* is build imaginative bridges and forge intellectual bonds between what we remember about our past and how we perceive ourselves in the present. Thus even as the social context varies drastically, the practice of using popular-culture media to control memories of war and, with them, to grapple for control of "Americanness" itself has not changed. Nor do we believe it will so long as there are wars and movies.

Final Act, Scene 1: The Archive

The canon of American war movies constitutes an archive—one that preserves the ideas, characters, themes, and imagery through which we have understood the fundamental stuff of Americanness. Or, more simply put, war movies function as an archive of us imagining ourselves. With *Martial Culture, Silver Screen,* we intend to show what lies behind the proverbial curtain. Spoiler alert: once you look, there's no going back. But our intention is not to ruin treasured films or to dispel the mystique of dimmed lights, popcorn, and a projector humming. Quite the opposite, in fact—because we love many of the films being "decoded" in this book, too. Thereby, as devoted cinephiles *and* as cultural historians, we genuinely hope that revealing the true power of war movies in everyday American life will lead theatergoers to appreciate them more, not less, and to engage with the likes of Benjamin Martin, Aldo Raines, and John Rambo on an entirely new level.

NOTES

1. On the relationship between Ford and Wayne, see Nancy Schoenberger, *Wayne and Ford: The Films, the Friendship, and the Forging of an American Icon* (New York: Doubleday, 2017).

2. Winter describes "civilianization" as the First World War process through which industrialized war specifically against civilians became normal—and which opened the door for the large-scale slaughter and cleansings of the Second World War.

3. Stephen Cohen, "How America Misremembers Russia's Central Role in World War II," *The Nation*, May 6, 2015, www.thenation.com/article/stephen-cohen-how-america-misremembers-russias-central-role-world-war-ii/.

4. See Douglas Brinkley Jr., *The Boys of Pointe du Hoc: Ronald Reagan, D-Day, and the U.S. Army 2nd Ranger Battalion* (New York: William Morrow, 2005); Max Hastings, *Inferno: The World at War, 1939–1945* (New York: Alfred A. Knopf, 2011), 436; Chris Bellamy, *Absolute War: Soviet Russia in the Second World War* (New York: Vintage, 2007), 4; Alexander Hill, *The Red Army and the Second World War* (Cambridge, UK: Cambridge University Press, 2017), 3–5; Peter Kenez, *A History of the Soviet Union from the Beginning to the End* (Cambridge, UK: Cambridge University Press, 1999), 156; Eric Hobsbawm, *The Age of Extremes: A History of the World, 1914–1991* (New York: Vintage, 1994), 7, 84.

5. Winston Churchill, *The War Speeches of Winston S. Churchill, Vol. III* (London: Cassell, 1951), 107.

6. William Jordan, "US Receives Most Credit for Defeat of Nazi Germany," *YouGov*, May 5, 2015, today.yougov.com/topics/politics/articles-reports/2015/05/03/us-receives-most-credit-defeat-nazi-germany; "Quelle est la nation qui a le plus contribué à la défaite de l'Allemagne en 1945?" *Les Crises*, May 8, 2019, www.les-crises.fr/la-fabrique-du-cretin-defaite-nazis/.

7. On changed American attitudes as Russia shifted from wartime ally to Cold War enemy, see Ronald Smelser and Edward J. Davies, *The Myth of the Eastern Front: The Nazi-Soviet War in American Culture* (Cambridge, UK: Cambridge University Press, 2008).

8. John Bodnar, "*Saving Private Ryan* and Postwar Memory in America," *American Historical Review* 3 (June 2001): 805–17; A. Susan Owen, "Memory, War and American Identity: *Saving Private Ryan* as Cinematic Jeremiad," *Critical Studies in Media Communication* 19 (Fall 2010): 249–82.

9. Paul Fussell, *The Boys' Crusade: The American Infantry in Northwestern Europe, 1944–1945* (New York: Modern Library, 2003), 34–35.

10. Timothy Snyder, *Bloodlands: Europe Between Hitler and Stalin* (New York: Basic Book, 2010), xiii–xv. On how the American relationship to Dachau, as well as its success as a memorial, has enlarged its perceived historical significance, see James E. Young, *The Texture of Memory: Holocaust Memorials and Meaning* (New Haven, CT: Yale University Press, 1993), 60–72.

11. Eric Hobsbawm and Terence Ranger, eds., *The Invention of Tradition* (Cambridge, UK: Cambridge University Press, 1993), 9.

12. Hobsbawm and Ranger, eds., *The Invention of Tradition*, 1–2.

13. Anthony D. Smith, *National Identity* (London: Penguin, 1991), viii.

14. Eric J. Hobsbawm, *Nations and Nationalism since 1790: Programme, Myth, Reality* (Cambridge, UK: Cambridge University Press, 1990), 170.

15. Louis Althusser, *Lenin and Philosophy and Other Essays*, trans. Ben Brewster (New York: Monthly Review, 2001), 112.

16. Terry Eagleton, *Ideology: An Introduction* (London: Verso, 1991), 14; Antonio Gramsci, *Prison Notebooks, Volume II*, trans. Joseph A. Buttigieg (New York: Columbia University Press), 175.

17. Eagleton, *Ideology*, xiii.

18. Louis Althusser, "Ideology and Ideological State Apparatuses," in Julie Rivkin and Michael Ryan, eds., *Literary Theory, An Anthology* (Malden, MA: Blackwell, 1998), 299.

19. On France, see Henry Rousso, *The Vichy Syndrome: History and Memory in France since 1944* (Cambridge, MA: Harvard University Press, 1991), Naomi Greene, *Landscapes of Loss: The National Past in Postwar French Cinema* (Princeton, NJ: Princeton University Press, 1991), and H. R. Kenward and Nancy Woods, eds., *The Liberation of France: Image and Event* (London: Bloomsbury, 1995). On Great Britain, see Geoff Eley, "Finding the People's War: Film, British Collective Memory, and World War II," *American Historical Review* 106, no. 3 (June 2001): 818–38.

20. John Bodnar, *The "Good War" in American Memory* (Baltimore: Johns Hopkins University Press, 2010).

21. Chris Hedges, *War Is a Force That Gives Us Meaning* (New York: Public Affairs, 2002), 3.

22. Christian G. Appy, *American Reckoning: The Vietnam War and Our National Identity* (New York: Penguin Books, 2015), 143.

23. Linda Dittmar and Gene Michaud, eds., *From Hanoi to Hollywood: The Vietnam War in American Film* (New Brunswick, NJ: Rutgers University Press, 1990), 4.

24. See, Matthew C. Hulbert, *The Ghosts of Guerrilla Memory: How Civil War Bushwhackers became Gunslingers in the American West* (Athens: University of Georgia Press, 2016); and Jenny Barrett, *Shooting the Civil War: Cinema, History, and American National Identity* (London: I. B. Taurus, 2009), 58–93, 188.

25. Richard Godfrey and Simon Lilley, "Visual Consumption, Collective Memory and the Representation of War," *Consumption Markets and Culture* 12 (Fall 2009): 275–300.

26. Bodnar, *The "Good War" in American Memory*, 130–65.

27. On the retrieval element of collective memory, see Barry Schwartz, "The Social Context of Commemoration: A Study in Collective Memory," *Social Forces* 61 no. 2 (December 1982): 374–97.

28. Maurice Halbwachs, *On Collective Memory*, rpt., ed. Lewis A. Coser (Chicago: University of Chicago Press, 1992), 25.

29. Halbwachs, *On Collective Memory*, 19.

30. Benedict Anderson, *Imagined Communities: Reflections on the Origins and Spread of Nationalism* (London: Verso, 1983).

31. Geoffrey Perret, *A Country Made by War: From the Revolution to Vietnam* (New York: Random House, 1989).

32. Eric Hobsbawm, *The Age of Capital, 1848–1875* (London: Weidenfeld & Nicolson, 1975), 167.

33. Jim Cullen, *The Civil War in Popular Culture: A Reusable Past* (Washington, DC: Smithsonian Institution Press, 1995), 6.

34. Max Horkheimer and Theodor W. Adorno, eds., *Dialectic of Enlightenment,* trans. Edmund Jephcott (Stanford, CA: Stanford University Press, 2002), 94–136.

35. On "official" and "vernacular" memories, see John Bodnar, *Remaking America: Public Memory, Commemoration, and Patriotism in the Twentieth Century* (Princeton, NJ: Princeton University Press, 1992).

36. Dittmar and Michaud, *From Hanoi to Hollywood,* 11.

37. Althusser, *Lenin and Philosophy,* 117.

38. W. E. B. Du Bois, *Black Reconstruction in America, 1860–1880* (New York: Simon and Schuster, 1935), 723.

History, Sir, Will Tell Lies as Usual

Founders, Patriots, and the War for Independence on Film

KYLIE A. HULBERT

T he air hanging over the cobblestone streets of Colonial Williamsburg was thick and humid. Shafts of sunlight broke through the clouds. The sundry rays began to dissipate the fog which enveloped the dwellings bordering the Palace green. A few stray beams shone through the paned windows of one such home, casting light on a small group of tourists gathered together on the second floor of the George Wythe house. The majority of the assemblage listened intently as a reenactor, portraying Wythe—Virginia delegate to the Continental Congress, signer of the Declaration of Independence—described his role during the early years of the American Revolution. One tourist, a bespectacled, mustachioed, middle-aged man, standing beside his wife, cleared his throat and proclaimed, "I hate to think what the Founders would say about the United States today. Our current government is in shambles. I sure wish we had men like you here now to help us figure this mess out." The reenactor, surprised by the outburst, continued on with his monologue. However, the man would not be deterred. He continued to extol the virtues of the Founding Fathers, noting how "the Founders knew how to run a government." He claimed the United States needed men, like the Founders, "now more than ever" as the current politicians were not up to the job; in fact, the man argued, they were failing miserably. Only the Founders, he contended, would be able to save the country and restore order to a broken system.

The opinions voiced by this strident tourist are not unusual in our current political state. This idea, which permeates large parts of society, holds up the Founders as the gold standard of American government. These were men— Washington, Adams, Jefferson, and Franklin among others—who had ideals; men who argued and debated, but also compromised and created. In the minds of many Americans, the men of the Revolution are the ultimate public servants. They established the nation, wrote the Declaration of Independence and the Constitution, and set the United States on a course for greatness. This nostalgia for a bygone selfless, capable public servant infuses Americans' understanding of the Revolution and their perceptions of the founding period, but it does not tell the entire story.

In the eyes of Americans, the Revolution was fought on two fronts: one principled, one savage, one of gentlemen and above disrepute, one masculine and violent. The first, the noble cause, was hashed out in a civilized manner, within the four walls of the Pennsylvania State House in Philadelphia (now Independence Hall). Here it was that those untouchable men, the famed Founders, used words and wit to fight for liberty. One need only look at the popular biographies displayed in bookstores to understand America's fascination with these men of character and charisma. David McCullough's *John Adams,* Ron Chernow's *Washington: A Life,* and Walter Isaacson's *Benjamin Franklin: An American Life,* to name just a few, paint vivid pictures of these larger-than-life men and their supposedly justified cause. Written with an eye toward the popular audience, these works reflect the idealistic view of the Revolution.[1]

Yet there is another point of view held by Americans about their founding, one rooted in masculinity and bravado, one where Americans—specifically men—define themselves by their ability to effectively wage war against the British Empire. This is the fight for freedom in the backwoods and at home. While the high-browed Founders sit in session and "piddle, twiddle, and resolve," these men wage a bloody war. A key component is that this war is not violent for violence's sake. Rather, their actions are justified through British cruelty and underhanded tactics. Once the British use less-than-gentlemanly means to achieve their aims, American patriots are more than justified to meet violence with violence. Interestingly, there are no popular biographies of these common men. No monuments are built in their names, no parks created in their honor. The actions taken by these men were indeed necessary in the course of the war, but they are distant from the hallowed hall in Philadelphia. These two visions of Revolution are distinct and separate in the American mind, yet both play key roles in the national understanding of the country's founding.

Historians have grappled with questions surrounding the Revolution for decades. Some maintained focus on these distinct stories, choosing to study the elite Founders versus the everyday man. Others began shifting attention to underrepresented characters and classes. In more recent years, rather than accept these separate spheres, scholars have attempted to combine them to truly understand the Revolutionary period, intermingling the noble stand and the seedy underbelly of the war into a single environ of creation. For example, the violent aspects of the war provide the central theme for a new study by Holger Hoock, *Scars of Independence: America's Violent Birth,* which specifically highlights the brutal, at times sadistic, nature of the War for Independence, perpetrated by both sides. Historians are constantly struggling to educate a public that is interested in their nation's origins, but relies more on movies and television than historical studies for their knowledge of the period. Scholars are not as adept at reaching the popular audience as movie producers and screenwriters who bank on a good story inspired by historical scholarship rather than being strictly bound by it.[2]

The Revolution on film has also received treatment from a variety of historians and scholars. Studies, articles, and books cover a range of topics from historical inaccuracies to the reasons behind the dearth of material on the period. Cotton Seiler contends the Revolution was one "of ideology and of language" which "seems to have presented obstacles to constructing strong films." Studies focus on the Founders specifically and whether they are suitable for cinematic treatment. Some argue for the humanizing aspects of the films and their success in making the Founders relatable, while others, such as Lawrence L. Murray, allege that movies like *1776* are "a parody of the Founding Fathers" and create more work for historians in highlighting the real Founders. Popular articles note that the Revolutionary period lacks major films because the era is simply bad for business. In one such study, Mark Glancy utilizes reception studies to highlight a special relationship he contends exists between Hollywood and Great Britain which affects the war's earning potential on the screen. At other times, the roadblock is stylistic. Michael Kammen argued that "most of the moving pictures" about the Revolution were "based upon historical novels" and "so derivative" that he did not even attempt "a systematic discussion and analysis of these films" in his work. He dismisses *The Devil's Disciple* because the play was "written by an arrogant Irishman" and, therefore, not American theater. Yet these plays and musicals—which were made into American films—are clearly part and parcel of American cinematic history. Hence they are worthy of analysis, regardless of their source material, as they were created for the American public. The dual identity of intellectual Founder and American fighter shapes what audiences see on-screen in various ways and, in turn, how the silver screen portrays the war and reinforces the American identity that audiences already possess. The question revolves not around historical in-accuracy or box-office earnings, but the identities Americans have created for themselves concerning the Revolutionary period and how movies cater to and reinforce these separate natures.[3]

Not surprisingly, studios, screenwriters, directors, and well-known actors want to play to their audience—an American audience—which neatly sepa-rates the two types of Revolutionary characters. Benjamin Martin, Mel Gib-son's farmer-turned-guerrilla who seeks revenge against a British officer in *The Patriot* (2000), is a far cry from the "obnoxious and disliked" John Adams, portrayed by Daniel Williams in *1776* (1972), who attempts to rally his fellow delegates at the Second Continental Congress from their summer lethargy. Cinematic representations of the War for Independence not only reflect this dual vision, but reinforce it. There is no film, as of yet, which seamlessly rep-resents both sides of this Revolutionary coin. The ideals of independence are written and signed by those far from the field of battle. For those Americans who learn history from what they view on the screen, rather than what they read in books, this is a self-fulfilling cycle. The conflict centers on either the intellectual or the masculine American with the British playing the necessary enemy, whether a witty and worthy adversary or a brutal and sadistic one.

Five American films, in particular, cater to and fortify this binary vision of the American Revolution. *The Scarlet Coat* (1955) and *The Devil's Disciple* (1959), two films produced in the post–World War II era, utilize the masculine, blue-collar colonist whose innate toughness and self-sacrifice make him a worthy representative of American identity. The main characters of these films engage in witty exchanges with their British enemy, take necessary actions to win the war, and succeed without much overt violence. The stand-out intellectual film is *1776* (1972), an adaptation of the Broadway stage musical, which centers on the actions and efforts of John Adams, Benjamin Franklin, and Thomas Jeffer-son, in the few months leading up to that fateful day in July 1776 when the Dec-laration of Independence was passed. The film exists in a bubble where the war reaches the delegates only through letters sent by George Washington, reinforc-ing the separate spheres of the intelligent Founder and the frontier badass. This masculine-fueled, revenge-filled colonist is featured front and center in the final two films, *Revolution* (1985) and *The Patriot* (2000). Al Pacino's and Mel Gibson's characters represent the Americans' innate ability to fight—everyday men living their lives, who only enter the war once they are forced to do so. Yet they are able to pick up guns and join the fray. Here is the idea that regular

Americans are capable of taking extraordinary actions. These are stories where colonists are filled with bloody rage and British violence is met with colonial violence; where the role of the commonplace man in the struggle for independence is highlighted. These five films encapsulate American identity and its Revolutionary origins. America was founded by political, ideological men, but also by those tough, intense colonists willing to sacrifice for cause and country.[4]

In the aftermath of World War II, as the United States emerged victorious alongside its closest ally, Great Britain, the silver screen made quick use of the relationship. *The Scarlet Coat,* released in 1955, features the tale of one self-sacrificing American revolutionary and one sympathetic British officer. The film claims to relate the untold story of a man named Gustavus engaged in espionage and treason during the Revolution. Furthermore, the story promised to relate how this spy was unmasked and to reveal his true identity: Benedict Arnold. Fictional Major John Boulton (played by Cornel Wilde) takes center stage in this melodrama about the quest to discover America's greatest traitor. Boulton is part of George Washington's secret spy ring, a select group charged with securing important information about British movements, plans, and personnel during the war. After killing a British spy at an inn, Boulton is sent into British lines as a double agent by his American commander. There he offers his services as a turncoat for the British. His main mission is to learn the identity of that American officer who is sharing vital information. In other words, Boulton is pretending to work for the British cause while actually serving as a spy for the Americans. All of this reconnoitering is done in an effort to uncover Gustavus's actual identity. Though the first British contact Boulton makes, Dr. Jonathan Odell (played by George Sanders), doubts the colonist's loyalty to the British Empire, Major John Andre of the British Army (played by Michael Wilding) is impressed with Boulton. Despite Boulton's claim that he is motivated only by money, Andre decides to trust this new man and offers Boulton the opportunity to prove himself in service to the Crown.

Boulton plays his part well, or at least well enough, to convince Andre. As part of his espionage routine, he claims to share critical information about American weaknesses and troop movements with the British on several occasions. There is always a grain of truth in what he discloses, which allows him to continue to build his relationship with Andre. All the while, Boulton is also sharing important material with his American commanding officer. Boulton's ability to infiltrate the enemy's inner circle and gain Andre's confidence highlights American ingenuity, resourcefulness, and commitment to the cause. At great personal risk, Boulton finds himself dining with the enemy, delivering official intelligence, and carrying out missions. He is nearly caught more than once, but manages to escape detection each time. Boulton is a prime example of that American bravado and virility touted by the public today. He embodies the ideals of a true American revolutionary with the masculine prowess to prove it. Engaged in fistfights and even two battles to the death, Boulton always emerges the victor. He risks his own life to find a traitor and help the cause he so ardently believes in, while also pursuing an amorous relationship. This commitment to principles is the one aspect Boulton cannot hide from Andre. At their first meeting, Andre asks, "You didn't believe in the ideals of independence?" Boulton replies, "I never found much comfort in ideals, sir." Yet Andre remains unconvinced, and he later notes that Boulton does indeed hold certain morals, such as "love, friendship, the essential good and dignity that all men possess in a greater or lesser degree." Boulton is a blue-collar patriot who cannot conceal his commitment to the cause.

Despite the red coat he wears, Major John Andre is a sympathetic, even likable, character, clearly reflecting the lingering good feelings of victory in World War II and the United States' investment in rebuilding Great Britain during the 1950s. Andre offers a contrast to Boulton's rough-and-tumble American. Andre is a gentleman, a man who is waited upon by a servant, who comports himself as an officer should, or at least, this is the vision the filmmakers wanted audiences—both in the United States and in England—to believe. The fateful hour draws near when Boulton is finally supposed to encounter Gustavus at a meeting with Odell, Andre, and Boulton himself. But the plan is foiled when Gustavus sends a messenger asking to see only Andre at a nearby home. As he prepares to depart for his meeting, he begins to change his clothes. Boulton stops Andre, whom the American now considers a true friend, and implores the Brit to wear his uniform to the meeting: "If you should be captured, let it be as an officer and not a spy." Andre dons his coat and departs. Boulton, ultimately, returns to American lines in an effort to trap Gustavus at the meeting, only to be delayed and given the runaround by an American officer who does not know Boulton is merely pretending to work with the British. By the time Boulton's true identity is revealed, Gustavus is gone. The only article Boulton recognizes in the closet at the meeting home is a scarlet British officer's coat— Andre's coat. Boulton learns that Gustavus is indeed Arnold through a pass bearing Arnold's signature. The pass grants access through American lines for a gentleman named Osborne; a gentleman whom Boulton discovers at that moment is none other than John Andre.[5]

All of the pieces finally fall into place. Andre is arrested as a spy because he was not wearing his officer's uniform, though Boulton assures the arresting soldier "he's to be treated with every courtesy." Despite his common clothing, Boulton notes Andre is a "gentleman." The news of Arnold's treachery, however, is learned too late. The general has already fled to the British. Andre is brought up on charges of espionage. Boulton attempts to save his friend. Pleading with the court, Boulton remarks, "Does humanity require adding another horror to the many horrors already brought about by this war? If so, then I say to you, sir, such a cruel example can never be the symbol of a great cause." But there is nothing to be done. Without Arnold to hold accountable, Andre is left to take the brunt of American anger at this treacherous behavior. He must serve as an example to any others who might consider the idea of turning traitor. Andre notes he will miss Boulton's friendship, and, in an encapsulation of that World War II–turned–Cold War alliance between America and Britain, he concludes that the two nations will "come together . . . for they have common blood." Andre is marched to his "rendezvous with history," ultimately meeting the hangman's noose, but still dying "like a gentleman."

In one of the earliest depictions of an American Revolutionary fighting man on film, John Boulton casts a mold that other actors and characters would follow. He is the embodiment of that oft-touted American Patriot: capable and resourceful, witty and smart, a gentleman in his own right, but not stodgy or prideful. When action is called for, he shows skill with weapons, whether fist or flintlock. Boulton only kills when necessary, often in hand-to-hand combat, but the violence hashed out in the film is muted even by the standards of the 1950s. In this way, Boulton reflects the ideal of an overly masculine, physically imposing, but still level-headed revolutionary. Though he dealt fraudulently with the British, he did so only as Benedict Arnold and the British dealt underhandedly in turn. In the character of Boulton, Americans found a man capable of doing the dirty work necessary to win the war, but he accomplished his task without tarnishing his reputation or the cause for which he fought. Indeed, while Andre is a sympathetic character, despite his intrigues against the Americans, Boulton looks upon Arnold with utter contempt. Andre and Arnold may both have been spies and enemies, but whereas Andre remained a gentleman, Arnold was a man of the worst kind. He was a traitor to his cause, a man who cared more about his career than about his country. Arnold was a turncoat and a coward. Boulton was a man of action and principles, a true American.

Four years later, studio executives turned to an Irish playwright, George Bernard Shaw, for another story about the Revolution. *The Devil's Disciple,* based on the play of the same name, centers on a case of mistaken identity wherein a rogue colonist, Richard Dudgeon (played by Kirk Douglas), claims to be a local parson, Anthony Anderson (played by Burt Lancaster), to protect him from the British gallows. At the outset, Anderson is a peace-seeking pastor in Websterbridge, Massachusetts, who strives to guide his flock through these troubling times. He attempts to save one of his parishioners accused of treason by the British Army from the gallows, but arrives too late. When the British refuse to cut down the body, Anderson tries to take a gun from a nearby soldier, but he is ultimately stopped and saved by a fellow colonist who claims ministers do not understand violence. Dudgeon, the eldest son of the victim, cuts down the body in cover of darkness and delivers it to the cemetery beside the church for burial. However, the British believe it is Anderson who has stolen and buried the body—hence, their interest in arresting him and Dudgeon's subsequent self-sacrifice.

Dudgeon and Anderson both reflect an innate American masculinity. Their toughness coupled with their sacrifice defines an Americanness prevalent following the "Good War." This strength of character is illuminated against a bantering, cocky British enemy, personified in the character of General John Burgoyne (portrayed by Laurence Olivier). Burgoyne is the perfect foil for this stout-hearted American model. He notes the skill of the Americans at obstructing the movement of his troops through the woods as they make their way from Springfield to Websterbridge. Snipers hide in the daytime and fell trees to block the path. Only the Natives, notes Burgoyne, seem to make any headway, but they take any scalp, and oftentimes those belong to friends as well as enemies. The general engages in witty repartee with his lieutenant, as well as with Dudgeon, posing as Anderson, at the latter's trial following his arrest. Dudgeon asks to be shot like a man. Burgoyne replies, "Have you any idea of the average marksmanship of the army of his majesty King George III . . . half of them will miss you and the rest will make a mess of the business." Considering the friendship between the United States and Great Britain in the 1950s, in addition to the cinematic market at play across the Atlantic, the appearance of a likeable, almost friendly, British enemy is none too surprising. While British Lieutenant Swinland and some of his men do indeed engage in acts against the Americans, such as hanging traitors, the violence portrayed is subdued. Burgoyne justifies their actions by claiming England is trying to maintain control of her American colonies. When Dudgeon accuses Burgoyne of fighting "because you're paid to do it," the general retorts, "If you knew what my commission cost me and what my pay is, you would think better of me." The British may have been our mortal enemies during the Revolution, but in the 1950s they were our allies and our friends.

While Dudgeon condemns himself before the British court, the actual Anderson has followed the Patriot militia to Springfield, where he makes the transition from parson to Patriot. He walks past retreating American rebels, through fire, and cannon shells splintering the church, into the center of town and straight into British headquarters. There he finds barrels of gunpowder alongside the building, which he decides to blow up. Anderson matches fists with a British officer who catches him in the act. A chair broken over his back barely slows the reverend down as he rises, takes two punches to the face, then proceeds to knock the lieutenant's lights out. He single-handedly moves a large wooden table to trap two soldiers, and then punches the lieutenant out—again. He finally succeeds in his goal by stabbing a burning log from the fireplace with a bayonet, carrying it to an open window, and throwing it on the pile of gunpowder-filled barrels. Anderson stands still smiling as the gunpowder explodes. He rips off his neckcloth, disappears behind closed doors with a British scout, and emerges fully clad in a Davy Crockett–inspired outfit made of buckskin. The transformation is complete; the backwoods Patriot rides to Websterbridge to save Richard Dudgeon and to inform Burgoyne, "now you will take the rope off that . . . American citizen."

Throughout the film, acts of strength foreshadow Anderson's potential power: lifting a wagon wheel out of a hole in the road, holding a giant millstone, pulling a burning log out of a fire with his hands, and finally proving himself proficient with a weapon. Yet up until those final scenes, Anderson is portrayed as a "man of peace" who tries to find a nonviolent way to save the man who has taken his place. Dudgeon, on the other hand, is the outcast. He is a man who has left his mother and younger brother to pursue his own selfish acts. Indeed, he explains to Anderson that he did not take his father's body out of filial duty, but rather to annoy the British. Dudgeon has already made a pact with the devil by his own admission, so his soul cannot be saved. Nevertheless, Anderson tells his wife that, though he does not like Richard Dudgeon, he cannot help but respect the man.

Together, these two men fulfill the American ideal. Both do what is necessary to complete their self-appointed mission, whether that is Dudgeon's righteous act of saving the parson or Anderson's efforts to save the man who saved him and took his place. Each represents an aspect of American identity entwined with the Revolution itself. When Burgoyne warns Anderson, "Don't take too much heart . . . you've only won a skirmish," Anderson proudly replies "You may occupy towns and win battles, General, but you cannot conquer a nation." *The Devil's Disciple* illustrates Americans born out of toughness, sacrifice, and patriotism to a fledgling country. Burgoyne predicts the ultimate outcome of the war when he explains to his lieutenant that no reinforcements are on their way under General Howe. "[Howe] received no orders, sir," Burgoyne sighs, "Some gentleman in London forgot to dispatch them. He was leaving town for his holiday, I understand. So to avoid upsetting his arrangements, England will lose her American colonies." In the final moments of the film, a voice-over narrative notes that General John Burgoyne surrendered at Saratoga three weeks later, indicating the war would indeed ultimately be won by those rebel colonists, though in reality the war would last another four years.

For nearly twenty years, the silver screen remained silent on the American Revolution. No new films appeared delving into the nation's founding. But as the bicentennial celebration of the signing of the Declaration of Independence drew near in the 1970s, producer Jack L. Warner sought to capitalize on feelings of patriotism and pride he thought would sweep the country. Enter stage right, a film version of the Broadway musical *1776*, released in theaters in 1972. Utilizing almost the entire original stage cast, the film depicts the debates and struggles surrounding the question of independence at the Second Continental Congress. John Adams (played by Daniel Williams) leads the charge for the creation of an American nation. In the midst of a hot Philadelphia summer, the American intellectual comes to the foreground. Rather than the backwoods badass of *The Scarlet Coat* or *The Devil's Disciple,* the intelligent, self-sacrificing, noble Founding Fathers fill the screen. Their actions highlight the political ideals, the rights of men, and the role of government still touted—at least in theory—by Americans today.

John Adams is the consummate American. He fulfills and, in many ways, defines the intellectual mold of the two-sided Revolutionary coin. A frontier fighting American like Boulton or Anderson he was most certainly not, but he could match wits with the best of men. He despises the British and their lack of respect for the colonies. He blames King George III for taxation and violence against the colonists. He urges his fellow delegates to rouse themselves and to take action. In the opening scene of 1776, he berates the assembly, stating, "I have come to the conclusion that one useless man is called a disgrace, that two are called a law firm, and that three or more become a Congress." Adams's main adversary is John Dickinson of Pennsylvania (played by Donald Madden). Dickinson notes there are benefits of a relationship with Great Britain. The Pennsylvanian does not want to rush into a separation which may not be necessary or advantageous. Meanwhile, Edward Rutledge of South Carolina (played by John Cullum) is concerned about the sovereignty of the individual states and how a nation would affect the ability of those states to govern themselves—in other words, who would have the authority to decide whether or not to allow slavery. Adams, however, is adamant that the colonies must break away and form their own country. Benjamin Franklin (played by Howard Da Silva) hits the nail on the proverbial head when he states, "We've spawned a new race here . . . rougher, simpler, more violent, more enterprising, less refined. We're a new nationality. We require a new nation." In those few words, Franklin explains the idea (and quite frankly, hope) of that new American identity of the 1770s which still permeates society today.

Frustrated by the Congress's lack of action, Adams works alongside Franklin to secure a proposal for independence. The two men enlist the help of Richard Henry Lee of Virginia, who returns from his colony with a resolution for independence. Adams—along with Franklin, Thomas Jefferson (played by Ken Howard), Robert Livingston, and Roger Sherman—is appointed to a committee charged with drafting a declaration. Ultimately, the task of writing said declaration falls to Thomas Jefferson. While Jefferson struggles to put pen—or rather quill—to paper, Adams and Franklin anxiously wait. Various dispatches arrive from George Washington addressed to the Congress, bemoaning the state of his Continental Army and the conditions they must endure. These letters contain the only glimpses of the British enemy, and for that matter, the American Army itself. Nowhere in the film is that adversary represented in flesh and blood, nor are Washington's men in mass numbers, Continentals or militia. When the dispatch rider, a young boy, describes the field of battle in song, no delegates are present. The congressional custodian, Andrew McNair (played by William Duell), exclaims, "Well, you don't see them [the delegates] running off to get killed, do ya?" They are "great ones for sending others," but as men of intellect, they remain far removed from the actual bloodshed. The separate spheres of noble Founder and frontier fighter are clearly delineated in

1776, where the two never coexist on screen. When Samuel Chase of Maryland (played by Patrick Hines) visits George Washington's troops at New Brunswick, he does so off-screen. He returns to Congress convinced of the army's potency after seeing them shoot a flock of birds. To say the war is nonexistent would ignore the few brief reports from the front and the dispatch rider's musical description of Lexington and Concord. Nevertheless, those scenes are described and not seen.

The majority of the film focuses on the Founders themselves as they quarrel over the question at hand. Independence was not a foregone conclusion. Rather, it took ingenuity, intellect, gumption, bravado, and dedication on the part of Adams, Franklin, Jefferson, and others to secure the votes necessary for independence. Some of the same traits touted by Boulton, Dudgeon, and Anderson can be found within these Founders, but they are utilized in a different way. The delegates engage in battles of wit and words, not fists and fire—with the exception of one brawl between Adams and Dickinson. Once the draft of the Declaration is read aloud, Congress spends days dissecting, revising, and "piddling" over the document. Adams is, once again, beyond frustrated. He berates the assembly: "We have endured 85 separate changes and the removal of close to 400 words. Now would you whip it and beat it until you break its spirit? I tell you that document is a masterful expression of the American mind." The message is clear: the Founders are men of verbiage and brainpower. Their might lies in their knowledge, not in their brute strength.

Despite Adams's claims of perfection, the inclusion of slavery and the clause which blames King George III for its existence in the colonies proves a dilemma. The southern colonies will not vote for independence, explains Rutledge, if the slavery clause remains in the Declaration of Independence. Though Adams believes "posterity will never forgive us," Franklin reminds his ally that "first thing's first . . . Independence. America." Besides, jests Franklin, "what will posterity think we were, Demigods?" Ultimately, it is Jefferson in an emblematic moment who takes up a quill and scratches out the problematic clause. South Carolina proceeds to vote in favor of independence, followed by the southern block.

Pennsylvania is the last vote. Dickinson maintains his position and will not vote for independence. Believing himself to be a noble, principled man, he cannot join his fellow delegates in voting the affirmative. However, when the resolution on independence is adopted, Dickinson vows to join in the fight for America's defense, though he believes it hopeless. Once Dickinson resigns his position as a logical Founder, he can pick up a weapon and become a soldier in the fight for freedom. He has left the intellectual bubble of the Congress and crossed the line to enter the field of battle. The dichotomy between the scholarly, political process of revolution encapsulated by the delegates in Congress versus the military campaign in the trenches and fields—as depicted in earlier films by Boulton, Dudgeon, and Anderson—is clearest in 1776. George Washington and his army are a mockery. In one dispatch, Washington bemoans, "My army is absolutely falling apart." This same sentiment is echoed in a later scene when Chase notes, "You've heard General Washington's dispatches. His army has fallen to pieces." Indeed, the Continental Army—which was not in reality falling apart in the spring and early summer of 1776—is described as a laughingstock, unworthy and incapable of meeting the British forces. Not even George Washington, the ultimate symbol of the Revolution, escapes unscathed. He is far from the halls of Congress and, as Adams explains, Franklin's role will exceed them all for "Franklin did this. Franklin did that. . . . Franklin smoked the ground and out sprang George Washington fully grown and on his horse. Franklin then electrified him with his miraculous lightning rod and the three of them, Franklin, Washington, and the horse, conducted the entire revolution by themselves."

The play, and later the film, encapsulate the ideal of American Founders who used words to fight for liberty rather than weapons. Indeed, these men fought among each other at times, but at the end of the day they came together to create that new nation Franklin described. The army would not have existed without their efforts. "An army needs something to fight for in order to win," Adams argues. The delegates' results make them untouchable in the minds of many Americans who idealize their actions and their ideas. Indeed, the Colonial Williamsburg visitor at the George Wythe house subscribed to just such a notion. These were men who wielded quills and quotes; they performed the *real* work of the Revolution as they wrote, revised, even "piddled and twiddled," but ultimately resolved and declared the United States a new and independent nation. They are unique unto themselves, in word and, in this case, in song.

A decade after Adams, Jefferson, and Franklin danced and sang their way through the Declaration, Hollywood took a drastic, 180-degree turn away from those triumphant Founders. While historians sought to illustrate and highlight the Revolutionary experiences of the urban and lower classes, director Hugh Hudson decided to shed light on their story in film. *Revolution*, released in 1985, tells the tale of fur trapper Tom Dobb (played by Al Pacino) and his son,

Ned (played by Sid Owen and Dexter Fletcher). Dobb is not interested in the war, the rights of men, or his alleged patriotic duty. He is interested only in selling his fur and protecting his son. Yet Dobb is pulled into the conflict when Ned signs up for the army under the promise of five shillings and 150 acres of land at war's end.[6]

From the beginning of the story, Dobb is a man set against the war, at odds with Congress, Patriots, and the British. His boat is confiscated by a mob in New York City, who claim, "Citizen, it is your duty, your responsibility," to relinquish your boat to the cause of independence. When Dobb argues his son was not at the age of consent to enlist, the American officer replies, "all willing to shed their blood fighting tyranny" will be accepted. Ned is forced to serve by an authoritarian enlistment agent. In short, he is tricked into signing his name by the so-called Patriots. Tom Dobb himself is threatened at the point of a sword, forced to enlist or risk never seeing Ned again. The father tells his son to stick close to the officers for they will never risk getting hurt in battle. The Patriot cause at the outset appears neither noble nor just.

Dobb does not comport himself as a hero in early battles. Nor does he exhibit the American characteristics of masculinity and bravery embodied by Boulton and Anderson. Rather, director Hudson attempts to show the horrors of battle. As Dobb describes the scene, "There was shouting and men just start falling all around us"; the chains from the cannon "cut men down . . . cut them in half." As British troops lined up in formation and advanced across a valley, the Continental troops retreated in haste and disarray. Dobb drags his son from the field of battle. He exclaims, "The war's over for us." The two return to New York City, where Dobb works in a rope factory, while Ned runs with a street gang of youths harassing and aggravating the British Army.

The enemy is characterized as cruel, merciless, and unsympathetic—a drastic contrast to the friendly, likeable characters of General John Burgoyne in *The Devil's Disciple* and Major John Andre in *The Scarlet Coat*. Dobb is enlisted to participate in a "fox hunt," where he and another man carry an effigy through the fields as they are pursued by hounds and British officers on horseback. When Ned is taken by the British, he is disciplined after biting a British officer. The punishment—the "Gunner's Daughter"—finds Ned strapped to a cannon, while Sergeant Major Peasy (played by Donald Sutherland) whips the bottom of the boy's feet until they are cracked and bleeding and the skin has been ripped away. In their pursuit of the Continentals during battle, the British run right over the American lines. One officer picks up a pike and proceeds to run men through with the weapon. Herein lies the painful, ugly, gritty birth of the American nation, according to director Hugh Hudson, written in the blood, sweat, and tears of unknown men, not the ink from Thomas Jefferson's quill.

Tom Dobb is spurred into action only when his son is taken from him by the British. He steals a boat and tracks Ned to the enemy camp. Utilizing the skills of a trapper and tracker, Dobb finds Ned and his friend Merle (played by Eric Milota) and rescues them. They proceed through the woods as they are pursued by Iroquois scouts, allies of the British. In a defining scene, when forced to face the Native threat to his son and his own life, Tom Dobb transforms from a reluctant Revolutionary into a frontier fighting, knife-wielding, ultimate combatant. In essence, like Boulton and Anderson before him, Dobb has made the "Rambo turn." He is all at once an American combatant with the skills necessary to fight for his life and for his son. When threatened, Dobb instantly had the capacity to kill. The trio is taken in by the Huron, and as Ned recovers he tells his father, "You saved me, Pa. I thought you was a coward, but you're not a coward." Tom Dobb is at that moment an American in the vein of Boulton and Anderson, or so it seems.[7]

Dobb joins the fight as a scout, working alongside the Hurons he befriended. He is shown braving the difficult winter at Valley Forge, marching through Philadelphia late in the war, and then ultimately engaged in battle with the British at Yorktown. Clouds of smoke fill the air as the camera pans over dead bodies. Dobb and Ned are serving as snipers when they see a group of British soldiers, led by Sergeant Major Peasy, attempting to outflank the American troops along the beach. Dobb and company take off in pursuit of the enemy. They encounter Peasy and his men on the beach, where the British meet the power of American gunfire. As the battle subsides, blood and death are illustrated on both sides. A silhouette of the Patriot forces standing on the battlements reveals everyday men covered in the scars and dirt of combat. The war is over. Dobb and his son return to New York City. But they do not return triumphantly.

As hinted previously, Dobb's transformation into that frontier fighting, noble American is never truly complete. He encapsulates the fierce nature of the American with his proficiency in combat and his capacity for killing, surpassing the violence perpetrated by his British foe, Peasy, by movie's end. But Dobb is disillusioned with the war and with the cause. In many ways, he is akin to a mercenary whose skills align with the Huron more than with the Americans. He has become an expert tracker and killer, but he lacks the ideological underpinnings and nationalistic motivations which justify his actions and make the

American fighting man so attractive. Ultimately, Dobb fails to fulfill the patriotic aspects of the mold set by Boulton in *The Scarlet Coat* and continued by Anderson in *The Devil's Disciple*. While Dobb failed as an American man, the Revolution failed to fulfill its promise of money, land, and opportunity for Tom Dobb. When he attempts to collect the redemption for his boat and the back pay owed him, he receives only forty dollars for the seventy assured. When Dobb inquires about the 150 acres promised him, he is told they were sold by Congress to pay for the war debt. Ned is given the opportunity to begin a new life, but not Tom Dobb. He sends his son north along the Hudson River to settle, but Dobb himself says he cannot go. He has been "treated like a dog." Tom Dobb may have been a man of action, but in this revolution, he was not a man of *American* principles.

Revolution bombed at the box office. Perhaps not surprisingly, American audiences did not want to see a fighting American who did not ultimately sing the praises of the Revolution itself in the end. He made the "Rambo turn" to fight for his life and his son, but by war's end, Dobb had not gained anything for his troubles. He resented the war and the cause. Independence was won, but at the expense of Tom Dobb. *Revolution* lambasts the triumphant narrative hailed by many Americans, blaming Congress for the troubles caused by the war and the lack of supplies available to troops. Ned comments, "Congress, I hear they fight a lot." There is no John Adams singing his way through the signing in this version of events. George Washington, the only Founder seen on screen, is barely glimpsed during a parade review as the crowd shouts, "Long live Washington." If one blinks, that brief moment is missed. No character, not even Ned, is promised a successful future or a successful nation. The lower classes were dragged into the war with a promise of a brighter tomorrow, but that tomorrow turned out to be just as dismal and disheartening as before the war began.

The failure of the film cannot be placed wholly at the feet of this diminished, lackluster American identity illustrated by Dobb. Though the setting may be realistic to the eighteenth century, the look is consistently drab and dismal. Even at moments of victory, there is an underlying depression to the film. The color palette and aesthetic align with the "New Hollywood" turn, a dark, gritty, and earthy presentation of the colonies. The choice lends itself to the story of social revision and division highlighted in the film, but it is far from uplifting or upbeat for audiences who expected to see America's moment of national genesis on film. The dialogue is painfully awkward at points, made worse by actors who, despite their talent in other films, did not rise to the challenge here. The story arc does not flow in a logical manner, and the characters are overall unlikeable and unsympathetic. Even Hugh Hudson's attempt to resurrect and restore the film with a 2009 director's cut, titled *Revolution Revisited,* fell far short of the mark. Tom Dobb may have been dragged into the war, and he may have saved his son, but he was not an American man the nation and audiences could or would rally behind.[8]

The American Revolution once again went dormant on the big screen—this time for nearly fifteen years. Following the flop of *Revolution,* it seemed studios were unwilling to take a chance on a period film which weighed heavily in the minds of Americans and in their nation's history. The next, and to this point final, revolutionary film required a big-name star and someone with proven box office clout. Following the successes of *Maverick* (1994), *Braveheart* (1995), and *Lethal Weapon 4* (1998), Mel Gibson seemed a logical choice. *The Patriot,* directed by Roland Emmerich, centers on Benjamin Martin (played by Gibson), a South Carolina farmer, French and Indian War veteran, and widower, who tries to stay out of the American Revolution, but is ultimately pulled into the conflict by the actions of his sons and his quest for revenge.

In the opening scenes of the film, Martin is enjoying a happy, prosperous life on his South Carolina plantation. He is a family man with seven children who grows tobacco, employs free black workers, and prefers to stay disengaged from the revolutionary fervor building around him. Martin's eldest son, Gabriel (played by Heath Ledger), does not share his father's pacifism. He longs to join the fight. When an assembly is called in Charles Town, Martin and his family make the journey to the city. There, at a meeting, Martin declares that, while he is upset about taxation without representation, he will not fight. He has seen the horrors of combat during the French and Indian War. He understands "this war will be fought . . . amongst us, among our homes. Our children will learn of it with their own eyes and the innocent will die with the rest of us." Since Martin will not fight, he will not send others to do so in his stead. Yet the assembly votes to join the Patriot cause, and Gabriel, without his father's permission, signs up to join the Continentals.

Gabriel writes letters home describing conditions in the North, a campaign marked by defeat, and the death of his friend. Martin, meanwhile, hides his violent past from his family in a trunk in his bedroom, until violence comes to his doorstep on the heels of Gabriel's return. A battle between the British and the Continentals rages in the fields outside Martin's home. Gabriel is wounded while trying to get through the lines with a dispatch. He takes shelter with his family, where he and other injured soldiers—American and British alike—are given care, food, and treatment. As the morning dawns, British cavalry, led by Colonel William Tavington (played by Jason Isaacs), ride up to Martin's front porch. Ignoring the fact that Martin cared for wounded British soldiers as well, Tavington orders the firing of the house and barns as a punishment for harboring the enemy. He also takes possession of the dispatches. When Gabriel admits to carrying them, Tavington commands, "Take this one to Camden. He is a spy. Hang him and put his body on display." Martin tries to intercede, citing the rules of war, but Tavington threatens the farmer and his children. He orders his men to shoot the rebel wounded and turns to leave. Thomas, Martin's second eldest son (played by Gregory Smith), attempts to help his brother escape. He lunges at the British soldiers holding Gabriel captive. Tavington raises his pistol, takes aim, and shoots Thomas in the back before his father can intervene. As Martin holds his dying son in his arms, Gabriel is led off, and the family home begins to burn.

In this moment, as Benjamin Martin feels the life fade from his son's body, something in the veteran snaps. He tells his children to stay put, then enters his home, unconcerned with the flames licking the walls around him. He emerges from the ashes of his old life—a life focused on family, prosperity, and hard work, built alongside his now-deceased wife—carrying muskets and his tomahawk. He calls to his next two eldest sons, Nathan and Samuel, to follow him, while the eldest daughter, Margaret, he tells to care for the rest of the children. On the road leading toward Camden through the forest, Martin and his sons track down the British soldiers who have taken Gabriel captive. Martin reminds his sons of the skills he has taught them, to "aim small, miss small," and to shoot the officers first. Then, after a short prayer, Martin unleashes hell upon the British. With this reversion to violence, Martin makes his "Rambo turn." He returns to what he knows. He recalls the skills he gained during the French and Indian War. Tomahawk in hand, he descends upon the redcoats like a "ghost." No longer is he a pacifist farmer trying to forget the horrors he once witnessed. Now he is a man bent on saving his son Gabriel and seeking revenge against those who killed Thomas.

In his initial actions against the British, Benjamin Martin takes justice into his own hands. He utilizes irregular tactics. Covered in blood, he bashes in the skull of a British soldier. Terrifying his own sons, their father becomes unrecognizable to them in that moment—overkill, to put it mildly. But he succeeds in freeing Gabriel. He volunteers his services to the Patriot cause. He is given the rank of colonel and placed in charge of a militia. Martin recruits other veterans and men who are skilled in the ways of the woods and frontier fighting. These are men far more concerned with killing the enemy than with the civility displayed in the process. They fire from the cover of the trees, plan ambushes, and practice a Native style of warfare. When British men who are about to surrender are killed by these American men, Gabriel cries, "We are better men than that." Martin agrees and establishes limits and boundaries. The war waged by his militia will be efficient and effective, but it will not be savage. There will be a distinction between American and British actions. As Gabriel reminds his father, "There will be a time for revenge. Until then, stay the course."

The British enemy, encapsulated by Tavington, is a sadistic, brutal foe. Tavington purposefully disregards the rules of war and gentlemanly conduct. American traitors are hung from trees outside towns as a warning. Women and children are attacked and killed. General Charles Cornwallis (played by Tom Wilkinson) claims his officers practice "civilized warfare," and Martin is not exhibiting "the conduct of a gentleman." Martin retorts, "If the conduct of your officers is the mark of a gentleman, I'll take that as a compliment." On the surface, Cornwallis follows those gentlemanly rules, but when he is outwitted by Martin, he turns a violent page. Cornwallis gives Tavington free rein to do whatever is necessary to catch the wily American. Tavington notes this manhunt will "require the use of tactics that are, what was the word your lordship used, brutal." If he does "what is necessary," he knows he "can never return to England with honor." Cornwallis quietly acquiesces. Tavington rides out to attack Martin's family personally. He burns the house of Martin's sister-in-law and kills the house slaves. He acquires a list of names of those fighting in Martin's militia and proceeds to burn their homes, killing whoever resists. John Billings (played by Leon Rippy) is so distraught over the death of his wife and son that he takes his own life.

In perhaps the most barbaric and tragic scene, Tavington orders an entire town's population into the local church. He promises to forgive anyone who shares the whereabouts of Martin and his men. After one townsperson shares the coveted information, Tavington orders the doors and windows shuttered. He does not release the informant. Instead, he orders a Loyalist, Captain Wilkins (played by Adam Baldwin), to burn the church. Wilkins replies, "There is no honor in this." "The honor is found in the end not the means," explains Tavington, "This will be forgotten." When Martin and his men come upon the town, they find the church burned to the ground. The only pieces left standing are the church doors with a lock around the handles. Gabriel and a group of men pursue Tavington. In hand-to-hand combat, Gabriel is stabbed by the British officer. Martin arrives on scene just in time to once again hold a dying son in his arms.

The loss of another son is the ultimate test for this American fighting man. He has shown his skill with tomahawk and musket, following in the footsteps of Boulton, Anderson, and even Dobb. He is clearly a transcendent fighter, and in this film, leader of men. For a brief moment, though, it seems Martin will fall the way of Dobb. His friend and fellow officer, Colonel Harry Burwell (played by Chris Cooper), asks Martin to continue in the fight following Gabriel's death. Burwell wants Martin to take part in an upcoming battle. He implores his friend to again "Stay the course." Martin cannot be convinced. He does not understand why men think they can "justify death." He seems disillusioned, beaten down, marked by loss.

Yet even in death, Gabriel serves as his father's conscience. In Gabriel's messenger bag, Benjamin Martin finds a patched-up flag Gabriel had saved and sewn back together. The triumphant music begins to play. The first sight to enter the frame is the flag fluttering in the wind. Martin on horseback appears. Shouts of "huzzah" ring out from the American troops, and Martin takes his place alongside Burwell and a Frenchman, Jean Villeneuve (played by Tcheky Karyo). During a planning session, he speaks confidently of the militia and their skills. On the field of battle, he stands in the front lines. Arrayed against British regulars, he gives the command to fire two shots, then orders the retreat. In the chaos of battle, the British believe the Americans are truly retreating. In actuality, they are luring the redcoats into a trap. All at once, Tavington appears on the scene. Martin sees his chance to take down his sons' murderer. Then the American line begins to falter. Martin must decide: take action for the cause or take his revenge. In true frontier man fashion, Martin makes the decision to save the line. He calls out, "No retreat. Hold the line! Hold the line! Hold!" He rushes forward, carrying a flag, and his men rally to his side.

Benjamin Martin takes his revenge as well. He unhorses Tavington and faces his enemy in hand-to-hand combat, tomahawk versus sword. Martin sustains several wounds. He falls to his knees. At the very moment America is winning, it would seem Benjamin Martin will lose. But this is an American rebel, a born frontiersman, a seasoned warrior; he ducks Tavington's sword before stabbing the redcoat through the throat with a bayonet. Cornwallis orders a retreat. In a voice-over, Martin relates how the tide has turned. The American forces are victorious at Yorktown. Cornwallis bemoans the British loss to "an army of rabble peasants"—representing once again the trope of the aristocratic British officer vis-à-vis the American everyman—while Martin tallies what has been won and lost.

Martin is unique among the American fighting men on film. Boulton and Anderson are both fully vested in the political cause of revolution while waging war, but the fate of neither is illustrated at war's end. They make the "Rambo turn," but the audience never sees the full-on result of that shift. Only Dobb and Martin exist during the entirety of the war. Dobb does not see how his wartime actions have changed anything about the world he inhabits. He is no better off than he was before the struggle began. Unlike Dobb, who felt trampled down at the conflict's conclusion, Martin is lifted up by those around him. He still has hope as he understands the "sacrifices borne by so many" for the Patriot cause. Ultimately, in Martin's world, the ends—that is, American freedom and an American nation—justified the means and the losses. Martin may have buried two sons during the war, but he returns to his plantation, where his men are building him a house on the ashes of his old foundation. He will live in this new home with his new wife and a new baby in a new nation, full of promise. Here is the American fighter embodied by Benjamin Martin: masculine, brave, skilled, resourceful. Indeed, filmmakers made specific choices so American audiences could and would cheer for Benjamin Martin. In an ahistorical scenario, Martin employs free black workers rather than owning slaves. A long-standing hypocritical aspect of the Revolution—men fighting for independence and freedom while they own other human beings—is averted in Martin's character. He now adds another tool to his box of ultimate Americanness: he is portrayed as antislavery as well. Whereas Dobb bemoaned the lack of rewards and broken promises following the war, Benjamin Martin reveled in all the hope and promise America had to offer. The likability of Mel Gibson's character (and of the actor himself, at least at the time) led to *The Patriot*'s box office success compared to *Revolution*'s failure.

John Boulton, Anthony Anderson, Tom Dobb, and Benjamin Martin are Hollywood's representation of the common American fighter during the American Revolution. John Adams, Benjamin Franklin, and Thomas Jefferson are the intellectual men behind the revolution itself. Through these characters, the five films discussed exemplify the two-sided coin of American identity born from the War for Independence. Everyday Americans want their history both ways. They want a pure, bloodless, intellectual Revolution, a war in which their nation is founded on the principles of liberty by sacred Founders wearing white wigs and britches. These men are untouchable and must be represented as such on film. If Adams, Jefferson, and Franklin were just like everyone else, then why are there no men like them today? The answer is simple. Though Franklin laughs when he asks Adams, "What will posterity think we were, Demigods?" in 1776, the joke is only funny because that is exactly what audiences in 1972 did think. Even audiences today often expect to see the knowledgeable, high-browed, philosophical Founders, whether on film or in popular culture. Despite the recent success of *Hamilton* on Broadway, the idea that the Founders were just like everyone else has yet to take root across the American landscape. The stereotype of these founders is long-standing and Americans are often loath to let go of myth and folklore they have held dear for generations and, in this case, since the beginning of American folklore itself. Not to mention, if Adams and Jefferson were mere mortals, then Americans would have to grapple with the idea that their founding was not as exceptional or as special as they are wont to believe. The identity of Americans is entrenched in this founding myth and the idea that noble, principled men gave birth to the nation which stands for liberty and freedom.

On the reverse side of that identity coin, audiences find the personification of all-Americanness when men pick up guns with an innate ability to fight. John Boulton sets the standard for backwoodsmen engaged in the fight for freedom. They must be skilled with weapons, resourceful, tough, masculine, and violent when necessary. Anthony Anderson seamlessly transitions from peace-seeking pastor to buckskinned militia captain. As he explains to General Burgoyne, "In the hours of trial, sir, a man finds his true profession." Tom Dobb begins as a reluctant revolutionary. But when his son is in distress, Dobb takes on a one-man rescue mission before becoming a tracker and scout. Benjamin Martin is the family man attempting to build the perfect rocking chair in his barn. Pulled into the war, he becomes a tomahawk-wielding guerrilla fighter. He is the fusion of all those characters who have come before. Martin has Boulton's ability to move with ease between the worlds of the general's tent and backwoods rendezvous, Anderson's principles, and Dobb's scouting and tracking abilities. These are the common men of the war who bled for and earned their freedom, men who have the uncommon ability to invoke violence when needed and turn the savage side off when the war is done. They are the picture of regular Americans who can do great things when called upon to fight.

Audiences want to cheer for this American fighter. They want to see him fight the bloody British and raise the American flag in triumph at Yorktown. And they want to believe that, deep within themselves, embedded in their DNA, is that same American fighting spirit and ability. Though Americans probably know this dual identity is not realistic, they continue to create films which reflect it. In actuality, the men who fought the Revolution inhabited a middle ground; they fell somewhere between the fighter and the Founder, but Americans cannot bring themselves to fuse the two. The dual identity serves a purpose in the stories Americans *want* to tell about themselves and their history, stories of the nation's origins and birth which form the basis of the distinct, exceptional American identity touted still today.

The British are molded to serve as fuel for this American-identity fire in these cinematic representations. In the post–World War II era, General John Burgoyne and Major John Andre are friendly, even likable, characters who offer witty banter and levity to a serious moment in history. This enemy is no match intellectually for the Founders, so they are not even portrayed in the great hall in Philadelphia. Nor do they belong in the celebratory triumph surrounding the bicentennial. In more recent years, the British are ruthless, vindictive, and cruel. Sergeant Major Peasy and Colonel William Tavington seem to take plea-sure in their brutality. Their uncivilized and ungentlemanly violence justifies the use of an equally uncivilized violence by Americans, violence exercised by the likes of Dobb and Martin. In those moments, they are not an empire trying to retain control of their colonies. Rather, the British are the oppressors, the enemy of freedom, liberty, and the rising American nation.

The intellectual American and the American fighting man are two distinct stereotypes employed by filmmakers and Americans to accomplish different work. One highlights the rational, idealistic founding, while the other com-memorates the bloody birth of the nation. One is based in words and so-called wisdom, the other in battle and physical sacrifice. Where is the story in be-tween these two? Hollywood has neglected all those others involved in the war: redcoats, Hessians, women, slaves, Natives. They do not fit neatly into the dual narrative. They would force Americans to see the failures of the war and the nation's founding. They might even force Americans to grapple with the idea that Britain had valid reasons for fighting a war to keep her colonies. Studio executives are not looking to push their viewers too far. After all, the bottom line is turning a profit. Audiences balked so strongly at *Revolution*, a less-than-triumphant narrative, that the next film, *The Patriot*, included a main character who, on some level, fought for the ideals of liberty and freedom. Yet while those ideals and principles partially motivated Martin, the lofty men themselves—that is the Adams, Jefferson, and Washington of the crew—were missing. There are separate spheres for the intellectual and the fighter.

The absence of George Washington in these Revolutionary films is of note. Here is the man who could potentially cross the streams: an intellectual of sorts and a fighter, a symbol of all the ideals of the Revolution. Washington is present for parts of the Continental Congress, and he is a strong force behind the Continental Army and its success. While he is mentioned and sends letters in 1776 and he is briefly glimpsed on screen, though not identified as such, in *Revolution* and *The Patriot,* he is never portrayed as a true character. Washington encapsulates the ultimate American Founding identity, and therein lies the problem. Washington is *too* great. There is no biopic or cinematic treatment of this First American. In some ways, his legacy, his value as an American myth and Founder, is still too great to risk besmirching. How would Americans receive a Washington who owned slaves, lacked confidence at times, showed a hot temper, and challenged particular political views? In some ways, Washington is the only untouchable Founder left; to unmask him would be to unmask the very Americanness claimed by generations. Audiences may not yet be ready to grapple with the idea that George Washington —who has monuments and cities named after him, who is featured on money and postage stamps, who was the man for the job when the new nation needed its first president—was perhaps a human being after all. And if audiences are not willing to see it, Hollywood will not make it.

Thus, despite the success of *The Patriot* at the box office, the American Revolution has once again fallen to the wayside as a viable vehicle for a successful film. Made-for-TV movies, television series, even Broadway musicals, have found material in our nation's founding, but Hollywood stands silent on the subject. Meanwhile, Americans continue to advance their parallel stories about the nation's founding—one intellectual in nature, the other rugged and masculine. General John Burgoyne may not have been right when he said, "History, sir, will tell lies as usual." However, history *will* be appropriated by those who need it to tell different stories about the same event. For the foreseeable future, Americans will continue to use their history to suit their own ends, and whether the Revolution was won by intellectuals or fighters will depend on the person telling the story and the movie playing on the screen.

NOTES

1. David McCullough, *John Adams* (New York: Simon & Shuster, 2001); Ron Chernow, *Washington: A Life* (New York: Penguin Press, 2010); Walter Isaacson, *Benjamin Franklin: An American Life* (New York: Simon & Shuster, 2003).

2. Gordon S. Wood, *Revolutionary Characters: What Made the Founders Different* (New York: Penguin Press, 2006); Gary B. Nash, *The Unknown American Revolution: The Unruly Birth of Democracy and the Struggle to Create America* (New York: Viking, 2005); Mary Beth Norton, *Liberty's Daughters: The Revolutionary Experience of American Women, 1750–1800* (Boston: Little, Brown, 1980); Gordon S. Wood, *The Radicalism of the American Revolution* (New York: Alfred A. Knopf, 1991); Pauline Maier, *American Scripture: Making the Declaration of Independence* (New York: Alfred A. Knopf, 1997); Joseph J. Ellis, *Revolutionary Summer: The Birth of American Independence* (New York: Alfred A. Knopf, 2013); Holger Hoock, *Scars of Independence: America's Violent Birth* (New York: Crown Publishing, 2017).

3. Mark C. Carnes, ed., *Past Imperfect: History According to the Movies* (New York: Henry Holt and Co., 1995); Nancy L. Rhoden, "Patriots, Villains, and the Quest for Liberty: How American Film Has Depicted the American Revolution," *Canadian Review of American Studies* 37, no. 2 (2007): 205–38; Cotton Seiler, "The American Revolution," in *The Columbia Companion to American History on Film: How Movies Have Portrayed the American Past,* ed. Peter C. Rollins (New York: Columbia University Press, 2003); Cotton Seiler, "The Founding Fathers" in *The Columbia Companion to American History on Film,* ed. Rollins; Lawrence L. Murray, "Feature Films and the American Revolution: A Bicentennial Reappraisal," *Film and History* 5, no. 3 (September 1975): 1–6; Alan Kulikoff, "The Founding Fathers: Best Sellers! TV Stars! Punctual Plumbers!" *Journal of the Historical Society* 2 (Spring 2005): 155–87; Andrew M. Schocket, *Fighting over the Founders: How We Remember the American Revolution* (New York: New York University Press, 2015); James Malanowski, "The Revolutionary War Is Lost on Hollywood," *New York Times,* July 2, 2000; Mark Glancy, "The War of Independence in Feature Films: *The Patriot* (2000) and the 'Special Relationship' between Hollywood and Britain," *Historical Journal of Film, Radio and Television* 25, no. 4 (October 2005): 523–45; Michael Kammen, *A Season of Youth: The American Revolution and the Historical Imagination* (New York: Alfred A. Knopf, 1978), 143, 135.

4. *The Scarlet Coat,* dir. John Sturges, 101 min., Metro-Goldwyn Meyer, 1955, DVD; *The Devil's Disciple,* dir. Guy Hamilton, 83 min., Hill-Hecht-Lancaster Productions, 1959, DVD; *1776,* dir. Peter H. Hunt, 141 min., Columbia Pictures, 1972, DVD; *Revolution,* dir. Hugh Hudson, 126 min., Warner Brothers, 1985, DVD; *The Patriot,* dir. Roland Emmerich, 165 min., Columbia Pictures, DVD.

5. Michael Kammen notes a similar shift in the characterization of British figures featured in novels about the American Revolution, though he delineates the period from 1933 to 1948. Authors faced the issue of painting our current ally as our past enemy, contends Kammen, a task most novelists decided to avoid by highlighting other villains. He claims novels chose to focus on Loyalists, neutrals, or Natives as the evildoers instead. The films noted above did not quite follow this trope, but the reluctance to portray the British as sadistic, vicious killers in the post–World War II period is a clear parallel (*A Season of Youth,* 173–75).

6. The film *Revolution* is part of a greater cinematic turn towards action movies in the 1980s. Led by muscular, physically fit actors such as Arnold Schwarzenegger, Bruce Willis, and Sylves-

ter Stallone, these feature films are chock full of guns, explosions, fistfights, and action-packed sequences. In this vein, *Revolution* ratcheted up the violence factor as well, reflecting the expectations of American audiences in addition to the shift in historiographical studies.

7. The term "Rambo turn" is a reference to the character John Rambo, who made his feature-film debut in *First Blood* (1982). Following his service in the Vietnam War as a Green Beret, Rambo attempts to peacefully reinsert himself into American society. However, when circumstances push him beyond his breaking point, Rambo reveals his innate abilities to wage war, from wielding a knife to utilizing any and all potential weapons within reach. Eventually, Rambo takes the fight to his enemies, highlighting his wrath, vengeance, and unique set of combative skills.

8. "New Hollywood" or "New Wave" films of the 1960s, 1970s, and 1980s reflected both the shattering of America's Cold War consensus and the demise of the Old Hollywood studio system. These pictures are often marked by realistic, graphic violence, antiheroes and antiestablishment themes, unresolved endings, and gritty visual aesthetics. Well-known examples include: *Bonnie and Clyde* (1967), *The Dirty Dozen* (1967), *Easy Rider* (1969), *Straw Dogs* (1971), *The Godfather* (1972), *Badlands* (1973), and *Apocalypse Now* (1979). For a general introduction to the genre, see Geoff King, *New Hollywood Cinema* (New York: Columbia University Press, 2002).

Attacking Antebellum Slavery on Screen

Hollywood Portrayals of Militant Emancipation, 1937–2016

JASON PHILLIPS

The war against slavery spanned centuries and continents, engulfing millions of captives, hunters, traders, sailors, soldiers, and civilians. This conflict continues today, with an estimated forty million enslaved people across the world. During the nineteenth century, slaves revolted across the Western Hemisphere, nations criminalized human bondage and trafficking, and navies first patrolled the seas against slavers. Before the Civil War made American violence against slavery a declared war, the nation's antebellum conflict resembled the Cold War. Both conflicts were defined by looming anxieties, polarizing ideologies, global ambitions, underground organizations, and proxy wars. The Cold War spawned conspiracy theories and red scares; the slave war spread rumors of the Slave Power and the Secret Six. The Cold War pitted capitalism against communism in a struggle for world domination; the slave war placed free labor against bondage in a similar contest that spanned continents, altered global economies, and shaped empires.[1]

Though scores of Hollywood films interpret the Cold War, only a handful of big studio productions shed light on the antebellum war against slavery. Some of its most compelling figures, like John Brown, have vanished from the cinema for more than sixty years. Other abolitionists have never received the Hollywood attention they deserve. I will analyze portrayals of John Brown and militant emancipation at the box office by contrasting three films on the war against slavery from the golden age of Hollywood to three recent movies about the conflict. Comparing *Souls at Sea* (1937), *Santa Fe Trail* (1940), and *Seven Angry Men* (1955) to *Amistad* (1997), *Django Unchained* (2012), and *The Birth of a Nation* (2016) reveals enduring themes but also important changes in Hollywood depictions of violence against slavery. Films from both eras rarely accept human bondage itself as a justification for violence, and they often criticize religious motivations for attacking slavery. The American identity these films promote is secular, masculine, and martial—these reluctant warriors are always right, never rash, and fight for freedom only after more patient approaches fail. As a result, John Brown, abolitionism, and slave revolts appear wrongheaded at best and responsible for the Civil War at worst in these films. Perhaps the standard interpretation of the war against slavery in American cinema is best expressed by the title of a Thomas Dixon 1927 screenplay about John Brown that never made it to the big screen: "The Torch: A Story of the Paranoiac Who Caused a Great War."[2]

Critiquing the historical interpretations of movies instead of criticizing their factual errors will explain how the war against slavery has appeared in theaters over time. Hollywood's mistakes and omissions distort how Americans imagine the past and understand the historian's craft. Movies shape the historical knowledge of millions of people who do not appreciate how collective memory differs from history. Given the importance and controversies surrounding American slavery and abolition, films on the subject have sparked disputes between professional historians and filmmakers. When *Amistad* premiered, the film's production team circulated "educational" packets to grade schools across the country to promote the movie and criticize scholars. "The real history," they claimed, "has been castrated—left out—and great historians have done it." Head-scratching statements like this one, and Hollywood's general disregard for scholarship, led Howard University Professor Abiyi Ford to call filmmakers "toddlers with automatic weapons, capable of doing great harm, but without any capacity for understanding the ramifications of their actions." Spilling ink over the bad blood between Hollywood and historians, however, would only obscure what historians and filmmakers have in common.[3]

Drawing distinctions between historical facts and Hollywood fictions minimizes how all of us—directors, actors, scholars, moviegoers, and readers—make sense of the past by telling stories. All historians, however dry or quantitative their subjects may be, are storytellers. Explaining cause and effect requires a plot and every plot belongs to a genre. Providing the historical context for an event means setting the scene; restoring a subject's agency requires finding your character's motivation; organizing claims in the most compelling sequence may demand flipping the script. Likewise, filmmakers perform tasks familiar to historians, such as imagining the past, interpreting its meaning, selecting who and what matter, and suggesting how history resonates today. Film studies often focus on directors and producers when analyzing the interpretive powers of Hollywood, but movie stars also shape the historical consciousness of their films. We can consider the "historiography" of John Wayne or Meryl Streep as well as Eugene Genovese or Drew Gilpin Faust.[4]

Bashing movies for mistakes also misses their fundamental difference from scholarship. What distinguishes historians and filmmakers isn't so much their methods or fidelity to the past; their goals divide them. Historians tell stories to convey arguments; filmmakers tell stories to make money. Occasionally, both tell stories to make art. Every decision that a historian makes about her work, from the questions she asks and the sources she interprets to the historiography she engages and the conclusions she draws, serves an argument about the past that seeks to expand our knowledge and understanding. Every choice that a filmmaker makes about her work, from set design and costumes to casting, cinematography, and editing, considers how the film will perform at the box office. The historian and the filmmaker share a storytelling tradition, and they may both care deeply about artistry, but their stories and art serve different purposes.[5]

With words and actions, John Brown embodied the war against slavery. While others considered abolition a social movement or a political issue, Brown conducted a personal, open war against slavery. In June 1856 he started the first actual battle over slavery when he coordinated an assault against proslavery militia at Black Jack, Kansas. For three hours the battle raged between over a hundred men, killing and wounding many, until the proslavery captain surrendered to Brown. During fundraising tours across New England, Brown requested weapons, ammunition, and camp equipment—not prayers or votes. While other abolitionists used newspapers, pamphlets, and petitions to attack slavery, Brown ordered a thousand pikes to kill slavery's defenders.[6]

Hollywood has portrayed Brown's militant, private war against slavery as reckless and hypocritical. In *Seven Angry Men*, a free-soil settler, Elizabeth Clark (Debra Paget), judges Brown "a dangerous fanatical man who is doing our cause much wrong." Clark and Owen Brown (Jeffrey Hunter) fall in love but continue to debate the justice of war against slavery. Owen credits his father's violence for giving antislavery settlers enough security to stay in the territory and vote for freedom. Clark counters that such methods are no better than bondage. "You stand for everything I've always hated," she explains to Owen, "violence and bloodshed." *Santa Fe Trail* questions the sincerity and sanity of

John Brown's private war. When Brown learns that US cavalrymen are riding to capture him in Kansas, he abandons a barn full of fugitive slaves by cynically telling them, "My children, the hour of deliverance I promised you has come." When they ask him for direction and help, he offers biblical verses about Gideon slaying thousands and says they must fend for themselves. Raymond Massey portrays Brown as a violent, troubled character in both films. In *Seven Angry Men*, he is convinced that slavery will only die through bloodshed. In *Santa Fe Trail*, he seems driven by madness and monomania, someone whose religious beliefs distort reality and convince him that he is God's avenger.

The darker portrait of John Brown in *Santa Fe Trail* seems unmoored from the historical record given the films many inaccuracies; however, scholarship was equally critical of Brown during the 1940s. In *John Brown and the Legend of Fifty-Six* (1942), historian James Malin argued that Brown had no genuine interest in the free-state cause in Kansas. Ignoring northeastern hagiography and relying solely on evidence from Brown's time in Kansas, Malin portrays Brown as a crazy, dishonest, violent man who looted and killed for no cause. Malin found no strategy or objective behind Brown's violence. "Without plan, so far as the evidence goes, Brown's activities continued during the summer [of 1856] on the level of highway robbery and outlawry, and under the sufferance of the free-state cause which dared not expose him." Malin even argues that Brown's role in Bleeding Kansas would have been forgotten along with the actions of similar frontier brigands had he not attacked Harpers Ferry years later.[7]

While John Brown appeared this way in historiography and cinema during the golden age of Hollywood, he looked very different in poetry, art, and popular culture. A renaissance of interest in John Brown occurred across American arts and letters during the first half of the twentieth century. Stephen Vincent Benét's epic, *John Brown's Body*, which sold millions of copies when it appeared in 1928 and won the Pulitzer Prize for poetry, treated Brown as a mysterious prophet who foresaw an inevitable war over slavery. "You can weigh John Brown's body well enough," Benét wrote, "But how and in what balance weigh John Brown?" For Benét, Brown was as hard, unreasoning, and destructive as stone. The private war that Brown waged in Kansas and Virginia was a cosmic struggle.

> Sometimes there comes a crack in Time itself.
> Sometimes the earth is torn by something blind.
> Sometimes an image that has stood so long

It seems implanted as the polar star
Is moved against an unfathomed force
That suddenly will not have it any more.

In 1953, Massey performed dramatic readings of the poem on Broadway. In 1940, the year that *Santa Fe Trail* premiered, artist John Steuart Curry finished his mural of John Brown for the Kansas State Capitol. Curry depicted Brown as a literal giant who stood above contentious settlers with a Bible in one hand and a rifle in the other. Citizens criticized Curry for focusing on violent, sensational subjects. The Kansas Council of Women protested, "The murals do not portray the true Kansas. Rather than reveal a law-abiding progressive state, the artist has emphasized the freaks in its history—the tornadoes, and John Brown, who did not follow legal procedure." When the state legislature sought to limit Curry's project, he stepped down, refused to sign the murals, and left the state.[8]

Kansans may have been touchy about Brown's larger-than-life presence in their capitol because of his adoption by the American Communist Party and its cultural front. The 1936 Communist Party candidate for president, Earl Browder, was from Kansas, and his campaign linked Browder and communism to Brown and his uncompromising stance against oppressed labor. Banners of John Brown decorated the party's convention. Meanwhile, Mike Gold, a leading voice in the party's cultural front, wrote *Battle Hymn* in 1936, a play that praised Brown's faith and principles. Gold and his coauthor, Mike Blankfort, interpret Brown as a devout, hardworking farmer compelled to battle slavery because of the violence that masters and slave catchers commit against his family and neighbors. "A man's life is the most precious thing in the world," Brown tells his sons, "Bloodshed is sin." The play's chorus placed Brown in a pantheon that advanced America's march toward "peace, liberty, and the good and secure life." The group included Tom Paine, Sam Adams, Daniel Shays, and Nat Turner. When Brown embraces violence in the play, he criticizes William Lloyd Garrison and other abolitionists who have done nothing but talk for twenty-five years. "We are the chosen ones; we are the soldiers of God," he tells the men who have volunteered to raid Harpers Ferry. "Our blood will water this land into free earth."[9]

Though supported by the WPA Federal Theater Project, *Battle Hymn* reflected the communism of Mike Gold and the cultural front rather than New Deal liberalism. As historian Michael Denning observes, Abraham Lincoln, not John Brown, appealed to "mainstream New Deal populism." John Ford's film *Young Mr. Lincoln,* Aaron Copland's *Lincoln Portrait,* and the works of Carl Sandburg illustrate how artists known as "Roosevelt's image brokers" preferred a rational, legal approach to reform over the terrorism of rogue revolutionaries. In Gold's famous essay, "Towards Proletarian Art," he, like Brown, welcomed Armageddon. "In blood, in tears, in chaos and wild, thunderous clouds of fear the old economic order is dying," he prophesied. Gold considered the Civil War years the "Golden Age" of American culture and adopted the name of a Civil War veteran (his real name was Isthok Granish). Gold was "not appalled or startled by that giant apocalypse before us," and emulated John Brown's anger, vision, and heroism. Denning insightfully argues that Gold and other leaders of the proletarian avant-garde favored a "belligerent masculinism" when the Depression threw men out of work and America's birth rate declined. In *Battle Hymn* the militancy, virility, and patriarchy of John Brown implies that workers and revolutionaries are exclusively male. The play's pantheon of American heroes excluded women.[10]

Santa Fe Trail counters *Battle Hymn* and challenges the cultural front's attempt to link communism with an American tradition of dissent. Beneath the film's fantastical plot, *Santa Fe Trail* conveys the message that radicals like Brown scheme against American democracy to foment a class war that workers abhor. When the film appeared in 1940, liberals in Hollywood's establishment fought the Popular Front's attempts to frame anti-capitalism and racial tolerance as American traditions. In 1939 *Gone With the Wind* scored points (and made millions) for the Hollywood establishment in this culture war, and the studio hoped that *Santa Fe Trail* would replicate that success a year later. At the start of the film, abolitionists plant an agent, Carl Rader, at West Point. Fellow cadets catch Rader distributing propaganda that calls for the overthrow of the federal government and the establishment of a new nation founded on emancipation. The academy's commandant, Robert E. Lee, dishonorably discharges Rader for "the traffic and violent exchange of political ideas, which are not the affairs of an American soldier." Rader joins John Brown's conspirators in Kansas and Virginia, where they repeatedly commit violence against citizens and soldiers who try to maintain peace and order. The film's hero, J. E. B. Stuart (Errol Flynn) confronts Brown for his violent ways. "Why blood?" Stuart asks, "The people of Virginia have considered a resolution to abolish slavery for a long time. They sense that it's a moral wrong, and the rest of the South will follow Virginia's example." According to Stuart, Brown's agitation would bring civil war, not abolition. Only the peaceful mechanism of democratic reform could liberate the slaves. When Brown abandons fugitive slaves to escape capture, Stuart saves them from a burning barn and asks them why they followed Brown. A mammy replies, "John Brown said he was gonna give us freedom, but shuckin's, if this here counts as freedom, then I ain't got no use for it, no sir." Her husband agrees, confessing, "I just want to get back home to Texas and set till kingdom come." The film's director, Michael Curtiz, was a Hungarian Jew who fled to the United States after the communist government took control of the nation's film industry in 1919. Curtiz was an avid reader of American history and became a US citizen shortly before he made *Santa Fe Trail*.[11]

Fifteen years later, during the civil rights movement, *Seven Angry Men* complicated the cardboard villainy that defined John Brown in *Santa Fe Trail*. In Curtiz's film, the abolitionists start every fight, from Rader's tussle at West Point to the Harpers Ferry raid. *Seven Angry Men* upends this portrayal in the opening scene when border ruffians confront Brown's sons on a train, and the abolitionists protect themselves and a woman onboard. In *Santa Fe Trail* Brown corrals African Americans in a barn like animals. In *Seven Angry Men*, he lives beside African Americans in an idyllic interracial community. When Martin White, a proslavery agitator, threatens Brown and his neighbors and bullies them to leave the territory, Brown describes himself as a "homesteader" and vows "no blood has been shed here nor will be unless you shed it first." Brown's war against slavery begins after White and other border ruffians assault the peaceful free-state town of Lawrence.

Though the title of the film implies a unified family of Brown men outraged by bondage, *Seven Angry Men* explores the morality of antislavery violence by pitting John Brown and his sons against each other over the right course of action. Owen questions his father's tactics but refuses to abandon him. Frederick, Jason, and John Jr. challenge their father after he massacres proslavery settlers. Indeed, Brown's graphic violence causes John Jr. to lose his sanity, and Jason decides to find him medical treatment. Salmon and Oliver Brown oscillate between following their father and their conscience. In the film's climactic scene, Owen listens to the gunfight at Harpers Ferry from across the river where he and a black comrade are guarding weapons. They planned to circulate the arms to slaves. When no one comes, Owen has to decide whether he will cross the river alone to join his father or find a way out of the predicament his father has caused. His friend, far more compassionate and intelligent than the stereotypical blacks in *Santa Fe Trail*, convinces him that together they should find their way to safety. The film closes with them turning their backs on Brown's violence and walking down the road together. Historian Peggy Russo insightfully notes that the film reflects "youthful rebellion against paternal authority," a popular theme of 1950s films like *The Wild One* (1953), *Rebel without a Cause* (1955), and *Blackboard Jungle* (1955). *Seven Angry Men* also anticipated 1960s debates between nonviolent resistance and militancy within the civil rights movement.[12]

When Owen turned his back on John Brown in *Seven Angry Men*, who could have guessed that his actions foreshadowed Hollywood's abandonment of Brown ever since? The studios have ignored this complicated character who underlines and undermines American identity. John Brown lived for the Declaration of Independence and died a traitor. He preached the Golden Rule and led a massacre. He collected Bibles and knives. He assaulted white supremacy and upheld patriarchal authority. Except for comical cameos, like Johnny Cash's portrayal of Brown in the television miniseries *North and South*, America's most militant abolitionist has disappeared from film and television since the 1950s. Promising material for screenplays is not to blame. Major novels like Russell Banks's *Cloudsplitter* and James McBride's *The Good Lord Bird* await adaptations. Julia Davis's superb play *The Anvil* tells John Brown's story where he gained immortality, not in Bleeding Kansas or the Harpers Ferry enginehouse, but rather in the Charlestown courtroom and jail. Brown captured the imagination of the North and the South when he mesmerized a small Virginia courthouse, received dozens of visitors in his cell, and wrote public letters that explained his actions and framed himself as a martyr for America's sin. This act, his most memorable performance, has received scant attention in Hollywood. *Santa Fe Trail* never tries Brown for treason; it skips from his capture to his hanging, thereby avoiding any debate over his and the nation's guilt. *Seven Angry Men* concludes with a brief courtroom scene before Brown's execution, but neither film permits the moral questioning that a courtroom drama would provide. Davis's play relied heavily on trial transcripts and premiered in the same Charlestown courthouse where Brown was convicted. It is curious that Hollywood has avoided the most famous trial of the war against slavery.[13]

Historical contexts in recent years have not aligned to promote a blockbuster John Brown movie. More recent films about the war against slavery pay more attention to African American responsibility for freedom. Since the civil rights movement, Hollywood and television have portrayed enslaved Americans with more complexity, sensitivity, and power. Recent movies like *Amistad*, *Django Unchained*, and *The Birth of a Nation* focus on black resistance to bondage. In *Amistad* and *Django Unchained*, worldly white Americans provide mentorship to black characters, but the primary contest in each film, and *The Birth of a Nation* as well, pits black protagonists against white representatives of an oppressive system. White abolitionists do not exist in *Django* and *Birth*; in *Amistad* they appear irrelevant.[14]

Other changes in American society since the 1950s suggest why Hollywood studios would doubt the box office success of a John Brown film. Brown's religious zeal may seem bizarre, not devotional, to an increasingly secular American society. Biblical dramas like *The Robe* (1953) and *The Ten Commandments* (1956) thrived during Hollywood's golden age, a time when more Americans were church members, but recent attempts to replicate that success, like *The Passion of the Christ* (2004), have stirred controversy in a more religiously diverse (and averse) America. Some recent historical films on religion, like *The Mission* (1986) and *The Apostle* (1997), explore frightening, violent dimensions of proselytizing that could work in a Brown biopic, but that critical approach to faith, militancy, and human rights drew criticism for *Malcolm X* (1992). Perhaps the biggest obstacle to John Brown's return to Hollywood in the twenty-first century is his terrorism. After 9/11, which studio will risk telling a story about a small band of American terrorists who improbably attack society and the government, expose the nation's vulnerability, and start a war in the name of religion and global injustice?[15]

One film has dared to tell that tale, albeit about a different freedom fighter, Nat Turner. Nate Parker's *The Birth of a Nation,* unlike other recent movies like *Amistad* and *Django Unchained,* portrays the war against slavery as a religious war. The film begins with slaves practicing their African faith in a secret ceremony that prophesies Turner's greatness when he's a child. When a young Turner begins to fulfill those expectations by teaching himself to read, his sympathetic plantation mistress gives him a Bible. In adulthood, Turner's comprehension of all scripture puts him in a difficult position when his owner rents him to brutal slaveholders who expect a "nigger preacher" to proselytize obedience and the sanctity of slavery. Among the six movies treated in this essay, *The Birth of a Nation* alone explores how white southerners twisted scripture to defend their violence and greed. *Santa Fe Trail* and *Seven Angry Men* portray John Brown's faith, not the beliefs of slave owners, as a pervasion of Christianity. In both films, Brown conceals rifles in crates labeled "Bibles," implying that he not only justified but also facilitated murder by abusing religion. In *The Birth of a Nation,* when Turner can stand bondage no more, he debates scriptures with a corrupt, proslavery preacher. During the pivotal scene, these ministers of dueling gospels trade verses that condemn and condone slavery until Turner's master sends him to the whipping post.[16]

Amistad argues that resorting to law, not religion, is the appropriate way to end slavery. In one scene, the movie contrasts abolitionist Louis Tappan's religious zealotry to Roger Baldwin's legal pragmatism. Baldwin (Matthew McConaughey) thinks the Amistad case is simple. For him the captives were legally akin to livestock. "The only way one can purchase or sell slaves is if they are born slaves," he explains. "Ignore everything but the preeminent issue at hand—the wrongful transfer of stolen goods." Appalled by Baldwin's casual comparison of people to stolen goods and cattle, Tappan (Stellan Skarsgård) insists, "This war must be waged on the battlefield of righteousness," not "on the vagaries of legal minutiae." "Did Christ hire a lawyer to get him off on technicalities," Tappan asks. No, "he went to the cross, nobly." "But Christ lost," Baldwin replies. Throughout the film Tappan and other white abolitionists appear out of touch with reality. He later admits to a black abolitionist, Theodore Joadson (Morgan Freeman), that it might be better for the cause of abolition if the Amistad Africans lost their case and died as martyrs. Joadson can't believe his ears. When a procession of abolitionists sings hymns to comfort the jailed Africans, the prisoners puzzle over their purpose and identity. "Who are they, do you think?," one captive asks their leader, Cinque (Djimon Hounsou). "Looks like they're going to be sick," Cinque answers with disgust. He decides they must be "entertainers" but can't fathom why "they look so miserable."[17]

Cinque's dismissal of white abolitionists in *Amistad* reflects a shift in recent films toward black, not white, resistance to bondage. In a chilling scene in *Django Unchained,* planter Calvin Candie (Leonardo DiCaprio) explains that he has lived his whole life surrounded by enslaved black people and the only question he has ever asked is, "Why don't they kill us?" Candie shows his dinner guests the skull of a faithful slave, Old Ben, who shaved his father for fifty years without slitting his throat. Cracking open Ben's skull, Candie finds his answer to the mystery. According to Candie, the part of the brain associated with submissiveness is bigger in Africans than in any other species on earth. Whereas white skulls, like Isaac Newton's, would reveal dimples where the brain expanded its creativity or intelligence, black brains, even of exceptional

specimens like Django (Jamie Foxx), are predisposed toward servility. *Amistad,*
Django Unchained, and *Birth of Nation* challenge Candie's phrenology and other
arguments that insist black people were content as slaves.[18]

Though recent films acknowledge black resistance to the brutality of bondage, something other than slavery itself causes people to fight for freedom.
Rape is a common cause for wars against slavery in these movies. Django hunts
white people as he searches for his enslaved wife, Broomhilda (Kerry Washington), who was sold as a "comfort girl" to Candie. Django's mentor, King Schultz
(Christoph Waltz), explains the quest of Siegfried, a noble knight who scales
the mountain and slays the dragon to save his love, Broomhilda. Throughout
his Deep South quest, Django sees his love in hallucinations and dreams, thus
confirming that she, not the institution itself, is the reason why he is fighting.
When he liberates her at the end of the film and ignites Candyland, Django's
war is over. Even *The Birth of a Nation,* in many respects the most radical film
in this genre, explains Nat Turner's revolt as a defense of a woman's honor.
Though troubled about slavery from childhood, Nat does not resort to killing until after slave patrollers gruesomely abuse his wife, Cherry (Aja Naomi
King). The plots of both films imply that the ultimate offense committed by
white southerners was not capturing, owning, and killing black people but dis-
regarding the sanctity of black marriages.[19]

By focusing on the middle passage, *Souls at Sea* and *Amistad* are the only
films that condone violence against slavery without resorting to other crimes
or causes for justification. Africans revolt onboard slave ships in the opening
scenes of both films. In *Souls at Sea,* the ship captain tries to thrash captives for
singing, but chained men grab his whip, yank him into the depths of the hold,
and beat him senseless. After the captain dies on deck and order resumes, two
white sailors decide the attack was justified. "If the slaves hadn't gotten him,
someone else would," they agree. As workers who labor under tyrannical conditions and suffer the lash themselves, the sailors in *Souls at Sea* empathize
with their human cargo. One of them, Michael "Nuggin" Taylor (Gary Cooper),
explains that the "floor of the ocean is paved with the bones of slaves." Taylor
reads *Hamlet* to his friend and compares their own fate to the blacks below
them. "To be or not to be," when suffering such inhuman treatment, sailors
and slaves must decide whether they would rather live or die. In the following
scene Taylor and his comrade suffer a cruel maritime discipline, hanging by
their thumbs, a punishment common among slaves. Likewise, in *Amistad,* the
film opens with captives killing a slave ship captain during the middle passage.

Amistad's plot most clearly presents bondage itself as the reason for revolt. The protagonist, Cinque, does not kill to avenge violence against himself or the rape of others. He breaks his chains, attacks his captors, and takes control of the ship simply to be free. When he learns enough English to express his cause, Cinque chants, "Give us free."

By focusing on slave-ship captains and crews instead of masters and slaves, *Souls at Sea* explores the war against slavery from a unique perspective. The protagonist is Taylor, an American sailor who conspires with the British Navy to fight the illegal, international slave trade during the antebellum period. A remarkable film for its time, *Souls at Sea* is the only movie under consideration that frames the war against slavery as a high seas adventure. Its approach showcases brilliant cinematography of clipper ships dancing over the waves in scenes that resemble pirate movies from the golden age of Hollywood. Other films set the war against slavery as a western (*Santa Fe Trail, Seven Angry Men,* and *Django Unchained*), a plantation epic (*The Birth of a Nation*), or a courtroom drama (*Amistad*). *Souls at Sea* begins and ends with courtroom scenes, but it succeeds in focusing on the harrowing naval war against slavery, whereas *Amistad* misses that opportunity. The Amistad captives spend the vast majority of the film in jail, not at sea where they performed their most remarkable feats: freeing themselves, overtaking the crew, and successfully navigating the ship to safety.[20]

At the beginning of *Souls at Sea*, Taylor stands trial for murdering panicked passengers who clamored for lifeboats during a shipwreck. The prosecutor identifies him as "a slaver" who destroyed the lives of thousands of innocent Africans. "Do these facts present to you a philanthropist? A generous, warm-hearted saver of human lives? They do not. They present him for what he is— an incredibly intolerant, callous, cold-hearted mass murderer." As a spy for the British Navy, Taylor sabotages slave ships and shares information about the clandestine slave trade, its secret ports and routes, with authorities. Revealing this work to the court would save his life but ruin the efforts of the British Navy and the lives of thousands of captives they sought to save. Taylor stoically awaits his fate while the rest of the film flashes back to reveal his true identity.

The biggest mystery throughout the film is Taylor's motives. Like John Brown, Taylor fights a personal war against slavery. Before the British Navy recruits him, Taylor purposefully steers a slave ship toward a naval patrol to ensure its capture, runs another slave ship aground off the coast of Africa to let thousands of captives swim to safety, and sets a third vessel on fire before it could collect its illegal cargo. Unlike Brown, Taylor disavows any religious justifications for his actions. When British officers confront him with his record of "waging a private war against the slave trade," Taylor asks why they "persist in regarding [him] as a Quaker or an abolitionist." Circumspect and clever, he never reveals why he risks his life to free the slaves. Equally confounding is his conduct on the shipwreck. During the chaos onboard the sinking vessel, Taylor fights a slave-ship agent and drowns him. Then, when too many people seek safety on a crowded lifeboat, Taylor fires three shots at them, presumably killing people. With no warning shots, no attempt to restore order by barking commands, not even an anguished look on his face, Taylor kills some men to save others. When the film premiered, one critic thought the scene was "a truly appalling shipwreck which only the strongest nerves could accept as entertainment." No other film from the era attacks slavery like *Souls at Sea*. When Taylor denigrates Quakers and abolitionists, he voices his preference for violence against slavery over pacifism and reform. In *Santa Fe Trail* and *Seven Angry Men*, John Brown is executed for making the same choice. In *Souls at Sea,* the court finds Taylor guilty, too, but a British minister reveals his secret identity, and the judge grants Taylor a new trial. Noble ends justify the means in this film.[21]

Cooper's enigmatic character in *Souls at Sea* illustrates a theme that pervades films about the war against slavery: human bondage distorts American identities. In *The Birth of a Nation,* Cherry shows Nat a dress her mother gave her before the slave trade separated them. Inside the garment, her mother stitched Cherry's real name so that she would never forget her family. In *Souls at Sea,* Taylor's friend pretends to be a merchant instead of admitting to a woman that he is a slaver. While Taylor works secretly for the British Navy, a British officer secretly works for the slave trade. No one in *Django Unchained* is who s/he appears to be, because the immorality of slavery twists people and demands disguises. Slaveholders prefer nicknames like "Big Daddy" and "Monsieur" to conceal their brutality beneath a veneer of false paternalism or fake sophistication. Klansmen wear hoods that comically hinder their ability to ride and shoot. A group of slave breakers, the Brittle Brothers, use aliases to conceal their criminal records. A Texas sheriff turns out to be a wanted man. Even a traveling dentist proves to be a bounty hunter, because like slave traders, he works in a "flesh for cash business." In *Django Unchained,* negotiating the Slave

South requires dishonesty, because every aspect of society, from the grandeur of its plantations to the fine print on its property deeds, is built on a terrible lie. Black wives are "comfort girls" to white men. Black men are gladiators forced to fight to death for entertainment. When Django is sold to the LeQuint Dickey Mining Company, he loses his name for a number. In this world, only wanted posters tell the truth.[22]

Like Taylor in *Souls at Sea*, the men who attack slavery in these films must assume false identities and betray people's trust to fulfill the reckonings they seek. Django (Jamie Foxx) and King Schultz (Christoph Waltz), the bounty hunter/dentist, pretend to be a slave driver and master to infiltrate Candyland. John Brown and his conspirators assume false identities to attack slavery in *Santa Fe Trail* and *Seven Angry Men*. When Brown orders a thousand pikes under the alias Mr. Smith, he asks the blacksmith to ship them to Harpers Ferry in boxes labeled "farm machinery" to avoid suspicion. Owen Brown even keeps the raid a secret from his wife. Nat Turner was his master's childhood playmate and most trusted slave in *The Birth of a Nation*, until he butchers him. The Amistad court cases hinge upon the true identity of the captives. It is a telling contrast that a white prisoner in *Souls at Sea* avoids a guilty sentence when one British diplomat testifies to his secret identity whereas the black prisoners of *Amistad* are not liberated until after they prove their identity in three trials.

The uncertainty that enshrouds actors' identities and motives in these films affects how audiences identify with characters who fought for and against slavery. Who is defined as a "true American" varies greatly in these movies, as society's understandings of race and violence have shifted over time, but these changes are not necessarily progressive. Though he stands trial for being a slaver and murderer in the opening scene of *Souls at Sea*, Gary Cooper's character is unquestionably a true American from the second audiences see him on screen. "Nuggin" Taylor's Americanness quietly fights for freedom and justice because he believes in human decency and follows his moral compass instead of falling for radical propaganda or arcane scripture. Likewise, audiences know that Errol Flynn's character in *Santa Fe Trail* is a true American, but he defines the ideal differently. As an American, Stuart matches Taylor's bravery but disagrees with his reliance on federal authorities and foreign powers that meddle in citizens' affairs, like slave ownership. When Stuart and his classmates graduate from West Point in the film, Jefferson Davis delivers the patriotic commencement address. In *Seven Angry Men*, Owen Brown, not his father, is defined as the true American. Jeffrey Hunter's character is loyal to his family and treats all races equally. He would prefer that democracy ends slavery peacefully, and he's willing to use violence to ensure that ballots are counted in Kansas, but he turns his back on the Harpers Ferry raid and its terrorism. In Hollywood's golden age, the true American was a white man who did what was right without rocking the boat, a reluctant warrior who believed that America's good heart would magically solve the slavery problem.

In more recent films on the war against slavery, American identity becomes more inclusive in some respects but not in others. In *Amistad*, the true Americans are, once again, recognizable to audiences as the film's biggest stars— Morgan Freeman who plays Theodore Joadson, Matthew McConaughey who plays Roger Baldwin, and Anthony Hopkins who plays John Quincy Adams. All three men hope that the American Revolution and Constitution will legally end slavery in time, because their nation was founded on liberty, not the oppression of millions. They oppose violence and religious fanaticism because both resort to unreason, the antithesis of the Enlightenment ideals that will abolish slavery in the end. In *Django Unchained*, the true Americans are Schultz and Django, an odd couple bound together by an urge to hunt criminals and avenge oppression. As a German immigrant, Schultz's Americanness suggests that the nation's ideals diminish over time and need to be revived by newcomers like him who are drawn to America's possibilities, freedoms, and equality. Django's prodigious skill with a pistol makes him a true American, but his wits, not his gunplay, save him and Broomhilda in the end, disproving Candie's phrenology lesson. Finally, in *The Birth of a Nation*, the true Americans are Nat Turner (Nate Parker) and his followers, African Americans who seek the same freedoms that George Washington and Patriots sought, and by the same means, bloodshed. Unlike Django, Turner fits the reluctant-warrior stereotype of American identity. Like Django, Turner is a prodigy, an exceptional black man, implying that blacks who are true Americans must be extraordinary. Ordinary black people are victims in these movies.

Unfortunately, none of these films on the war against slavery portrays the true American as a woman. The violence of war films privileges masculinity. Actresses in these movies question the morality of militant emancipation or serve as casualties who inspire resistance to bondage, but they do not fight this war. The long struggle over slavery involved millions of women on all sides, women who joined abolitionist societies, owned slaves, or felt the lash firsthand. Hollywood depicts this conflict as a man's concern and often defines the triumph of slaves as an assertion of their masculinity rather than their humanity. Perhaps future films on this subject will capture the brilliance of runaways like Linda Brent, the moral courage of the Grimké sisters, and the pathbreaking work of Maria Lydia Child and Elizabeth Cady Stanton. Hopefully *Harriet* (2019), Kasi Lemmons's biopic of Harriet Tubman, starts this vital revision. Until other films follow its lead, American cinema portrays a fraction of the antebellum war against slavery that fails to resonate with the plight of millions of enslaved women fighting bondage today.[23]

NOTES

1.For analysis of American war films, see Glen Jeansonne and David Luhrseen, *War on the Silver Screen: Shaping America's Perception of History* (Lincoln, NE: Potomac Books, 2014); Peter C. Collins and John E. O'Connor, *Why We Fought: America's Wars in Film and History* (Lexington: University Press of Kentucky, 2008).

2. *Souls at Sea,* dir. Henry Hathaway (Hollywood: Paramount Pictures, 1937), film; *Santa Fe Trail,* dir. Michael Curtiz (Burbank, CA: Warner Brothers, 1940), film; *Seven Angry Men,* dir. Charles Marquis Warren (Los Angeles: Allied Artists Pictures, 1955), DVD; *Amistad,* dir. Steven Spielberg (Glendale, CA: Dreamworks, 1997), DVD; *Django Unchained,* dir. Quentin Tarantino (Hollywood: Columbia Pictures, 2012), DVD; *The Birth of a Nation,* dir. Nate Parker (Los Angeles: BRON Studios, 2016), DVD; Jim Cullen, *The Civil War in Popular Culture* (Washington, DC: Smithsonian Books, 1995); Gary Gallagher, *Causes Won, Lost, and Forgotten: How Hollywood and Popular Art Shaped What We Know about the Civil War* (Chapel Hill: University of North Carolina Press, 2008); Matthew Christopher Hulbert and John C. Inscoe, eds., *Writing History with Lightning: Cinematic Representations of Nineteenth-Century America* (Baton Rouge: Louisiana State University Press, 2019); Thomas Dixon, *The Torch: A Story of the Paranoiac Who Caused a Great War* (New York: Thomas Dixon, 1927), screenplay.

3. Educational packet and Ford quoted in Casey King, "Abolitionists in American Cinema: From The Birth of a Nation to Amistad," in *Prophets of Protest: Reconsidering the History of American Abolitionism,* ed. Timothy Patrick McCarthy and John Stauffer (New York: New Press, 2006), 268–69; Mark C. Carnes, ed., *Past Imperfect: History According to the Movies* (New York: Henry Holt and Co., 1995); James Oliver Horton and Lois E. Horton, eds., *Slavery and Public History: The Tough Stuff of American Memory* (New York: New Press, 2006).

4. Vivien Ellen Rose and Julie Corley, "A Trademark Approach to the Past: Ken Burns, the Historical Profession, and Assessing Popular Presentations of the Past," *Public Historian* 25, no. 3 (Summer 2003): 49–59; Jim Cullen, *Sensing the Past: Hollywood Stars and Historical Visions* (New York: Oxford University Press, 2013).

5. Jason Phillips, ed., *Storytelling, History, and the Postmodern South* (Baton Rouge: Louisiana State University Press, 2013).

6. Franklin B. Sanborn, ed., *The Life and Letters of John Brown: Liberator of Kansas and Martyr of Virginia* (Boston: Roberts Brothers, 1891), 508–10; Jason Phillips, *Looming Civil War: How Nineteenth-Century Americans Imagined the Future* (New York: Oxford University Press, 2018).

7. James C. Malin, *John Brown and the Legend of Fifty-Six* (New York: Haskell House, 1971), 759; Stephen B. Oates, *To Purge This Land with Blood: A Biography of John Brown* (Amherst: University of Massachusetts Press, 1984), 390.

8. Stephen Vincent Benét, *John Brown's Body* (New York: Rinehart and Co., 1954), 52–53; Kansas Historical Society, "Kansas State Capitol—Curry Murals," *Kansapedia*, www.kshs.org/kansapedia /kansas-state-capitol-curry-murals/16864 (accessed December 9, 2018); R. Blakeslee Gilpin, *John Brown Still Lives! America's Long Reckoning with Violence, Equality, and Change* (Chapel Hill: University of North Carolina Press, 2011), 144–57.

9. *Battle Hymn* was adapted from a biographical tribute of Brown that Gold published in 1923; it was his first published work. Michael Blankfort and Michael Gold, *Battle Hymn* (New York: Samuel French, 1936), 28, 12, 99–100; Michael Denning, *The Cultural Front: The Laboring of American Culture in the Twentieth Century* (London: Verso, 1996), 499n32; Earl Ofari Hutchinson, *Blacks and Reds: Race and Class in Conflict, 1919–1990* (East Lansing: Michigan State University Press, 1995), 97.

10. Denning, *The Cultural Front*, 499n32, 137; Michael Folsom, ed., *Mike Gold: A Literary Anthology* (New York: International Publishers, 1972), 291, 62; James D. Bloom, *Left Letters: The Culture Wars of Mike Gold and Joseph Freeman* (New York: Columbia University Press, 1992), 45–47. The red scare and censorship in Hollywood barred communist interpretations of John Brown from the big screen during Gold's career. See Larry Ceplair and Steven Englund, *The Inquisition in Hollywood: Politics in the Film Community, 1930–1960* (Urbana-Champaign: University of Illinois Press, 2003).

11. Nicole Etcheson, "From 'Bleeding Kansas' to Harpers Ferry via *Santa Fe Trail*," in *Writing History with Lightning*, ed. Hulbert and Inscoe, 137–47; Peggy A. Russo, "John Brown Goes to Hollywood: Santa Fe Trail and Seven Angry Men," in *Terrible Swift Sword: The Legacy of John Brown*, ed. Peggy A. Russo and Paul Finkelman (Athens: Ohio University Press, 2005), 195. Russo argues that Curtiz framed *Santa Fe Trail* as a criticism of America's isolationist policies before the Second World War. She interprets Rader's propaganda as fascist. I contend that the film's heroes espouse isolationism by favoring peace and insisting that the South should be left alone to solve slavery. Moreover, Rader's passionate championing of equality and emancipation is not fascist but communist. Nina Silber concurs with my reading. See Silber, *This War Ain't Over: Fighting the Civil War in New Deal America* (Chapel Hill: University of North Carolina Press, 2018).

12. Russo, "John Brown Goes to Hollywood," 205.

13. Russell Banks, *Cloudsplitter: A Novel* (New York: Harper Perennial, 1999); James McBride, *The Good Lord Bird* (New York: Riverhead Books, 2013); Julia Davis, *The Anvil: The Trial of John Brown, A Two-Act Drama* (Evanston, IL: Harper and Row, 1963).

14. Zachary Price, "Economies of Enjoyment and Terror in *Django Unchained* and *12 Years a Slave*," *Postcolonialist* 2, no. 1 (January 2015): 2–15.

15. Eric Michael Mazur, "Film and Religion in America," in *Oxford Encyclopedia of Religion in America,* ed. John Corrigan (New York: Oxford University Press, 2019).

16. John Brittle reads scripture while whipping a slave in *Django Unchained,* but the film does not explore religion.

17. Steven Mintz, "Spielberg's Amistad and the History Classroom," *History Teacher* 31, no. 3 (May 1998): 370–73.

18. For analysis of how Hollywood has depicted slaves over time, see Natalie Zemon Davis,

Slaves on Screen: Film and Historical Vision (Cambridge, MA: Harvard University Press, 2000); Donald Bogle, *Toms, Coons, Mulattoes, Mammies, and Bucks: An Interpretive History of Blacks in American Films*, rev. ed. (New York: Bloomsbury Academic, 2016).

19. Matthew C. Hulbert, "Review of *The Birth of a Nation* (2016)," *Film and History* 26, no. 2 (Winter 2016): 108–11. Even *Spartacus* (1960), perhaps the most famous film about a slave revolt, justifies the revolt by focusing on how the slave trade separated two lovers, Spartacus (Kirk Douglass) and Varinia (Jean Simmons). As in *Django Unchained* and *The Birth of a Nation*, the main character in *Spartacus* attacks slavery to avenge an outrage committed against his woman.

20. Marcus Rediker, "History White-Washed: Reflections on Steven Spielberg's Amistad," in *Writing History with Lightning*, ed. Hulbert and Inscoe, 95–102.

21. King, "Abolitionism in American Cinema," 280.

22. The Old South is stereotypically gothic in both *Django Unchained* and *The Birth of a Nation*, which was shot on a Georgia cotton plantation, not a historically accurate Virginia tobacco farm. For more on the South in film, see Jack Temple Kirby, *Media-Made Dixie: The South in the American Imagination* (Athens: University of Georgia Press, 1986); and Deborah E. Barker and Kathryn McKee, eds., *American Cinema and the Southern Imaginary* (Athens: University of Georgia Press, 2011).

23. Gender bias is most evident in *Birth of Nation* and *Django Unchained*. Roxanne Gay, "Nate Parker and the Limits of Empathy," *New York Times*, August 19, 2016; Kenneth S. Greenberg, "Birth and Rebirth: Filming Nat Turner in the Age of Fake News," in *Writing History with Lightning*, ed. Hulbert and Inscoe, 84–94; Glenda R. Carpio, "'I Like the Way You Die, Boy,' Fantasy's Role in *Django Unchained*," *Transition*, no. 112 (2013): 1–12; *Harriet*, dir. Kasi Lemmons (Hollywood: Focus Features, 2019), film.

No, Will, He Just Died

The Abandonment of Triumphalism in Recent Civil War Films

BRIAN MATTHEW JORDAN

William H. Mitchell fumed with indignation as he took the stage at Topeka's Memorial Hall on Friday, April 11, 1924. The previous year, the state panel tasked with reviewing and censoring motion pictures reversed its earlier decision to ban D. W. Griffith's twelve-reel feature *The Birth of a Nation* (1915) from theaters throughout Kansas. Reed thin and bespectacled, sporting a graying goatee on his chin and an American flag on his lapel, Mitchell looked every bit the part of a Grand Army of the Republic department commander. "Now the old veterans have flaunted in their faces a film picture which characterizes them as an army of vagabonds and libertines," he objected, "and which parades the leaders of treason against their country as saints from the throne of glory. In this picture the traitor R. E. Lee, robed in his uniform of treason, is represented as a hero and held up as an exemplary character and model for American youth to emulate and pattern after, while U. S. Grant, who brought this arch traitor to his knees at Appomattox, is relegated to the background and help us as an insignificant chump, unworthy of recognition as an American defender." Deeming Griffith's silent epic "the last remnant of the last vomit of rebellion and treason, spewed out upon an unsuspecting public," the grizzled veteran of the Twenty-Fourth Indiana Volunteers urged his fellow ex-soldiers to "accept this challenge," and to "denounce and fight treason to-day with the same spirit and determination" they had displayed at Shiloh and Vicksburg.[1]

The Birth of a Nation, of course, would hardly be "the last" celebration of rebellion and treason on the silver screen. Still, the outrage that its racist depiction of the Civil War and Reconstruction provoked among Union veterans reminds us that Hollywood has always been an important battleground in the ongoing struggle to define the meaning and legacy of the nation's bloodiest conflict.[2] The episode in Kansas likewise indicates that films (not unlike the histories we produce) very often engage the past in an effort to address contemporary social, cultural, and political anxieties. Griffith's film, of course, had little difficulty attracting an audience in a state that became a hothouse of Klan activity in the 1920s.[3]

Since Appomattox, Civil War memory has functioned as a reliable index of society's ideas about race, war, and national identity. Sterilized and segregated tales hawked in the twentieth century remembered a mythic past that at once promoted the nation's quest for empire, excused Jim Crow, and affirmed American exceptionalism. "The Civil War," mused the southern novelist Robert Penn Warren, "is our only felt history—history lived in the national imagination."[4] For decades, Hollywood helped Americans to feel—and feel *good* about—their Civil War past. But more recently, filmic representations have cast the war into question—a move that reflects a broader national ambivalence about both military conflict and the health of our democracy. Five recent films betray much about the shifting and unstable place of the Civil War in the contemporary American imagination. Costly wars, racist violence, and political brinksmanship have exposed the fragility of our experiment in self-government and renewed questions about who we are as a nation. On cue, filmmakers have dismantled alluring myths in search of a new national story.

For much of the twentieth century, cinematic representations of the Civil War ennobled its combat—and only rarely contemplated the war's charge or consequences. As Bruce Chadwick has noted, polemical representations of the war (such as the one rendered by D. W. Griffith) quickly yielded to nonideological hymns of sectional reconciliation and national redemption. Whether as a nostalgic, magnolia-shaded escape from the demands of modern American life or as a celebration of a supposedly simpler, heroic time when men fought for what they believed in, Civil War motion pictures almost always sought to affirm that 1861–65 was the crucible of American national identity. "The mythmakers," Chadwick contends, "gave us a past that demeaned African-Americans and ignored much of actual history, a glorious and honorable past that probably never was, but a past we would like to have had." Filmmakers spent little time "worrying" about the war or its substantive issues, effacing the complexities of "a troubled time in American history by framing it in a positive way."[5] The war became an annealing fire that forged a brawny nation.

It was this motif that filmmaker Ken Burns so successfully exploited in his blockbuster nine-episode PBS documentary, *The Civil War* (1990). The film opens with the wistful strains of Jay Unger and Molly Mason's "Ashokan Farewell" wailing in the background. As the camera pans across iconic period photographs, narrator David McCullough makes clear that this was "our" war. The opening narration is littered with unironic references to Americans: "more than three million Americans fought" in the Civil War, the script informs. "Americans slaughtered one another wholesale here, in America, in their own cornfields and peach orchards, along familiar roads and by waters with old American names." For "two days at Shiloh, on the banks of the Tennessee, more American men fell than in all previous American wars combined." After cutting to quaint, creaky newsreel footage of the 1938 Blue-Gray Reunion in Gettysburg—the final meeting of Union and Confederate veterans—novelist Shelby Foote appears on screen to declare in his distinctive drawl: "Any understanding of this nation has to be based, and I mean really based, on an understanding of the Civil War." Though an "enormous catastrophe," he contends, "it defined us. . . . It was the crossroads of our being, and it was a hell of a crossroads." For Foote, no less than for Burns, the war's tragedy was eloquent poetry—a quintessentially American tale of "regeneration through violence."[6]

But perhaps no depiction of the Civil War on the silver screen did more to imbue the war's losses with redemptive meaning than *Glory* (1989). Director Edward Zwick's film is bookended by powerful combat sequences. The film first depicts the bloodiest single day of the war—the September 17, 1862, battle of Antietam, in which the twenty-four-year-old Captain Robert Gould Shaw leads a company of the Second Massachusetts Volunteer Infantry into the bloody cornfield. Men attempt to dodge the leaden hail that rains around them. Clipped in the neck by an enemy slug, Shaw stumbles to the ground. Hugging the earth, the wounded soldier watches with bemused horror as the battle rages around him. After the shooting stops, the camera surveys a field littered with discarded cartridge boxes, disabled cannon, and dead and wounded men—the inevitable debris of battle. An all-black burial crew, reminiscent of the one depicted in Alexander Gardner's 1865 print, "A Burial Party, Cold Harbor, Virginia," roams the field, shovels and spades slung over their shoulders. John Rawlins, a member of the crew, rouses Captain Shaw, who winds his way to a crowded field hospital. Not unlike Gardner's haunting photograph, the sequence's deliberate juxtapositions hold out the promise that the war's great violence will redeem the nation by ridding it of slavery. Effectively, the scene conveys what Massachusetts Governor John A. Andrew announces at the Boston soiree where a recuperating Captain Shaw decides to take command of the newly organized, all-black Fifty-Fourth Massachusetts: Antietam was "a great and a terrible day," the victory that inspired President Lincoln to issue his preliminary emancipation proclamation.[7]

Shaw and his men—no less than the nation itself—are "redeemed" by the inescapable logic of the war's events. Captain Shaw must overcome not only the scenes of Antietam, which continue to annex him, but his own, not insignificant, reservations about the capabilities of black men in blue uniforms. "I don't know these men," Shaw confesses with anguish in a letter to his mother. At the same time, Trip—a sardonic escaped slave turned Union soldier—must set aside the conviction that he will "never be anything in the eyes of a white man other than an ugly ass chimp"—and embrace the opportunity to demonstrate his manhood to the nation.

The slights suffered by the regiment—a division quartermaster who ignores requisitions for socks, shoes, and supplies; the inferior pay initially dispensed to black soldiers; and superior commanders who sneer at the thought of African Americans engaging in combat—incense Shaw, but in the end serve only to steel his convictions. "If you men will take no pay, then none of us will," he declares in a dramatic sequence as the troops gleefully rip their pay stubs to shreds.

Even more dramatic is Trip's baptism in wartime waters. When the skeptical soldier informs the newly appointed sergeant major that he "ain't nothing but the white man's dog," Sergeant Major John Rawlins musters a forceful response, observing that Trip is "full of hate" because of his experiences in bondage. "Well, that might not be living, but it sure as hell ain't dying. And dying's what these white boys have been doin' for going on three years now, dying by the thousands! Dying for you, fool! I know, 'cuz I dug the graves. And all the time I keep askin' myself, 'When, O Lord, when gonna be our time?' Gonna come a time when we all gonna hafta ante up and kick in like men."

The dressing-down has an effect, for although Trip announces to Shaw that he "ain't fightin' this war for you, sir," he ultimately concedes that seeing the Union war effort through to victory is the only way to end slavery and begin racial healing. "It stinks, I suppose," Shaw tells him. "Yeah, it stinks bad," Trip replies. "And we all covered up in it. Ain't nobody clean. Be nice to get clean though." The only way to "get clean," he determines, is to "ante up and kick in." Trip's transformation mirrors the triumphal interpretation of the war touted by exponents of the self-emancipation thesis: namely, that wartime events rushed toward freedom with an inexorable force.[8]

Not unlike Shaw's, Trip's transformation comes full circle with the storming of Battery Wagner, which supplies the plot for the movie's moving, final sequences. Military service facilitates his personal metamorphosis. The evening before the battle, the men send up prayers around the dancing sparks of a campfire. With great emotion, Trip announces that the regiment has become his family. "Y'all's the onliest family I got," he says, professing his "love" for the unit. "Ain't much a matter what happen tomorrow. 'Cause we men, ain't we?! We men, ain't we?!"

The next day, a choir of bells toll as the Fifty-Fourth Massachusetts charges toward the zagging Rebel works. Though they suffer heavy losses and fail to wrest the fort from Confederate hands, the film makes clear that the men have triumphed in death. A Confederate burial detail heaves Colonel Shaw's lifeless body into a mass grave with his men, their attempt at indignity remade (as many reviewers noted) into an inspiring moment of racial reconciliation. The film concludes with a title card declaring that the bravery of the Fifty-Fourth Massachusetts "turned the tide of the war"—one final note of redemption in a "heart tugging" and "self-congratulatory" film that "eschews the ironic for the heroic."[9] Though it gives the lie to the myth of the loyal slave, *Glory* departs not at all from popular post–civil rights era interpretations of the war, in which "both blacks and whites found some commonality of purpose."[10]

Making its box office debut four years later, director Ronald F. Maxwell's *Gettysburg* (1993) also found something noble and affirming in the war's calamities. Because the film fails to situate the battle in a larger context (a decision at once faithful to Michael Shaara's novel and necessary to ensure that the audience develops empathy for both armies), questions about the ideological purpose of the war or its causes are all but irrelevant. The battle instead emerges as a venue for soldiers to demonstrate their daring and martial prowess. "Show me, for the thousandth time, Joshua Lawrence Chamberlain on Little Round Top, exhorting his exhausted men to make one last charge to win the day," Martin Pengelly confessed in *The Guardian*, "and I will feel a thrill and a catch in the throat."[11]

Not surprisingly, *Gettysburg* is a "guilty pleasure" for Civil War aficionados; a number of its devotees insist on the director's cut, now available on blu-ray.

"Despite flaws," one Civil War enthusiast commented on an Internet discussion forum in anticipation of the film's twenty-fifth anniversary, "it's still one of my favorite movies." In 2018, its adoring fans crowded into Gettysburg's sold-out Majestic Theater to once again watch the film on the big screen—and to attend a postshow "meet and greet" with cast members Stephen Lang (Major General George E. Pickett), Patrick Gorman (Major General John Bell Hood), Andrew Prine (Brigadier General Richard B. Garnett), Patrick Stuart (Colonel E. Porter Alexander), and Brian Mallon (Major General Winfield Scott Hancock).[12]

While the appeal of *Gettysburg* owes something to the film's "poetic" cinematography and Randy Edelman's stirring soundtrack—who can forget the chirpy whistle of "Fife and Drum," as the Iron Brigade pushes into Herbst's Woods, or the mystical strains of the main title?—even more significant was the way in which Maxwell posited the Civil War as an antidote to the trials of modern American life. *Gettysburg* debuted in theaters at a moment when the nation was showing signs of stress fracture. The confident, hawkish optimism of the 1980s—put on display at the flag-waving 1984 Olympic Games, and seemingly confirmed by the smashing of the Berlin Wall and the end of the Cold War—could no longer efface deep divisions at home in culture, politics, and the media. Riots and racial unrest, for instance, gripped Los Angeles in the spring of 1992 after a bystander's camcorder captured grainy footage of five white police officers beating Rodney King, an African American, following an intense, high-speed chase along I-210. The following spring, it was federal agents' fifty-one-day siege of a Branch Davidian compound on the outskirts of Waco, Texas, that invited the nation's rapt attention. In Washington, DC, the newly inaugurated president, Bill Clinton, became no stranger to controversies. Beguiling technological developments, together with a sputtering economy, disoriented Americans as they lurched toward the new millennium. By celebrating the uncommon pluck and mettle of soldiers North and South—by admiring the clenched jaws and burnished bayonets that both attacked and defended Little Round Top—Maxwell urged modern Americans to rise to the occasion by mustering the same manly resolve put on display the first three days of July 1863.[13]

Punctuated by panoramic shots of reenactors, Maxwell's *Gettysburg* rendered an idealized picture of the Civil War's bloodiest battle.[14] Following a brief prelude, Maxwell transports his viewers to Tuesday, June 30, 1863. It is on this day that "Harrison," a fictional, waggish actor turned enterprising Confederate scout, plies General James Longstreet with the news that "the Yankee cavalry" and seven corps of Federal infantrymen are within striking distance. From there, the scenes alternate between officers and men on both sides, documenting their participation in the three-day engagement. Each day of the fight is reduced to a single set-piece action: Buford's stalwart delaying action west of town on July 1, the fight for the rock-strewn slopes of Little Round Top on July 2 and Pickett's Charge on July 3. While faithful to Shaara's novel, this decision nonetheless noiselessly effaces the battle's ugliest and most confusing combat—as well as actions (the fight north of and in town on July 1, and the battle for the Wheatfield on July 2, for example) that would highlight the participation of non-native soldiers and civilians.[15]

In Maxwell's *Gettysburg*, the leaders of both armies display a heroic fatalism; they accept that battle is their destiny, a conviction that sometimes mutes deep-seated reservations. In an especially memorable scene, General Buford surveys the ridges that undulate west of Gettysburg. Turning to Colonel Thomas C. Devin, who leads one of his brigades, the cavalry division commander remarks, "I've led a soldier's life, and I've never seen anything as brutally clear as this. It's as if I can actually see the blue troops in one long, bloody moment, going up the long slope to the stony top. As if it were already done . . . already a memory." Buford forecasts that the army's new commander, Major General George Gordon Meade, will "come in slowly, cautiously." But even as the gritty cavalryman envisages another bloody reverse, he cannot resist the fight. "You must even take part, and help it fail," he adds. Confederate commanders are equally resigned to whatever fate awaits them. Preparing for the second day of battle, Lee muses to Longstreet, "We do not fear our own death, you and I. . . . When you attack, you must hold nothing back. You must commit yourself totally."

Since men on both sides of the fight are resigned to their circumstances, they are not especially political. James Longstreet, for example, tells the British military observer Sir Arthur Fremantle that southerners should have "freed the slaves and then fired on Fort Sumter." In one of the movie's final scenes, a pensive Lee, regretting the catastrophe of Pickett's Charge, asks rhetorically, "And does it matter after all who wins? Was that ever really the question?" The theme of fatalism feeds naturally into the trope of reconciliation. "*Gettysburg*, in the end," one reviewer noted soon after the film's release, "is about the tragic cost of national division and the hope of reconciliation."[16]

★ ★ ★

In 1993, of course, it was still possible to celebrate the swiftness of sectional reconciliation after the Civil War. Beginning that very year, however, and over the course of the next decade and a half, Civil War historians eagerly embraced memory as a powerful, analytical tool. By the early 2000s, in the words of one leading scholar, historical memory studies had become "not merely a cottage industry but a boon trade." Collectively, this scholarship considered the significant cost effects of sectional reconciliation: namely, how national healing was achieved at the expense of any real reckoning with the war's cause, conduct, and consequences. In particular, historian David W. Blight's prize-winning *Race and Reunion: The Civil War and American Memory* (2001) revealed how sterilized, nonideological tales of the war both harmonized with and advanced the politics of racial segregation.[17] Once disarming, the spectacle of "Blue-Gray fraternalism" now emerged as a stubborn reminder of the war's "unfinished work"—and of the nation's consistent unwillingness to confront the painful legacies of a bloody rebellion waged on behalf of chattel slavery.

The influence of this scholarship was profound. At symposia in Nashville and Washington, DC, the National Park Service looked to overhaul its interpretive efforts at Civil War battlefield sites—long focused on military minutiae to the exclusion of the war's crucial social, cultural, and political contexts. Though many important stakeholders and battlefield preservationists craved "rectangle, triangle, and arrow" history, believing that battlefield sites were military classrooms, scholars of Civil War memory correctly pointed out that a fixation on tactical and operational details had served to overwhelm any consideration of the reasons the war was fought. Without making slavery and race central to discussion of the war, a distorted picture of the conflict emerged that prevented any real understanding of what was at stake between 1861 and 1865. The cause of the war became increasingly difficult even for popular audiences to deny after the publication of historian Charles B. Dew's *Apostles of Disunion* (2001), a concise and accessible text that relied on the words of southern secession commissioners to demonstrate that the Confederacy was founded to maintain slavery and white supremacy.[18]

If memory studies offered the first significant challenge to the reconciliation paradigm, the horrific events of 9/11—followed closely by costly, seemingly unending wars spanning (at this writing) nearly two decades and three presidencies—provided the second. A mounting cynicism about the efficacy of military force, mocking uncertainties about the meaning of war's human toll, and racial tensions that burst (with tragic frequency) into deadly violence supplied the backdrop for the Civil War's sesquicentennial commemoration (2011–15). Not surprisingly, Civil War films released in this period served only to amplify the nation's restless anxieties about war, power, gender, and race. While motion pictures like *The Conspirator* (2010), *Lincoln* (2012), *Copperhead* (2013), *Free State of Jones* (2016), and *The Beguiled* (2017) each addressed specific, contemporary concerns, collectively they betrayed a certain uneasiness about the Civil War's meaning in modern American life.[19] By giving voice to the conflict's messiness—its ambiguities and intraparty battles, internecine divisions and antiheroes—these films also reflect important trends in recent Civil War historiography, which itself seems stunningly unable to achieve any meaningful synthesis of the conflict's signal accomplishments—the abolition of slavery and the preservation of the Union—with its "dark" underside of grisly violence, atrocity, and human destruction.[20]

The war maintains a brooding presence in Steven Spielberg's *Lincoln* (2012). On the floor of the US House of Representatives, a knot of dismayed congressmen scan lengthy casualty lists that annex the entire front page of James Gordon Bennett's *New York Herald*. An anguished Mary Lincoln implores her husband to prevent their eldest son, Robert, from enlisting in the Union Army; in a vain attempt to satisfy her, the president invites his son to accompany him on a visit to the Richmond-Petersburg front. While his father visits with grievously wounded men in a makeshift army hospital, Robert waits outside—just long enough to watch as hospital stewards trundle a bloody wagon heaped with freshly amputated limbs to a nearby burial pit. In one of the film's most powerful sequences, Lincoln removes his stovepipe hat and rides mournfully along the siege lines of Petersburg, now littered with dead soldiers. "I've never seen the like of it before," he tells Ulysses S. Grant, who rides alongside him. "We've made it possible for one another to do terrible things." Even Major General Daniel E. Sickles's shattered tibia, mounted for public display in a glass case at Washington's US Army Medical Museum, makes a cameo appearance—as though we need one more reminder of what the war did to human bodies.[21]

Beginning with its opening sequence, *Lincoln* presents a war that is anything but ennobling. The title card fades to an especially brutal battle scene—in a dark, drenching rain, soldiers use their muskets as clubs and stab with their bayonets. A voice-over instructs that this is the battle at Jenkins' Ferry, Arkansas, a vicious engagement during Maj. Gen. Frederick Steele's Camden Expedition. Just twelve days before at a place called Poison Spring, Confederate General James Marmaduke's victorious troops "refused to take [African American] prisoners," twisting, in the words of one historian, "a glorious Confederate triumph . . . into Arkansas's most notorious war crime." The men of the Second Kansas Colored Infantry regiment vowed to seek revenge. On April 30, 1864, a righteous rage carried them through the fight. Shouting "Poison Springs" as they stormed the Confederate gunners, the black soldiers left no doubt about what motivated their "acts of merciless cruelty."[22]

Spielberg not only recreates the vicious battle, but affords two African American veterans of the fight—Corporal Ira Clark and Private Harold Green, now enlisted in the 116th United States Colored Troops and ready to shove off to the port of Wilmington—the chance to speak directly to their commander in chief. The men do not squander the opportunity, upbraiding Lincoln for the second-class treatment black soldiers receive in the Union armies. "Now that white people have accustomed themselves to seeing negro men with guns fighting on their behalf, and even getting the same pay," Clark jeers, "in a few years perhaps they can abide the idea of negro lieutenants and captains." While no less determined, courageous, or ideological, these men are not the soldiers of Zwick's *Glory*. They do not fight to demonstrate their manhood, nor do they have any patience for the false pieties of recruiting posters or war propagandists. Clark, for one, presciently anticipates the challenges yet ahead for African American veterans. When Lincoln asks the soldier what he intends to do after the war, Clark replies that he will go to work. "But you should know," he adds assertively, "I get sick at the smell of bootblack and I can't cut hair."

Two white soldiers interrupt this remarkable exchange. When they announce that they had attended the dedication of the Soldiers' National Cemetery in Gettysburg two years before, Lincoln's attention is piqued. Somewhat self-consciously, the president asks if they could hear what he said. Lincoln gets his answer when they begin reciting, "mechanically" and with perfect accuracy, the words of the Gettysburg Address. Before they can finish, the troops are ordered to move out; the white soldiers and Private Green disappear into the fog, but Corporal Clark lingers on the screen a moment longer. "That we here highly resolve these dead shall not have died in vain," he says, picking up the speech where the white soldiers left off. "That this nation, under God, shall have a new birth of freedom—and that government of the people, by the people, for the people shall not perish from the Earth."

Some reviewers criticized this admittedly contrived opening sequence, finding it implausible that Union soldiers would have committed the words of Lincoln's speech to memory within the space of two years.[23] Nonetheless, the scene movingly establishes Spielberg's purpose: to depict black freedom as the war's unfinished charge, not its unequivocal consequence. The sense of urgency that animates the film is the need to secure passage of the Thirteenth Amendment before the end of the war—a keen reminder that the conflict could have ended without destroying slavery in the states of the former Confederacy.[24]

While the historian Kate Masur and other scholars scolded *Lincoln* for "generic, archetypal" African American characters who "do almost nothing but passively wait for white men to liberate them," less noticed was the way that the *war's* agency was likewise diminished. Much more than battlefield pluck or sure-footed idealism, it is pragmatism—in turn dubious, exploitative, dissembling, and unsightly—that ultimately triumphs in *Lincoln*. Principle alone cannot win the day; securing the votes for the amendment ending slavery in America requires promises of patronage and concessions made to political opponents. It is a lesson that chastens even the film's hero, the club-footed Pennsylvania abolitionist Thaddeus Stevens.[25]

Spielberg's *Lincoln* powerfully conveys that the Civil War left behind unfinished business. Following the president's assassination (a scene Spielberg opts to not recreate), the film ends with a stunning recreation of his Second Inaugural Address. Before the screen fades to the credits, Lincoln reads the speech's lyrical last line, in which he urges his countrymen to "bind up the nation's wounds, to care for him who shall have borne the battle, and for his widow, and his orphan—to do all which may achieve and cherish a just and lasting peace." Rather than end the film in the back room of William Petersen's boardinghouse, where the sixteenth president would draw his last breath, Spielberg's unexpected intervention—an ethereal, dreamlike flashback—prods us to reflect on Lincoln's eternal message, a speech in which "neither vindication nor triumphalism is present." As the speech's most careful student concludes, Lincoln "saw that the issues at hand would not be solved by either emancipation or armistice" and "offered his sermon as the prism through which he himself strained to see the light of God."[26] Lincoln's eloquent chastening of the nation is an altogether fitting ending for a film in which the war neither affirms nor resolves.

★ ★ ★

Notwithstanding its significant departures from the popular narrative of the Civil War as an unambiguous moment of national redemption, *Lincoln* was merely a portent of what was to come in director Gary Ross's *Free State of Jones*

(2016). Hailed by historians but earning regrettably mixed reviews from critics, Ross's film was a 139-minute assault not just on the Lost Cause, but on the idea that the Civil War was a "fulcrum of freedom." In no small part, the film achieves this through its periodization—stretching from the second battle of Corinth in October 1862 to the collapse of Reconstruction on the ground in 1876. This is the "long" Civil War on screen—made even longer by periodic flash-forwards to the 1948 trial of anti-rebel Newton Knight's great-grandson, Davis, indicted for violating Mississippi's anti-miscegenation statue. The war here is not only unfinished, but unending.[27]

From the outset, Ross makes clear his intent to upend conventional narratives. A line of gray-and-butternut-clad soldiers charges up a hill littered with dead bodies; at the crest, they are greeted with sheets of enemy musketry, which knock Rebels out of the ranks by the dozens. After the battle concludes, the camera surveys the gruesome costs of the futile attack: maggots feast on a decapitated head, a stiffened hand clutches a framed tintype, and a stretcher-bearer hurries wounded Rebels to an overwhelmed field hospital, where surgeons hack away with bone saws, nurses wring out bloody bandages, and the wails of dying men form an orchestra. The sequence scorns any suggestion of combat as glorious or heroic. In camp that evening, the men read about the so-called Twenty Negro Law, a much-reviled provision of the 1862 Confederate Conscription Act that exempted from military service "one white man on every plantation with twenty slaves or more." Newt joins the measure's choir of critics. Contemplating the impending discharge of some wealthy slaveholders, he declares, "I'm tired of helping 'em fight for their damn cotton." When another soldier announces, "I'm fighting for honor," an agnostic Knight mocks him. "Oh, that's *good*," he replies.[28]

When the battle resumes the next day, an especially accurate sharpshooter's bullet claims the life of Newton Knight's nephew, Daniel, who, despite his youth, has been conscripted into the Rebel Army. Hurrying through the maze of Confederate works, Newt manages to deliver his nephew to a field hospital, only to find that blood-spattered surgeons are too busy to tend to Daniel's injuries. Instead, Newt is left to pillow his dying nephew's head and comfort him in his final moments. Later, when one of Newt's comrades assures him that the boy "died with honor," Knight immediately corrects him. "No, Will," he replies, "he just died." With this remarkable exchange, it is clear that the redemptive Civil War metanarrative has been buried in that simple Mississippi churchyard grave, too.

Devastating the Lost Cause narrative that white southerners waged a heroic rebellion against an overweening federal government determined to trample their way of life and local, home rule, Ross's film depicts a Confederate war bureaucracy that, in its efforts to preserve slavery and white supremacy, became more and more intrusive in the lives of ordinary men and women. Confederate cavalry officers and tax agents stalk the home front, rounding up hogs, emptying corn cribs, drafting men, and hunting army deserters as though they were fugitive enslaved persons. The Rebels stifle dissenters with hand-turned nooses. Newt Knight thus rejects the war and creates the Free State of Jones— his own biracial Confederacy—in a snake-choked swamp. While anything but color-blind, the Free State of Jones is nonetheless committed to the principle that "every man is a man."[29]

As Joseph Beilein Jr. and other commentators have noted, one of the film's most evocative scenes depicts Knight and his followers lowering the Rebel flag that flaps in the breeze over the Jones County Courthouse. Yet Ross's real cinematic coup is not in hauling down the Stars and Bars, but rather in demonstrating just how ineffectual the exercise proved to be in the blood-spattered years of Reconstruction. In an index of the public's dim memory of the years following the Civil War, titles appear on the screen to convey important narrative details and historical facts related to Reconstruction. One of the most effective titles places the word "emancipation" in quotation marks as rows of African American sharecroppers tend to the fields of their former masters. From voter intimidation and uncounted ballots to farcical loyalty oaths and cold lynch mobs, Ross's film demonstrates the myriad ways the war went on.

Both *Lincoln* and *Free State of Jones* darkened and destabilized the narrative of the war. Sofia Coppola carried this work forward in *The Beguiled* (2017), her haunting remake of Don Siegel's 1971 Southern Gothic. Critics commented that the war appeared "distant" in the film.[30] "Death and danger," writes one, are "lurking just out of sight."[31] Yet if uninterested in the war as a military *event*, the film is profoundly interested in the war as a human *experience*. The film offers a powerful meditation on some "lesser appreciated" battlefields of the conflict: the struggles of wartime women to maintain their emotional health and satisfy their sexual desires. Indeed, that critics and the viewing public did not immediately appreciate *The Beguiled* as Civil War cinema speaks volumes about the degree to which our "heroic national narratives" of the conflict "necessarily involve selective celebration along patriarchal lines." As historian Stephanie McCurry recently pointed out, the "writing out of women from histories of war reflects a deep investment in the gender order itself and a desire to limit the destructiveness of war."[32]

In Coppola's film, the war is neither a source of identity nor an occasion for courage; much to the contrary, it cruelly displaces and sows maddening doubt. Amelia Dabney, for instance, the young pupil who first stumbles upon Corporal John McBurney in the woods and invites him to the boarding school, announces that her "home is in Georgia"; she remains in Virginia because her "mother decided it would be better" with "General Sherman down there so close to Atlanta and all." Amelia reports that all of the men have marched off to the front (among them is her older brother, who was killed the previous year in Tennessee). She further informs Corporal McBurney that the "slaves left"— a remark that at once excludes African American voices from the film while subtly undermining the trope of the "loyal slave."[33] As an Irish immigrant lured into the ranks of the Sixty-Sixth New York Volunteer Infantry regiment by a $300 bounty, even the "unwelcome" Yankee visitor has been displaced by the war he cravenly attempts to escape.

More subtly but no less significantly, Coppola, like Ross, has the Lost Cause in her crosshairs. Postwar histories revered white southern women as indefatigably loyal to the Confederate war effort—prepared to place everything on the "altar of sacrifice." But such narratives effaced, in the words of historian Drew Gilpin Faust, the degree to which "emotional and material deprivation took their inescapable psychological toll." For elite, white southern women, the war occasioned a painful reckoning with the antebellum "bargain" that exchanged male protection for female domesticity. Forced to step into new and uncomfortable roles that confronted them with the intellectual bankruptcy of the plantation way, many elite southern women lost hope in the Confederate project. Unable to live any longer in a "feminine sphere," they urged their men to return home, encumbered by "profound doubts about what lay within their power to accomplish" and "serious questions about the desirability of female independence." For elite white southern women, the demands of "self-preservation" prevailed over sacrifice. "Faced with the unrelenting hardship of war," Faust contends, "they had begun inevitably to think about themselves."[34]

Acknowledging debts to Faust's important scholarship, Coppola treats the war as a gendered experience. "I wanted to tell the story of the isolation of these women, cut off from the world and in denial of a changing world," she writes. Not unlike Ross's war, which levies increasingly unreasonable demands, Coppola's suffocates; it promotes self-interest, not self-abnegation, and ultimately explodes in frenzy—dispatching the Yankee visitor who has charmed and repelled. "Throughout the film, we see students and teachers trying to hold on to their crumbling way of life," Coppola continues. "Eventually, they even lock themselves up and sever all ties to the outside world in order to perpetuate a reality that has only become a fantasy."[35]

For decades, the Civil War itself was a reality that came to us as a fantasy—in print and on celluloid, in reenactments and on computer screens. Recent events, however, have prompted a popular and scholarly rethinking of the Civil War's meaning and its place in our narratives of the past. Once the inspiring hinge of our national identity—that "time when we threw off the slavery of our inheritance and became truly American"—the Civil War's legacy is today far more complicated, ambiguous, and uncertain. "Soon enough, if not already," historian Stephen Berry wrote as the sesquicentennial loomed, "the Civil War will be understood not as a test this country passed—a kiln in which the nation was fired—but as a test we failed when we couldn't, short of war, give up our original addiction to 'black gold.'"[36] Indeed, in recent years, Civil War narratives have frayed and fragmented. As art historian Kirk Savage anticipated, by abandoning the "self-congratulatory rhetoric of 'reconciliation'" and refusing to shoehorn "the Civil War and civil rights movement into a simplistic narrative of national redemption," recent scholarship has recovered "historical actors as the human beings they were."[37]

Attentive to war as a human experience, aware of its substantial costs, and mostly agnostic about its accomplishments, recent depictions of the Civil War on the silver screen have also abandoned triumphalism. And while the enduring appeal of the Lost Cause was made evident with director Ronald F. Maxwell's *Gods and Generals* (2003), in the wake of the white-supremacist violence in Charleston and Charlottesville, Hollywood may never again dream of loyal slaves or salute the Confederate flag.

One can only speculate about what William H. Mitchell would make of these developments. The old veteran would doubtless cheer the retreat of the Lost Cause and nod approvingly at the overdue acknowledgment of the war's human toll. At the same time, the Kansas Republican who celebrated his comrades for "t[aking] our declaration of independence out of the class of fiction" might sound a note of caution: if we are left to find redemption in the future, then we first need to divine some inspiration from the past.[38]

NOTES

1. *Journal of the Forty-second Annual Encampment of the Grand Army of the Republic, Department of Kansas* (Topeka: B. P. Walker, State Printer, 1923), 75–76; Sheridan Ploughe, *History of Reno County, Kansas* (Indianapolis: B. F. Bowen & Co., Inc., 1917), 48–49. On the censorship of *The Birth of a Nation* in Kansas, see Gerald R. Butters Jr., *Banned in Kansas: Motion Picture Censorship, 1915–1966* (Columbia: University of Missouri Press, 2007), 78–100.

2. Recent takes on Hollywood's Civil War include Brian Steel Wills, *Gone With The Glory: The Civil War in Cinema* (Lanham, MD: Rowman and Littlefield, 2007); Gary W. Gallagher, *Causes Won, Lost, and Forgotten: How Hollywood and Popular Art Shape What We Know About the Civil War* (Chapel Hill: University of North Carolina Press, 2008); Jim Cullen, *The Civil War in Popular Culture: A Reusable Past* (Washington, DC: Smithsonian Institution Press, 1995); Barbara A. Gannon, *Americans Remember Their Civil War* (Santa Barbara, CA: Praeger, 2017), 99–112, and Matthew C. Hulbert and John C. Inscoe, eds., *Writing History with Lightning: Cinematic Representations of Nineteenth Century America* (Baton Rouge: Louisiana State University Press, 2019).

3. See Linda Gordon, *The Second Coming of the KKK: The Ku Klux Klan of the 1920s and the American Political Tradition* (New York: Liveright, 2017), and Brent M. S. Campney, *This Is Not Dixie: Racist Violence in Kansas, 1861–1927* (Urbana: University of Illinois Press, 2015).

4. Robert Penn Warren, *The Legacy of the Civil War* (New York: Random House, 1961), 3.

5. Bruce Chadwick, *The Reel Civil War: Mythmaking in American Film* (New York: Vintage, 2001), 1–16, quotes at 13 and 16.

6. See also Robert Brent Toplin, ed., *Ken Burns's* The Civil War: *Historians Respond* (New York: Oxford University Press, 1996). Richard Slotkin has argued that "regeneration through violence became the structuring metaphor of the American experience." See his *Regeneration Through Violence: The Mythology of the American Frontier, 1600–1860* (Norman: University of Oklahoma Press, 1973), 5.

7. On the Fifty-Fourth Massachusetts, see Douglas R. Egerton, *Thunder at The Gates: The Black Civil War Regiments That Redeemed America* (New York: Basic Books, 2016). For superb meditations on the Gardner photograph, see Anthony W. Lee and Elizabeth Young, *On Alexander Gardner's Photographic Sketchbook of the Civil War* (Berkeley: University of California Press, 2007).

8. My analysis here draws on W. Scott Poole, "'Ain't Nobody Clean': *Glory!* and the Politics of Black Agency," in *Memory and Myth: The Civil War in Fiction and Film from Uncle Tom's Cabin to Cold Mountain*, ed. David B. Sachsman, S. Kittrell Rushing, and Roy Morris Jr. (West Lafayette, IN: Purdue University Press, 2007).

9. Kevin Thomas, "'Glory' An Epic of Wanting Proportions," *Los Angeles Times*, December 14, 1989. Zwick's film considers neither the final year of the war for the Fifty-Fourth Massachusetts, which included an ugly, costly defeat at Olustee, Florida, nor the difficulties and discrimination

faced by African American Civil War veterans in the postwar years. On the atrocities at Olustee, see Robert Broadwater, *The Battle of Olustee, 1864: The Final Union Attempt to Seize Florida* (Jefferson, NC: McFarland & Co., 2006). On the hardships of black Civil War veterans, consult Donald R. Shaffer, *After the Glory: The Struggles of Black Civil War Veterans* (Lawrence: University Press of Kansas, 2004).

10. Edward Zwick as quoted in Michelle P. Perry, "*Glory* Director Edward Zwick Discusses His Motivations Behind the Film," *The Tech* 109, no. 60 (January 24, 1990): 11; Edward L. Ayers, "Worrying About the Civil War," in *What Caused the Civil War? Reflections on the South and Southern History* (New York: W. W. Norton, 2005), 107.

11. Martin Pengelly, "My Guilty Pleasure: Gettysburg," *The Guardian*, March 21, 2014.

12. Quote from Civil War enthusiast posted to CivilWarTalk forum, civilwartalk.com/threads /gettysburg-movie-25th-anniversary-in-2018.134920/page-2 (accessed March 24, 2019); on the twenty-fifth anniversary screening of the Ronald F. Maxwell film at Gettysburg's Majestic Theater, see Gettysburg College's Majestic, www.gettysburgmajestic.org/calendar/event_detail.dot?id =3f84ada2-a7a1–4c11-a210-ab3e9a8b3430 (accessed March 24, 2019).

13. Kevin Kruse and Julian Zelizer, *Fault Lines: A History of the United States Since 1974* (New York: W. W. Norton, 2018).

14. Michael Shaara, *The Killer Angels* (New York: David McKay Co., Inc., 1974).

15. Margaret S. Crieghton, *The Colors of Courage: Gettysburg's Forgotten History: Immigrants, Women, and African Americans in the Civil War's Defining Battle* (New York: Basic Books, 2005). Lesley Gordon makes this point in "And Does It Matter, After All, Who Wins? The Movie Gettysburg and Popular Perceptions of the Civil War," in Hulbert and Inscoe, eds., *Writing History With Lightning*, 172–80.

16. Ken Ringle, review of Ron Maxwell's *Gettysburg, Washington Post*, October 10, 1993.

17. Michael Vorenberg, "Recovered Memory of the Civil War," *Reviews in American History* 29, no. 4 (December 2001): 551. See, for example, Nina Silber, *The Romance of Reunion: Northerners and The South, 1865–1900* (Chapel Hill: University of North Carolina Press, 1993); Kirk Savage, *Standing Soldiers, Kneeling Slaves: Race, War, and Monument in Nineteenth Century America* (Princeton, NJ: Princeton University Press, 1997); David W. Blight, *Race and Reunion: The Civil War in American Memory* (Cambridge, MA: Harvard University Press, 2001).

18. See Robert K. Sutton, ed., *Rally on the High Ground: The National Park Service's Civil War Symposium* (Washington, DC: Eastern National, 2001); Charles B. Dew, *Apostles of Disunion: Southern Secession Commissioners and the Causes of the Civil War* (Charlottesville: University of Virginia Press, 2001).

19. Based on Harold Frederic's 1893 novel, Ronald F. Maxwell's *Copperhead* was preoccupied by the question of dissent during a time of war. Since he has been an outspoken critic of the United States' interventionist foreign policy and its "disastrous and costly" wars in the Middle East, it should come as little surprise that Maxwell's latest film embraced Lincoln's critics and the most determined opponents of the Union war effort. On Maxwell's foreign policy views, see Ronald F. Maxwell, "America Last?" www.breitbart.com/politics/2017/04/08/ron-maxwell-america -last/ (accessed March 24, 2019). At the same time, harkening back to a much older scholarship disinclined to see John Wilkes Booth's dastardly crime as premeditated or ideologically motivated, director Robert Redford's *The Conspirator* presumed Mary Surratt's innocence in an effort to critique the precarious state of civil liberties during wartime.

20. Edward L. Ayers issued the first call for a neo-revisionism in Civil War historiography. See his "Worrying About the Civil War," 103–30. On the so-called "dark turn" in Civil War historiography, see Yael Sternhell, "Revisionism Reinvented? The Antiwar Turn in Civil War Scholarship," *Journal of the Civil War Era* 3, no. 2 (June 2013): 239–56; Drew Gilpin Faust, *This Republic of Suffering: Death and the Civil War* (New York: Alfred A. Knopf, 2008); Michael C. C. Adams, *Living Hell: The Dark Side of the Civil War* (Baltimore: Johns Hopkins University Press, 2014); and Diane Miller Sommerville, *Aberration of Mind: Suicide and Suffering in the Civil War–Era South* (Chapel Hill: University of North Carolina Press, 2018). For important critiques of neo-revisionism, see Eric Foner, "Battle Pieces," *The Nation,* January 10, 2008, and Gary W. Gallagher and Kathryn Shively Meier, "Coming to Terms With Civil War Military History," *Journal of the Civil War Era* 4, no. 4 (December 2014): 487–508.

21. Around the same time, academic historians were no less fascinated with amputation, perhaps one consequence of the visibility of amputees from the wars in Iraq and Afghanistan. See Megan Kate Nelson, *Ruin Nation: Destruction and the American Civil War* (Athens: University of Georgia Press, 2012); Shauna Devine, *Learning from the Wounded: The Civil War and the Rise of American Medical Science* (Chapel Hill: University of North Carolina Press, 2012); Brian Craig Miller, *Empty Sleeves: Amputation in the Civil War South* (Athens: University of Georgia Press, 2015); and David Seed, Stephen C. Kenny, and Chris Williams, eds., *Life and Limb: Perspectives on the American Civil War* (Liverpool: Liverpool University Press, 2016).

22. Gregory J. W. Urwin, "'We *Cannot* Treat Negroes as Prisoners of War': Racial Atrocities and Reprisals in Civil War Arkansas," in *Black Flag Over Dixie: Racial Atrocities and Reprisals in the Civil War,* ed. Gregory J. W. Urwin (Carbondale: Southern Illinois University Press, 2004), 133, 143–44.

23. Gabor S. Boritt, *The Gettysburg Gospel: The Lincoln Speech That Nobody Knows* (New York: Simon and Schuster, 2006), contends that the speech was not immediately remembered, but historian Jared Peatman notes that, "from the beginning, the words had been in the public eye." Jared Peatman, *The Long Shadow of Lincoln's Gettysburg Address* (Carbondale: Southern Illinois University Press, 2013), 3.

24. Kevin M. Levin extracted this very lesson from the film in "The Civil War Almost Didn't End Slavery," *Daily Beast,* December 6, 2015.

25. Kate Masur, "In Spielberg's 'Lincoln,' Passive Black Characters," *New York Times,* November 12, 2012.

26. Ronald C. White Jr., *Lincoln's Greatest Speech: The Second Inaugural* (New York: Simon & Schuster 2002), 202–3.

27. Aaron Sheehan-Dean, "The Long Civil War: Recent Writing on the Outcomes of the U.S. Civil War," *Virginia Magazine of History and Biography* 119 (June 2011): 107–53. Recent historians have challenged the war's traditional periodization. See, for example, Gregory P. Downs, *After Appomattox: Military Occupation and the Ends of War* (Cambridge, MA: Harvard University Press, 2015), and Brian Matthew Jordan, *Marching Home: Union Veterans and Their Unending Civil War* (New York: Liveright, 2015). Ross's film is based on John Stauffer and Sally Jenkins, *The State of Jones: The Small Southern County That Seceded From the Confederacy* (New York: Anchor Books, 2009), and Victoria E. Bynum, *The Free State of Jones: Mississippi's Longest Civil War* (Chapel Hill: University of North Carolina Press, 2001).

28. Scott Reynolds Nelson and Carol Sheriff, *A People at War: Civilians and Soldiers in America's Civil War, 1854–1877* (New York: Oxford University Press, 2008), 339.

29. Historians debate vigorously the extent to which conscription, confiscation, and other centralizing policies undermined the project of Confederate independence. Richard E. Beringer, Herman Hattaway, Archer Jones, and William N. Still, Jr., *Why the South Lost the Civil War* (Athens: University of Georgia Press, 1986), and Emory M. Thomas, *The Confederate Nation, 1861–1865* (New York: Harper and Row, 1979), powerfully suggested a loss of will and internal collapse, while Gary W. Gallagher, *The Confederate War: How Popular Will, Nationalism, and Military Strategy Could Not Stave Off Defeat* (Cambridge: Harvard University Press, 1997), emphasizes external factors and battlefield defeats.

30. Apart from a barrage of period photographs, the war was not especially present in Siegel's film, either. "Eastwood's quirky *The Beguiled* (1971), though set in Confederate Louisiana," observes historian Gary W. Gallagher, "could just as easily have been made as a dark comedy set anywhere at any time" (*Causes Won, Lost, and Forgotten*, 55).

31. A. A. Dowd, "Sofia Coppola Twists an Old Clint Eastwood Vehicle, *The Beguiled*, into Arty Pulp," *A/V Film*, June 22, 2017.

32. Stephanie McCurry, *Women's War: Fighting and Surviving the American Civil War* (Cambridge, MA: Harvard University Press, 2019), 204–5.

33. This decision prompted much censure from critics. For a good summary of the debate, see Sonia Rao, "Sofia Coppola's 'The Beguiled' Criticized for Leaving Out a Slave Narrative from the Confederate South," *Washington Post*, June 22, 2017.

34. Drew Gilpin Faust, *Mothers of Invention: Women of the Slaveholding South in the American Civil War* (Chapel Hill: University of North Carolina Press, 1996), 234–35, 256.

35. Qtd. in "Sofia Coppola Responds to 'The Beguiled' Backlash—Exclusive," www.indiewire .com/2017/07/sofia-coppola-the-beguiled-backlash-response-1201855684/ (accessed March 24, 2019).

36. Ayers, "Worrying About the Civil War," 118.

37. Kirk Savage, "War/Memory/History: Toward a Remixed Understanding," in *Remixing the Civil War: Meditations on the Sesquicentennial*, ed. Thomas J. Brown (Baltimore: Johns Hopkins University Press, 2011), 185, 186, 188.

38. *Journal of the Forty-second Annual Encampment of the Grand Army of the Republic, Department of Kansas*, 75–76; Scott Sandage, "A Marble House Divided: The Lincoln Memorial, the Civil Rights Movement, and the Politics of Memory, 1939–1963," *Journal of American History* 80, no. 1 (June 1993): 139. Recently, Jill Lepore has argued that we need a "new national history." See her "A New Americanism: Why a Nation Needs a National Story," *Foreign Affairs*, February 5, 2019.

The Indian Wars for the American West

Custer, Costner, and Colonialism

ANDREW R. GRAYBILL

Some of the first Hollywood movies were westerns—such as D. W. Griffith's *Old California* (1910) and Cecil B. DeMille's *Squaw Man* (1914)—and studios churned out hundreds of them during the film industry's classical era. While many of these early movies focused on the Native American experience and especially the intimate relationships between indigenous people and white newcomers, by the 1920s the focus had turned largely to dramatizing the so-called Indian Wars, which roiled the American West during the second half of the nineteenth century. In terms of story lines, the subject was hard to beat: "savage" Indians and "civilizing" Anglos, struggling for control of an alluring but untamed wilderness.

Despite periodic revivals, the genre has been in decline since its mid-twentieth-century heyday, derided as formulaic or substituting violence for plot. And yet the sheer number of such films demonstrates their enduring cultural significance. In their sustained engagement with the original sin of American history—Native dispossession—westerns showcase the evolution in American thinking about the conquest of the region. What began as a celebration of US martial prowess has morphed into a lament for the suffering endured by both sides in this bloody and sweeping conflict. In short, if the subjugation of Indians has been central to the (white) American experience, in history as well as myth, the shifting narratives of the western over the last century suggest a growing unease with this uncomfortable truth.

Classic Cinema

George Armstrong Custer is perhaps the most enduring historical figure from the era of the Indian Wars. He was famous for his military exploits and dashing style, and many films have memorialized the annihilation of his command at the Battle of the Little Bighorn in June 1876. Custer was already the subject of nearly a dozen movies before noted director Raoul Walsh took up his story in a 1941 epic, *They Died with Their Boots On*. The movie paired two of the biggest names of Hollywood's golden age, Errol Flynn and Olivia de Havilland, in their eighth collaboration in just six years. The movie also reunited de Havilland with Hattie McDaniel (Callie, the maid), the era's most renowned African American film star; both women had been nominated for the Academy Award for Best Supporting Actress for their roles two years earlier in *Gone With the Wind* (McDaniel won).

Although a heavy, Indian-sounding drumbeat accompanies the opening credits, Native Americans do not appear on-screen until the movie is more than half over. Rather, *They Died with Their Boots On* is a truncated—and liberally fictionalized—biopic of Custer (Flynn), beginning in 1857 with his arrival at the US Military Academy as an incoming cadet from Monroe, Michigan, dressed in full regalia, sporting a pack of hunting dogs, and accompanied by a black manservant.[1] When asked by fellow cadet Ned Sharp (Arthur Kennedy) why he has chosen the military as a career, Custer answers haughtily: "Glory, Mr. Sharp, glory. I want to leave behind me a name that the nation will honor." Custer's struggles to observe protocol at West Point are played for laughs, as he piles up demerits and infuriates his superiors, especially Major Romulus Taipe (Stanley Ridge).

They Died with Their Boots On is an example par excellence of Custer as the irresistible rogue, his vanity and insubordination redeemed by his code of personal honor and especially his bravery in combat, qualities on full display in the film's Civil War scenes. Mistakenly promoted to general, Custer assumes command of the Michigan Brigade; sizing him up, one of his colonels remarks slyly, "He's got more gold braid on him than a French admiral." After chastising the officers for their ineptitude, Custer ignores orders to concentrate his troops and hold them in reserve, instead leading his men "to the sound of the guns" at Gettysburg, where he saves not only the day but also the Union itself.

In these earlier sequences the script remains lightly tethered to the historical record; Walsh cuts the story loose from fact altogether once the action shifts to the Dakota Territory in the West. Viewers learn that the instability there stems not from rapacious white settlers or the troops sent to protect them, but mainly from the workings of the unscrupulous corporation run in part by Custer's West Point nemesis, Ned Sharp, with help from Major Taipe, now a devious politician. Horrified to discover that the company is selling guns to "friendly" Indians and plying the troops at Fort Lincoln with alcohol, Custer banishes the offenders and soon whips his men into fighting shape, building camaraderie by abstaining from liquor himself and adopting "Garryowen" as the regimental anthem.

As the movie begins its final act, a title card explains, "so was born the immortal 7th US Cavalry which cleared the Plains for a ruthlessly advancing civilization that spelled doom to the red race." Then follows a series of jump cuts showing fierce (if sanitized) combat between Custer's troops and the Sioux, led by Crazy Horse (a svelte Anthony Quinn). Worn down by the constant skirmishing, the warrior eventually asks for a parley with "Long Hair," as Custer is by then widely known. In the halting English spoken by cinematic Indians of the day, Crazy Horse offers to quit fighting, provided that the Americans will forever respect the sanctity of the Black Hills. Custer promises that he will intercede with the government, and a treaty is struck.

But the peace does not hold. In need of customers, Sharp spreads false rumors of gold in the Black Hills in order to lure settlers, igniting a fresh round of conflict. Aware of the long odds faced by his regiment as well as the steely resolve of his Native foe, Custer bids his wife, Libbie (de Haviland), a tender goodbye, and leads his troops out of the fort and toward his rendezvous with immortality. All this, of course, is precisely backwards. For one thing, it was Custer's 1874 expedition, with its express purpose of locating mineral deposits in the Black Hills, that brought on open warfare with the Sioux. For another, Custer was famously—even notoriously—aggressive, eager to press the attack lest his Native targets slip away and he miss out on a share of the laurels. But in Walsh's hands the slaughter at the Little Bighorn is a noble sacrifice instead of a terrible blunder born of Custer's overconfidence, the fault of corrupt businessmen and their political enablers.[2]

Most remarkable is the film's inattention to Indians, since for many moviegoers they were one of the principal draws. Quinn has only a few scenes and but a handful of lines; the rest of the Native characters are an undifferentiated mass. Given the era in which the film was made, one hardly expects a sustained and clear-eyed consideration of the Indians' perspective. Even so, Native people are strangely absent from a movie that depicts their single greatest battlefield triumph over the United States (and one of the most storied engagements in American military history). Instead, Indians serve as little more than a mirror in which Custer's honor and decency are reflected for the audience, underscored by Libbie's posthumous reading of her husband's final letter, in which Custer demands that President Ulysses S. Grant uphold the right of the Sioux to remain in their own country.

If Indians are largely missing from Walsh's film, they are a ubiquitous, menacing presence throughout *The Searchers,* director John Ford's 1956 classic starring John Wayne.[3] This was the sixth of eight westerns the two made together, starting with *Stagecoach* (1939) and including Ford's celebrated "Cavalry Trilogy"— *Fort Apache* (1948), *She Wore a Yellow Ribbon* (1949), and *Rio Grande* (1950). Native people appear on-screen in only some scenes in *The Searchers,* but the terrifying threat they pose is etched onto the faces of the white characters who populate the story. Moreover, unlike *They Died with Their Boots On,* there are no pitched battles in *The Searchers;* rather, Ford opens a different window onto the Indian wars, in which the fighting is a nasty guerrilla struggle to the knife between isolated but determined settlers and vicious, implacable Indians.

Based on Alan LeMay's 1954 novel of the same name (itself drawn from the true story of Cynthia Ann Parker, a white girl abducted by Comanches in Texas in 1836), *The Searchers* is a cinematic version of the captivity narrative, an American literary genre dating to seventeenth-century New England.[4] Such tales featured the kidnapping of women and sometimes children by Indians and the efforts of loved ones to effect their repatriation to civilized society. This is the plot of *The Searchers,* in which Ethan Edwards (Wayne), a hardened Confederate veteran, grimly devotes himself to the hunt for his two nieces, Lucy (Vera Miles) and Debbie (Natalie Wood), stolen by Comanches during a murderous raid upon his brother's Texas ranch (shot beautifully, if incongruously, in Ford's beloved Monument Valley, located hard on the border between Arizona and Utah, west of the Four Corners).

Embedded in the captivity narrative is what historian Richard White calls "the inverted conquest," in which white colonizers are depicted as the victims of Indian aggression. Viewed this way, Native violence justifies retribution by the newcomers, which leads ultimately to the Indians' dispossession.[5] This formulation suffused the dime novels popular in the late nineteenth century and reached its apotheosis in Buffalo Bill's Wild West Show, which ran from 1883 to 1913. For much of its run, that spectacle culminated in a set piece, the Attack on the Settler's Cabin, in which a pioneer family is beset by a party of marauding Indians who are run off—just in the nick of time—by Buffalo Bill Cody himself, with help from a posse of cowboys.[6]

Even more than property, what Cody defended in the climax of his extravaganza was (white) female virtue. Coursing through the captivity narrative is the dread of rape, imagined, perhaps especially by the victim's male relatives, as a fate worse even than death. So it is with *The Searchers*. Upon discovering the smoldering ruins of his brother's ranch, Ethan peers into one of the outbuildings. While the audience cannot see inside, Ethan's pained reaction and especially his strenuous effort to block his adoptive nephew, Martin (Jeffrey Hunter), from gaining access conveys to viewers the awful truth: Martha (Dorothy Jordan), Ethan's cherished sister-in-law, has been raped and killed. Likewise, later in the film, Lucy's fiancé, Brad Jorgensen (Harry Carey Jr.), seems more distraught by the fact of Lucy's sexual violation at the hands of the Comanches than her murder; consumed by fury, he charges the Indians' camp and is promptly shot down.

Ethan, however, has a different concern: that after five years of captivity Debbie has become a wife to Scar (Henry Brandon), leader of the Comanche band that killed her parents and took her captive. To him, such defilement is an affront not only to the Edwards family but to white society at large. Thus, as he indicates to Martin, upon tracking her down Ethan intends to kill Debbie, since "she's been living with a buck." And upon locating her he nearly succeeds, stopped only when Martin steps between them and shields Debbie with his own body. This scene—and others in which Ethan explains that such captives, after years of living with the Comanches, can no longer be considered white— taps into the primal American fear of interracial mixing on the frontier, bad enough when it involved white men and Native women, but so much worse with the roles reversed.[7]

Ethan makes clear his revulsion to such relationships throughout the movie, starting with his reintroduction to Martin—whom he rescued as an infant— after many years gone. Staring him down in one of the opening scenes, Ethan remarks, "Fella could mistake you for a half breed," to which Martin replies flatly, "Not quite. I'm [an] eighth Cherokee, the rest is Welsh and English, at least that's what they tell me." Thereafter Ethan takes pains to remind Martin that they are not blood related, and that he should not call him "uncle" nor refer to other members of the Edwards family as "kin." On another occasion, he refers to Martin derisively as "blanket head," mocking his Native ancestry.

Despite such cruelty, Martin remains devoted to Ethan throughout the movie, sticking with the search for Debbie long after all the others have fallen away.

Ethan's abuse of Martin and his wish to kill Debbie point at the dark heart of the film: the deep-seated racism that animates Ethan's character. In his mouth "Comanch" is an epithet equal to "redskin." Upon discovering the corpse of an Indian killed in the aftermath of the raid on his brother's ranch, Ethan shoots the dead man twice in the face, explaining that, according to Comanche belief, "[if] he ain't got no eyes he can't enter the spirit land, [and] has to wander forever between the winds." And after Martin kills Scar while liberating Debbie, Ethan relishes scalping the chief. Ford, in keeping with his earlier films, clearly paints the Natives as savages, with Ethan occupying a liminal space between them and polite Anglo society, captured in the iconic closing scene. Having delivered Debbie safely to the Jorgensen ranch, Ethan pauses at the threshold of the cabin, then turns and walks away as the door closes on him and the movie itself. Despite his undeniable heroism, Ethan is barred from entering the world he has defended.[8]

Vietnam War

Less than a decade after the release of *The Searchers*, the United States had committed nearly 200,000 troops to crush a Communist insurgency in Vietnam. As popular sentiment turned against the conflict, Hollywood took notice, and several westerns adopted an explicitly antiwar perspective. The genre was in some sense the perfect vessel for such a message, considering that—as on the nineteenth-century American frontier—the Vietnam War pitted the technologically superior US military against a nonwhite indigenous foe. Premiering in August 1970 and starring Candice Bergen and Peter Strauss, director Ralph Nelson's *Soldier Blue* was the most controversial (and maligned) of these revisionist films.[9]

An ominous crawl suggests from the start that this is not your grandfather's western. It reads in part, "The climax of 'Soldier Blue' shows specifically and graphically the horrors of battle as blood lust overcomes reason. Brutal atrocities affect not only the warriors, but the innocent as well . . . the women and children." And yet the opening scenes are standard captivity narrative fare. A military detachment in Colorado is escorting Cresta Marybelle Lee (Bergen), a young white woman abducted two years earlier by the Cheyenne, to the post where her fiancé is stationed. But unlike Ethan Edwards in *The Searchers*, who seethes at the prospect of white female violation, a leering solider says to Private Honus Gant (Strauss), "Two years captive with them red bucks. Don't it make you wonder, though . . . how many of them got to her? Don't it get you all worked up?" He is plainly aroused, not disgusted.

Further subverting the genre is the film's feminist sensibility. After a Cheyenne war party attacks the caravan, killing Gant's twenty-one fellow soldiers, it is Cresta—all the while chewing on a blade of grass—who calmly leads the greenhorn private to safety on a bluff overlooking the slaughter. She tells him to expect a long wait before they can move out, since "they're gonna be messing with those bodies down there for hours." Gant then watches in stunned indignation as Cresta strips off her bloomers ("'cause it's hotter than hell and they're itching") and relaxes on her stomach, as if at a picnic. Even more upsetting to the prudish soldier is Cresta's obvious affection for her captor. When she explains that it was the Cheyenne chief Spotted Wolf (Jorge Rivero) who led the assault, Gant demands to know how she can be so sure. With a telling, wistful smile, she says, "I know him," explaining casually a moment later that "I was his wife."

But for Gant the worst is yet to come. As the two strike out on their own for Fort Reunion, Cresta chides him about the role of the US military in the West, revealing an unmistakable sympathy for the Natives. "What good, brave lads, coming out here to kill themselves a real, live 'Injun,' putting up their forts in a country they've got no claim to." Gant pushes back, appalled by her lack of patriotism, but Cresta will have none of it. "You ever seen an Indian camp after the army's been there? Huh? You ever see the women and what was done to them before they were killed? Ever see the little boys and girls stuck on the long knives . . . stuck and dying? Well, I have." Gant—whom she mocks contemptuously as "Soldier Blue"—meekly replies, "you're lying," but he lacks any courage of conviction.

The scales soon fall from his eyes. Of necessity he and Cresta separate (but not before becoming lovers), she returning to the Cheyenne camp and he catching up with his unit, the Colorado Eleventh Volunteers. Convinced by Cresta that, if given the chance, Spotted Wolf might treat for peace, Gant beseeches Colonel Iverson (John Anderson) to delay his offensive against the Natives. Iverson shouts him down, insisting that, given the murder of Gant's comrades, "a price will be paid, soldier!" Cresta, by contrast, is warmly received among the Cheyenne, surrounded by adoring children and embraced by Spotted Wolf. Although some of his warriors urge him to rouse the tribe to fight, the chief insists that peace with the whites is the only way forward. Meanwhile, Colonel Iverson is shown in his tent, swilling liquor and sharpening the edge of his saber.

The troops appear before the Cheyenne camp the next morning, and Spotted Wolf rides out to meet them, flying an American flag and a white handkerchief. Colonel Iverson orders his men to commence shelling anyway, and then leads the troops in a cavalry charge. The violence is at once horrifying and cartoonish. Nelson had recruited amputees as extras and the set boasted "a prosthetics wagon . . . stocked with seemingly every conceivable body part," deployed to gruesome effect.[10] A terrified woman carrying a swaddled infant runs directly toward the camera and is decapitated by a mounted soldier. Most disturbing, perhaps, are scenes of female sexual mutilation.[11] Gant, who had tried to stop the cannons, wanders aimlessly among the smoldering lodges, mumbling unintelligibly as he witnesses precisely what Cresta had described, including infants spitted upon bayonets. For her part, Cresta directs a group of women and children to safety in a ravine, only to be dragged away, screaming, as the soldiers butcher all of her companions.

In the end, Gant is led off in chains and Cresta is left to contemplate the razed camp. As the camera pans away, a voice-over describes the Sand Creek Massacre of November 1864, which has clearly informed *Soldier Blue*, even if many of the details have been altered (such as the names of historical figures as well as the season of the year in which the actual carnage took place). Some have speculated that this is because Nelson wanted his movie to conjure contemporary events unfolding in Vietnam, especially the March 1968 My Lai Massacre, news of which broke in November 1969, shortly after the filming of *Soldier Blue* had begun (although a leading authority on the film disagrees).[12] In any event, such allegorical connections—intended or otherwise—were not lost on critics at the time. Many found the movie persuasive, while others denounced what they considered its exploitative violence, something that the film's marketing had touted in the publicity campaign, featuring posters that billed *Soldier Blue* as "THE MOST SAVAGE FILM IN HISTORY!" This may explain why the movie performed modestly in the United States but was the third-highest-grossing film of 1971 at the British box office. By the time of its release, American audiences wanted no additional reminders of US martial brutality.

In December 1970, four months after *Soldier Blue* appeared in theaters, another revisionist western hit the screens, this time to much wider acclaim and enduring cultural significance. Adapted from the celebrated 1964 novel by Thomas Berger, *Little Big Man* starred Dustin Hoffman, who had recently shot to fame on the strength of Oscar-nominated performances in *The Graduate* (1967) and *Midnight Cowboy* (1969).[13] Although covering much the same ground as *Soldier Blue,* director Arthur Penn's movie eschews the overweening self-seriousness of its counterpart, using satire and dark humor more than graphic violence to heighten the contrast between white society and the Native communities it sought to displace.

The film opens at a nursing home in the present day, where a historian (William Hickey) is interviewing Jack Crabb (Hoffman), who claims to be 121 years old and the "sole white survivor of the Battle of Little Bighorn." Patiently but pedantically, the scholar explains that he is interested in hearing about the "primitive lifestyle" of the Plains Indians rather than Crabb's tall tales, and that anyway, the American defeat in Custer's Last Stand was the exception to the rule of US military aggression, which he indicts as genocidal. The younger man then adds casually, "But of course I wouldn't expect an old Indian fighter like you to agree with me." At that point, a visibly agitated Crabb insists that his guest activate his tape recorder and shut up, so that Crabb might tell all that he has seen.

Crabb's story, recounted in flashback, starts as yet another captivity narrative, beginning in 1859 when his entire family, save for Jack and his teenaged sister, Caroline (Carole Androsky), is slaughtered by Pawnees during their ill-fated crossing of the Plains. The two white children are rescued by a lone Cheyenne warrior, Shadow That Comes in Sight (Ruben Moreno), and conveyed back to the Indians' encampment, where Caroline fully expects to be raped and murdered. Instead, the newcomers are kindly welcomed, although Caroline manages to slip away to safety on their first evening. Thus begins Crabb's shuttling between white and Native worlds, in which he encounters legendary figures such as Wild Bill Hickok and George Armstrong Custer.[14]

In its depictions of Native people, *Little Big Man* is far more nuanced than most of its cinematic predecessors, steering a deliberate path between the portrayal of Indians as either mindless savages or noble victims. Rather, Indians are fully realized human beings, none more than Old Lodge Skins (Chief Dan George), who becomes Crabb's adopted grandfather and christens him Little Big Man after the diminutive Crabb saves a fellow Cheyenne from death at the hands of a Pawnee warrior. Part of this humanizing process stems from the Native characters speaking in English, giving viewers access to their interior lives. But Penn resists the temptation to valorize Indians, showing them—especially Crabb's nemesis, Younger Bear (Cal Bellini)—alternately as petty, boastful, and superstitious. Moreover, with light humor, Penn conjures a range of Indian stereotypes, from their fondness for dog meat to their sexual practices.

White people, meanwhile, do not come off nearly so well. Captured by soldiers during his first battle against the US military, teenaged Jack is turned over to Reverend Silas Pendrake (Thayer David) for "moral guidance and a Christian upbringing." The preacher thinks that corporal punishment is the best way to cure his young charge of any sinful ways, especially those he might have picked up from the Indians. His wife, Louise (Faye Dunaway), meanwhile, takes a keen interest in the young man, who falls under her spell and enters what he calls "my religion period," attending church and even getting baptized. But this idyll ends abruptly when Jack discovers Mrs. Pendrake committing adultery with a shopkeeper. Blindsided by her hypocrisy, he joins forces with Llardyce T. Merriweather (Martin Balsam), a snake-oil salesman he finds honest by comparison, but who chides Jack for his scruples, which compromise his ability to perpetrate the fraud. As Merriweather explains, "The one that ruined you was that damned Indian [Old Lodge Skins]. . . . He gave you a vision of moral order in the universe, and there isn't any."

Little Big Man saves its harshest criticism for the US military. After unsuccessful stints as a gunfighter and a merchant, Crabb ends up serving as a mule skinner in a cavalry detachment and joins the unit in a raid on a small Indian village. Watching from a distance until the few able-bodied warriors have left the camp, the commanding officer issues a desultory order to "spare the females and children, if possible." He then leads a merciless charge, despite Jack's frenzied efforts to stop the butchery. Later repatriated to the Indians, Jack is living among the Cheyenne when Custer (Richard Mulligan) directs the Seventh US Cavalry in an assault on the Natives' winter camp on the banks of the Washita River. Crabb watches in agony as his wife, Sunshine, and their newborn child are cut down in a hail of gunfire. For his part, Mulligan plays Custer as a preening fool, drunk on vanity and unearned pride, all of which spell his doom at the Little Bighorn, witnessed by Crabb firsthand before his rescue by Younger Bear, who then reunites Crabb with Old Lodge Skins.

There is a poignant moment, just before the Battle of the Washita, when, holding his infant son, Crabb explains in a voice-over that "I reckon right then I come pretty close to turning pure Indian." This speaks to a very real possibility that existed briefly in the West, just as it had on successive American frontiers, where white men and Native women intermarried and had children that moved easily between worlds.[15] But the onrushing tide of white settlement and the military violence that shored up and extended those territorial gains closed that window in the years following the Civil War. Ultimately, unlike the searing indignation of *Soldier Blue,* the tone of *Little Big Man* is elegiac, mourning not only the terrible losses endured by the Natives but also the duplicity of the US government, which had promised the Cheyennes "land where they could live in peace . . . [for] as long as grass grow, wind blow, and the sky is blue." For those Americans outraged by the Vietnam War, including the incursion into Cambodia in spring 1970—contradicting President Richard M. Nixon's campaign promise to end the conflict—the representation of such brazen deceitfulness surely struck a chord.

Modern Era

After a string of leading roles in hit movies, including *The Untouchables* (1987) and *Field of Dreams* (1989), actor Kevin Costner made his directorial debut in 1990 with *Dances with Wolves*. Based upon his friend Michael Blake's eponymous 1988 novel, Costner's effort was credited by many with reviving and updating a fading genre (which received another big boost in 1992 with director Clint Eastwood's Oscar-winning *Unforgiven*).[16] The movie achieved iconic status through blending elements from the classic and Vietnam eras. John Barry's Oscar-winning score, coupled with gorgeous, on-location filming in South Dakota and Wyoming, summoned the romance of golden age westerns. And like a handful of previous revisionist films, chief among them Delmer Daves's *Broken Arrow* (1950), John Ford's *Cheyenne Autumn* (1964), and Martin Ritt's *Hombre* (1967), Costner's sympathies lay clearly with Native peoples.

Dances with Wolves begins on a fictional Civil War battlefield in Tennessee in spring 1863, where US Lieutenant John Dunbar (Costner), faced with losing an injured foot to the surgeon's knife, decides instead to commit suicide by riding directly in front of the Confederate line. He survives, miraculously, and the distracted Rebel troops are overrun by Dunbar's Union comrades. As a reward for his unwitting heroism, Dunbar is offered any assignment of his choosing. He opts for a posting to the Great Plains, since, as he explains to the commanding officer who receives him at Fort Hays, Kansas, "I've always wanted to see the frontier . . . before it's gone." Dunbar is then sent to Fort Sedgwick, "the furthermost outpost in the realm," discovering upon his arrival that the small stockade has been deserted by the troops stationed there. He resolves to stay, and orders Timmons (Robert Pastorelli), the uncouth wagon driver, to unload the post provisions and depart.

As in *They Died with Their Boots On*, Indians are rumored but not seen until well into the movie, and when they first appear they are of the terrifying, savage variety. A small band of Pawnee warriors, spotting the cooking fire of the homeward bound Timmons, weighs his fate from a distance. They are a fearsome looking bunch, with mohawks and red face paint, and their unnamed leader (Wes Studi)—speaking in dialect, with English subtitles (as do all Native characters in the film)—insists on killing the trespasser, despite his companions' entreaties to leave the white man be. In the end, the Natives ambush Timmons, their leader shooting him with arrows before drawing his knife, with a flourish, and scalping his shrieking victim, brandishing the gory prize to his whooping confederates.

Dunbar's Lakota neighbors, however, are presented in an entirely different light. Curious about the lone soldier living nearby, Kicking Bird (Graham Greene), a Sioux holy man, visits the post and tries to steal Dunbar's horse.[17] Dunbar runs him off, but later observes in his diary that "the man I encountered was a magnificent looking fellow." In time, the Indians befriend the interloper, and through his eyes the audience comes to view the Lakota as almost perfect. As he writes in his diary: "I had never known a people so eager to laugh, so devoted to family, so dedicated to each other, and the only word that came to mind was 'harmony.'" Dunbar even finds dignity in their brutal, collective dispatching of a Pawnee foe, saying of the battle that preceded it: "There was no dark political objective. This was not a fight for territory or riches or to make men free," but rather to defend resources and protect women and children.

Dunbar lionizes the Sioux, and the soldier gradually becomes one of them, spending time in the Natives' camp and learning their language and customs from the elders, who name him "Dances with Wolves" after watching Dunbar frolic with Two Socks, a wolf he has befriended. Having won their trust and affection, he marries into the tribe when he weds Stands With a Fist (Mary McDonnell), a white woman who has lived with the Sioux ever since her family was killed by the Pawnee when she was a little girl. Like Jack Crabb in *Little Big Man*, Dunbar is on the brink of becoming "pure Indian" when the film's true villains—white people—appear during the last act and threaten to destroy his new world.

Up to that point, in a tidy inversion of *The Searchers*, it is the Americans who are the phantom menace, sensed but rarely seen. With a furrowed brow, Kicking Bear presses Dunbar repeatedly for information about the whites, questions that the soldier deflects at first, worried that honest answers would constitute treason. But Dunbar's attitude towards his countrymen hardens, especially after seeing a field of skinned bison left to rot by white hide hunters, whom he judges "a people without value and without soul." When whites do finally show up—in the guise of military reinforcements sent to Dunbar's post— they mistake him for an Indian and shoot his horse out from under him; later, the soldiers take pot shots at Two Socks, who refuses to desert the imprisoned Dunbar, killing the wolf. The message is clear: white people sow death.

The Americans' depravity yields the ultimate reversal, as the audience finds itself rooting hard for the Sioux in their resistance to the US military, which culminates in the Natives' attack on a caravan transporting Dunbar back to Fort Hays (and presumably the gallows pole). With help from Dunbar, who, despite his shackles, drowns the odious Private Spivey (Tony Pierce), the Sioux slaughter the entire detail, and then convey Dunbar to their winter camp. However, as Dunbar explains to the council, he fears that the army will pursue him ruthlessly, as a traitor. Chief Ten Bears (Floyd Red Crow Westerman) demurs, explaining, "The man the soldiers are looking for no longer exists. Now there is only a Sioux named Dances with Wolves." But Dunbar, like the audience, knows better, and thus the movie ends as he and Stands With a Fist ride away on their own, hoping to spare the camp the military's wrath. A title card explains that, "Thirteen years later . . . the last band of free Sioux submitted to white authority. . . . The great horse culture of the plains was gone and the American frontier was soon to pass into history." The sense of loss is crushing.[18]

The title card at the start of director Scott Cooper's 2017 movie *Hostiles* features a quotation by D. H. Lawrence that seems to prepare viewers for another round of violence against Native people by the US Army. It reads: "The essential American soul is hard, isolate, stoic, and a killer. It has never yet melted." Instead, reminiscent of scenes from *The Searchers* as well as John Farrow's *Hondo* (1953) and Robert Aldrich's *Ulzana's Raid* (1972), the beginning of *Hostiles* depicts a vicious Indian attack. At her New Mexico homestead, Rosalie Quaid (Rosamund Pike), witnesses the slaughter of her husband and three children by a band of Comanches but manages to flee into the hills behind her home. The action then shifts abruptly to a small cavalry detachment encircling an escaped Apache warrior, whom the troops lasso and drag to the ground while nearby a Native woman and her young child wail in terror. Cooper's use of the Lawrence quote thus assumes a different meaning: the "essential American" in *Hostiles* apparently applies to both Natives and newcomers.

Captain Joe Blocker (Christian Bale) strenuously rejects this equivalence. A renowned Indian fighter with decades of experience in the West, he is hardened against the indigenous peoples he has helped to subjugate, having lost numerous men under his command. As he hisses to an eastern journalist (David Camp) who taunts Blocker for his cruel treatment of the Natives: "I've killed savages. I've killed plenty of 'em. Cause that's my fucking job. . . . I hate 'em. I've got a war bag of reasons to hate 'em." But such animosity does not stop his commanding officer (Stephen Lang) at Fort Berringer from assigning Blocker to a most unpleasant duty: conveying a party led by Yellow Hawk (Wes Studi), Blocker's bitterest adversary, from New Mexico to Montana, so that the elderly and cancer-ridden Cheyenne chief might die in the land of his birth. The captain accepts only when threatened with a court-martial and the loss of his pension.[19]

Blocker's rage is palpable. After playing along with the colonel's publicity stunt and posing for pictures with his Native charges, Blocker gamely leads the group out of the fort. But he soon stops the caravan, ordering his corporal to place the chief and his son, Black Hawk (Adam Beach) in chains and, staring coldly at the two adult women in the party, to "take the braids out of the bitches' hair." But Blocker slowly recognizes the Indians' humanity, moved by the compassion they show Rosalie, whom the group discovers sitting with her slain children in the burned-out ruins of the family cabin. Moreover, the two Cheyenne warriors team up with Blocker and his soldiers in fending off an attack by the same band of Comanches that killed the Quaid family, and then once again later in the film when they rescue the women, who have been kidnapped by a party of fur trappers. In short, the former enemies forge a tenuous bond in facing down common foes, whether they are Natives or whites.

Blocker's right hand, Master Sergeant Tommy Metz (Rory Cochrane), undergoes a more profound transformation. From the start of the movie, he seems haunted, even vacant. As he explains to Blocker in an early scene, "I think I've reached the end of my soldiering. They say I'm not fit. They said that I have the melancholia." But Blocker says "there's no such thing," recruiting him for the mission. Later, on night watch during the trip to Montana, Metz explains to Lieutenant Kidder (Jesse Plemons), a green West Point graduate, that "I've killed everything that's walked or crawled—men, women, children, all colors. If you do it enough, you get used to it, doesn't mean a thing." To which Kidder replies, "That's what I'm afraid of." And yet it is not only post-traumatic stress that dogs Metz, but also a deep sense of guilt. In camp one evening, in the midst of a driving rainstorm, he kneels before Yellow Hawk and says in Cheyenne (which Blocker also speaks), "Our treatment of the Natives cannot be forgiven." Then, offering a gift of tobacco, he implores the chief to "have mercy on us." He eventually commits suicide, and Black Hawk assists with the burial.

For his part, Blocker follows a different path to redemption. On the one hand, throughout the movie he rejects the moralizing of white liberals, first the journalist and then the wife of the commanding officer at Fort Winslow, Colorado, where the party stops for provisions and to treat its wounded. At dinner, and to the clear discomfort of Rosalie, Mrs. McGowan (Robyn Malcolm) muses aloud about the terrible mistreatment by the government of Native peoples in the West, who, after all, "were here first, [and have been] dispossessed, at our own hand." And yet Blocker clearly struggles to reconcile all that he has done in the name of war, which is hurled in his face by Sergeant Charles Wills (Ben Foster), who fought with Blocker at Wounded Knee. Now, however, Wills is a prisoner whom Blocker must deliver to the post that he deserted, where he will hang for the murder of a Native family. As Wills says to Blocker, "I seen you butcher women and children. It ain't right judging me." Blocker's eyes suggest that he agrees with Wills.

Ultimately, the kindness and dignity of the Cheyenne as well as Blocker's reflection on the extraordinary human cost of warfare lead to a poignant scene between the soldier and the chief. Upon reaching Montana, Blocker crouches alongside Yellow Hawk, who is close to death, and begins recounting the names of friends who were killed by the chief and his warriors. Yellow Hawk looks away in sadness or shame, but Blocker then acknowledges, "I have lost many friends and you have lost many as well." The chief replies, "They are a great loss for us both, but we know that death comes to us all." The two adversaries lock eyes, and then Blocker extends his hand, saying to Yellow Hawk: "Don't look back, my friend. Go in a good way. A part of me dies with you."

Whatever optimism this scene engenders is washed away at the end of the movie. As the group buries Yellow Hawk, a white man, Cyrus Lounde (Scott Wilson), rides up with his three adult sons. He demands that the interlopers "get your shit, your dead Cheyenne, and get the hell out of here." Blocker refuses, and in the ensuing gun battle all perish save for Blocker, Rosalie, and Little Bear (Xavier Horsechief), Yellow Hawk's young grandson. In the aftermath, Blocker tallies up the dead Indians, then takes a knife and approaches one of the dying Loundes, pulling the man to his feet and disemboweling him. However satisfying, viewers know that there is an endless stream of Loundes headed west (or already there) who will force any indigenous stragglers to accommodate themselves to the world of white America. Such is the message of the closing scene, in which Blocker puts Rosalie and Little Bear on a train bound for Chicago, where the boy will grow up in an alien world. Wordlessly, Blocker decides at the last moment to join them, and in an apparent homage to *The Searchers* hops on the back of the train and pauses at the door of the caboose before opening it and walking inside.[20]

Classic westerns featuring the Indian Wars achieved what the nineteenth-century US military could not: they made Natives vanish wholesale. Indigenous people in these films stood no chance against the onslaught of white settlers and especially the soldiers who facilitated the newcomers' advance and shored up their territorial gains. The confidence in white racial superiority shared by moviemakers and their audiences made the disappearance of Indians seem inevitable, the natural order of things. Thus in films like *They Died with Their Boots On*, Natives could be treated almost wistfully, noble but doomed, safe to be romanticized since they posed no real existential threat. Released at the end of this era, *The Searchers* bears some of these hallmarks, especially in terms of the movie's racial politics, meant to elicit sympathy for the besieged whites. But the fascinating character of Ethan Edwards points to a new idea: the ambivalence of conquest. Ethan's prejudice and brutality reveal the costs—not only for Indians but also for whites—of colonialism, in which the dispossession of Indians, however justified in the eyes of moviegoers, stripped at least some of the colonists of their claims to innocence, and prevented them from enjoying all the fruits of their victory.

The revisionist westerns of the Vietnam era seized upon this notion and pushed it further, resulting in a perfect chiasma: the Indians became the innocent victims of savage violence committed by the US military. Informed by the political cynicism of the era, in which government officials misled the American public on the prosecution of a bloody and increasingly unpopular conflict, movies like *Soldier Blue* and *Little Big Man* quite literally flipped the scripts of many golden age westerns. No longer were vulnerable white homesteads under constant threat from cruel Natives, but rather just the opposite. In such films, indigenous peoples of the United States (with a nod to their nonwhite counterparts in Southeast Asia) were cast as the sympathetic targets of senseless aggression by a pitiless foe, whose vicious behavior is made all the more unbearable by professions of duty, honor, and sacrifice in service to the nation. These movies seemed designed to provoke and teach rather than merely to entertain, a far cry from the boots-and-saddles epics made only a few decades before.

Perhaps it is no surprise that the revival of the genre in the contemporary period began with a reconsideration of the Native-white struggle for the West, given the enduring popularity of such themes. *Dances with Wolves* continued the 1970s trend of casting whites in general, and the US military in particular, as the villains, except for the heroic John Dunbar, who plays the role of white savior. But Natives were now divided into two opposing camps: warlike savages (in this case, the Pawnee), hearkening back to the stereotypes of the golden age; and enlightened beings (the Sioux) living in balance with the nonhuman world. Its simple message must have been the visual equivalent of comfort food for audiences unsettled by the political confusion of the late 1980s, marked especially by the fall of the Berlin Wall and growing tensions in the Persian Gulf. *Hostiles,* however, hoses away any such complacency, forcing viewers to grapple with the legacies of violence upon which the nation was built, a reckoning with the past that is at once vital and long overdue. Given the infrequency of major studio westerns, it could be a long wait to see if future films will revisit this perpetually unsettling question about the origins of our nation and just how we choose to confront it.

NOTES

1. The historical literature on Custer is enormous; supposedly, he trails only Lincoln as a biographical subject. For the best recent treatment, see T. J. Stiles, *Custer's Trials: A Life on the Frontier of a New America* (New York: Knopf, 2015).

2. Angela Aleiss argues that, in some ways, this shifting of blame also exonerates the Indians from what had long been seen as their brutality at the Little Bighorn. See her *Making the White Man's Indian: Native Americans and Hollywood Movies* (Westport, CT: Praeger, 2005), 71–75. Other classic westerns that indict corrupt white traders rather than the US military include Cecil B. DeMille's *The Plainsman* (1936) and Norman Z. McLeod's *The Paleface* (1948).

3. For a thorough and careful study of the film, see Glenn Frankel, *The Searchers: The Making of an American Legend* (New York: Bloomsbury, 2013).

4. Alan LeMay, *The Searchers* (New York: Harper and Brothers, 1954). The first half of Frankel's *The Searchers* offers an excellent account of the Parker story. For another recent—if highly sensationalized—version, see S. C. Gwynne, *Empire of the Summer Moon: Quanah Parker and the Rise and Fall of the Comanches, The Most Powerful Indian Tribe in American History* (New York: Scribner, 2010).

5. Richard White, "Frederick Jackson Turner and Buffalo Bill," in James R. Grossman, ed., *The Frontier in American Culture* (Berkeley: University of California Press, 1994), 7–66, esp. p. 27.

6. Louis S. Warren, "Cody's Last Stand: Masculine Anxiety, the Custer Myth, and the Frontier of Domesticity in Buffalo Bill's Wild West," *Western Historical Quarterly* 34, no. 1 (Spring 2003), 49–69, esp. 54–58. See also Warren's *Buffalo Bill's America: William Cody and the Wild West Show* (New York: Knopf, 2005).

7. There is a burgeoning historiography on Native-white intermarriage in the West. For the most comprehensive recent treatment, see Anne F. Hyde, *Empires, Nations, and Families: A New History of the North American West, 1800–1850* (Lincoln: University of Nebraska Press, 2011).

8. This scene, one of the most famous in cinematic history, has been treated extensively, most recently by journalist and film historian Glenn Frankel. See his *The Searchers*, 309.

9. For an extended consideration of the movie, see P. B. Hurst, *The Most Savage Film:* Soldier Blue, *Cinematic Violence, and the Horrors of War* (Jefferson, NC: McFarland & Co., 2008). The movie was based on Theodore V. Olsen's novel *Arrow in the Sun* (New York: Doubleday, 1969).

10. Hurst, *The Most Savage Film*, 114.

11. A sequence in Oliver Stone's *Platoon* (1986)—when US troops raze a Vietnamese hamlet—features much of the same violence, including graphic scenes of rape, witnessed with horror by Private Chris Taylor (Charlie Sheen), just as with Honus Gant in *Soldier Blue*.

12. Hurst argues that any overlap is largely unintentional, given the lateness of the breaking news about My Lai, and that, given the scripted denouement (which was meant to conjure not only Sand Creek but also the 1890 slaughter at Wounded Knee), "the film would always have ended with an extremely bloody extermination." See *The Most Savage Film*, 124–30; quotation on 130.

13. Thomas Berger, *Little Big Man* (New York: Dial, 1964).

14. In an interview with journalist Allen Barra in 1996, Berger objected to what he believed were the film's excessive attempts to serve as a parable to the Vietnam War, especially the My Lai Massacre. (Berger was also irritated by later descriptions of Jack Crabb as the "Zelig of the West," since Woody Allen's *Zelig* appeared nearly two decades after the publication of Berger's novel, and thirteen years after the cinematic adaptation.) See Allen Barra, "The Little Big Man Hoax?" *True West,* November 4, 2014: truewestmagazine.com/the-little-big-man-hoax/ (accessed April 14, 2019).

15. See, for instance, Andrew R. Graybill, *The Red and the White: A Family Saga of the American West* (New York: Liveright, 2013).

16. Michael Blake, *Dances with Wolves* (New York: Fawcett, 1988). For the complicated relationship between Blake and Costner, including disagreements about the movie, see Aleiss, *Making the White Man's Indian,* 144.

17. It is worth noting that Greene was nominated for the Academy Award for Best Supporting Actor, only the second time a Native person had received an Oscar nomination—the first came

two decades earlier, for Chief Dan George in *Little Big Man;* neither won. See Aleiss, *Making the White Man's Indian,* 146.

18. Not all reviewers saw it this way. For a sample of critical opinion, see Aleiss, *Making the White Man's Indian,* 144–46.

19. As noted by Matthew Hulbert in an email to the author, "In some ways, *Hostiles* is the modern depiction of Nathan Brittles [from *She Wore a Yellow Ribbon*], but with all of the brutality and hate and PTSD that couldn't be on screen in [the] 40s." This is an insightful observation, and I thank him for it.

20. Film critic A. O. Scott makes precisely this point in his review of the film (*New York Times,* December 21, 2017).

Manifest Mythology

Cinematic Distortions of Antebellum American Imperialism and Manhood

JAMES HILL "TRAE" WELBORN III

I n 1854 the United States of America stood squarely amid the tumult and throes of geographic expansion. Having only recently extended its national boundaries "from sea to shining sea" following the 1848 Mexican Cession that followed US victory in the Mexican War, the nation had grown roughly 60 percent in geographic size in an instant. Intensifying domestic disputes between antislavery "free state" and proslavery "slave state" interests in national politics somewhat tempered expansionist enthusiasm and its seemingly boundless prospects, however. Much of this dissension centered upon the future of slavery in western territories, and that already troubling question became even more pernicious with the most recent territorial gains from Mexico. The competing proslavery and antislavery visions for America's future managed to strike a contentious compromise in 1850 regarding the territory added from Mexico, but tension and conflict persisted as older territories gained in the 1803 Louisiana Purchase began to apply for statehood, Kansas first and foremost among them. The tumult over the Kansas-Nebraska Act in 1854, in which each state's slave status would be determined by "popular sovereignty" opened the door for already contentious sectional compromises to give way to overt sectional conflicts in the last half of the decade and, infamously, into the next as southern secession fomented national civil war.[1]

But as much as these tempests occupied the nation in the mid-1850s, so too did furthering that nation's expansionist designs, especially among proslavery southerners who, though they recognized the threat of a shifting balance of domestic political power toward an antislavery agenda, maintained considerable clout regarding the nation's foreign policy, which they wielded in decidedly proslavery and imperialistic ways. While these official political contests unfolded, other quasi-political expansionary endeavors emerged alongside in the form of American "filibusters" in the Caribbean and Central America. These efforts, most avidly supported by proslavery southerners but tacitly sanctioned more broadly by the still nationally dominant though southern-centric Democratic Party, touted the benefits of extending the scope and scale of the nation's "manifest destiny" beyond its current reach from the Atlantic to the Pacific. Filibuster schemes looking northward into Canada had gained national support in the decade prior to the Mexican War but had largely subsided by the mid-1840s due to repeated failures and a southward shift in priorities among expansionist visionaries. Latin America assumed primacy for filibusters from the mid-1840s through the 1850s, and proslavery southerners constituted the dominant voice endorsing them. Collectively these expansionist schemes, whether privately funded and directed expeditions or formal national military invasions, exposed the overtly imperialistic agenda as well as the proslavery undertones and white supremacist overtones of the nation's alleged "manifest destiny."[2]

One prominent proslavery southerner, William Gilmore Simms of South Carolina, commenced a national lecture tour amidst these trends in 1854, resulting in three lectures collectively entitled *Poetry and the Practical* that took up this theme and considered its reverberation throughout antebellum American society and culture in its increasingly expansive yet vulnerable state. Simms openly doubted whether his words would be heard over the din of Americans clamoring for commercial expansion, whether they would be heeded by those so "eagerly listening for the roll of those mighty engines which are to bring you the treasures of Ophir from the shores of the Pacific!" In his view this pursuit of the nation's manifest destiny constituted undeniable progress—for the white "Anglo-Norman" race, American manhood, and, through the exploits of both, the very nation itself: "We have gone fearlessly forth upon the high seas, declaring them our common; and have passed with the flight of an eagle, from the little spots along the Atlantic shores, first dotted by our infant settlements, to the far waters of the Great Pacific. . . . we have achieved wondrously, if not always well, and the very fact of our successes in the single field of progress, would seem to be held a sufficient argument against our exercise in any other." As an unapologetic apostle of the American gospel of progress through expansion, Simms, like many of his fellow white southerners, joined in antebellum America's faithful adherence to the doctrine of manifest destiny, tinged as it was by a prevailing belief in an American exceptionalism still rooted in white supremacy.[3]

But Simms's faith mirrored that of many across the sectional divide as well in that it did not preclude a critical concern over imperial excess as the corruptive, corrosive agent portending this ideal America's potential demise: "The result of all this achievement . . . is to exaggerate in the national estimate. . . . we thus learn to confound possessions with power; accumulations with developments; enjoyments with endowments; and to place the very faculties which conduct us to the conquest, in subordinate relation to the spoils which they acquire." Simms questioned both the means and the ends of such conquests and warned that they could just as well prove destructively all-consuming: "Indulging but a single great appetite, it swallows up the rest. Sworn only to the acquisition of material things, we ignore all the endowments of the soul. In just that degree in which the one passion prevails, will be the absorption of all other attributes." "Is this to be the unvarying record of the great nation?" Simms then rhetorically pondered: "Is it to be nothing but a convulsive progress of storm, and blood and fire, shouts and exultation—then, loathsome, pitiable ruin?" Neither he nor by extension the nation's leaders would or could reconcile themselves to this ultimate demise in the midst of their striving, however fraught with peril it might be. "I do not believe this to be the destiny," Simms asserted hopefully before concluding, "I find it written neither in the book of God, nor in the volumes writ by man. I believe that these contain the secret of our securities, which, properly read, received in faith, rendered strong and confident by loving sympathies, will confer upon us safety, continued growth and youth, duration to the end."[4]

By voicing his misgivings in the same long-winded breath in which he celebrated the exploits from whence they had been born, William Gilmore Simms placed a finger on the ever-quickening pulse of antebellum Americans as they simultaneously exalted the most promising hopes and confronted the most portentous fears attending their fervent pursuit and alleged fulfillment of manifest destiny. Such duality of mind pervaded the era, as tensions between North and South, free and slave, white and black intensified amidst the ongoing contests with American Indians, European powers, and neighboring countries. By the end of the 1850s, the productive *and* destructive potential of this perpetual combat had plagued Simms's mind and the national psyche for decades, despite every conscious attempt to justify themselves to themselves, to the world, and to memory.[5]

The martial ardor with which many an American (white) man had mustered into service of the nation's manifest destiny during the antebellum era and the overtly patriotic remembrance of their efforts in American historical memory since have obscured the often-brutal means by which they fulfilled that destiny and perpetuated that memory to posterity. Nowhere do the silver linings surrounding the darkest moments of this history appear brighter than when depicted on the silver screen. The cinematic distortions of antebellum American imperialism and manhood in *The Alamo* (1960), *The Alamo* (2004), *Ravenous* (1999), and *Walker* (1987) at once reveal the tendency of American popular memory to sanitize history, the power of film to shape American popular memory, and, perhaps most significantly, the persistence with which historical complexities involving issues of class, gender, race, and religion refuse to fully conform to such mythological distortions predicated on patriarchal, white supremacist, and American exceptionalist paradigms.[6]

Each of these films captures essential aspects of this dynamic between collective American identity, memory, and popular culture, whether by leveling harsh cultural criticisms and harping on uncomfortable historical truths as evidenced in *Ravenous, Walker,* and *The Alamo* (2004), or by reinforcing prevailing assumptions of cultural superiority from the past for the present as *The Alamo* (1960) does so conspicuously. In the end none of these films succeeds in remaking the broader national narrative regarding how Americans became Americans—how we became us—because their message either affirms what we think we already know (1960 *Alamo*) by reinforcing "patriotic and redemptive stories of reverence toward the nation" while simultaneously seeking to justify "counter-themes of military overreach, defeat, and imperial retreat" predicated on "violence, belligerency, and supremacy" by reifying "oppositional postures toward different or antagonistic 'others'" as the bedrock of a national identity that supersedes internal divisions of class, religion, gender, race, and language to galvanize "centripetal impulses of 'us' and 'them,' 'we' and 'they,'" or refutes these biased assumptions so fervently (2004 *Alamo*, 1999 *Ravenous*, 1987 *Walker*) that we typically ignore their criticism by rejecting these productions as "bad cinema." In general, only those films that show us as we wish to be portrayed garner praise for their "entertainment value," however rife with historical omissions and prejudicial depictions, while those films that confront the darker side of American history by exposing the more nefarious means and motives by which the United States has progressed through time become forgotten box-office flops.[7]

Gone to Texas: American Filibusters and the Texas Revolution

Filibustering dates to the founding era in US history, but such efforts became more conspicuous and numerous in the twenty years before the American Civil War. Though some of the earliest filibusters sought territorial gain above the northern US border in Canada, the bulk focused upon geographic and political expansion southward, and during the first three decades of the nineteenth century much of this agenda centered upon former Spanish colonies in the southernmost reaches of North America (Florida and northern Mexico), in the Caribbean (Haiti, Cuba, and Puerto Rico), and extending into Central America (Nicaragua, Honduras, and Guatemala), and even in some cases South America (Venezuela). Aside from Florida (finally and officially ceded to the United States by Spain in the Adams-Onis Treaty in 1819 following the conclusion of the First Seminole War, after numerous prior filibusters into the region), these privately funded, sometimes publicly sanctioned attempted conquests generally failed, in large part because official US policy prohibited such militaristic expansionism through a series of "neutrality" enactment between 1794 and 1838, the most prominent and, for filibusters, pernicious, of which was the Neutrality Law of 1818. This official policy, combined with higher priorities focused on the settlement of more immediate continental claims and acquisitions (the Old Northwest beginning in the 1780s, the old Southwest beginning in the 1790s, and the Louisiana Purchase beginning in 1803) that intensified precipitously from 1810 to 1840 tended to minimize the prominence of filibustering before 1840. The beginning of this end occurred in Texas during the 1830s. The infamous "Alamo" in San Antonio figured prominently in that historical process and has continued to loom large in historical memory since, especially in the two most iconic films depicting the period, the first released in 1960 as *The Alamo* starring John Wayne as Davy Crockett, the second appearing forty-four years later under the same title and starring Billy Bob Thornton in the role of Crockett.[8]

However, the road to "The Alamo," historically and in memory, began much earlier in the Early Republic era of the United States, when Spanish imperial suspicion of US designs upon the Spanish colonies along the Gulf Coast of North America ultimately proved well-founded, first with several militaristic invasions of Spanish Florida that eventually prompted the formal cession of the territory to the United States in 1821 following the signing of the Adams-Onis Treaty in 1819, then in the wake of the Louisiana Purchase with a series of Anglo-American filibusters between 1812 and 1822 into Spanish Texas from the newly acquired Louisiana Territory, all of which transpired as the Mexican War for Independence from Spanish imperial authority raged.[9]

Mexican revolutionaries achieved independence from Spanish rule in 1821, and though the newly independent Mexican regime initially encouraged Anglo-American settlement of its northernmost region of Texas as a means of stabilizing the area that had long been dominated by the Comanche, the Mexican government also inherited the suspicions of American expansionism from their former imperial rulers. These suspicions intensified contests between what one historian of the Texas borderlands described as the "three forces that combined to determine the ultimate fate of the region: the rise of the global cotton economy, the international battles over slavery that followed, and the struggles of competing governments to control the territory. These were the three driving forces—cotton, slavery, and empire—that . . . then shaped the unlikely evolution of this borderlands territory from Comanche hinterland to American state."[10]

Predictably, much of this complex history fails to appear on the silver screen. But despite the combination of glaring omission and myopic revision typical of American popular memory in general, especially as reflected in (and formidably shaped by) cinematic depictions, some of this more sordid story of imperialistic expansion, proslavery motivation, and white supremacist discrimination does subtly inflect both film adaptations of The Alamo and its significance within this pivotal, complex moment in antebellum American history.

Both pictures project several common tropes, namely an assumption of American exceptionalism with regards to dominant ideologies and the motives cited for extending the influence of those ideals abroad, a general conflation of American culture with its masculine manifestations and expressions, and a marginalization of the role of slavery in the Texas Revolution. But even within each of these mutual cinematic characteristics, each film varies in the degree to which it follows these well-trodden thematic paths. The result is two films that reify persistent truisms about American cultural and historical development while diverging in crucial ways that reflect the specific moments in which each film was produced and the evolution in prevailing historical memories in those moments.[11]

Though both films consciously engage the national and international contexts in which, and to some degree for which, they were produced, they do so in ways that mirror important historical developments and associated shifts in perspective. The Alamo (1960) embodies post–World War II American confidence at home and abroad, but also alludes to emerging Cold War tensions with the Union of Soviet Socialist Republics (USSR) in global diplomatic affairs. However, the film demurs from direct references to the domestic social anxieties stemming from both the Cold War and burgeoning social movements such as that for African American civil rights. The leading characters in the film all personify American ideals as first expressed in the Declaration of Independence: life, liberty, and the pursuit of happiness, including the limited application of those ideals across racial and gender lines. All characters seek to improve their individual prospects, but all give credence to a higher calling, a more noble cause greater than themselves; all swear utmost allegiance to the continued prosperity of the United States of America. Though Texas during the 1836 tumult at the Alamo had yet to formally seek or gain annexation to the United States, the prominence of white American settlers in the region and their pervasive adherence to quintessential American ideals of liberty and freedom figure prominently in the film's narrative and tone.[12]

One scene best captures this persistent undertone running throughout the film. In the early scenes, Colonel William Travis meets Colonel Davy Crockett in the bar where Crockett's newly arrived men have commenced their typically boisterous conviviality. Amidst the cacophony of shouts, Travis and Crockett find a quite side room for each to gauge the manner and manly qualities of the other upon this first meeting. In their exchange, they find that, despite seemingly divergent appearances, they share certain core values and perspectives, especially a commitment to American cultural and political ideals. Crockett reveals that he knows the intentions of Travis, Sam Houston, and others to seek US annexation of the Republic of Texas upon securing independence from Mexico, and when Travis acknowledges that likelihood, Crockett asserts his support of securing independence regardless of what follows by exclaiming: "Republic. I like the sound of the word. Live free. Free to go or come, buy or sell, to be drunk or sober, however they choose. Some words give you a feeling. Republic gives me a tightness in the throat. Same tightness a man gets when his baby takes his first steps, his first baby shaves, makes his first sound like a man. Some words give you a feeling that makes your heart warm. Republic is one of those words." Such ideological assurance as depicted on-screen reinforces progressive collective conceptions of America's past and served to promote faith in the sanctity, stability, and sustainability of the nation's founding ideals during a time in which all were believed to be fundamentally threatened by the communist ideals of the USSR.

Other poignant scenes reinforcing this theme abound, none more than one toward the end of the film when the fate of the Alamo's defenders is all but sealed and in which several soldiers consider the fate of their souls and reflect upon their religious views as they come within sight of their own deaths. All express fervent belief in God and his forgiveness, and confidence that their sacrifice will be rewarded in eternity, that their sins will be forgiven, their lives divinely pardoned if not sanctioned. The only dissenting voice is of Mexican descent, a notable contrast in that this Mexican did not share the cultural values of his white American compatriots and therefore fell prey to moral doubt and even derision. He thus denies the existence of God, God's final judgment, and an afterlife in either heaven or hell as a result of that judgment, instead claiming that man's fate is simply to return to the earth as his body decomposes in his grave. This portrayal of avowed faith among the majority of white American defenders of liberty and freedom at the Alamo constitutes a not-so-subtle condemnation of alleged communist atheism and an affirmation of the purported Christian moral principles permeating the cultural ideals and capitalist society of the United States. As the Alamo's commander, Colonel William Travis, had earlier proclaimed, "We stand here ready to do our duty, and cognizant of the will of God." Travis might well have been talking as much to Moscow in 1960 as to Mexico City in 1836.

While both *Alamo* films assume the superiority of American ideals and intentions abroad, the 1960 version generally portrays those tasked with extending these ideals to fulfill these intentions as heroes, while the 2004 adaptation presents the most prominent historical actors in ways that render them more flawed and conflicted, less heroic and more human. *The Alamo* (2004) certainly reflects the prevailing cultural, political, and military confidence of a nation engaged in a global "War on Terror," but also exposes the fault lines of this perceived confidence, especially as manifested in the increasingly divided opinions regarding the "proper" response to the international threats embodied in the 9/11 attacks, debates that centered upon expansions in government surveillance of the citizenry and aggressive deployment of military force.[13]

An American braggadocio tinged with latent insecurity pervades the 2004 *Alamo* and its depiction of American ideals in action. The film's portrayal of Sam Houston's personal and political ambitions parading beneath the guise of promoting and protecting the higher ideals of liberty, democracy, and freedom poignantly illustrate this central tension. From the opening scenes showing glimpses of the Alamo defenders' fate, the film then transports the audience to the camp of Sam Houston's army as the news of the Alamo's fall arrives. Upon hearing this news Houston retires to his tent, staring resolutely into a flickering candle and reflecting on the previous year and the role he had played in setting these events in motion. This introspection takes Houston back to Washington, DC, one year earlier, in which most people he encountered looked upon him and his pleas for national support of Texas independence with some combination of curiosity, skepticism, and disdain. He comes off as a frontier rube lacking sophistication, an ungentlemanly ruffian from an unrefined, uncivilized place—a desperate man making desperate pleas for national recognition of Texas's promising prospects for American expansion and progress.

The only man shown to have given Houston's claims any credence in Washington, DC, is Davy Crockett, and his implied reasons for doing so appear motivated more by personal ambition than by any higher noble cause. The film portrays Houston as a drunkard, a man increasingly frustrated by a surplus of military and political ambition and the lack of opportunity to satisfy either. Crockett similarly appears little more than a common charlatan and crooked politician who has exploited his fame as a frontier legend to ascend the social ranks, as the subject of a popular play (which he and Houston are shown to attend together in the capital) and as congressman from Tennessee. Yet despite this modicum of success, Crockett too seems unsatisfied, still searching for fulfillment. Both he and Houston walk the same fine line between the archetypal frontier hero and men of dubious repute; they appear both confident and insecure in their self-conceptions, both celebrated and derided in public reputation. The flashback then returns to Texas and a meeting of the Texas assembly, a boisterous affair that symbolizes the tension pervading the newly declared republic's aspirations for sustained nationhood and potential annexation to the United States and its alleged frontier barbarity as a foreign territory. Houston is shown thriving in this contentious, liminal space in stark contrast to his obvious discomfort in Washington. He is promptly joined at the assemblage by fellow frontiersman-turned-politician Jim Bowie. Bowie, like Crockett, toes the line between genteel refinement in manner and speech and a more virile, brawling nature born of a long frontier existence, and he meets with similar respect from the assembly. Bowie and Houston together sway the vote to marshal the republic's military resources for defense against the looming threat of Mexico's General Santa Anna and his approaching army.

The fourth character upon which the film projects these conflicted and contested identities and ideologies, Colonel William Travis, then arrives in San

Antonio to assume command of the garrison at the Alamo. Travis, unlike Houston, Crockett, or Bowie, affects an elite gentility that contrasts sharply with these other men. The film reinforces the contrast by showing Travis as young and inexperienced, ambitious, idealistic and naive, driven to achieve a notion of manly, martial glory the other men longer in the tooth long ago dismissed as foolhardy. Bowie and Crockett, upon meeting at the Alamo, find kindred spirits in one another, much as Crockett and Houston had done previously in Washington, in keeping with the like-minded respect held between Bowie and Houston. The film depicts all three men as representing a shared perspective forged in the frontier settings of the ever-expanding American "West," but only implies their common identity as white *southern* men, privileging instead this "westernized" narrative of frontier men seeking some semblance of personal redemption in Texas.

All four men, Houston, Crockett, Bowie, and Travis, find common ground, however, in this implied identity and purpose, as southern men offered a second chance in Texas. Though Bowie and Crockett and their men view Travis with suspicion because of his perceived "dandification" and elitism, the film counters these tensions between them by emphasizing that Travis, too, seeks personal redemption through martial glory in Texas, as flashback scenes reveal his decision to divorce his wife in Tennessee before setting out westward. His personal insecurities as a man emanate from his guilt over this decision and infuse his bravado as a soldier and commander, and though the latter of which initially rankles Crockett's Tennesseans and Bowie's Texian militiamen, the film ultimately emphasizes how these men's common convictions prevail in the face of impending Mexican military might and the death it portends. They all set aside their differences and develop a mutual respect based on a shared valor predicated on their collective willingness to sacrifice themselves for the higher cause of Texas independence and, by extension, American ideals.[14]

Such patterns of convergence and divergence in the two *Alamo* films' depictions of American cultural values and foreign-policy motives and methods extend, then, into their portrayals of white American manhood, which both pictures generally presume to be the predominant mode of expressing such values and intentions. Nowhere is this more prevalent than in the portrayal of martial manhood—and its latent tension with more restrained conceptions of manhood—that pervades both movies (personified in both films by Bowie and Crockett and their respective militias as contrasted with Travis's insistence upon soldierly discipline among his "regular" troops). In the 1960 *Alamo,* such martial manhood stands as an exalted ideal almost beyond reproach and, when properly pursued, its exploits constitute progress of the highest order. Though tensions arise among the film's martial men over what degree of violence and aggression is acceptable in the performance of manly duty, all agree that fulfilling this duty demands some level of violence and aggression, and more "restrained" manhood ideals find little resonance among any of the men depicted in the film. Even as they observed the military might of Santa Anna's army assembling for their own destruction, the Alamo's defenders summed up this conception of martial manhood: "Fancy clothes don't make a fightin' man," one anonymous defender asserts, prompting his compatriot's reply, "They're just off two years puttin' down revolts; they're fightin' men." Later another anonymous soldier completes the thought by declaring, "[It] speaks well for a man if he ain't afraid to die if he thinks right's on his side." And as the 1960 film makes clear, right was on the side of the American defenders at the Alamo, just as it remained on the side of American Cold Warriors in their global fight against communism.[15]

By contrast, post–Vietnam era doubts and insecurities inflect the perspectives of soldiers and the purpose of combat in vital ways that are repeated throughout the 2004 *Alamo*. Whether making a defiant stand against Santa Anna's much larger army will enable the four leading men and those under their command to realize the redemption they seek remains in doubt as the action unfolds and constitutes the primary dramatic tension in the film. Crockett gives these doubts most fervent expression during a campfire recounting of his previous military service as a young man in the Red Stick War. Despite much of his publicly celebrated reputation stemming from this service—indeed he is prompted to relate the tale by one of his fellow soldiers at the Alamo obviously elated to be serving alongside the famous Davy Crockett—Crockett has consistently disparaged the legitimacy of this reputation throughout the film. He exhibits this insecurity in one poignant exchange with Bowie in which Crockett observes, "People expect things," to which Bowie replies simply, "Ain't it so," sending Crockett into a confession: "If it was just simple old me, David from Tennessee, I might drop over the wall one night and take my chances. But this Davy Crockett feller, they're all watching him. He's been fighting on this wall every day of his life." This self-effacement and its implied prevalence among many if not most of the men at the Alamo call into question the very manly ideals purportedly holding these men to their "duty" in that place, a cynicism Crockett further exposes in his blatantly inglorious and lamenting, almost shameful, recanting of his military "exploits" and the "successes" of American forces against the Red Sticks. The initial enthusiasm of those gathered around him quickly fades as Crockett's account of war as ignoble murder—the perpetration of regrettable violence and needless slaughter—casts a melancholy pall over the entire garrison as the scene closes. The underlying meaning seems clear: the efforts of the United States to "reform the world" in 2004 unfolded with less self-righteous conviction and met with more concerted criticism at home and abroad than that attending the Cold War crusades of the United States in 1960.[16]

Despite such scenes of antiwar sentiment, the film ultimately projects a more assured tone by showing how the conflicted individual men tasked with defending the Alamo against the impending Mexican onslaught resigned themselves to their fate by convincing themselves that theirs was a higher purpose, a more noble cause greater than themselves: the security of the Republic of Texas and by extension the United States itself, threatened as they were by the allegedly maniacal, egotistical, and despotic Santa Anna and his army. Travis's final address to the men on the eve of their final stand captures this reconciliation between men and their ideals assertively: "Texas has been a second chance for me. I expect that might be true for many of you men. It has been a chance not only for land and riches, but also to be a different man, I hope a better man. . . . I'd like each of you men to think of what it is you value so highly that you are willing to fight and possibly die for it. We will call that Texas."[17]

Both *Alamo* films relegate the issues of slavery and white supremacy so embedded in the history of antebellum American culture and the specific events surrounding the Texas Revolution to the margins, but the manner in which they do so differs widely. The 1960 picture only nominally confronts the racial causes and consequences of the Texas Revolution, whether concerning black slaves or the Hispanic population in the region. Early in the film, Davy Crockett expresses a personal maxim tinged with irony, given the prominence of slavery among the causes of the conflict: "It rankles me when somebody tries to force somebody to do something." This despite Crockett fighting on the side of the Texians, many of whom hailed from the slave regime of the US South and whose primary conflict with Mexico's General Santa Anna revolved around his government's antislavery edicts. The film subtly transforms the contentious nature of slavery's prominence in the American settlement of Texas and its status as the major cause of the conflict into a secondary concern in other ways as well. The only black character of note in the film, Jim Bowie's slave Jethro, perpetuates long-standing racial stereotypes of African Americans in his broken dialect, his obedient nature, and his deferential attitude toward his master's authority, despite Bowie's alleged excesses in violence and drunkenness and their striking contrast with Jethro's own strong faith and simple, sober piety. Bowie matter-of-factly manumits Jethro on the eve of the final, fateful fight at the Alamo, and exhibits little indecision or regret in doing so. But Jethro fulfills his role as the ubiquitous "loyal slave" by choosing to remain with his former master, asserting that his ability to decide is "what you men is fightin' for." Slavery and the higher ideals of American culture and manhood are incompatible in the collective American memory, so the most controversial issue of the era in the region becomes ancillary to the narrative of a "just war" in defense of American liberty and freedom against Mexican tyranny and oppression.[18]

Racially prejudiced views of Mexicans and Mexican Americans in both the antebellum era and in the popular conception of mid-twentieth-century American society and culture find repeated expression in the 1960 *Alamo*. Soon after assuming command of the Alamo, Colonel Travis receives military intelligence from Juan Seguin, depicted as a wealthy landowner of Mexican descent in the region, regarding the whereabouts of General Santa Anna's approaching army. Travis listens to Seguin's account, based upon the observations of Native Americans in the vicinity, with obvious impatience and disdain before finally dismissing Seguin in short order without crediting the information he's shared. When confronted by Bowie about his cold reception of Seguin and his conspicuous dismissal of the intel delivered before the Alamo's garrison, Travis bristles, citing higher priorities than the personal feelings of a local Mexican landowner. When pressed by Bowie, Travis explains that, though he personally regrets the possibility of offending Seguin and doubts the viability of successfully defending the Alamo, as commander of the fort his first obligation is to dissuade such doubts among his men, and to fulfill his duty to defend the Alamo as a crucial stopgap against Santa Anna's "invasion" of Texas. This offhand dismissal of Mexican perspectives in favor of an American agenda symbolizes prevailing American racial attitudes in the region in 1836 as well as 1960.

Other scenes reiterate such prejudicial perspectives. When Davy Crockett encounters Señora "Flaca" Lopez in the hotel in San Antonio, she is engaged in heated conversation with a Mexican aristocrat, Emil Sande. Crockett eavesdrops upon their conversation, which centers on the arranged betrothal of Sande and Lopez that has been orchestrated by General Santa Anna. In this exchange, Lopez asserts her unwillingness to accede to the arrangement, whereupon Sande forcefully asserts that she will either marry him according to his and Santa Anna's wishes, or else. This ominous threat prompts Crockett to intervene directly, gun in hand, and only Lopez's conciliatory admonitions prevent violence between Crockett and Sande, the latter of whom departs after repeating his threat. In the series of exchanges between Crockett and Lopez that follows, Crockett repeatedly places himself in an overtly patriarchal role as male protector of a dependent woman, though these gestures are laced with chivalric and paternalistic undertones. Symbolically, Mexico as personified in Señora Lopez becomes increasingly dependent upon American protection as personified in Crockett and his compatriots at the Alamo, a thinly veiled allegory intended not only to exalt the motives of white American settlers in Texas during the antebellum period but also those of Americans engaged in the global Cold War against communism in the twentieth century.

Even when Mexican society and culture garner praise from American characters in the film, such praise exudes an overt sense of superiority and the assumed prerogative to cast judgment upon others. A scene between Jim Bowie and Davy Crockett personifies such biased assumptions best, as Bowie admits his admiration for the Mexican people and their courageousness by declaring, "they are not afraid to die, and more importantly they're not afraid to live. Yankees might say that's lazy, but I call it living." But such limited expression of cultural admiration pales in comparison to the film's overarching tendency toward prejudicial portrayals. In its depiction of the soldiers engaged at the Alamo, the film consciously asserts the individuality of the American defenders of the Alamo and sets these hyper-individualized portrayals against those of the largely nameless, faceless "horde" of Mexican "enemies" under the command of General Santa Anna, who himself appears as a largely distant, though menacing and imposing, figure. This symbolic "othering" of Santa Anna and his Mexican force highlights the alleged racial and ideological superiority of Americans over their declared enemies, a prejudiced perspective that speaks as much to the mindset of Cold War America and its historical memory and present foreign policy as it does to the cultural biases animating antebellum Americans in Texas. These prejudiced portrayals collectively serve to reinforce the film's depiction of the Texas Revolution against Mexico as a noble defense of freedom against an ignoble, racially inferior, and rapacious dictatorship.[19]

The 2004 film ascribes more agency and less racial stereotyping to the black and Hispanic actors than does the 1960 iteration, though the contentious debates over the status of both groups in antebellum Texas still found limited time on-screen. The presence of two slaves at the Alamo, William Travis's slave, Joe, and Jim Bowie's slave, Sam, symbolizes the presence of slavery in Texas during the period. Two poignant scenes symbolically acknowledge the ongoing divisions over slavery in the adjacent antebellum United States and in the relationship between the Republic of Texas and the Mexican government from which Texas had just declared itself independent. The first scene shows both the elder Joe and the younger Sam engaged in digging a new well for the Alamo garrison, and Joe seizes the opportunity to dissuade his younger companion from risking his life for Travis by declaring, "You clean up they shit, take care of they horses, wash 'em, feed 'em. Damn if you ain't gonna die for 'em too!" Joe then tells Sam to remember the phrase "Soy negro, no desparo," when the Mexican forces overrun the Alamo in order to take advantage of Mexican antislavery laws. Their conversation in the well exhibits the slaves' knowledge of Mexican antislavery laws and their recognition that Mexican victory and American defeat might well mean their freedom. The second scene shows Bowie, at this point laid up with tuberculosis on his deathbed, granting Joe permission to leave the Alamo with the other noncombatants, but when Joe asks if this means he's being granted his freedom papers, Bowie fervently denies it, saying, "You're my property, and you'll be my property until my last breath," threatening to hunt Joe down wherever he goes should Bowie survive both his sickness and the impending assault upon the Alamo. Thus Bowie appears as an unapologetic slaveowner clinging to his slave property through the last few hours before his death, a metaphor for the hold that slavery itself had taken upon the white American settlers in Texas. The film attempts to soften this hard-edged criticism of slavery's pernicious place in antebellum Texas and the United States, however, in one of the final scenes, showing Sam, Travis's young slave, dutifully clutching his recently killed master's personal effects while repeatedly uttering the phrase, "Soy negro, no desparo." Even in critically confronting the uncomfortable truth of slavery in the history of Texas and American expansion there, the trope of the loyal slave persists in this conflicted moment for Sam, who simultaneously seizes upon the opportunity for freedom offered him while embracing Travis's satchel and sobbing over his death.[20]

Such complexities also pervade the portrayals of Mexican and Mexican American characters in the 2004 *Alamo*. Early in the film, as the various American militia and military forces coalesce at the Alamo, an exchange between the "Texican" Juan Seguin and another anonymous compatriot of Mexican descent sees them observing a dispute between Bowie, Travis, and their respective commands and discussing their own role and purpose alongside. Both Seguin and his companion express their opinion that the American Texians were greedy and grasping "low-lifes," but Seguin nevertheless asserts that "the enemy of my enemy is my friend," alluding to his aversion to Santa Anna and his government. His companion retorts, "Yeah, but Santa Anna only wants to rule Mexico, these disgraces want the whole world." The motives and methods of the American Texians at the Alamo specifically and in Texas at large when considered from across the racial and ethnic line imposed by Americans themselves appear far more sanguineous.

Here again, however, the film softens the proverbial blow to the collective American psyche by emphasizing the multiethnic makeup of the army Sam Houston marshals in the wake of the Alamo's defeat. Juan Seguin, whom Travis dispatched to Houston prior to the final assault on the Alamo by Santa Anna's army, personifies this demographic among the Texian army and its convicted-though-conflicted place within it, as he earnestly demands that he and his men remain to fight Santa Anna when Houston expresses his concern that his American troops are likely to fire upon "anything and anyone that looks Mexican" in the heat of battle. Seguin's commitment to stay deflects Houston's allusion to the prevailing racial and ethnic prejudice among the white Texian troops towards Mexicans and Texicans alike. Such deflection again figures prominently after Houston's army defeats Santa Anna's at the Battle of San Jacinto and Seguin drops to his knees in thanks for this outcome and for Santa Anna's subsequent agreement (though consistently contested within Mexico for the next decade) to concede Mexico's claims to the Texas territory. This serves as the symbolic epitaph to the Alamo's defenders who ultimately did not die in vain, as the film notes that none other than Juan Seguin himself returned to inter their bodies with the honor due them.[21]

South of the Border, Westward Ho!
The Mexican War and the Antebellum Wild West

The turmoil in Texas during the 1830s and 1840s, rooted as it was in the extension of proslavery economic interests and the associated cultural values of white supremacy, ultimately engulfed both Mexico and the United States in a brief but bloody military conflict that quickly escalated from its border war origins into a war of invasion. Historians have delved deeply into the complexities of this escalation, and though some of this scholarship focuses on the military history of the conflict exclusively, most scholars situate the war within the broader context of antebellum America, especially its relation to the burgeoning dissension over slavery, both as a domestic sectional dispute and as a transnational ideological contest.[22]

But that pivotal moment in the rise of antebellum American imperialism seldom garners the attention befitting its historical significance in American collective memory. "In spite of its importance to the expansion of the United States in the nineteenth century, the US-Mexican War is often perceived as being the nation's forgotten war," observes one historian of the conflict and its legacies, further asserting that "many historians believe that the US-Mexican War has slipped from the memory of many Americans because it highlighted their nation's aggression and was then eclipsed by the bloodier Civil War. The US invasion of a fellow republic has been embroiled in controversy since the day the conflict began," the author continues, arguing that "modern Americans, like their nineteenth-century compatriots, have struggled to reconcile the gains of the war with the means by which it was initiated. Forgetting the conflict has therefore proven to be a convenient means of easing the national conscience." Those "means" blatantly included expanding the scope and scale of a proslavery foreign policy agenda as well as the influence of white supremacy through the extension of US political power and associated cultural ideals. Much of the often-willful historical amnesia afflicting the American memory of the Mexican War in particular and the antebellum era generally can be attributed to a pervasive unwillingness to confront these uncomfortable historical truths that seemingly undermine the exceptional promise of American ideals as typically conceived in collective memory and popular culture.[23]

Like the contests in the Texas borderlands from whence the conflict sprang, the modern popular memory of the Mexican War in the United States, when remembered at all, tends to situate it within a western context, and often the war itself appears only as the spark that ignited the westward expansion of the United States, an expansion that spawned the mythological "Wild West" that enveloped the vast territory stretching westward from the Mississippi River to the Pacific Ocean and spanning southward from the Canadian border to the Rio Grande. In short, the territorial gains that resulted from the conflict assume center stage, while the motives and means by which such gains were made fade into oblivion. Reasons for this trend abound, but the most compelling ones revolve around the nature of antebellum American imperialism and the extent to which prevailing cultural ideals of white supremacy and sectional proslavery politics animated this expansionism, all of which many modern Americans consider anathema to national ideals and their perpetuation throughout the United States' triumphant march into the present and toward the future.[24]

As one of the few films to engage the Mexican War at all, *Ravenous* (1999) in many ways follows this "westernized" script, as the bulk of the action involving the lead character, Mexican War veteran Captain John Boyd, focuses on his postwar experience at a remote outpost in California's Sierra Nevada, with his experience in the war itself merely setting the stage for his postwar experiences in the far West. And the film makes almost no effort to directly engage the history of racial tension and slavery inherent in the westward expansion of the antebellum United States, though it does subtly allude to racial tensions with American Indians attending this expansion. Though the racialized impact remains largely implied, elements of the darker history of American imperialism in Mexico and the West seep into the narrative of manifest destiny as portrayed in *Ravenous* to a greater extent than the cinematic depictions of the fight at the Alamo, most poignantly in the critical tone with which that conception of American expansion is discussed and the often-horrifying scenes in which the film symbolically exhibits its execution.[25]

The film's overtly critical tone condemns antebellum America's alleged attempts to bring civilization and order, liberty and freedom, to the purportedly untamed western wilds by emphasizing the extent to which the so-called high ideals animating the nation's pursuit of Manifest Destiny—south of the border in the Mexican War and in the wake its territorial gains, west to the Pacific shore—fall victim to the base savagery and rapaciousness lurking just beneath the surface. The film sets this tone from the opening scene in which Capt. John Boyd is being recognized before a military tribunal in the immediate wake of the American victory in the Mexican War (1847) "for heroism above and beyond the call of duty, for successfully infiltrating the enemy's ranks and securing victory independently, with cunning and honor." But the internal strife afflicting Boyd as he flashes back in his mind to harrowing battle scenes that portray little of the heroism, cunning, or honor for which he is being commended is revealed in the expression of visceral pain upon his face throughout the ceremony and the banquet that follows. The soldiers surrounding him at the banquet table set upon their steaks with vigor, passing the bottle of wine with enthusiasm, while Boyd surveys the scene with visible disgust. The rare, bloody steaks and the image of soldiers devouring them turns his stomach and brings forth further visions of bloody bodies writhing in pain on the battlefield amidst pools of crimson, until Boyd abruptly leaves the party to vomit. Boyd's commander, General Slauson, follows him out in order to deride Boyd's commendation, proclaiming, "You're no hero Boyd!" before informing him of his "promotion" to an isolated post at Fort Spencer, California, "as far away from my company as possible." Despite this contempt for Boyd's character and manhood, however, the scene closes with General Slauson himself avidly directing his orderlies in the placement of the sundry material spoils of victory for his personal office as Boyd hurriedly departs, highlighting the degree to which prevailing conceptions of manly honor, courage, and character ring hollow amid the greed that accompanies imperialistic "progress."

Captain Boyd then arrives at Fort Spencer, an isolated, tumbledown fort of little consequence in eastern California, high in the snowcapped western Sierra Nevada. Though this was technically a promotion, Boyd finds himself second in command at his new post behind Colonel Hart and surrounded by a misfit company of army rejects that includes Lieutenant Knox, the notorious drunkard; Private Cleaves, the drugged-out cook; Private Reich, the military zealot; Private Toffler, the slow-witted army chaplain; as well as two American Indians, George and his sister Martha, who Colonel Hart simply says "came with the place." This isolated outpost promises to shackle Boyd to his own troubled memories of death and gore in Mexico, imprisoning him in a haunted existence possessed not only by specters of the destruction he witnessed but also the craven way he faced (and continues to face) them. In relating his "act of heroism" and subsequent commendation to the party at Fort Spencer, Boyd tells how his success in capturing the command post from behind enemy lines stemmed from having "played dead" during and after the battle, to be buried beneath the corpses of his commanding officers, their blood running down his throat. It was then, he asserts ominously, that "something changed," and the flashback scene shows him wantonly killing Mexican soldiers in a rampage. The very honor for which Boyd was so dubiously rewarded and promoted, then, is also his shame—and that of the army's and the nation's in its misguided Mexican "conquest."

The film proceeds to depict California not as the land of bounty justly bestowed upon the United States in its triumphant march towards its manifest destiny, but rather as a landscape of horrors in which the alleged promise of American manhood succumbs to the vile urges of wanton savagery. In transgressing south of the Mexican border, American imperialists had not ushered in some golden era of progress but had instead wrought a series of hellish returns in which supposedly high ideals would be sundered to satisfy more barbaric and unholy desires in the West, desires that implicitly included persistent tensions and conflicts with various American Indian peoples in the region as well as the tensions and conflicts between proslavery and antislavery forces that would ultimately rend the nation in civil war. The film itself falls well short of making these tangible historical connections, instead focusing on the immediate peril portending American westward expansion, not from those encountered in this pursuit, but rather from the inherent, insatiable greed for greater dominion over more and more territory among white Americans themselves.

A dark turn consumes the film henceforth in its effort to drive this point home, beginning with the arrival of a severely frostbitten, nearly dead Scottish immigrant named F. W. Colqhoun at Fort Spencer. After almost too quickly recovering from his frostbite following a hot bath, Colqhoun proceeds to relate his harrowing tale of the fate that befell his wagon train as they traveled west, the party numbering seven in all and led by a Colonel Ives whom Colqhoun describes as a brutal, savage man. When severe winter weather caught them exposed high in the Sierra Nevada, they sought shelter in a cave. Facing starvation, Colqhoun recalls with evident horror that, when one of their party died, they all agreed to cook and eat him. But despite his aversion to the deed, Colqhoun also admits that he thanked the Lord for the nourishment. He then describes how the savagery of the party's hunger increased after that first cannibalistic act and they proceeded to set upon one another, killing and eating one after the other until only four remained. At this point Colqhoun admits that he abandoned the party out of fear, and credits Providence for his arrival at Fort Spencer.

Having heard this shocking tale, the garrison at Fort Spencer takes pity on Colqhoun and considers it their duty to attempt the rescue of the other remaining members of the wagon train still holed up in the cave and who, at least according to Colqhoun's account, remained at the mercy of Colonel Ives and his growing cannibalistic fervor. Before the rescue party departs for the cave, the Indian George relates a story from Native American lore about a cannibalized man-beast named Windigo, whose appetite for human flesh once whetted becomes increasingly insatiable with each subsequent cannibalistic act, each feast fortifying his body and mind further. When Captain Boyd and Colonel Hart both express doubts about the veracity of this native legend, especially the alleged superhuman powers its cannibalism affords, George critically observes that such cannibalism is not so foreign and savage as these white men make it out to be, for after all, do not white Christian communion practices represent a similar vein of sacralized cannibalism? With this foreboding message fresh in their minds, the rescue party sets out from Fort Spencer for the cave.

Upon their reaching the cave, the Windigo legend comes to life when it's revealed that Colqhoun had been no hapless victim of cannibalism but rather the primary perpetrator, having devoured his companions with relish and wholly given himself over to his newfound cannibalistic craving. He turns upon the fort's garrison with rabidity, adding their corpses to his grisly banquet. Only Boyd survives the ordeal, but he injures his leg making his escape from Colqhoun and falls into a deep pit along with Private Reich, who dies in the fall. Without the ability to walk and find sustenance, Boyd himself is forced to filet flesh from his dead comrade's leg to stay alive in the pit. After several days of doing so, his leg quickly heals and he begins the trek back to Fort Spencer, to be further haunted by this new specter of Colqhoun falling upon him (or perhaps he himself falling prey to the very same cannibalistic fervor now that he too has partaken of human flesh). Thus the Windigo of Indian legend becomes a thinly veiled symbol of American expansionist greed and the insatiable desire for ever more territory, wealth, power, and dominion that promises not to reward those who partake but instead to corrupt them beyond recognition and possibly destroy them.

Colqhoun then resurfaces at Fort Spencer claiming to be Colonel Ives, having been recently appointed by General Slauson to replace the deceased (by Colqhoun's hand) Colonel Hart. Boyd resists Ives's appointment to command of the fort to no avail, as General Slauson already deems Boyd deficient as a soldier and a man, and Boyd's increasingly wild ravings about Colonel Ives's previous cannibalistic atrocities under the guise of Colqhoun only intensify the general's disdain. Ives then relates his personal story to Boyd, admitting to being formerly plagued by "tuberculosis, depression, and suicidal ambitions," all of which had put him en route to a "sanatorium to convalesce, more likely to die" in the far West. At least, that had been his expected fate until he heard a "strange story" from an Indian scout about a man who consumes another man's flesh, and from it draws that man's strength. "Well," Ives confesses, "I just had to try. Coincidentally, I ate the scout first and you know he was absolutely right; I grew stronger. Later through circumstance my wagon train grew lost in the Rockies," Ives continues, "and I ate five men in three months. Tuberculosis vanished, as did the black thoughts. I reached Denver that spring feeling happy. And healthy. And virile. . . . Here I am a year later feeling more alive than ever before. And that's what surprises me about you, Boyd. You've tasted it. You've felt its power. Yet you're resisting. Why?" Boyd vehemently answers, "Because it's wrong!" to which Ives mockingly replies, "Ah! Morality. The last bastion of a coward. Oh, I'm sorry. Did I offend you?" This dichotomy between Ives's embrace of cannibalistic power and Boyd's resistance to and rejection of it becomes symbolic of the tension between imperialism and anti-imperialism in the antebellum United States as the nation sought to expand its political and economic power throughout the Western Hemisphere. This expansion, like the burgeoning need for human flesh that consumes the cannibal, feeds upon what Ives calls "the growing, killing need to replenish."

What the film largely implies to this point it makes abundantly clear in the final scenes that follow, first with Colonel Ives revealing to Boyd that he's begun recruiting others to his gruesome cause, including Colonel Hart, whom Ives had not eaten but instead had nurtured back to health with the flesh of the other members of the ill-fated rescue party at the cave. And Ives seeks to enroll Boyd as well, imploring him to give in and satisfy his urge to taste the flesh and blood of his fellow man by appealing to his manhood. "It's not courage to resist me, Boyd. It's courage to accept me," Ives asserts before observing, "you're already one of us. Well, almost. You hunger for it. You just won't resign yourself to it. It's not so difficult really. Acquiescence. It's easy actually. You just, give, in." Ives then touts this conversion experience not only as a personal revelation but as the means of national salvation, soliloquizing, "Manifest Destiny. Westward Expansion. Come April it will all start again. Thousands of gold-hungry Americans will travel over those mountains on their way to new lives passing right through here. We won't kill indiscriminately. No. Selectively. Good God, we don't want to break up families," he mockingly proclaims in a subtle aspersion of the antebellum proslavery defense and its paternalistic claims before continuing, "We don't want to recruit everyone, we've got enough mouths to feed already. We just need a home. And this country is seeking to be whole. Stretching out its arms. And consuming all it can. And we merely follow." Here the film confronts the uncomfortable truths lurking beneath the nation's ideals and the antebellum efforts to extend them across the continent and the hemisphere: not everyone qualified for the full life, liberty, and pursuit of happiness promised in the Declaration of Independence. Class, gender, racial, and religious limits precluded many from drinking from the fount of American progress in the antebellum era, and the pursuit of manifest destiny to fulfill that progress rendered many social groups little more than fodder for the imperial feast of white America upon the land and the people and cultures already inhabiting that land.

The projected confidence with which white antebellum Americans pursued this manifest destiny obscured the latent insecurities of an ever-changing nation, however. Doubts and misgivings about the means and ends of antebellum imperial expansion abounded during the era itself, though such nuance has generally been lost in the collective memory of the period. Such tensions find a voice in *Ravenous,* not only in Captain Boyd and his concerted resistance to Ives and the temptation to satiate his cannibalistic urges, but in the newly recruited Colonel Hart as well. Hart expresses the cynicism that ultimately enabled him to embrace cannibalism by arguing that, "for two millennia struggling with the nature of man, the ideal society? And morality? Boil it down, it's the same issues we can't solve today. Happiness, and how to achieve it . . . and truth! Ha! I lived my whole life according to what I thought was right and true and look where it got me: Fort Spencer. . . . Don't you understand?" Hart continues, "All you have to do is kill. Kill! You have to kill to live."

But such violent assertions take their toll and prove unsustainable for even the most ravenous of men. Colonel Hart eventually concedes to Boyd that, despite the power it brings, the rapacious spirit required of the cannibal in his constant consumption corrupts absolutely. He then tells Boyd to "take the knife," obviously expecting Boyd to use it to slay Ives and bring the sordid banquet to a close. "But you have to do me a favor before you go," Hart demands, "you have to kill me. I can't live like this anymore." Boyd fulfills this request then sets about the other, to kill Ives and himself and eradicate the cannibalistic urge before it consumes everything good and decent and just. He confronts Ives in the fort's stables, and in grappling with one another they fall together into a massive bear trap that Boyd had previously triggered for the purpose. Both men perish in this final ghastly embrace. But the film denies the audience an optimistic ending, for despite this dual killing of Ives and Boyd, which Boyd enacted as the only way to exorcise the cannibalistic demon, the film portends the demon's persistence in the final scene, wherein General Slauson is seen lapping up the sordid stew of human flesh that remained simmering over the fire. And so the film implies that the demon goes unvanquished to continue to feed its voracious, destructive appetite with the lives of all those in its path: American imperialism continued/continues unabated.[26]

Filibusted: Proslavery Offensives and White Supremacy
in Central America

The Treaty of Guadalupe-Hidalgo that formally ended the Mexican War in 1848 did little to quell the rising tide of sectional discord *or* imperialistic intent in the United States, but rather intensified both to unprecedented levels in the decade before the American Civil War. The former generally preoccupied American politicians during the decade, beginning with the contentious Compromise of 1850, continuing with the tumult surrounding the Kansas-Nebraska Act of 1854, and then rapidly spiraling out of control between 1856 and 1861 as conflict displaced compromise in "Bleeding Kansas" and the Brooks-Sumner Affair (1856) and the overtly sectional responses to them as well as the subsequent Dred Scott Decision (1857), John Brown's Raid on Harpers Ferry (1859), and Abraham Lincoln's election as president (1860).[27]

But alongside this domestic sectional firestorm an equally important foreign policy fixation smoldered among proslavery southerners and their sympathizers who, despite the shifting balance of power toward antislavery politics on the home front, continued to promote a national expansionist policy abroad, especially with regards to Latin America. Many politicians advocated for overt militaristic expansion like that just successfully pursued in Mexico, and some even lamented the territorial concessions that had been made in negotiating the end of that war, having aspired to the complete conquest of Mexico by promoting the "all Mexico" movement throughout the conflict and into its wake. From this point forward, such prominent names as Stephen Mallory, Judah Benjamin, John Slidell, Stephen Douglas, and Lewis Cass combined with a host of lesser-known expansionists to foment the dream of an "American Empire" in the tropics of the Caribbean and Central America. A southern accent set the tone and direction for much of this imperialistic agenda, with some conservative northern Democrats such as Douglas and Cass lending their voices to the chorus as all united around repeated refrains of white supremacy, even if they lacked harmony in its most radical proslavery applications. These internal divisions within the still-dominant Democratic Party combined with increasingly formidable antislavery Republican opposition to temper the official pursuit of such an imperial vision, however, as the US government balked at several opportunities for official territorial annexation in the wake of the prolonged trouble in Texas that culminated in the Mexican War.[28]

This official reticence reflected in policy did not dissuade and in no way condemned expansionist endeavors during the decade, however. Southern

Democrats, despite their languishing hold on Congress, maintained a powerful presence in the executive branch through the office of the president (in succession from John Tyler to James K. Polk to Zachary Taylor to Millard Fillmore to Franklin Pierce to James Buchanan) and his cabinet, especially those offices which determined foreign policy and directed military affairs. But beyond these formal channels, American expansionist enthusiasm spilled over into the private realm, and the American filibuster reached the zenith of his infamous yet influential career during the 1850s. Though the United States continued its official policy of prohibiting and prosecuting such privately funded expansionist expeditions, the conviction with which it did so during the decade frequently fell well short of anti-imperialist expectations and served to infuriate the foreign nations most often targeted in such filibustering schemes.[29]

Here again historians have spilled considerable ink in chronicling and analyzing the often controversial exploits of these late-antebellum filibusters, beginning with those stemming from both the "all Mexico" movement and its designs on southern Mexico's politically unstable Yucatan region in 1848–49, as well as the bevy of expeditions into Mexico's northern frontier under a litany of American and French adventurers from 1851 to 1860, all of them born of unresolved border disputes and persistent American ambitions in the region. Long-standing American designs upon Cuba have also drawn much historical interest, especially Narciso Lopez's pair of ill-fated expeditions to the island in 1850 and 1851 and the many similarly conceived though ultimately unhatched schemes, those of Mississippi's John A. Quitman in 1854–55 foremost among them. Failed expansion efforts in Ecuador under General Juan Jose Flores in 1851, and revived efforts in 1855, both garner historical attention as well.[30]

But by far the most renowned and thoroughly studied American filibuster of this veritable "age of filibustering" was William Walker, the so-called "gray-eyed man of destiny" who steadfastly pursued the expansionist agenda in Central America from his first forays into Mexican territories in Baja California and Sonora to his infamous expeditions to Nicaragua, the first of fleeting success from 1855 to 1857 when Walker established himself as president of the Republic of Nicaragua, the second undergoing several false starts beginning in late 1858 and continuing through 1859 before finally ending with Walker's arrest by British naval forces and subsequent execution by firing squad at the behest of Honduran authorities in September 1860. Walker's death signaled the symbolic death of the "age of filibustering" at large and with it the popular faith in the doctrine of manifest destiny.[31]

The secession crisis, four bloody years of Civil War, and the turbulent postwar Reconstruction era would all drive additional nails into this proverbial coffin. Though Americans would resurrect their imperialistic ambitions in the 1890s, the potential for a resurgence of filibustering failed to materialize, as the formal military might of the American nation would assume primacy in this turn-of-the-twentieth century rise of a global American empire that no longer sought to shroud its expansionist aims behind the veil of a now obsolete manifest destiny.[32]

Somewhat ironically, the most consciously anachronistic of the four featured films focused on antebellum American imperialism, *Walker* (1987), most successfully counters the prevailing tendency to exalt American exceptionalism in the nation's collective historical memory. It does so by openly mocking the commitment to democracy's manifest destiny that purportedly motivated William Walker and his men in their militaristic descent upon Nicaragua and by bluntly injecting contemporary criticisms of the Reagan administration's support of the Nicaraguan *contras* during the mid-1980s into the epic portrayal of Walker's mid-nineteenth-century "Immortals." But even this blatantly critical tone so infused with presentist political perspectives fails to wholly shed progressive perceptions of America's past, as much of the film's ridicule centers not upon the expressed ideals of Walker and his compatriots (and by extension, those of the Reagan administration) but upon the flawed men themselves and the fallacious manner of their ideological expressions. In short, the film implies that Walker (like Reagan) misappropriated otherwise sound American ideals for nefarious purposes that undermined the sanctity of those very ideals and their erstwhile progress.[33]

Throughout the film William Walker personifies the absurdity of American claims to righteousness regarding the nation's repeated incursions into Central America, past or present. This absurdity spews repeatedly from the mouth of Walker himself, who consistently fails to acknowledge or recognize the disparity between the means by which American ideals are being transported to the region and the extent to which such means fundamentally undermine those very ideals. For Walker, if American ideals are sound, then they should be expanded, and any means of achieving this expansion justifies that ultimate end. Walker's apparent conviction that "where there's a will there's a way" constitutes the surest means of achieving glory and perpetuating progress finds expression in his closing statement at the trial in San Francisco for his alleged violation of American neutrality laws in Sonora, Mexico. "Unless a man believes that there is something great for him to do he can do nothing great. A great idea springs up from a man's soul, agitates his entire being, transports him from the ignorant present and makes him feel the future in a moment. It is the God-given right of the American people to dominate the western hemisphere," Walker insists before concluding, "It is our moral duty to protect our neighbors from oppression and exploitation. It is the fate of America to go ahead. That is her manifest destiny." Walker's aspirations are America's aspirations, but Walker's flaws are also America's flaws, and the film emphasizes these flaws as the primary obstacle to America's ability to discern noble aspirations from base ambitions, to distinguish between progress and profits, to differentiate between expanding freedom and eroding it for the sake of expansion.

In spite of his constant sermonizing as to the righteousness of his cause and the higher moral standards by which they would pursue and fulfill it in Nicaragua, both Walker and his men consistently fail to uphold these tenets, a contrast placed in stark relief throughout the film in order to challenge American claims to moral and ideological superiority over those they summarily conquered. After debarking in Nicaragua Walker begins an address to the locals at Realejo with a quote from Proverbs 11:3, "'The integrity of the upright shall guide them but the perverseness of transgressors shall destroy them,'" before pronouncing, "Soldiers we are now embarked on a glorious destiny: nothing short of the entire regeneration of this republic. Ours is a sacred trust. And any man who betrays that trust by creating an act of transgression against the hospitality of the Nicaraguan people will be judged and dealt with accordingly. There will be no excessive drinking, no seducing and no swearing in public places. Gentlemen," he continues, "we are honored guests here and we will act that way according to the moral dictates of God, science, and hygiene."

Such moralizing remonstrance does little to temper the soldiers' hedonism, however, as they proceed to engage in various forms of debauchery among locals, with several of them even eyeing a corral of sheep with lascivious intent. When one of the party questions their designs, another exclaims, "stay out of it. Walker says this is a democracy." This equivalent to "this is a free country, I can do what I want," captures the film's absurd, almost juvenile portrayal of Walker and his men, who espouse high ideals and a commitment to high moral character in the same breath with which they execute heinous acts of violent brutality and undemocratic assertions of authority. The film deliberately and repeatedly juxtaposes such contradictions in expression and action, including this "sheep scene" which is followed by the short quip: "Walker realized that he would need to keep a firm hand on the moral conduct of his men."

Other examples include Walker's proclamation to his men prior to their march on the city of Rivas: "It is our mission to introduce into the family of enlightened and civilized nations a new sister. To help us in our just cause are two of Nicaragua's Liberal Party, and defenders of democracy, Generals Castellon and Munoz. We march for Rivas. As God is on our side, victory will be ours." But later when Timothy Crocker, one of his most trusted men, confesses, "I feel I have to tell you . . . the men are awfully confused about just what exactly we're fightin' for here. I mean I know and they know that the Liberals are our friends and the conservatives are our enemies, but to tell you the truth, I can't tell them apart. They all seem the same to me." Walker responds simply, "That is no concern of yours, Timothy, or of the men either. All you have to remember is that our cause is a righteous one." Walker and his men are subsequently ambushed upon entering Rivas, but Walker proceeds forward without pause, untouched and seemingly immune to the bullets and bloodshed surrounding him. When a bleeding, dying Timothy asks what he's doing, Walker asserts, "I'm doing the only thing I know how to do, advance." Timothy then calls him a "dumb shit," prompting a ludicrous reprimand from Walker in the heat of battle, "There's no reason for you to talk to me that way, Timothy." Timothy apologizes by saying, "I'm sorry sir. It's just that you'll get yourself and everyone else killed," to which Walker callously replies, "Then we'll be together again, won't we."

A self-righteous manly bravado permeates Walker's characterization, but his words and his actions often contradict one another, a point of emphasis throughout the film that consciously calls into question the allegedly high-minded motives and methods animating antebellum American filibusters like Walker to action. Issues of race, slavery, and white supremacy figure most prominently in such contradictory portrayals. Early in the film, Walker disavows his support of slavery by declaring to his fiancé, "Ellen. You know I despise . . . I despise slavery!" And yet, once established as president of Nicaragua and confronted with the possible collapse of the government and nation he has constructed, Walker denies the impending collapse before announcing, "Men, I have found a solution to our problem. Slavery." When Captain Hornsby, his black chief lieutenant, objects by saying, "what do you mean?! We don't need no slavery!" Walker ignores him and proclaims, "we will introduce slavery into Nicaragua. The South will have no choice but to rally to our cause."

A later scene shows Walker sitting alone with Hornsby, reviewing his journal chronicling their Nicaraguan expedition (what would later be published as *The War in Nicaragua*) and attempting to justify his recent decision to enact slavery in the country: "The Indian of Nicaragua, in his fidelity and docility and in his capacity for labor approaches nearly the Negroes of the United States. In fact, the manners of the Indian towards the ruling race are now more submissive than those of the American Negro to his master. The advantage of Negro and Indian slavery in Nicaragua will therefore be twofold. While it will furnish a certain labor for the use of agriculture it will also tend to separate the races and destroy the half-castes who cause the disorder." This embrace of slavery to court the favor of the antebellum American South highlights the prominence of proslavery proponents and white supremacist ideals in driving the US expansion agenda into Central America during the period.[34]

The film emphasizes that this embrace developed not on the whim of a moment for Walker, but as a result of long-standing proslavery proclivities, as evidenced by two prophetic scenes earlier in the picture. The first scene occurs in Walker's San Francisco parlor, where a Mr. Squier engages in a heated exchange with Walker's fiancée, Ellen Martin, after declaring, "we must move southward. Only by expanding can we hope to avoid a civil war and save those institutions we hold most dear." Ellen retorts, "I assume you're including slavery, are you not, Mr. Squier?" "I most certainly am!" Squier replies, "we must not be sentimental if we hope to preserve that which is most precious to us." Ms. Martin then rejoins, "well perhaps not all our institutions are worth saving," prompting Squier's boisterous replay, "well perhaps not, however I'm sure the little lady will agree that we must preserve our way of life at any cost! Otherwise, the barbarians will surely stone the gates and then where will we be?" Ellen departs in obvious distemper, prompting Walker's earlier, though ultimately disingenuous, disavowal of slavery in San Francisco. The second scene takes place in Nicaragua and shows a black woman discussing her situation and that of the country with one of the soldiers (presumably her husband), describing the privations at home ("no water, no toilet paper, no beer"), then later asserting, "Next thing you know they've be institutin' slavery. It's the same racist, macho, sexist shit we turned our backs on." Though the film foists an uncertainty upon Walker's views of slavery that did not exist, this direct confrontation of the most uncomfortable truth about antebellum American history counters the prevailing tendency in American memory to sanitize the past by marginalizing both the proslavery motives and white supremacist views so essential to the period's expansionist schemes in Latin America.

Such irrational portrayals of Walker's ideological contradictions and the underlying white supremacy informing his worldview aren't limited to black-white race relations but permeate the relations with other ethnic and racial groups as well, especially those of Hispanic descent. Walker's smoldering desires for Yrena Corral, the wife of Grenada's mayor, personifies the American desire for dominion over Nicaragua itself, but in showing how Yrena manipulates Walker's desire to her advantage, effectively seducing him into a one-sided and tumultuous relationship, the film implicitly condemns US intervention in the region, past or present. Later in the film, after Walker has executed President Corral for treason in order to maintain political stability, Yrena joins the burgeoning resistance movement against Walker's government, and even returns in an attempt to assassinate him, which only goads Walker into more oppressive measures that run counter to the ideals of democracy and freedom he constantly purports to be spreading throughout the country.

Other scenes extend these prejudicial views from Walker to his men. When marching inland from the coast in Nicaragua, Walker's "Immortals" come upon a group of half-naked Nicaraguan women bathing in the river and promptly move to satisfy their sexual desires, a scene symbolic of America's nefarious desires for dominion in Central America at large. Later, when Walker decides to sever ties with his patron Cornelius Vanderbilt to better stabilize his military and political grip in Nicaragua, one of his officers, Major Hennington, objects, sparking a furious rebuke from another of Walker's adjutants of Hispanic descent, who declares, "I've had it with you, foreign weasel! You have the nerve to come over here barely speaking the language. Taking our jobs! Poleaxing our women! Take that! (striking him with a cane). And that! And that! You bastard!" The irony of such aspersions, given consistent nativist sentiment regarding immigrants from Central and South America throughout much of the twentieth century, could not be lost on a late-1980s audience. Similar anachronisms scattered throughout the film—the liberal use of "fuck" and "man" in conversation, the placement of plastic flowers upon the corpse of President Corral after his execution, Yrena Corral and her dead husband's advisors reading editions of *Newsweek* and *People* magazine featuring Walker's image on their covers, the sporadic appearance of modern technologies like automobiles and machine guns—likewise serve to remind that audience of the present pertinence of the past transgressions committed by Walker and his "Immortals."

The final scenes weave all of these critical threads together, from the intense moralizing of Walker in expressing his motives, purpose, and prospects, to the white supremacy and proslavery perspectives ingrained in both, to the blatant anachronisms that blur the lines between past and present in order to question the motives and ideals of both eras alike. After executing Corral, Walker's military and political control of Nicaragua quickly disintegrates in spite of his self-righteous denials and calculated embrace of slavery to recapture control. He becomes increasingly desperate and despotic in his exercise of authority, though as demonstrative as ever in claiming that such actions align with the highest ideals for which he and his government stand. Only a small band of Walker's most loyal men continue to follow him as he marches through the burning town of Granada, which Walker ordered his men to set ablaze following Yrena Corral's attempt on his life. At the cathedral, which has been requisitioned as a makeshift field hospital, Walker is seen assisting the doctor in a gruesome surgery with obvious relish when Major Hennington and Captain Hornsby report that they must leave immediately as they've lost nearly all of their men.

Walker, seemingly stupefied at this intelligence, insists upon speaking to his men and the general public one last time. Taking the pulpit, Walker repeats the first portion of his final statement from the trial in San Francisco several years earlier: "Unless a man believes that there is something great for him to do he can do nothing great. A great idea springs up in a man's soul. It agitates his entire being. It transports him from the ignorant present and makes him feel the future in a moment." But then Walker speaks more directly to the situation at hand and projects toward the future. "Reduced to our present position by the cowardice of some, the incapacity of others, and the treachery of many, we are yet writing a page in history that it will be impossible to forget or erase. You all might think that there will be a day when America will leave Nicaragua alone, but I am here to tell you, flat out, that that day will never happen, because it is our destiny to be here," he asserts before conclusively prophesizing, "it is our destiny to control you people. So no matter how much you fight, no matter what you think, we'll be back, time and time again. By the bones of our American dead in Rivas and Granada, I swear that we will never abandon the cause of Nicaragua. Let it occupy your every waking and sleeping thought. From the future, if not the present, we may expect a just judgment."

As the assembled crowd of doctors, nurses, and patients takes up the refrain of the battle hymn "Onward Christian Soldiers," Walker's men begin summarily executing the patients as they depart the cathedral. Once outside, a helicopter arrives and modern US troops file out, as if sent from the future Walker had just referenced. Their commander addresses Walker, saying, "I have been instructed by the State Department of the United States of America to return all American citizens to their homeland." Then to the crowd, "Yes, sorry, only American citizens," as all others are executed or abandoned, including Walker himself, who repeatedly declares, "I am William Walker, President of the Republic of Nicaragua," and is therefore denied passage. The final scene shows Walker being executed by firing squad and left ignominiously on the beach, followed by this historical epitaph: "William Walker was born in Nashville, Tennessee on May 8, 1824. He ruled Nicaragua from 1855 to 1857. He was executed in Honduras September 12, 1860." During the film credits, modern video footage surrounding the 1980s *contra* crisis in Nicaragua, including Ronald Reagan's speech in which he asserts, "Let me say to those who invoke the memory of Vietnam, there is no thought of sending American troops to Central America," is promptly followed by footage of US military maneuvers in Nicaragua and several interviews of US troops expressing their belief that their very presence is meant to send a message to the communist Sandinistas allegedly threatening US interests in the region. The ensuing conflicts in-country result in a massive death toll, and footage of Nicaraguan corpses punctuates the end of the film credits.[35]

Conclusion: Manifest Mastery and the Myths of American Empire in Memory

Historians frequently position the rise of modern American imperialism around the turn the twentieth century, and for good reason, given the United States' concerted and conspicuous embrace of imperialistic expansion in much the same mode as that pursued by European imperial powers during that era. Centering upon Africa, Asia, and the South Pacific, European empires— Britain, France, Germany, and Belgium most prominent among them—took up the so-called "white man's burden" to "civilize" the people of color who inhabited the "third world," all of which constituted a thinly veiled facade for the economic exploitation of these colonial territories through racially oppressive regimes. That the United States embarked on such endeavors at all exposed longstanding (and long denied and/or marginalized) incongruities between the celebrated promise of American democracy, liberty, and freedom and the gross inequality and prejudicial thinking animating much of the imperialistic vision, despite growing aversion to the term "imperialism" and its nefarious implications by the mid-twentieth century—a delusionary denial that in many ways persists into the present.[36]

Though the vigor with which the United States pursued such endeavors, along with the scale on which it did so, both distinguish the nation's expansionist agenda at the turn of the twentieth century, much of that same vision and the attendant ideological inconsistencies it entailed emerged much earlier, in the antebellum period. Despite the continued existence, even expansion, of racialized slavery during the antebellum era, however, American popular memory has largely failed to attach the same stigmas to this earlier period as those grafted upon subsequent eras. As perpetuated in the willful amnesia of American popular memory, this antebellum manifestation of the imperialistic impulse in the United States appears more benign, even enlightened, beneath the guise of manifest destiny.

But, as the simultaneous acclamations and admonitions of William Gilmore Simms revealed, many antebellum Americans recognized that impulse for exactly what it was, even if they avidly celebrated its results and consciously perpetuated its legacies in the most positive light. That Simms figured among the southern elite, a class many historians credit with the lion's share of antebellum expansionary vision and imperialistic fervor, looms especially large when considered in the broader context of historical memory construction and evolution. While historians have plumbed the depths of this earlier age of imperialism, exposing the deep social and cultural fissures belied by the era's almost unbounded enthusiasm for expansion and progress, such historical analyses connecting these eras of American imperialism across the nineteenth century through the twenty-first have been only nominally projected on screen and found little resonance in the popular memory. This trend certainly speaks to the insulated nature of the academy, but also to the persistence of progressive mythologies concerning American history and culture in the public mind.

Whether consciously or not, Americans' collective identity and historical memory posits much of the "frontier thesis" pioneered by historian Frederick Jackson Turner at the turn of the twentieth century: a thesis predicated on the assumption that the United States needed the frontier—the "West"—for its citizens to become true Americans; a thesis that celebrated the "winning of the West" as the progress of America and the supreme expression of American values; a thesis that lamented the passing of the frontier as the alleged death knell of such values deployed in pursuit of such progress by such citizens. Scholars now roundly reject this thesis and its bevy of white patriarchal assumptions that conveniently ignored how the United States "won" the West and why. And yet Turner's "frontier thesis" remains immensely powerful in shaping how Americans collectively conceive of national identity and nostalgically remember western expansion as an essential element of that identity.[37]

These four films exemplify this trend in American identity and memory creation and evolution as influenced by and reflected in cinema. Each film illustrates the entrenchment of the Turner thesis in the collective American psyche. Whether it assertively perpetuates the myths or consciously counters them, each film exposes the centrality of the "American West" in the nation's collective identity and memory, but in so doing they also expose the persistent tendency to mythologize that "West" by white-washing the memory of how it was won and for what purpose. That three of these films—*The Alamo* (2004), *Ravenous* (1999), and *Walker* (1987)—deliberately confront and criticize these inglorious means and motives undoubtedly accounts for their box-office busts and popular culture contempt. Conversely, *The Alamo* (1960) stands as the undisputed champion among the four in box-office success and popular appeal, no doubt because it evinces a more celebratory nationalistic tone that reifies persistent myths in collective identity and memory and marginalizes uncomfortable historical truths. These four films embody how collective memory consciously defends and preserves itself by perpetuating such myths in popular culture productions like film and thereby training audiences to reject the conspicuous critiques leveled in *Walker, Ravenous,* and even *The Alamo* (2004) in favor of films such as *The Alamo* (1960) that dispense with such critiques and continue the cycle of self-congratulation, celebration, and ultimately, willful self-delusion.[38]

The very phrase "American imperialism" exposes the most uncomfortable truths about American historical development and the prevailing and persistent misconceptions surrounding that history and the place of celebrated founding ideals within it. Attempts to confront the nation's many pitfalls in its pursuit of these ideals often meet with derision or abject denial in favor of more progressive conceptions of American historical development that either marginalize or omit instances where an exclusive application of these ideals fell woefully short of their immense promise. But this common tendency to conflate critical analysis for ideological or political opposition serves only to prevent holistic understanding and perpetuate divisive mythology by blurring the lines between the past, history, and memory. The evidence of American imperialism that abounds in the historical record and in the historiography places this intellectual and cultural dichotomy in stark relief. Each of the four films featured herein, which span the latter half of the twentieth century into the twenty-first, evince both the lamentable disconnect between scholars and the general public as well as the entrenched position of myth in memory. In an increasingly polarized historical moment rife with social tensions, cultural divisions, and polemical political partisanship eerily reminiscent of the strife that afflicted antebellum America, bridging the gap between the proverbial ivory tower and popular memory assumes primacy as the most promising path toward rectifying these problematic portrayals and perceptions of the past, in the present and for the future.

NOTES

1. Matthew Karp, *This Vast Southern Empire: Slaveholders at the Helm of American Foreign Policy* (Cambridge, MA: Harvard University Press, 2016), 125–49, 173–98; Robert E. Bonner, *Mastering America: Southern Slaveholders and the Crisis of American Nationhood* (New York: Cambridge University Press, 2009), xi–213; Walter Johnson, *River of Dark Dreams: Slavery and Empire in the Cotton Kingdom* (Cambridge, MA: Harvard University Press, 2013), 1–420; Adam Rothman, *Slave Country: American Expansion and the Origins of the Deep South* (Cambridge, MA: Harvard University Press, 2005), ix–226; Matthew Pratt Guterl, *American Mediterranean: Southern Slaveholders in the Age of Emancipation* (Cambridge, MA: Harvard University Press, 2008), 1–192.

2. Amy S. Greenberg, *Manifest Manhood and the Antebellum American Empire* (New York: Cambridge University Press, 2005), 1–282; Karp, *This Vast Southern Empire*, 1–225; Bonner, *Mastering America*, xi–213; Robert E. May, *Manifest Destiny's Underworld: Filibustering in Antebellum America* (Chapel Hill: University of North Carolina Press, 2002), 1–296; Frank L. Owsley Jr. and Gene A. Smith, *Filibusters and Expansionists: Jeffersonian Manifest Destiny, 1800–1821* (Tuscaloosa: University of Alabama Press, 1997), 1–192; Ed Bradley, *"We Never Retreat": Filibustering Expeditions into Spanish Texas, 1812–1822* (College Station: Texas A&M University Press, 2015), xiii–xx; Maria Angela Diaz, "At the Center of Southern Empire: The Role of Gulf South Communities in Antebellum Territorial Expansion," in *Inventing Destiny: Cultural Explorations of US Expansion*, ed. Jimmy L. Bryan Jr. (Lawrence: University Press of Kansas, 2019), 229–45; Christopher Childers, *The Failure of Popular Sovereignty: Slavery, Manifest Destiny, and the Radicalization of Southern Politics* (Lawrence: University Press of Kansas, 2012), 1–282; Tim Matthewson, *A Proslavery Foreign Policy: Haitian-American Relations During the Early Republic* (Westport, CT: Praeger, 2003), 1–149; Joseph A. Fry, *Dixie Looks Abroad: The South and U.S. Foreign Relations, 1789–1973* (Baton Rouge: Louisiana State University Press, 2002), 1–74.

3. William Gilmore Simms, *Poetry and the Practical*, ed. James E. Kibler Jr. (Fayetteville: University of Arkansas Press, 1998), 6, 7–8; Steven E. Woodworth, *Manifest Destinies: America's Westward Expansion and the Road to the Civil War* (New York: Alfred A. Knopf, 2010), xi–358; Frederick Merk, *Manifest Destiny and Mission in American History* (Cambridge, MA: Harvard University

Press, 1995), 3–266; Jay Sexton, *The Monroe Doctrine: Empire and Nation in Nineteenth-Century America* (New York: Farrar, Straus, & Giroux, 2011), 3–122; William C. Robbins, *Colony and Empire: The Capitalist Transformation of the American West* (Lawrence: University Press of Kansas, 1994), 1–198; A. G. Hopkins, *American Empire: A Global History* (Princeton, NJ: Princeton University Press, 2018), 10–238; *Inventing Destiny*, ed. Bryan, 1–39.

4. Simms, *Poetry and the Practical*, 8, 10–11; John C. Pinheiro, *Missionaries of Republicanism: A Religious History of the Mexican-American War* (New York: Oxford University Press, 2014), 1–172; Merk, *Manifest Destiny and Mission*, 3–266. William Gilmore Simms in many ways represented the antebellum extension of earlier "proslavery amelioration" precedents best explicated in Christa Dierksheide, *Amelioration and Empire: Progress and Slavery in the Plantation Americas* (Charlottesville: University of Virginia Press, 2014), 1–223. The tangible effects of such thinking, and the racial tensions it posed, are best analyzed in Daniel B. Rood, *The Reinvention of Atlantic Slavery: Technology, Labor, Race, and Capitalism in the Greater Caribbean* (New York: Oxford University Press, 2017), 1–201. For the religious undertones inflecting much of the "manifest destiny" mode of antebellum American expansionism, as well as opposition to it, see especially: Pinheiro, *Missionaries of Republicanism*, 53–66; Andrew Preston, *Sword of the Spirit, Shield of Faith: Religion in American War and Diplomacy* (New York: Alfred A. Knopf, 2012), 103–53; Emily Conroy-Krutz, *Christian Imperialism: Converting the World in the Early American Republic* (Ithaca, NY: Cornell University Press, 2015), 1–178, 205–13; Daniel J. Burge, "Stealing Naboth's Vineyard: The Religious Critique of Expansion, 1830–1855," in *Inventing Destiny*, ed. Bryan, 40–55.

5. Greenberg, *Manifest Manhood*, 1–17. Greenberg posits two generally oppositional yet frequently overlapping conceptions of American manhood—martial and restrained—as essential competing perspectives in shaping gendered expectations and conventions in American society affecting the direction and perception of antebellum American imperialism. William Gilmore Simms himself personified much of this gendered tension in his own life and gave it frequent voice in his writings, especially in the series of lectures referenced at length herein. Also see Ian Tyrrell and Jay Sexton, eds., *Empire's Twin: U.S. Anti-Imperialism from the Founding Era to the Age of Terrorism* (Ithaca, NY: Cornell University Press, 2015), 1–76; Burge, "Stealing Naboth's Vineyard," 40–55.

6. Stephanie LeMenager, *Manifest and Other Destinies: Territorial Fictions of the Nineteenth-Century United States* (Lincoln: University of Nebraska Press, 2005), 1–222; Michael A. Morrison, *Slavery and the American West: The Eclipse of Manifest Destiny and the Coming of the Civil War* (Chapel Hill: University of North Carolina Press, 1997), 1–279; Carroll Smith-Rosenberg, *This Violent Empire: The Birth of an American National Identity* (Chapel Hill: University of North Carolina Press, 2010), 1–468.

7. Matthew Christopher Hulbert and Matthew E. Stanley, "Introduction," *Martial Culture, Silver Screen: War Movies and the Construction of American Identity,* eds. Matthew Hulbert and Stanley (Baton Rouge: Louisiana State University Press, 2020); "Movie Comparison: *The Alamo* (1960); *The Alamo* (2004); *Walker* (1987); *Ravenous* (1999)," *The Numbers,* www.the-numbers.com/movies /custom-comparisons-extended/Alamo-The/Alamo-The-(2004)/Walker/Ravenous#tab=day_by _day_comparison (accessed October 7, 2019).

8. May, *Manifest Destiny's Underworld*, 1–14; Joseph A. Stout Jr., *Schemers and Dreamers: Filibustering in Mexico, 1848–1921* (Fort Worth: Texas Christian University Press, 2002), 1–5; Randall B. Campbell, *Filibusters and Expansionists: The Peculiar Institution in Texas, 1821–1865* (Baton

Rouge: Louisiana State University Press, 1989), 1–192; Bradley, *"We Never Retreat,"* xiii–xx; Matthewson, *A Proslavery Foreign Policy,* 1–149; Laurel Clark Shire, *The Threshold of Manifest Destiny: Gender and National Expansion in Florida* (Philadelphia: University of Pennsylvania Press, 2016), 1–202, and "Armed Occupiers and Slaveholding Pioneers: Mapping White Settler Colonialism in Florida," in *Inventing Destiny,* ed. Bryan, 89–117.

9. Matthewson, *A Proslavery Foreign Policy,* 1–149; Shire, *The Threshold of Manifest Destiny,* 1–202, and "Armed Occupiers and Slaveholding Pioneers," 89–117; Bradley, *"We Never Retreat,"* 1–231; Andrew J. Torget, *Seeds of Empire: Cotton, Slavery, and the Transformation of the Texas Borderlands, 1800–1850* (Chapel Hill: University of North Carolina Press, 2015), 1–266; Stout, *Schemers and Dreamers,* 6–55; Campbell, *Filibusters and Expansionists,* 32–81, 103–80.

10. Campbell, *An Empire for Slavery,* 1–114, 190–208; Torget, *Seeds of Empire,* 5–6; Pinheiro, *Missionaries of Republicanism,* 1–52; David M. Pletcher, *The Diplomacy of Annexation: Texas, Oregon, and the Mexican War* (Columbia: University of Missouri Press, 1973), 1–610.

11. *The Alamo,* dir. John Wayne (Batjac Productions, 1960); *The Alamo,* dir. John Lee Hancock (Buena Vista Pictures, 2004).

12. *The Alamo* (1960); James E. Crisp, "Delineating Davy, Defining Ourselves: *The Alamo* in 1960 and 2004," in *Writing History with Lightning: Cinematic Representations of Nineteenth-Century America,* ed. Matthew C. Hulbert and John C. Inscoe (Baton Rouge: Louisiana State University Press, 2019), 58–72.

13. *The Alamo,* dir. John Lee Hancock (Buena Vista Pictures, 2004).

14. *The Alamo* (2004).

15. *The Alamo* (1960); *The Alamo* (2004); Greenberg, *Manifest Manhood,* 1–17.

16. *The Alamo* (1960); *The Alamo* (2004); Crisp, "Delineating Davy, Defining Ourselves," 58–72; Ian Tyrrell, *Reforming the World: The Creation of America's Moral Empire* (Princeton, NJ: Princeton University Press, 2010), 1–246.

17. *The Alamo* (1960); *The Alamo* (2004); Crisp, "Delineating Davy, Defining Ourselves," 58–72.

18. *The Alamo* (1960); Crisp, "Delineating Davy, Defining Ourselves," 58–72.

19. *The Alamo* (1960); Crisp, "Delineating Davy, Defining Ourselves," 58–72.

20. *The Alamo* (1960); *The Alamo* (2004).

21. *The Alamo* (2004).

22. Pletcher, *The Diplomacy of Annexation,* 1–610; Robert E. May, *Slavery, Race, and Conquest in the Tropics: Lincoln, Douglas, and the Future of Latin America* (New York: Cambridge University Press, 2013), 5–56; Karp, *This Vast Southern Empire,* 50–198; Bonner, *Mastering America,* xi–213; Amy S. Greenberg, *A Wicked War: Polk, Clay, Lincoln, and the 1846 U.S. Invasion of Mexico* (New York: Alfred A. Knopf, 2012), xiii–110; Pinheiro, *Missionaries of Republicanism,* 53–86; David A. Clary, *Eagles and Empire: The United States, Mexico, and the Struggle for a Continent* (New York: Bantam Books, 2009), 1–455; James M. McCaffrey, *Army of Manifest Destiny: The American Soldier in the Mexican War, 1846–1848* (New York: New York University Press, 1992), 1–210.

23. Greenberg, *A Wicked War,* 111–279; Robert W. Johannsen, *To the Halls of the Montezumas: The Mexican War in the American Imagination* (New York: Oxford University Press, 1985), 3–312; May, *Slavery, Race, and Conquest in the Tropics,* 1–59; Pinheiro, *Missionaries of Republicanism,* 109–72; Laura E. Gomez, *Manifest Destinies: The Making of the Mexican American Race,* 2nd ed. (New York: New York University Press, 2018), 15–47; Michael S. Van Wagenen, *Remembering the Forgot-*

ten War: The Enduring Legacies of the U.S.-Mexican War (Boston: University of Massachusetts Press, 2012), 5–6.

24. Campbell, *An Empire for Slavery*, 1–2; Van Wagenen, *Remembering the Forgotten War*, 1–40, 59–80, 101–27, 192–246.

25. *Ravenous*, dir. Antonia Bird (Twentieth Century Fox, 1999).

26. *Ravenous* (1999); Johannsen, *To the Halls of the Montezumas*, 270–312; Clary, *Eagles and Empire*, 402–55; Lemenager, *Manifest and Other Destinies*, 1–19; Morrison, *Slavery and the American West*, 1–125.

27. Stout, *Schemers and Dreamers*, 6–55; Greenberg, *Manifest Manhood*, 54–134; May, *Slavery, Race, and Conquest in the Tropics*, 5–56; Morrison, *Slavery and the American West*, 126–279.

28. Karp, *This Vast Southern Empire*, 150–98; Bonner, *Mastering America*, xi–213; Robert E. May, *The Southern Dream of a Caribbean Empire, 1854–1861* (Athens: University of Georgia Press, 1989), 3–45; May, *Slavery, Race, and Conquest in the Tropics*, 57–204.

29. Karp, *This Vast Southern Empire*, 1–9, 32–49, 125–225; Bonner, *Mastering America*, xi–213; May, *The Southern Dream of a Caribbean Empire*, 3–45, 190–205; May, *Slavery, Race, and Conquest in the Tropics*, 57–204; Matthewson, *A Proslavery Foreign Policy*, 1–149; Aims McGuinness, *Path of Empire: Panama and the California Gold Rush* (Ithaca, NY: Cornell University Press, 2007), 1–204.

30. Greenberg, *Manifest Manhood*, 170–96; May, *Manifest Destiny's Underworld*, 19–296, and *The Southern Dream of a Caribbean Empire*, 46–76, 136–89; Charles H. Brown, *Agents of Manifest Destiny: The Lives and Times of the Filibusters* (Chapel Hill: University of North Carolina Press, 1980), 3–173; David C. Keehn, *Knights of the Golden Circle: Secret Empire, Southern Secession, Civil War* (Baton Rouge: Louisiana State University Press, 2013), 1–61.

31. Michel Gobat, *Empire by Invitation: William Walker and Manifest Destiny in Central America* (Cambridge, MA: Harvard University Press, 2018), 1–293; Greenberg, *Manifest Manhood*, 135–69; May, *Manifest Destiny's Underworld*, 19–296, and *The Southern Dream of a Caribbean Empire*, 77–135, 206–58, and *Slavery, Race, and Conquest in the Tropics*, 205–76; Keehn, *Knights of the Golden Circle*, 1–76; Brown, *Agents of Manifest Destiny*, 174–467.

32. Edward B. Rugemer, *The Problem of Emancipation: The Caribbean Roots of the American Civil War* (Baton Rouge: Louisiana State University Press, 2008), 1–302; Thomas Richards Jr., "The Lansford Hastings Imaginary: Visions of Democratic Patriarchy in the Americas, 1842–1867," in *Inventing Destiny*, ed. Bryan, 181–204; Patrick J. Kelly, "The Cat's Paw: Confederate Ambitions in Latin America," in *American Civil Wars: The United States, Latin America, Europe, and the Crisis of the 1860s*, ed. Don H. Doyle (Chapel Hill: University of North Carolina Press, 2017), 58–81; Fry, *Dixie Looks Abroad*, 75–105. On the late-nineteenth-century resurgence of American imperialistic designs on Central America, see Thomas D. Schoonover, *The United States in Central America, 1860–1911: Episodes of Social Imperialism and Imperial Rivalry in the World System* (Durham, NC: Duke University Press, 1991), 1–179; Walter LaFeber, *Inevitable Revolutions: The United States in Central America*, 2nd ed. (New York: W. W. Norton & Co., 1993), 31–60. On the more general expansion of American imperialism in the late nineteenth and early twentieth century and into the twenty-first, see especially: Gail Bederman, *Manliness and Civilization: A Cultural History of Gender and Race in the United States, 1880–1917* (Chicago: University of Chicago Press, 1995), 1–240; Kristin L. Hoganson, *Fighting for American Manhood: How Gender Politics Provoked the Spanish-American and Philippine-American Wars* (New Haven, CT: Yale University Press, 2000), 1–208; Tyrrell, *Reforming the World*, 1–246; Hopkins, *American Empire*, 239–738; Sexton, *The Monroe Doctrine*, 123–250;

Tyrrell and Sexton, eds., *Empire's Twin,* 79–242; LaFeber, *Inevitable Revolutions,* 60–368; and Fry, *Dixie Looks Abroad,* 106–298.

33. *Walker,* dir. Alex Cox (Universal Pictures, 1987); LaFeber, *Inevitable Revolutions,* 271–368; William M. LeoGrande, *Our Own Backyard: The United States in Central America, 1977–1992* (Chapel Hill: University of North Carolina Press, 2009), 1–590.

34. *Walker* (1987); William Walker, *The War in Nicaragua* (Mobile, AL: S. H. Goetzel & Co., 1860), 261–63.

35. *Walker* (Universal 1987); LaFeber, *Inevitable Revolutions,* 271–368; LeoGrande, *Our Own Backyard,* 1–590.

36. Bederman, *Manliness and Civilization,* 1–240; Hoganson, *Fighting for American Manhood,* 1–208; Tyrrell, *Reforming the World,* 1–246; Tyrrell and Sexton, eds., *Empire's Twin,* 79–242; Bryan, ed., *Inventing Destiny,* 1–39; Sexton, *The Monroe Doctrine,* 123–250; LaFeber, *Inevitable Revolutions,* 60–368; Schoonover, *The United States in Central America,* 1–179; Fry, *Dixie Looks Abroad,* 106–298.

37. Frederick Jackson Turner, *The Frontier in American History* (Mineola, NY: Dover Publications, Inc., 2010), 1–38.

38. "Movie Comparison: *The Alamo* (1960); *The Alamo* (2004); *Walker* (1987); *Ravenous* (1999)," *The Numbers,* www.the-numbers.com/movies/custom-comparisons-extended/Alamo-The/Alamo -The-(2004)/Walker/Ravenous#tab=day_by_day_comparison (accessed October 7, 2019).

To End War and Bring Peace

World War I, Peace, and Antiwar Films

LIZ CLARKE

T he successful superhero movie *Wonder Woman* (2017) is set during World
War I. An American pilot crashes and becomes stranded on an island entirely populated by the all-female Amazon warriors. Though the Amazons
are warriors, they live a peaceful life, isolated from the world. Steve Trevor
(Chris Pine) is the American soldier whose arrival disrupts peace on the island.
With him comes an invasion of German soldiers, along with a battle on the
beach reminiscent of World War II combat films such as *Saving Private Ryan*
(1998). The Amazon princess, Diana (Gal Gadot), and the other female warriors are finally forced into battle to defend their land after years of peaceful
training. Diana is staunchly in favor of peace, despite her warrior upbringing.
Although simplistic and heavy-handed in its message, the film suggests humans
are capable of love and goodness, even though they are at war with each other.
For the film's message, World War I functions as the perfect backdrop precisely
because, in popular memory, it has come to represent the senselessness of war
and the valor of reluctant warriors.

World War I in American film is often used to represent themes of pacifism
and antiwar messages. More often than not, the films do not contextualize or
depict the reasons for the conflict. *Wonder Woman* is no different; in fact, the
reason for the conflict is attributed to the mythical Ares (David Thewlis), god
of war. It would be difficult to set a Hollywood movie in any other real conflict in which the United States has fought. World War I, however, has come
to signify something other than its political origins. However, there is another
interesting layer to the opening of *Wonder Woman*. American films about World
War I prior to American entry were often narrativized representations of the
preparedness debates: fears of foreign invasion were stoked by those promoting
military preparedness, while peace and isolationism were also strongly held
positions. Again, prior to American entry into World War II, American films

about World War I, such as *Sergeant York* (1941), repeated the formula: a reluctant pacifist discovers the need to fight in order to bring about peace. World War I in popular American memory has come to symbolize the complicated questions between the necessity for war, peace, and strong military preparedness. These questions exist at the center of *Wonder Woman,* as well.

Starting with *Wonder Woman,* not strictly a war movie, will show both what the history of World War I in American film was, from before American entry and throughout the first decades after the war, to where it is now, almost divorced from the causes of the war. In other words, American films about World War I not only changed over time—the same could be said about any war or historical subject—but increasingly came to represent antiwar themes. Although there is not one distinct trend that can describe all the films, one could argue that the war has increasingly come to symbolize the senselessness of war; some of the most canonical films about World War I are distinctly antiwar. What is fascinating, then, is how these antiwar themes are employed differently throughout the twentieth and early twenty-first centuries in relation to the popular conception of the United States as a military powerhouse. In short, the paradox of a society of peaceful warriors in *Wonder Woman* serves as an apt metaphor for the tension between American ideals of anti-imperialism, military strength, and democratic freedom at the heart of certain depictions of American national myth. In particular, tracing the way that World War I appears in American films during and since the war reveals these tensions. World War I in popular memory serves equally as a symbol of antiwar themes and the idea of the United States as a reluctant but strong military force, only entering into war for the greater good.

As David Williams demonstrates, historians and scholars have debated whether there exists a great divide between the history of the war and the myth of the war that emerges from literature and other forms of popular culture, to the point where the myth of World War I as "unhistorical" prevails over the reality of the war.[1] What Williams seeks to clarify is not fact from fiction but, rather, the less-examined connection between film and memory. Both the war and film mark the emergence of modern life, and with the change in medium for representing contemporary or historical events comes a change in the way temporality and memory are both represented and perceived.[2] What is key here, though, is the link between cinema and the myth of World War I in popular culture. On literature of the First World War, John T. Matthews suggests that, "because thousands of miles of ocean lay between the US and the battle in Europe, and because American troops did not participate in major action until the last years of hostilities, the First World War remained a virtual phenomenon to many US residents."[3] In other words, "American writing of the war *was* the war." Without attempting to contradict or argue against the importance of literature, journalism, and other written forms that Matthews highlights, I would add to that list film, which requires not just attention to the films as texts but to Hollywood as an industry that worked with the American government to shape Americans' attitudes toward the war during the war, and later as an industry intent on exploiting popular sentiment for ticket sales. What does World War I signify in American film? How is the war popularly understood? How did its meaning shift over time? The concluding analysis of *Wonder Woman* posits that World War I was the only American-fought war that functions well as the backdrop of that particular story because the pairing emphasizes themes of peace, love, and the chaos of war. This is not because of anything unique to the political realities of the actual war but, rather, about what the war came to signify in American popular memory.

World War I had a short lifespan as a popular subject in American film. Jeanine Basinger argues that the World War I genre was cut short by the arrival of World War II, and that it became "frozen" in the state of pacifism.[4] A strong impulse toward isolation and pacifism through the interwar period led to a number of filmic representations of the war with strongly antiwar themes or, at the very least, critical depictions of war. Alternatively, World War II quickly became known as "Good War," which was fought for "essentially noble causes, including the American struggle for independence and the campaign against the Nazis in order to 'save democracy.'"[5] Thus, even in the years after World War II, there was never a sustained return to World War I because the "Good War's" form of heroism shaped the Hollywood war genre in the years that followed. World War I's rare reappearance in films after the 1940s is in films that are critical of war, more generally. In other words, the reasons for the war's fade from popular memory is in part because the films themselves concern the suffering of soldiers and the loss of young lives, rather than the heroism of fighting for a noble cause.

For Hollywood films, World War II had a more clear-cut purpose and easier to convey stories of heroes versus villains. While very early World War I films employed the Hun-as-villain trope, it very quickly fell out of favor, so much so that by 1930 the popular *All Quiet on the Western Front* sympathetically portrayed young German soldiers as protagonists who suffered the real consequences of their leaders' decisions to go to war. The films about World War I that had a lasting impact on popular memory often contain no enemies, yet they depict heroism on both sides. As a result, World War I in American film represents pacifism, and military heroism despite a reluctance to fight. Like the Amazons depicted in *Wonder Woman*, symbolically World War I allows for an America that values peace while also maintaining its image as a nation with strong military power.

Preparedness or Peace: American Films, 1914–1918

The American entry into World War I was not quite as clear-cut as the reasons for European nations; the postwar effects were less concrete—the United States did not have to rebuild—so much so that Pierre Sorlin argues that American films about World War I never directly address the why of the war, only the loss of lives.[6] Perhaps, then, we can divide the films about the war into two categories, broadly speaking, accounting for distance in time when the films become less about *the* war to become either about the myth of the war or critiques of war more generally. Arguably, World War I became synonymous with war as a concept rather than the historical facts of the war—at least in Hollywood renderings—precisely because the films so frequently turned to larger questions of war versus peace, the senselessness of war, the loss of life, and, less frequently, the adventure of war rather than depicting the causes or specific battles.[7] World War I also became a signifier of the complicated relationship between American anti-imperial ideologies and the nation's growing military dominance worldwide in the latter half of the twentieth century.

At the time, the attitude of filmmakers and exhibitors to the war was complex. In fact, the years between the outbreak of the war and the US entry into it were fascinating for the variety of political positions on display in American films. Most striking is in the films that either directly or indirectly depicted the war, but that took a stance as to whether the nation should build up its military in preparation for war—or defense—or, on the contrary, maintain an isolationist foreign policy. The film *Civilization* (1915) was pro-peace. Like many of the other American films made in the early years of World War I, it is not about the war itself. In *Civilization* the horrors of war are depicted through a fictional war set in the kingdom of Wredpryd, with a final appearance by Jesus, teaching those who have created the war about the pain and suffering they have caused. Although the war and the country are fictional, the imagery of war, including men dying in trenches, is an obvious reference to the war that was happening in Europe at the time. While *Civilization* performed well and had an extensive road-show run, it was not endorsed as heavily by US officials as a preparedness picture, *The Battle Cry of Peace* (1915).

This Vitagraph film was written and directed by J. Stuart Blackton and based on Hudson Maxim's "Defenceless America." *The Battle Cry of Peace* was not a depiction of the war "over there," but rather envisioned a scenario in which New York City was invaded—an extension of the European war—and the US military was not properly prepared. Numerous officials were cited for participating in the production, including Secretary of State Lansing and Secretary of War Garrison.[8] The filmmakers, Blackton in particular, stressed the need to manufacture munitions, without which even an army of "a million men" would not last long.[9] The film's message of preparedness was presented through a young couple engaged to be married. The man is a preparedness advocate, while the woman's father is involved in a number of peace groups. The film involves an invasion of New York City and culminates when the peace advocate is shot, the preparedness advocate is killed in front of his fiancée, and then she is killed by her mother, in an attempt to save her from falling into the hands of invaders.[10] The melodramatic film was endorsed by Theodore Roosevelt as a film "every American should see."[11] Preparedness films and serials were more frequent than peace-advocating films in the US industry at the time. *The Nation's Peril* (1915), *Fall of the Nation* (1916), *Pearl of the Army* (1916), and *Patria* (1917) were all instrumental in promoting the need for military preparedness to audiences across the nation.

What the *Battle Cry* example demonstrates, however, was the connection between politicians and filmmaking that became central to the film industry during World War I. Leslie Midkiff DeBauche has written extensively on this connection, using the term "practical patriotism" to describe the benefits to film producers and stars support for the war could offer.[12] In addition to fiction films about the war, stars attended rallies and promoted Liberty Bonds throughout the war. When the United States entered the war in April of 1917, the promotion of some of these preparedness films and serials—among others such as *Joan the Woman* (1916) and *Womanhood, The Glory of the Nation* (1917)— shifted to include parades promoting enlistment and recruitment tables set up in theater lobbies.[13] Multiple parts of the film industry, from production to promotion and exhibition, were enlisted to promote patriotism and the war effort. This did not necessarily mean that filmmakers suddenly started making films about US involvement in World War I; however, by 1918 and 1919 films about the heroics of American men in war were more frequent. Films such as *The Unbeliever* (1918), *The Lost Battalion* (1919), and *Behind the Door* (1919) celebrated the heroics of American men during World War I.

Taken as a whole, the war-era films made in the United States reveal how film was one of a number of media and entertainment forms that were shaped by and helped to shape public opinion about isolationism, military preparedness, patriotism, and celebration of the United States' participation in war. This short period, however, also demonstrates the way World War I became emblematic of the struggle between pacifism and military strength. The interwar period, which saw the highest concentration of World War I films produced in Hollywood, continued to depict narratives of the war that oscillated between pacifism, antiwar themes, and celebration of valor and military strength.

Hollywood War Films, 1920s–1930s

The 1920s and 1930s are among the most interesting decades for depictions of the Great War on film. While World War I fell out of favor for American filmmakers after World War II, its importance to the history of the war genre cannot be underestimated. In the 1920s, films like *What Price Glory?* (1926) and *The Big Parade* (1925) stand out as exemplary, in part due to the popularity of author Laurence Stallings at the time, and in part because they laid the groundwork for later combat pictures.[14] Stallings was an author who had lost his leg during the war, later writing short stories, plays, and screenplays about the horrors and heroics of trench warfare. Stallings wrote the short story that *The Big Parade* was based on, as well as the stage play *What Price Glory*, which was made into a film in 1926. Stallings's depictions of war were praised for their gritty realism, which contributed in large part to the turn away from formulaic hero-versus-villain narratives of the war—in other words, the Hun-as-enemy—and a turn toward examining the camaraderie, heroism, and masculinity that emerged during wartime, away from the rules that govern modern society.[15] While Stallings was indeed a large contributor to how World War I took on a more critical look at war, temporal distance from the war also made apparent the loss of American lives. In short, while the combat films of the 1920s depicted war as a terrain in which American heroism, courage, and valor could flourish, these films can also be interpreted as antiwar through their emphasis on loss, suffering, and the horrors of warfare for the men and women who participated, and for the families who waited for their return.

But the 1920s also saw a number of melodramatic films about World War I—notably, *7th Heaven* (1927)—or comedic films—*Corporal Kate* (1926), *The Better 'Ole* (1926).[16] In short, a variety of genres made up the corpus of American-made World War I films during the interwar period. The Hollywood war films of the 1920s and 1930s depicted World War I as either an adventure for young protagonists or a meaningless war during which a young generation of men—and sometimes women—sacrificed their lives. Due to what Michael Isenberg calls the "ocean of prosperity and progress" of the 1920s, even seemingly anti-war films of the decade took up the theme of "war-as-adventure."[17] Whether comedic or dramatic, the films of the 1920s had a common theme that war collapsed class differences. Michael Isenberg argues that the themes of "democracy as class leveler and democracy as melting pot" were common in the late 1910s and continue throughout the 1920s in films about World War I.[18] One way this theme was consistently repeated in World War I films of the 1920s and 1930s is in how characters overcome class differences. Guy Westwell describes such World War I narratives: "These movies show war erasing previous social demarcations: upper-class American protagonists befriend and learn from lower-class comrades and ineffective military leadership (associated with upper-class ineptitude) is compensated for through the hard work and commitment of the lowly infantryman. The narratives show class antagonism being overcome in order to defeat aristocratic militaristic Prussia, and as a result confirm a particular brand of American liberal democracy."[19]

The theme of overcoming class differences is found in various films about World War I, from melodramas, combat films, and comedies. Whether antiwar or war-as-adventure, the prevailing celebration of democratic ideals existed in many of the World War I films of the interwar period.

Pierre Sorlin argues that Hollywood films centered on narratives about individual psychology rather than the causes of the war: "This tradition of emphasizing private destinies at the expense of collective concerns helped American film-makers to transform the problem of war responsibility into a moral conflict, the resolution of which was, by definition, psychological. American movies never tackled the tricky question of cause but their depiction of warfare was extremely impressive. It is through these pictures rather than historical studies that successive generations have learned the history of the conflict."[20]

That World War I films really only flourished during the interwar period—World War II is by far more favored by Hollywood filmmakers—makes it hard to know if the subgenre of World War I in film "froze" with World War II, as Jeanine Basinger posits, or if it would have shifted over time.[21] Basinger's argument is that World War I films stayed at the pacifist stage and, as a war depicted in popular culture, never moved beyond that. However, one might also ask if the style and narrative drive of 1920s and 1930s war films—those that "never tackled the tricky question of cause"—also froze World War I's mythology as a war untethered from its historical causes, at least in popular American film.

Basinger argues that, with the coming of sound (after 1927), World War I movies took two directions: "some that presented the glory of World War I in memory and retrospect, and some that were powerfully antiwar." The types of films made about the war either emphasized trench warfare or air battles. The films of trench warfare take on pacifist and antiwar meanings by depicting "death, futility, and the waste of youth in war," while the films of the air concern themselves with elite forces.[22] *Wings* (1927) was the first airplane movie, and it spawned a number of air movies during the 1930s. The protagonists come from different class backgrounds; they form a bond of friendship; and their experience of war is filtered through a melodramatic story about love, friendship, and adventure. The film concerns Jack Powell (Charles Rogers) and David Armstrong (Richard Arlen), two men who enlist in the Air Force and leave their hometown and families to fight in World War I. David is from a wealthy family while Jack is not. They fight over the same woman, Sylvia (Jobyna Ralston), while Jack's neighbor, Mary (Clara Bow), is in love with him. The audience sees Jack and David first train as fighter pilots and then go to war together. Unbeknownst to Jack, Mary has also enlisted, as an ambulance driver. David is shot down near the end of the war. He survives the crash and steals a German plane in the hope of making it back to his unit. Unfortunately, Jack, now out for revenge, sees the German plane and shoots it down just as peace is declared. He lands his plane and finds that it was David all along. The two embrace and kiss moments before David's death. Jack returns home and brings David's stuffed bear back to his parents.

Several things stand out in this narrative. First, the love triangle between Jack, David, and Sylvia—with Mary vying for Jack's attention—provides motivation for rifts between Jack and David that punctuate their time together. David knows that Sylvia loves him and intended to give him the picture that

Jack wears around his neck, but David spares Jack's feelings by not revealing the truth. This reaches a climax when the picture falls from Jack's locket and David sees that there is a note inscribed to him on the back. Instead of risking that Jack would see the note, David tears up the picture and sacrifices their friendship to save Jack's feelings. This is the last time they speak before Jack finds David dying in the small farmhouse. The melodramatic storyline—a love triangle between friends, a lie to save another from learning the truth, forgiveness just in time to say goodbye to a loved one—is extended with David's death scene. The two men embrace and kiss, suggesting that Sylvia was the odd one out in this triangle, as Jack begs everyone around him to call a doctor. The war is ending, but Jack is unable to save David. The film's narrative is about the friendship that developed between Jack and David throughout their experiences: at training camp, when they found respect for each other during a fistfight, at the flight-training camp, where they bonded with their tent-mate (Gary Cooper) just moments before his death, and in battle where they flew together in various dogfights, always coming home safely until their last flight. The war exists as a background to their developing friendship and adventures. No reasons or details are given for the causes of the war or the battles in which they fight.

This is not to say that the war is treated lightly, nor that David's death is the only melodramatic element of the film. Throughout the narrative, both David and Jack transition from naive adventure-seekers to experienced and mature men. The film uses war as a coming-of-age trope, where the men's earlier grins are replaced with solemn faces, long before David's death. This element of the film does not reach a level that would categorize it as antiwar. Rather, it seems to present the change in both Jack and David as maturation, compounded with a melodramatic sorrow when Jack returns home alone. Rather than uniting with Sylvia, because the love triangle no longer exists, Jack simply apologizes to David's parents, returning the stuffed bear that David's mother gave him when he left. Jack then meets with Mary, who he initially regarded only as a friend. Presumably Jack and Mary will live happily ever after, yet the film can be read in another way. Jack has lost the most important person in his life, and the return home will always be clouded with that loss. This ending, however, is neither about World War I nor a critique of war more broadly. While *Wings* and various other films of the 1920s and 1930s can be read as adventure-melodramas, a second, parallel, set of films about World War I was also popular.

World War I as Antiwar War Film

The most common theme of World War I films is that of antiwar or pacifism. Tom Pollard argues that, "during brief periods of pacifism and neutrality, Hollywood films tend to reflect such views. Here as later, when the U.S. enters into armed conflict, any semblance of pacifism evaporates as Hollywood producers gear up to create movies that embellish patriotic and militaristic themes."[23] This parallels popular sentiments of the interwar period, where isolationism and pacifism were strongly held positions.[24]

Perhaps the best-known World War I film from the 1930s is *All Quiet on the Western Front* (1930). It is about a group of young German students who, after a rousing speech by their teacher, enlist in the army. It becomes clear quite quickly that war is not the adventure and the honor they had been sold. The film proceeds much like the earlier war films, including training sequences and then a series of realizations of the horror of war. There is no true survivor at the end of the film. It ends with a man reaching out from a trench for a butterfly, a shot rings out and then the sound cuts. The final shot is of a graveyard with a superimposed image of men marching. Film of the 1920s would show the destruction of war through the deaths of many central characters, leaving one main protagonist alive to return home. In *All Quiet on the Western Front,* there is no sense of survival. The film ends with an explosion in a trench. The destruction is total but, above that, the reason for war is unclear.

The antiwar theme is apparent in the conversations between the men. They freely question the purpose of the war, debating why they are fighting. This conversation, although brief during the film's long war sequences, serves to emphasize the lives that young men sacrificed for a war that, at least in popular memory, had no clear purpose. First, they engage in a conversation about the absurdity of countries at war.

ALBERT: Ah, the French certainly deserve to be punished for starting this war.

DETERING: Everybody says it's somebody else.

TJADEN: Well, how do they start a war?

ALBERT: Well, one country offends another.

TJADEN: How could one country offend another? You mean there's a mountain over in Germany gets mad at a field over in France?

ALBERT: Well, stupid, one people offends another.

TJADEN: Oh? That's it. I shouldn't be here at all. I don't feel offended.

KAT: It don't apply to tramps like you.

TJADEN: Good, then I can be going home right away.

Tjaden points out the absurdity of every attempt to explain the war. First, he points out that a country is nothing more than a geographical area, unable to start wars. When Albert explains that it is people, not the land itself, that begin wars, Tjaden is still not satisfied. The people are not those who actually must fight the war. Although in jest, Tjaden's claim that he can go home because he "don't feel offended" encapsulates the popular myth of World War I: that young men went to war and sacrificed their lives for disputes in which they had no stakes. The conversation continues, next blaming the Kaiser for starting the war:

SOLDIER 1: Well, he never had a war before. Every full-grown emperor needs one war to make him famous. Why, that's history.

PAUL: Yeah, generals too!

SOLDIER 2: And manufacturers, they get rich.

ALBERT: I think it's more, a kind of fever. Nobody wants it in particular and then all at once. Here it is. We didn't want it. The English didn't want it. And here we are—Fighting!

KAT: I'll tell you how it should all be done. Whenever there's a big war coming on, you should rope off a big field and

SOLDIER 3: Sell tickets.

KAT: Yeah, and on the big day you should take all the kings and their cabinets and their generals, put them in the center dressed in their underpants and let them fight it out with clubs. The best country wins.[25]

The critique of leaders not fighting, yet encouraging the war, is further emphasized when Paul returns to the classroom in his hometown while on brief leave. The teacher who once encouraged him and his friends to enlist now has a new class of fresh-faced and attentive students, eager to hear from the soldier about his brave adventures in war. Rather than encourage a new group of students to enlist, Paul tells them his true feelings about the war. They call him a coward as he yells at the teacher before leaving.

Despite the discussion about the war's causes, ambiguity runs deep. The war, in a sense, becomes emblematic of the horrors and senselessness of war and thereby loses a connection with depicting the nuance of its history. Regarding the connection between pacifist and isolationist groups and the film industry, John Whiteclay Chambers writes, "A related question, of course, is whether Hollywood could make films that explored larger issues or clarified policy choices in an educated, sophisticated manner. Most of the antiwar films of the early 1930s merely encouraged excitement and revulsion against the horrors of warfare. Few of them explored in any depth the causes of wars or the moral issues raised by aggression. When Hollywood eventually became committed to the anti-Nazi cause in 1939–1941, the studios again produced rather simplistic, one-sided propaganda, this time in support of war."

What is clear, though, is that, whether the films of the 1920s and 1930s were depicting antiwar or war-as-adventure themes and narratives, the war was presented in a simplistic way. What *All Quiet* did differently was to turn the lack of clarity of the cause into a larger question about war. It is likely this film's popularity, its lasting impact, and its ability to turn the lack of clarity of causes of the war into profound questions about war that solidified World War I's legacy in film as a subject of the antiwar film. However, as Chambers indicates and other scholars have noted, for a few years leading into World War II, World War I was taken up by filmmakers to bolster themes of intervention and military preparedness.

From Pacifism to Intervention

Sergeant York (1941) is a film that celebrates World War I heroism, while also addressing the history of antiwar and pacifist readings that had previously been attached to films about the war. Jeanine Basinger notes that, in the late 1930s and early 1940s, films about World War I shifted in tone in order to rewrite the conflict for the growing possibility of the United States' entry into the war.[26]

While the film is based on a real decorated war hero from Tennessee, it spends very little screen time depicting combat. The majority of the film takes place in Tennessee, tracing Alvin York's (Gary Cooper) life leading up to his entry in the war. York is reluctant because of strongly held pacifist beliefs. Once in combat, however, York proves extraordinarily heroic, single-handedly taking many prisoners of war. The narrative not only served to promote military preparedness in the United States prior to the country's entry into World War II, but it reinforced the notion of American military strength coming from a place of pacifism rather than imperialism and expansionist aims. The message suggests that the skills needed to win wars are part of American life—York developed his skill not in military training but, instead, during his daily life in

Tennessee—and that hard-working American men have what it takes to form the strongest army, if the need arises.

The film begins in a church during a sermon, introducing the audience to the people who make up the town. The service is interrupted by the sounds of gunshots outside, which turns out to be York, who shot his initials into the trunk of a tree while he rode by on a horse. York is established as a wild, reckless man who drinks and has little regard for his family and the family farm until a near-death experience brings him to the church. After York finds the church, he also begins taking on any jobs that will help him to buy a plot of land so that he can set up a life for his family and his fiancée, Gracie (Joan Leslie). A significant portion of the film is devoted to tracing York's trajectory from irresponsible to hardworking, and to establishing this small Tennessee farming community as the heart of America. Later, when York meets other Americans at the training camp, they ask about his English because of his pronunciation of specific words, to which he responds, "Hain't no English people down thata way nohow. We're all Americans."

A key plot point in *Sergeant York* is that he is a conscientious objector because of his religion. When news comes that the United States entered the war and that men would soon be drafted, York applies for exemption on religious grounds. After his exemption is denied, York spends a portion of the film grappling with what seem to be two conflicting beliefs: duty to God and duty to his country. After reading a book about the history of the United States and learning about the country's commitment to freedom, he decides to go to war. His expert marksmanship singles him out as superior to other men, but it is his steadfast belief in peace that signals York's uniqueness. It is this focus on York's pacifism that allowed *Sergeant York* to not just reimagine what the war meant, representationally, but to use pacifism as a theme to support the possibility of fighting in another war. York was a hero not despite of his pacifism but precisely because of it. In the final scenes, set during York's time in battle, he kills a handful of German soldiers and captures 132 men. He later explains how he was able to kill, despite his pacifist beliefs:

MAJOR BUXTON: That night you reported back to me at Camp Gordon, you as much as told me you were ready to die for your country but—well . . . not to kill. What made you decide differently? . . . Of course, if you'd rather not say. . . .

ALVIN: Oh, I'm as much agin killin' as ever.

MAJOR BUXTON (puzzled): But. . . .

ALVIN: The way it were, Colonel . . . when I started out, I felt like ye said. But when I heerd all of them machine guns a-stutterin' like and fellers were droppin' all around me, I figgered them guns were killin' hundreds, mebbe thousands. And thar were nothin' anyone could do, 'cept to stop them guns . . . so that's what I done.

MAJOR BUXTON (a realization dawning on him): Let me understand you, York. You mean you did it to . . . to save lives?

ALVIN: (very simply) Yessir.[27]

York's heroic deeds spring from his convictions and, as the first half of the film sets up, his homegrown abilities as an expert marksman. A review in *Time* suggested, "By showing what he found in the U.S. worth fighting for the picture becomes Hollywood's first solid contribution to national defense."[28]

Sergeant York was a successful film, earning Gary Cooper an Oscar for best actor.[29] Michael Isenberg calls it "a film that, in its way, is probably as much a motion picture classic as *All Quiet on the Western Front*."[30] And yet the heroism and its rewards depicted in this film seem out of place amid American representations of World War I on film. The film itself is more a representation of attitudes toward war in the pre–World War II period as it is about World War I. What links it to so many other World War I films is the emphasis on pacifism, though it is used in order to promote war intervention. Tom Pollard argues that, "Of twentieth century armed conflicts, only World War II has been consistently portrayed as a good war, rekindling strong memories of patriotism, glory, and victory."[31] After the interventionist push of the late 1930s and 1940s, and then after the Second World War itself, World War I was less frequently the subject of American war films. When it did appear, it tended toward pacifist and antiwar messages.

Antiwar Film and Vietnam

Johnny Got His Gun (1971) is another example of World War I as the subject of an antiwar film. Based on Trumbo's novel from the 1930s, the film is read in relation to the ongoing Vietnam War.[32] The film is unrelenting in its depiction of the suffering of war. Joe is a soldier who wakes up in a hospital bed without any limbs, unable to speak, hear, or see anything. Trapped inside his body, his internal monologue plays as voice-over as nurses and doctors come in and out of his room. The film alternates between the present day of Joe's hospital room, his prewar life, and his wartime experiences. The film opens with historic footage of the war, including many shots of parades and politicians, cutting to a black screen and the sound of breathing. A voice-over explains the doctors' decision to keep Joe alive despite the loss of limbs and any ability to communicate. The first flashback scene begins with Joe and his girlfriend at home before he leaves for war. She tells him he should have applied for exemption because he risks dying; he tells her that many men come home. Joe's future is an ever-present reality for the viewer and exists in stark contrast to the two possibilities—life or death—that the young couple discuss. Her father then walks in on the two and tells them to go to the bedroom, where they have sex on Joe's final night. The authority of parents, doctors, and military officers, in contrast to Joe's awkward youthfulness, adapts the critique of war that World War I films from the 1920s and 1930s offer to the Vietnam era. In this film there is a strong critique of the authority figures that control Joe's life.

Conclusion: Myth, Mythology, and the Great War

Perhaps because it has remained in the shadow of World War II in Hollywood history from the 1940s onward, World War I has never signified American heroism quite in the same way that makes for a good Hollywood movie. Even as a signifier of antiwar sentiments, it has never had the specificity for American politics that the Vietnam War continues to represent, along perhaps with future war movies set in Iraq and Afghanistan. World War I occupies a liminal space: the allies won the war, but at what cost? Even the strongest antiwar films about World War I never imply that the United States should not have fought in the war—unlike Vietnam, where the antiwar protests and sentiment are as much a part of the popular memory of the war as the war itself. Yet the war never reached a point in popular representations that celebrated it as a fight worth fighting. Throughout film history, movies critical of World War I have been about the effects war has on the soldiers—seen from *The Big Parade* to *Johnny Got His Gun*—the horror of trench warfare, the massive and senseless loss of life, and of the leaders who created a war they themselves did not fight.

Setting *Wonder Woman* during this war maps the recurring themes of World War I in popular memory with the film's narrative, particularly the ambivalence toward leadership and those who must fight the war. First, there are no bad soldiers in *Wonder Woman*. The film takes up the question of leadership versus those who fight in the trenches, particularly through the villain, Ares (David Thewlis).[33] The relationship between Ares and the war itself is sometimes ambivalent. Diana continues to argue that human beings are good and are merely under the influence of Ares. Steve Trevor (Chris Pine) tries to remind her that people are fallible, that there is no easy answer to ending the war. Prior to the final battle with Ares, Diana kills another man, Ludendorff (Danny Huston), who she believes to be Ares. Had the film ended with Diana's reaction to seeing the war continue, even after the death of the man she believed to be Ares, it would have fit nicely with the themes of the senselessness of war and the difficulty in pinpointing with any accuracy what caused the war. That the film did not end here does not detract from the use of World War I as the setting; instead, it highlights this use.

World War I works in this narrative precisely because it has come to signify a war divorced of its politics in US popular culture. It becomes a war that represents the concept of war. To align any contemporary historical war with mythology (that Diana, Ares, and others are gods rather than humans or superheroes) that speaks to war conceptually—however simplistically—requires a war that has broken free from its historical causes. To be clear, this is not to suggest that World War I did not have clear historical causes, nor to suggest that they are unknown; rather, this film clarifies what World War I has become in popular representations. However, what separates this film from the war genre category—World War I, in particular—is the final confrontation between Diana and Ares, after which the war ends. When Diana defeats Ares, thus ending the war, the cause of the war becomes evident. It was Ares all along. The division between good and bad, war and peace, remains intact. The antiwar sentiment never disappears completely, but its message is changed when there is a clear-cut villain to blame. Instead of politicians, generals, and greed on both sides—as discussed by the soldiers in All Quiet—the war is caused by manipulation of a greater power. What is interesting to note is that Ares was not a German politician or general, as Diana assumed, but rather on the side of the Allies, a trusted individual. Again, this demonstrates the way the themes of World War I films were adapted and used in the context of a superhero film. This narrative only works when the popular memory of the war has no clear villains. Only then can these mythological heroes and villains be inserted into a historical event.

Diana's goal is love and peace. Although she was trained as a warrior from a young age, her objective throughout the film is to locate Ares and thereby end the war. As she attempts to end the war (and in her mind, all war), she states, "I believe in love." Her hope is that love will prevail, that humanity cares more for each other than they do for their wars. However, the final lines indicate that defeating Ares has not saved humanity:

I used to want to save the world. To end war and bring peace to mankind. But then, I glimpsed the darkness that lives within their light. I learned that inside every one of them, there will always be both. The choice each must make for themselves—something no hero will ever defeat. I've touched the darkness that lives in between the light. Seen the worst of this world, and the best. Seen the terrible things men do to each other in the name of hatred, and the lengths they'll go to for love. Now I know. Only love can save this world.

Her faith in love's ability to save the world, and her commitment to peace, lay the groundwork for her continued mission. Again, the ambiguity of World War I in popular culture and its use throughout film history as the antiwar war made it the perfect setting for a war film about peace in which the hero believes until the climax that ending *this* war will end all wars.

NOTES

1. David Williams, "Film and the Mechanization of Time in the Myth of the Great War Canon," *ESC English Studies in Canada* 41, nos. 2–3 (2015): 165.

2. In addition to his article "Film and the Mechanization of Time," Williams expands on this idea in his book *Media, Memory and the First World War* (Ithaca, NY: McGill-Queen's University Press, 2009).

3. John T. Matthews, "American Writing of the Great War," in *The Cambridge Companion to the Literature of the First World War,* ed. Vincent Sherry (New York: Cambridge University Press, 2005), 217.

4. Jeanine Basinger, *The World War II Combat Film: Anatomy of a Genre* (Middletown, CT: Wesleyan University Press, 2003), 80.

5. Tom Pollard, "The Hollywood War Machine," in *Masters of War: Militarism and Blowback in the Era of American Empire,* ed. Carl Boggs (Abingdon, UK: Routledge, 2003), 314.

6. Pierre Sorlin, "Cinema and the Memory of the Great War," in *First World War and Popular Cinema: 1914 to the Present,* ed. Michael Paris (New Brunswick, NJ: Rutgers University Press, 2000), 14.

7. This is not the case for films about World War I made by European countries, and there are exceptions to this even in Hollywood film.

8. "Prepare Against Invasion, Is Vitagraph Film Lesson," *Motion Picture News,* July 31, 1915, 49.

9. "Blackton Reasserts Strong Plea for National Defense," *Motion Picture News,* August 14, 1915, 48.

10. The film itself is lost, although plot summaries can be found throughout the trade journals published at the time. "'The Battle Cry of Peace' Is Epic of Patriotism," *Motion Picture News,* August 21, 1915, 82.

11. "'The Battle Cry of Peace' Is a Call to Arms in Boston," *Motion Picture News,* November 13, 1915, 47.

12. Leslie Midkiff DeBauche, *Reel Patriotism: Movies and World War I* (Madison: University of Wisconsin Press, 1997).

13. Elizabeth Clarke, "War and the Sexes: Gender and American Film, 1898–1927," PhD diss., Wilfrid Laurier University, 2013.

14. Basinger, *The World War II Combat Film,* 76–80.

15. Liz Clarke, "Ladies Last: Masculinization of the American War Film in the 1920s," *Journal of Popular Film and Television* 43, no. 4 (2015): 171–87.

16. Liz Clarke, "Vamps and Virgins: The Women of 1920s Hollywood War Romances," *New Perspectives on the War Film,* ed. Clémentine Tholas, Janis Goldie, and Karen Ritzenhoff (London: Palgrave Macmillan, 2019), 39–57.

17. Michael Isenberg, "An Ambiguous Pacifism: A Retrospective on World War I Films, 1930–1938," *Journal of Popular Film* 4, no. 2 (1975): 99.

18. Michael Isenberg, *War on Film: The American Cinema and World War I, 1914–1941* (Plainsboro Township, NJ: Associated University Press, 1981), 89.

19. Guy Westwell, *War Cinema: Hollywood on the Frontline* (London: Wallflower Press, 2006), 19.

20. Sorlin, "Cinema and the Memory of the Great War," 17.

21. Basinger, *The World War II Combat Film,* 80.

22. Basinger, *The World War II Combat Film,* 87, 82.

23. Pollard, "The Hollywood War Machine," 312.

24. Isenberg, "An Ambiguous Pacifism," 98.

25. Transcribed from *All Quiet on the Western Front* (1930).

26. Basinger, *The World War II Combat Film,* 91.

27. American Film Institute shooting script, *Sergeant York.*

28. Qtd. in Isenberg, *War on Film,* 94.

29. William Holmes also won for best editing, and the film earned a number of nominations.

30. Isenberg, *War on Film,* 94.

31. Pollard, "The Hollywood War Machine," 338.

32. Michael Ryan and Douglas Kellner, "Vietnam and the New Militarism," *Hollywood and War: The Film Reader,* ed. David Slocum (Abingdon, UK: Routledge, 2006), 240–41.

33. See also Richard Grippaldi's and Andrew McKevitt's essay in the present volume on World War II, which examines the contemporary trend toward superheroic soldiers and unnaturally strong villains.

Heroes and Superheroes

The Twenty-First-Century World War II Film

RICHARD N. GRIPPALDI AND
ANDREW C. MCKEVITT

F our-hundred sixty-four American servicemen received the Medal of Honor for actions during World War II.[1] Before the war, Audie Murphy would have seemed an unlikely future recipient.[2] Murphy was barely eighteen when he enlisted in the US Army in 1942. A previous attempt to join the Marines foundered on his small size: five feet, five inches, and 110 pounds. Nonetheless, he proved acceptable for the infantry. Despite only five years of schooling, combat in North Africa, Italy, and France revealed natural leadership qualities, ultimately earning him a direct commission as a lieutenant. That said, his actions on January 26, 1945 went beyond those expected of an American officer. Germans attacked his Company B, Fifteenth Infantry Regiment, with superior numbers, including armor.[3] Ordering his men to withdraw, Murphy stayed forward in order to call artillery strikes on the enemy. When this failed, he climbed aboard a disabled and burning US tank destroyer and fired its pintle-mounted machine gun until its ammunition was exhausted. During an hour of fighting, he suffered a leg wound while the tank destroyer threatened to explode. Murphy then retreated to the nearby woodline, reorganized his company, and successfully counterattacked. His actions far exceeded the level of devotion to duty expected of American officers in combat. Narratives of Murphy's heroism, like the autobiographical film *To Hell and Back* (1955), presented him as an ordinary man thrown into the most extraordinary of circumstances.

At the war's outset, Steve Rogers was also such an ordinary man. Born and raised in Brooklyn, Rogers repeatedly attempted to enlist in the armed forces after the war began. But as with Murphy, recruiters found him physically wanting. Standing alongside the other men waiting for their examinations, his puny frame looked malnourished and sickly. Unqualified to serve and on the point of despair, he agreed to receive an experimental serum that gave him superstrength and enhanced all of his physical qualities beyond their natural limits. Steve Rogers was, like Audie Murphy, simply ordinary—perhaps even less than—but, unlike Audie Murphy, he had to become extraordinary to become a hero, and indeed the transformation from ordinary to extraordinary made him a *super-hero*: Captain America. His story has been told repeatedly over the past seventy-five years, in comic books, on television, and, most recently, on film, in *Captain America: The First Avenger* (2011).

Like Steve Rogers's physical body, Hollywood films about World War II changed in the twenty-first century. At the previous century's end, director Steven Spielberg created one of the most iconic of films about the war, *Saving Private Ryan* (1998), a sensational example of a genre that film scholar Jeanine Basinger called the "World War II combat film."[4] At its root, the genre portrays a group of ordinary American men struggling to survive in the most extraordinary of circumstances. In the two decades that followed *Ryan,* however, filmmakers drifted away from the combat-film formula when it came to telling stories about World War II, retaining some of *Ryan's* defining features, but also adapting to Hollywood's new favorite blockbuster storytelling mode, the comic-book movie, in order to retell the American experience of the war. Reflecting broader social and political anxieties about the United States' wars of the twenty-first century, filmmakers portrayed the extraordinary circumstances of World War II as a war that could only be won by extraordinary men, by superheroes. For twentieth-century Hollywood, Audie Murphy would do; the twenty-first century needed Steve Rogers.

Tracing the lineage of the combat film, Basinger found *Bataan* (1943) the first to have all the familiar and repeated elements of the genre, while conceding that "no one film ever appears that is quintessentially *the* genre." In terms of story, there is a group of men drawn from different ethnicities and parts of the country. One of these, the "hero," occupies a leadership position, even if another formally leads or commands the group. There is an objective, the attainment of which will somehow involve a journey and death. The men wear military uniforms and equipment and exist in a geography defined or destroyed by military violence. Their bodies are far from home, but not their minds. Taken from their civilian lives, their group becomes a surrogate family. The filmmaker has a lesson for the audience. Teaching that lesson combines technical tools of the trade with information about the military or combat, some of it provided by military advisors, and ideas about war and "war films" the audience has learned by watching other movies.[5]

Captain America is a World War II movie, but it and many of its twenty-first-century contemporaries are better understood not as combat films in Basinger's mold. Instead they represent a different, twenty-first-century genre: the comic-book movie. Media studies scholar Liam Burke argues that the "comic book film adaptation" draws upon the western for its depictions of its heroes, noting that it "follows a vigilante or outside character engaged in a form of revenge narrative, and is pitched at a heightened reality with a visual style marked by distinctly comic-book imagery." He further concludes that "the emergence of a comic aesthetic is the most significant impact of the Golden Age of Comic Book Filmmaking." Said aesthetic can include limiting space and signifying transitions through visuals and lighting; the visualization of sound; minimalism as an aesthetic; the use of color, either by removing it, or intensifying it; the "bullet-time" sequence of films like *The Matrix* (1999), moving the camera around the performer at a fixed point, and subsequently blurring the action, to simulate motion lines; emphasizing key moments to emulate the restriction of print panels to the "chosen moment"; divergent alter egos; and, quoting legendary comic-book writer Frank Miller, "physicality [as] a metaphor for [characters'] interior reality."[6]

We will consider the contemporary run of World War II movies that emerged just after the fiftieth anniversary of the war's conclusion in light of the rise of the comic-book film. *Saving Private Ryan* was merely one of three critically acclaimed World War II films that premiered in 1998, but it was the one that came to dominate World War II cinema; two decades after its release, it is virtually shorthand in the United States for "World War II film."[7] *Ryan* is easily recognized as a World War II combat film in Basinger's mold, yet the relative paucity of World War II combat films in the nearly two decades before Ryan's premiere convinced those who had forgotten the genre, or never experienced it at its height, that Spielberg had created something new. In her review, for instance, *New York Times* critic Janet Maslin breathlessly declared that the "film simply looks at war as if war had not been looked at before," while *Wall Street Journal* critic Joe Morgenstern concluded that some scenes "differ little from the past."[8] To redefine what moviemakers and the public expected visually out of combat films, *Ryan* married familiar, almost tacit, conventions about World War II combat to a particular visual aesthetic, namely, wartime documentary footage; it harnessed the power of modern filmmaking and editing equipment; and it trucked in the cultural acceptance of explicit violence as a hallmark of authenticity. *Saving Private Ryan* also defined the average or ordinary GI as a "decent" American caught in circumstances beyond his experience or control. Its star, Tom Hanks, was himself shorthand for "everyman" in late-twentieth-century American movies.

Other twenty-first-century World War II movies, however, demonstrate the influence of Hollywood's new favorite genre, the comic-book film, its own success a product of both changes in the entertainment industries and the broader political culture of the United States' "Global War on Terror." Productions not drawing directly from the Spielberg-Hanks tree, even combat movies, conformed less rigidly to the *Ryan* standard and instead absorbed influences from the comic-book-movie genre epitomized by *Captain America*. *Fury* (2014), for example, largely abandons the concept of ordinary men in extraordinary circumstances. It is, instead, a movie about an extraordinary man, Staff Sgt. Don "Wardaddy" Collier, and his ability to make others extraordinary. In Quentin Tarantino's *Inglourious Basterds* (2009), the iconoclastic Hollywood director refights the war with a clandestine Nazi-hunting unit pulled from vengeance-themed comic-book fantasies. Other World War II movies wholly outside the combat genre feature fictional characters who fit the comic-book milieu, or actual, living persons re-imbued with the extraordinary nature of the comic-book hero. Both Spike Lee's *Miracle at St. Anna* (2008) and Angelina Jolie's *Unbroken* (2014) imagine characters facing extraordinary circumstances with supernatural forces on their side. In Mel Gibson's *Hacksaw Ridge* (2016), one finds the ultimate variant of genre: a superhero serves as a battlefield medic with the US Army during the battle for Okinawa. Gibson takes what distinguished PFC Desmond Doss from other real-life Americans of the period, his desire to serve in a combat unit despite a commitment to pacifism, and recasts it as something extraordinary. Doss's decency illuminates the fundamental indecency of the US Army and its soldiers. In Gibson's hands, this decency becomes Doss's superpower, not unlike Steve Rogers's superhuman strength.

Hacksaw Ridge challenged the notion that the United States stands for decency in the world. As expressed in *Ryan* and the World War II films it represents, this was central to a postwar masculine American identity. For Spielberg and Hanks, decency is civilization in the face of barbarism, moderation in a world of excess, compassion in the midst of a "war without mercy," to use John Dower's famous description of the war in the Pacific.[9] The American citizen-soldier had to preserve that decency, which stood in relief with the indecency of the empires of Europe and Asia. His duty was defined in both contrast and relation to women, who, while physically absent from combat, were ever present in thought. To be sure, this concept of decency elided actual US indecency toward many of its own people, toward African Americans who nevertheless fought in the "Double V" campaign against tyranny overseas and inequality at home, and toward the people populating the formal US empire in the Philippines or the informal sphere of influence in the Caribbean. But those contradictions do not unseat the concept of decency at the core of American identity, particularly a white, masculine, heteronormative identity, in the first half of the twentieth century. Spielberg attempted to recapture that decency, which also stood in contrast to the indecent war films of the 1970s and 1980s, critical appraisals of US military action in Southeast Asia.

Comic-book films grew in a different context, rising to prominence in the aftermath of the September 11, 2001, attacks on the United States and during the subsequent "Global War on Terror." Americans' most immediate frame of reference for a sudden attack on US soil was Pearl Harbor. The George W. Bush administration pitched the global battle against al Qaeda and its affiliates as an existential struggle on par with the Allied fight against fascism.[10] But while the political culture of 9/11 recalled the existential threats Americans faced during World War II, the Bush administration did not ask or expect Americans to sacrifice in the ways they had six decades earlier. The US government expected ordinary Americans to sacrifice during World War II—not just the ordinary men sent to battlefields across the globe but the ordinary people who contributed to the war effort on the home front. There would be no military draft for the War on Terror, however, no call to material sacrifice—"Go down to Disney World in Florida," President Bush told Americans. "Take your families and enjoy life the way we want it to be enjoyed."[11]

In the twenty-first century, American leaders would not call upon ordinary Americans to sacrifice their ordinary lives to fight an extraordinary existential threat; rather, they expected the United States' extraordinary resources to win the war. New military technologies, implemented after decades of preparing for the "revolution in military affairs," coupled with a reliance on special forces—the definition of the extraordinary soldier—were the military counterparts to the rise of comic-book superheroes and fantasy and science-fiction universes on Hollywood screens. As global military adventurism provoked political ambiguity in the decade after 9/11, comic-book film characters, narratives, and aesthetics offered storytellers reimagining World War II an affirmation of the moral righteousness of a global cause. In retelling the American experience of

World War II, filmmakers mixed the legacy of combat films up through *Saving Private Ryan* with a post-9/11 worldview expecting the extraordinary to save the ordinary among us.

Dropping a Documentary Unit into the Past:
The Spielberg-Hanks Film

In *Saving Private Ryan,* Spielberg sought to make as "authentic" a film as he could. He found inspiration both in the lived reality of World War II and in how the era's legendary directors documented it. John Huston filmed *The Battle of San Pietro* (1945), about the liberation of an Italian village, while leading a Signal Corps combat documentary crew. Critics hailed its authenticity, not knowing, as Mark Harris writes, that the movie "was a scripted, acted, and directed movie that contained barely two minutes of actual, unreconstructed documentation." Huston and his crew had arrived after the Thirty-Sixth Infantry Division had taken the town, but before its residents had returned to their daily lives. Huston had to mimic the combat documentary. Harris reviewed fourteen reels of unedited footage at the US National Archives, concluding that Huston sought "slightly imperfect images—a jumpy rather than smooth camera movement or a momentary loss of focus—as a badge of authenticity." At the same time, Huston had access to the kind of military advisors and "props" of which Steven Spielberg could have only dreamed a half-century later. The army allowed Huston to read oral histories taken from veterans of the battle, and the Signal Corps provided soldiers to "act" as the 143rd Infantry Regiment.[12]

Huston's initial cut of the film challenged viewers to question the meaning of the war. At one point late in the film, Huston showed a group of dead soldiers, with a voice-over of different men talking about their futures. In these scenes, deleted after high-ranking officers in Washington objected, Huston "had chosen to make a documentary that was true to his own emotional experience," Harris observes, "a film that emphasized the terrible cost of the Allied campaign in Italy rather than its strategic importance, tactics, or ultimate success."[13] These Americans were ordinary men in extraordinary circumstances. Those lost in combat would never be able to return home and, to paraphrase a line from the dying Captain John Miller in *Ryan's* penultimate scene, "earn this"—their postwar peacetime lives.

Spielberg, without knowing how much of *San Pietro* was fictional, chose to pattern *Ryan* after Huston's combat-documentary style. Reviewers like Maslin and Morgenstern, impressed with Spielberg's use of filmmaking technology and his ability to flout Hays Office–era restrictions on gore and violence, generally missed this historical context. In 2003, Basinger responded to such reviews by observing, "*Saving Private Ryan* became a major example of the struggle film historians face when dealing with modern critics who judge artistic events by the standards of their own time, and with viewers whose knowledge of the film of the past is thin, if not nonexistent."[14] *Ryan* clearly met the criteria of the combat-film genre. Basinger also reminded readers that the absence of graphic violence in older movies did not mean the audience was unfamiliar with it; furthermore, earlier filmmakers, like Huston, tried to conform to the visual style of contemporary newspapers, magazines, and newsreels rather than what might have passed for more "realistic" representations of violence.[15]

Film scholar Tanine Allison argues that Spielberg, in envisioning how his *Ryan* should look, was reacting to the disconnect between the World War II movies of his youth and the gore-filled Vietnam War footage shown on television in his young adulthood. This tension played out in Spielberg's methods.[16] On the one hand, he openly admired those shots in *San Pietro* that looked imperfect, or looked like the cameraman had put himself at grave risk to take.[17] Desaturating the color made his film look it had been shot during the war.[18] *San Pietro* had real soldiers, if mostly fake combat; Spielberg hired Dale Dye to put his actors through "boot camp," something Dye had first done for Oliver Stone's *Platoon* (1986).[19] On the other hand, *Ryan*, and the Omaha Beach scene in particular, is graphically violent. Spielberg told Roger Ebert that he wanted to immerse the audience in the combat experience, rather than let it be a mere spectator.[20] Digital technology allowed Spielberg to do this without putting cast and crew at excessive risk. As Spielberg and Hanks would executive-produce the HBO miniseries *Band of Brothers* and *The Pacific*, those series held fast to *Ryan*'s style. Remi Adefarasin, cinematographer on both series, described the style on *Brothers* as "like dropping a documentary unit into the past."[21]

Thematically, the Spielberg-Hanks film emphasizes how ordinary its men are, and how they simply want to pass through the extraordinary circumstances of wartime to return to an "ordinary" life. Jennifer Mittelstadt notes that over half of all American men eligible by age for conscription served in the armed forces during World War II: "The result was a military force unlike any other in the country's history. The massive mobilization forced the white middle classes to join in significant numbers."[22] This extended past socioeconomic distinctions to physical ones. As early as October 1942, men with loss of, or blindness in, one eye; complete deafness in one ear; the entire loss of one thumb, or three fingers on one hand; or a complete lack of teeth were not completely physically disqualified.[23] This near-total utilization of men not holding defense work-related draft deferments clarified and hardened basic tenets of American military culture. Adrian Lewis argues that "American beliefs about manhood, battle, and war were at odds with the value placed on young American lives, a value that compels Americans to expend every resource, almost unconditionally to remove man from the battlefield."[24]

The plot of *Ryan* takes Lewis's comment about "removing man" literally. The film focuses on a group of Army Rangers given the task of finding Pvt. James Ryan after General George C. Marshall is told three of Ryan's brothers died within days of one another. Captain Miller and his Rangers have been worn to a nub. Conversation between Miller and his top noncommissioned officer, Technical Sgt. Michael Horvath, reveal the two had survived operations at Anzio, a brutal fight in which two battalions of real Rangers were destroyed, and after which a third deactivated. As members of the Second Ranger Battalion, which in real life did participate in the Normandy invasion, Miller and Horvath see their comrades decimated. The force sent to save Ryan is a mere squad.

Elite though the Rangers might have been, Spielberg chooses to reveal their ordinariness and thus their common decency through their leader, Miller. To a certain degree, Spielberg relies on his audience knowing who Tom Hanks is. In a 1994 profile, *Time*'s Richard Corliss compared Hanks to "quiet types like Henry Fonda and Gary Cooper [who] played the extraordinary ordinary man."[25] This was not unprecedented. Basinger argues that, because "John Wayne's persona is clearly that of 'John Wayne never dies,'" his death in *Sands of Iwo Jima* (1949) is particularly effective. This suggests that "men like [Wayne's character John] Stryker are needed when they are needed, but that they are not needed for peacetime," and the war was long over when *Sands* premiered.[26] *Ryan* features the inverse. War has hardened Miller. When the squad encounters a family trapped in the middle of a fight, Private Caparzo tries to rescue the family's daughter, arguing it is "the decent thing to do." He dies for his trouble. Miller angrily declares, "*This* is why we don't pick up children!" as he removes one of Caparzo's dog tags.

Spielberg told the BBC's Mark Cousins in 1998 that, although he avoided revealing his movies' meanings when he could, decency was a running theme of *Ryan*.[27] Paul Bullock argues that Miller's anger is not actually at Caparzo, but at a world that punishes such decency. This helps explain Miller's choice later in the film to assault a German position that the squad easily could have bypassed, a choice that leads to the death of Technician Fourth Grade Wade, the squad medic.[28] The squad's debate over whether to summarily execute the lone Wehrmacht survivor of the assault ultimately ends in Miller setting the German free, to which Private Reiben sarcastically asks, "I guess that was the decent thing to do, huh, Captain?"

Reiben's anger leads to a sequence in which Sergeant Horvath threatens to shoot him, a fight which Miller brings to a dead stop by telling the squad his heretofore unknown civilian history: he teaches high-school English and coaches baseball: "Back home, I tell people what I do for a living, and they think, well, that figures. But over here, it's a big, a big mystery. So I guess I've changed some." Miller continues:

> Sometimes I wonder if I've changed so much my wife is even going to recognize me, whenever it is that I get back to her. And how I'll ever be able to tell her about days like today. Ah, Ryan. I don't know anything about Ryan. I don't care. The man means nothing to me. It's just a name. But if . . . You know, if going to Ramelle and finding him so that he can go home, if that earns me the right to get back to my wife, then that's my mission.

He then tells Reiben he can quit the mission if Reiben wants, and he won't stop him. But "I just know that for every man I kill, the farther away from home I feel."

Near the end of the film, after finding Ryan, only to learn that Ryan wants to stay and fight, Miller and Horvath discuss whether they should simply report Ryan's whereabouts and leave. Although no viewer would seriously expect the Rangers to do so, Spielberg uses this moment to make one last point about decency. Ryan's unit is holding a bridge that the First US Army must secure in order to advance. The Rangers leaving will increase the chances that the Germans will seize and destroy it. Horvath tells Miller that, if they stay and survive the coming battle, "Someday we might look back on this and decide that saving Private Ryan was one decent thing we were able to pull out of this whole godawful shitty mess." Recalling Miller's speech after Wade's death, Horvath adds, "Like you said, Captain, we do that, then we all earn the right to go back home."

For many of the characters, home is where the women are. Miller, his Rangers, and Ryan himself have positive memories of mothers, wives, or significant others. The MacGuffin is preventing Mrs. Ryan the heartbreak of having all four of her sons die in the war. Caparzo is decent toward a family's daughter. Wade reminisces about his mother working odd hours when he was a boy. Miller mentions his wife more than once. Reiben recalls a bosomy woman trying on a girdle in his mother's shop. Ryan himself tells a story about his brothers and a date gone horribly wrong. He remarks at the end of the story that this particular night was the last time he saw all of his brothers together.

Given that Ryan survives the war, the film's last five minutes are remarkably heavy-handed about the connections between the ordinary, the decent, and the stereotypical role of women in men's lives. Miller tells Ryan to "earn this," referring to his return to Iowa. In front of Miller's grave in a Normandy cemetery, an elderly Ryan asks his wife to assure him that he is a "good man"—"Tell me I've led a good life." The film ends with the American flag, backlit by the sun.

For Spielberg, decency is something the ordinary GI possessed because the ordinary prewar American male possessed it. Although the narratives of both *Band of Brothers* and *The Pacific* were constrained by their portrayal men who really lived, they also gave Spielberg and Hanks plenty of diggings from which to pan for gold. The miniseries carries through this practice of equating decency with ordinariness. Richard Winters is at the heart of *Brothers*. Over the course of the ten episodes, Winters is promoted from junior officer in E Company, 506th Parachute Infantry Regiment, to company commander, to executive officer of its parent battalion. He proves himself as a combat leader, despite being soft-spoken at other times. In the fifth episode, his conscience haunts him after shooting a young German. In the eighth episode, he tells a squad about to undertake a highly dangerous mission for the regimental intelligence officer to stay in their billet overnight and falsify the report.

Other characters in *Brothers* stand out for their decency. Lieutenant Lynn "Buck" Compton perhaps is too decent. He becomes overly familiar with the men of his platoon and then is devastated when they are wounded or killed. Carwood Lipton begins the series as an enlisted man, later becomes Easy Company's first sergeant, then earns a direct or "battlefield commission" to second lieutenant. Rather than bursting with the derring-do of Audie Murphy, Lipton is a steady presence who keeps the men going at a point when casualties are high, and the men's faith in their officers, low. Eugene Roe, the company medic, spends much of the sixth episode working at a hospital in the surrounded Belgian town of Bastogne during the German Ardennes counteroffensive. The effects of combat traumatize him, but in a way riflemen could not understand.

The Pacific recounts the stories of three real-life Marines: John Basilone, Robert Leckie, and Eugene Sledge. Although it, too, follows the Spielberg-Hanks theme of decency, it differs from *Ryan* and *Brothers* in two key respects. First, the trauma of combat unsettles the Marines far more than the Rangers of *Ryan* or the paratroopers of Easy Company. Basilone wins the Medal of Honor on Guadalcanal, only to spend most of the series adrift, selling war bonds and uncertain of his place in the corps. Leckie survives both Guadalcanal and Cape Gloucester, only to suffer so severe a case of battle fatigue that he is sent to a psychiatric ward. Sledge's war takes place on Peleliu and Okinawa. These were battles of such brutality that, on Peleliu, Sledge nearly removes a corpse's gold fillings to "bag me some Jap gold," and on Okinawa, he announces his desire to kill every Japanese he sees.

Second, *Pacific* features more intimate relationships between servicemen and women than either *Ryan*, where women are largely off-screen, or *Brothers*, where they appear rarely. Basilone, in the States, is portrayed as drunken and promiscuous in his off time. He meets Lena Riggi, a fellow marine, and by episode's end, the two are married, with a civilian-style honeymoon. A redeemed man, Basilone goes on to die in combat on Iwo Jima. Leckie, on leave in Australia, has an extended relationship with a woman who ultimately rejects him. Shortly thereafter in narrative time, he falls apart on New Britain. In the miniseries finale, he wins a date at home with his neighbor while wearing his dress blues. Sledge has the least positive interactions with women. His father is more sympathetic than his mother, to both his choice to enlist and his restlessness when he returns. Returning to a rear base after the grueling fight on Peleliu, he finds the presence of Red Cross girls incomprehensible. Back at home, when a female college registrar's clerk asks him if he learned anything in the Marines, he yells in response that they taught him to kill.

Pacific is the darkest of the three, but it most strongly ties together ordinariness, decency, and heteronormativity. Basilone chafes at being used to entertain, feels more a phony than extraordinary, and sleeps around. Leckie, away from both the United States and his wartime romance, comes to doubt God's existence. Sledge is given the most harrowing tests of decency. Ultimately, he neither mutilates the corpse for its gold-laden teeth nor brings himself to shoot a mortally wounded Okinawan. But alone of the three, Sledge never has a "normal" relationship with a woman. And alone of the three, he is not shown to be restored by his return stateside.

Has the day of the Spielberg-Hanks film passed? Perhaps not entirely. In

October 2019, Apple announced that, as part of its streaming Apple TV Plus service, the pair would executive-produce *Masters of the Air*, a miniseries about the Eighth Air Force and its contributions to the Combined Bomber Offensive against Germany.[29] Furthermore, the aesthetics, visuals, and violence of *Ryan* have spread to other twenty-first-century combat films. But the distinguishing mark of the Spielberg-Hanks film, the idea that war puts ordinary men into extraordinary circumstances which they survive via their prewar, civilian sense of decency, has not.

"You Will Stay Who You Are": Captain America, *Inglourious Basterds*, and the World War II Comic-Book Film

Band of Brothers premiered on the night of September 10, 2001. The World War II films that followed came from a world that changed not overnight, but a few hours after dawn. Filmmakers continued to portray war as hell. Increasingly, however, they told stories in which only extraordinary men survive extraordinary circumstances. As the United States fought new wars around the globe in the twenty-first century, wars in which there was no real national consensus on "the decent thing to do," World War II films reflected the instability of a masculine American identity linked to that notion of decency. If ordinary men once labored to preserve decency, extraordinary men would have to abandon it to overcome singular threats.

Captain America: The First Avenger provides the most obvious window through which to view Hollywood's transition from telling World War II stories of ordinary men to those of extraordinary ones. That shift was literally embodied in Steve Rogers's physical transformation in the film. Actor Chris Evans played Rogers, both as a diminutive hopeful enlistee and as a hyper-muscular superhero. Custom-made "Steve slimming" special effects turned the brawny Evans into the emaciated pre-serum Rogers.[30] When director Joe Johnston described Rogers as "an Everyman who in the course of a few minutes becomes the perfect human specimen," he revealed the twenty-first-century shift in attitudes toward World War II film, encapsulated in the comic-book-movie format: extraordinary challenges require extraordinary people to confront them.[31]

The film thus wrestles with the dichotomy between ordinary and extraordinary. As Dr. Erskine prepares Rogers for the administration of the super-serum, he cautions the future superhero not to lose sight of the value of his ordinary decency: "Whatever happens tomorrow, you must promise me one thing,"

Erskine pleads. "You will stay who you are: not a perfect soldier, but a good man." Ultimately, though, Rogers is changed fundamentally because it takes the perfect soldier to defeat an extraordinary threat. That threat comes not from Nazism or Hitler, or even the Wehrmacht, but from another superior being, the Red Skull, the supervillain alter-ego of Johann Schmidt, a high-ranking Nazi officer tasked with uncovering and weaponizing mythological technologies who was himself transformed by an earlier Erskine experiment. Erskine's plea for decency was motivated by Schmidt's own physical transformation, becoming a perfect soldier but also one devoid of decency, capable of malice and cruelty. At the beginning of the film, Schmidt finds the Tesseract, a powerful and mysterious cube of alien provenance—"not for the eyes of ordinary men," Schmidt warns. Nazism, it turns out, was merely Schmidt's cover for leading an even more nefarious organization, HYDRA, and the Tesseract discovery gives him the opportunity to splinter HYDRA off from Nazi Germany. Defeating Nazi Germany alone, then, proves too ordinary a task for Steve Rogers as Captain America, who must instead confront the ultimate evil, HYDRA, not a nation-state but, like al Qaeda, an international terrorist syndicate bent on nothing less than world domination.

Producer Stephen Broussard called *Captain America* the "Marvel Comics version of World War II." As the Marvel team considered the narrative for the film, they decided to confine most of it to the past because "WWII has exactly zero moral ambiguity," in the words of journalist Jeff Jensen, who interviewed the filmmakers about their vision. Director Joe Johnston had tackled a World War II–era superhero film once before, in *The Rocketeer* (1991), but this time relished the opportunity to ground the narrative in the realism of the war, "to make a superhero movie that felt real, that didn't have to rely on an overabundance of fantasy elements."[32]

To ground Cap's origin story in a historical reality, the screenwriters crafted a self-aware meta-narrative in which the new super-soldier is not rushed off to a battlefield in Europe or Asia, but instead becomes Captain America, a minor celebrity entertaining audiences and selling war bonds at home alongside a chorus line of dancing women in a USO show. Eventually the show goes overseas, where Rogers tries to entertain crowds of real soldiers weary from months at the Italian front. Here the film demonstrates the influence of the traditional combat film—these ordinary men look like they've been through the kinds of trials Captain Miller's Rangers faced. They mock Rogers for his ridiculous costume; one GI calls him "Tinkerbell," while the colonel commanding US forces at the front refers to Rogers as a "chorus girl," both implying he is not a man like these combat-hardened GIs. When Rogers pleads with the colonel to attempt a mission to rescue POWs behind enemy lines in Austria, he's rebuffed, at which point he undertakes the mission against orders, successfully liberating the POWs, who then become members of his own unit, the Howling Commandos. Fighting the war on the US Army's terms proved too ordinary for Captain America.

So too would be the case for First Lt. Aldo Raine and the Basterds. Even though he had no comic-book source material when he wrote the script for *Inglourious Basterds,* Quentin Tarantino nevertheless made a World War II comic-book film. The plot proceeds through a series of five chapters, each built around characters motivated for revenge though elaborately conceived means. The Basterds themselves are a special military unit organized for just such a purpose, modeled in form if not substance on Captain America's own Howling Commandos: a squad of American Jews sent behind German lines for no other reason than to kill every Nazi they encounter and terrorize those they don't. They are not there to preserve decency in the face of barbarism, as their comic-book character commander, Raine (played by Brad Pitt), makes clear: "We will be cruel to the Germans," he says, "and through our cruelty they will know who we are." He instructs the Basterds that, unlike Captain Miller's Rangers and the hundreds of thousands of other ordinary men invading northern France, they did not come to Europe "to teach the Nazis a lesson in humanity." Instead, they will kill Nazis indiscriminately, and Raine, who claims Native American ancestry, insists that each of the Basterds provides him with "100 Nazi scalps." "You probably heard we ain't in the prisoner-taking business," he explains to a captured Nazi soldier. "We in the killing-Nazi business, and cousin, business is a-booming."

Indeed, for the Basterds—for Tarantino—extraordinary indecency is the point. It is hard to imagine a scenario more extraordinarily indecent, in fact, than turning a unit of Jews into the kind of murderous hunters their enemies were, or "turning Jews into Nazis," as critic Daniel Mendelsohn put it.[33] "Hollywood movies always have Jews as victims," Tarantino said. "Let's see Germans that are scared of Jews."[34] Tarantino contrasts the Basterds' barbarism in the name of righteousness with the character of Hans Landa, portrayed brilliantly by Christoph Waltz, who displays all the outward signs of civilization and decency—he's polite and ebullient in a half-dozen languages—while making a name for himself as the infamous "Jew hunter," a dichotomy illustrated in the film's opening scene, where Landa charms a French farmer while trying to uncover a Jewish family hiding from him in terror.

"In a Tarantino war," wrote critic David Denby, "everyone commits atrocities," and Denby took issue with *Inglourious Basterds'* "moral callousness" in that regard.[35] Reviewer Christopher Orr also found that there was "no moral weight to the violence in the film," that what made *Inglourious Basterds* indecent was that it took the United States' most sacred bloodletting and parodied it.[36] Tarantino relied on the aesthetics and narrative tropes of the comic-book film, rather than the Spielberg-Hanks combat film, to accomplish such a task. The Basterds are ultimately too indecent—truly inglorious—to serve as the film's heroes. At the film's denouement, several members of the unit effectively become terrorists, suicide bombers ready to blow themselves up to kill the upper echelon of Nazi society as it attends a preview of the Reich's newest propaganda film. As the theater manager, a young French Jew named Shosanna whose family was murdered by Landa's troops in the opening scene, carries out her own parallel revenge plot, arranging to burn the theater to the ground as the Nazi elite watches the film, the Basterds attack. They fire machine guns into the crowd and then storm Hitler's private box to desecrate the Führer's corpse in a hail of bullets. There is no redemption to be found in the film's violence, no preservation or recovery of the sort of decency that motivated Captain Miller's men to storm beaches and sacrifice for each other. Americans can be as indecent—as inglorious—as their enemies.

In the end, Tarantino's superhero, the character that will save the protagonists from the ultimate evil, is not any one person or group bent on revenge, but the movies themselves. Inflammable nitrate film does the work of burning Nazis alive in the theater (and here again is Tarantino's indecent irreverence for the lived experience of Europe's Jews in World War II). When *Inglourious Basterds* was screened at the Cannes Film Festival in 2009, Tarantino boasted, "The power of the cinema is going to bring down the Third Reich—I get a kick out of that!"[37] Both the Basterds' and Shosanna's revenge plots converge on the burning theater in the film's final chapter, which Tarantino titled "Revenge of the Giant Face." The Nazi crowd takes in a new propaganda film, *Stolz der Nation* (Nation's Pride), which chronicles the exploits of Fredrick Zoller, "the German Sergeant York," an ordinary soldier who performs extraordinary murderous acts beyond the call of duty. As the film's body count escalates in tandem with the crowd's bloodlust, a "Giant Face," Shosanna's, appears on the screen, as both the herald and the catalyst for the Nazis' doom. In the conflagration that follows, most of the vengeance-minded protagonists perish with their Nazi foes. Meanwhile, Landa has taken custody of Raine, and while escorting him to a German camp reveals himself to be a traitor, willing to sell everything he knows to the Americans in exchange for postwar freedom and comfort. Raine is forced to accede to his superiors' eagerness to have Landa on their side, but not before carrying out one last indecency: he carves a swastika into Landa's forehead in a final scene illustrating both graphic and exaggerated comic-book violence.

Machine: *Fury*, *Miracle at St. Anna*, and the New World War II Combat Film

David Ayer's *Fury* came out in 2014, long after *Ryan*, and after Hollywood started cranking out comic-book movies. As such, it bears the aesthetic, visual, and violent hallmarks of the Spielberg-Hanks film. Nonetheless, the crew members of the titular tank are not ordinary in the Spielberg-Hanks sense. Most are not "decent," and while you could argue the tank's commander, "Wardaddy" Collier, struggles with the place of decency in his present world, there is no postwar world to envision, no wife to return to, no job as a high-school English teacher. Furthermore, the newest crew member, Pvt. Norman Ellison, is transformed by the violence and by Wardaddy into a warrior who volunteers for a suicide mission. If *Saving Private Ryan* argues that men like Captain Miller have to work to preserve their decency in war, *Fury* argues that war annihilates decency.

Although Ayer insisted in 2014 that he did "not base my look off of someone else's World War II movie look," *Fury*'s presentation matches that of the Spielberg-Hanks films.[38] Ayer sent the actors to a "boot camp," as Spielberg did for his cast, run by former US Navy SEALs. Kevin Vance, one of the instructors, told the *New York Times* that "my job was to get them miserable, wet, and tired." The drilling went considerably beyond this, however. An actor accidentally bayoneted a stuntman.[39] Ayer told an interviewer that he had the lead actors fight one another: "Mostly, it's a great trust-building exercise and a great bonding exercise. . . . There's nothing like having them do some heavy sparring, and then you do a rehearsal immediately afterward. There's just an honesty that comes from that." He added later in the interview that the method had created "a family that happens to live in a tank and kill people."[40]

The visuals also follow *Ryan*. *Fury* uses a denatured color palette. Mechanized vehicles vibrate too much for a combat cameraman to ride and shoot, but Ayer credited his cinematographer, Roman Vasyanov, with finding the solution in "some Soviet movies. . . . [T]he photography in them was brilliant, with a naturalistic feel, all done by using sticks and dollies and fluid heads and track. . . . Those films were a great inspiration for us." The two built a camera platform on a British armored personnel carrier, which both permitted the use of a crane and added a little vibration for realism.[41]

Finally, there was the violence. Daniel Eagan noted in his review of the film that the movie's "pounding battle scenes . . . seem to be taking place only a few feet away from theatre seats. Heads explode, limbs are shattered, bodies are pierced with shards of phosphorus."[42] A Panzerfaust destroys the tank leading a column. Fury enters a village, and the crew fires on soldiers emerging from a burning building. A different building explodes in an artillery strike. The last hour or so of the film is little more than the tank and German infantry exchanging fire. In *Ryan,* Spielberg used the Omaha Beach scene to bond the audience with the similarly inexperienced men of the Twenty-Ninth Infantry Division. Ayer defined his problem somewhat differently: "Most of the characters in *Fury* have been at war for three years. It's a miracle that they've survived, but surviving has made them cynical, which makes them hard to like. The film is taking the audience into a strange land, and the audience wants someone to relate to, someone who, as they are, is learning the ropes of combat."[43]

That character is Norman, a clerk-typist with eight weeks' time in the army. Ayer's comment that he created "a family that happens to live in a tank and kill people" is revealing. Brian Crim observes that giving Sergeant Collier the nickname "Wardaddy" overtly declares Ayer's thinking: he is "the father to war, the sociopathic 'daddy' to death."[44] Wardaddy adopts the audience into his family.

More importantly, Wardaddy adopts Norman. On his introduction, Norman does appear to be a mere two months out of civilian clothes, perfectly average and ordinary. The rest of the crew certainly does not. Grady "Coon-Ass" Travis is coarse and uncouth. Jon Bernthal, who portrayed Coon-Ass, remarked in an interview that he envisioned the character as a man from an isolated pocket of the South, "a guy with no mass communication, no real view or idea of what's out here in the big wide world." Furthermore, the faceless enemy shoots at him all day, but as the tank's loader, Coon-Ass is the only crew member who doesn't get to shoot back. Bernthal decided that Coon-Ass "walks around with this unsatisfied pressure, this unsatisfied urge to hurt, and kill, and fight back, because all he's doing is loading shells all day."[45]

Boyd "Bible" Swan, played by Shia LaBeouf, is intensely religious. Ayer told

Relevant magazine in 2014, "[B]ecause of [Bible's] faith, he's not unafraid of dying, but he's able to accept it and doesn't see it as the end of the road." The director added that Bible was the moral center of the crew, a position that required he keep some distance from his mates: "[T]hat idea of separation out of calling, responsibility or duty is very much a part of how the movie's structured."[46]

The final member of the crew is Trini "Gordo" Garcia, the tank's driver and machine-gunner, played by Michael Peña. Peña told the *Salt Lake Tribune* that Gordo is "battling depression, fighting war, constantly drinking."[47] He added, in an interview with the *Fresno Bee,* that "he imagined Garcia's parents were huge believers in the American Dream and that he was in that tank to protect it."[48] Gordo, although not ordinary, seems the most "normal" of the crew: filled neither with the rage of Coon-Ass, nor the preternatural calm of Bible, nor the mysticism that surrounds Wardaddy.

Make no mistake about it, Wardaddy does have a supernatural hold on his crew. Early in the film, he tells Norman, "I promised my crew a long time ago I'd keep them alive," a fact and sentiment each character confirms. For the crew to have survived that long, intact, was nothing short of miraculous. As an example, the Third Armored Division entered combat in Normandy on June 29, 1944, and underwent 231 days of combat.[49] Belton Cooper, an ordnance officer assigned to the Third Armored, recorded in his memoir that the division suffered a M4 Sherman loss rate of 580 percent; that is, on average the division replaced each of its tanks nearly six times.[50] Shawn Woodford, drawing on Trevor Dupuy's work, notes that over that period, for each tank lost by armored units assigned to the First US Army, as the Third Armored was, on average, one crewman was killed or wounded.[51] It is only in April 1945, two and a half years after Fury's first fight in North Africa, that the crew loses its first member, "Red," an assistant driver–machine-gunner. Wardaddy becomes emotional about it, albeit out of sight of the remaining crew.

There is nothing ordinary about this crew. The Spielberg-Hanks concept of decency does not exist in this film. There is no discussion of events before the war. There is no speculation about events after the war. For Fury's crew, the war simply is. In the other combat films discussed so far, women represent home, and thus ordinary circumstances: what was, what may be. In a twenty-minute sequence set inside a German home, women simply are. Wardaddy and Norman have entered the home of two German women. Wardaddy gives one of the women eggs and cigarettes, and asks for hot water for himself, so that he might shave. Norman attracts the attention of the younger of the two, and

Wardaddy encourages him to have sex with her: "She's a good, clean girl. If you don't take her in that bedroom, I will."

A short time later, Wardaddy and Norman are sitting at a dining-room table when Coon-Ass, Gordo, and Bible burst in. Their idea was to invite Norman to rape a woman whom they, in all probability, had just sexually assaulted, only for the trio to discover that Wardaddy has already provided Norman with an apparently consensual sexual opportunity. All five members of the tank crew then sit sullenly around the table. Brian Crim writes, with some amusement, "Bible seemingly abstains from sex (and liquor), but is offended on [Coon-Ass and Gordo's] behalf."[52] Tanine Allison regards this scene as "a compact demonstration of how war debases or perverts normal life."[53] A family, indeed. Eventually the crew returns to the tank, and the war. Shortly afterwards, German artillery destroys the "rest home."

Ayer suggested that the film's last hour, in which Wardaddy chooses to stay and attempt to carry out the mission of guarding the crossroads despite Fury having thrown a track, and having no way to repair it, is redemptive.[54] There are hints of this, none more important than Coon-Ass's declaration to Norman while investigating a barn near the crossroads: "I think you're a good man. That's what I think. I think maybe we ain't, but . . . I think you are. So, just . . . I wanted to tell you that." Crim, alternatively, suggests that Wardaddy is a literal title. Once Norman becomes sexually experienced, he "is lulled into believing in the fiction of his properly maturing masculinity."[55] Fathers prepare sons to act as adults. In the hour-plus before the crossroads mission, we have seen Norman face death, kill Germans, and, in Crim's telling at least, lose his virginity. He is now ready to join the crew and face their greatest test. Wardaddy can give himself up, and he will father no more sons.

Ayer's point is that war is transformative. Earlier in his article, Crim notes perceptively: "Ayer contests the assumption that American soldiers *in extremis* were reflexively decent, civilized. Decency in war required effort, the kind of civilizing energy that Wardaddy, of all people, spends in order to deflect the tide of his crew's bloodlust when they burst into the apartment."[56] Norman is worth the effort. Wardaddy has transformed him into someone who might survive the war, having suffered the least. Norman has acquired the faith in Wardaddy that the rest of the crew found years ago. That is why he is first to volunteer to stay and help Wardaddy defend the crossroads. Shortly thereafter, Norman is rechristened "Machine." Near the end of the film, in a tense moment when only Machine and Wardaddy are left alive, Wardaddy asks Machine to call him "Don." Don dies, but Machine lives, after a Waffen-SS trooper sees him but refuses to shoot. One might infer that Ayer believes, as Peña told the *Fresno Bee* about his concept of Gordo, that America is worth fighting for. But Ayer makes it just as clear that war is corrupting to the decency that Spielberg and Hanks found central to the GI.

The other noteworthy twenty-first-century World War II combat film featuring the influences of the comic-book era was Spike Lee's *Miracle at St. Anna* (2008). At first glance the film appears to be Lee's provocative attempt to correct a historical injustice: World War II films, and specifically the combat film, have long ignored the contribution of African Americans to the war effort. The film opens on an elderly Hector Negron, who we later discover served in the war as a corporal in the Ninety-Second Infantry Division, watching the classic World War II combat film *The Longest Day* (1962), which featured an ensemble cast of some of the era's biggest white male movie stars. As John Wayne appears on screen, Negron, with a touch of bitterness in his voice, addresses him directly: "Pilgrim, we fought for this country too." Much of the film is a flashback to Negron's memories of the Ninety-Second's time in Italy, which begins with a failed attack on German lines that leads to Negron and three other men from the Ninety-Second separated from the rest of the division. The men befriend residents of a small village, which serves as a base from which anti-Nazi partisans operate.

Lee's pitch would have seemed simple enough: in decades of dozens of film representations of the US war effort, never before had anyone made a Hollywood movie featuring black soldiers in World War II. More than 100,000 African Americans served their country overseas during the war, and it only stood to reason that their contributions to victory be commemorated on film. On closer inspection, though, Lee did not create a narrative of ordinary men sacrificing to protect and preserve decency. Instead, *Miracle at St. Anna* is a story of survival in an indecent world. Tanine Allison notes that the film "visualiz[es] the victimization of African-American soldiers, both by the Germans they are fighting and by the racist American authority figures who underestimate them and discriminate against them."[57] Germans on the battlefield want to kill these soldiers but also, as illustrated in a striking early scene, lure them to desert their white American commanders, who, as "Axis Sally" reminds them, treat them like "slaves" while German women covet black men. Those white commanders, in Lee's framing, have no respect for the men of the all-black Ninety-Second Division, refusing to believe their claims that they had made it across the river during the assault and then ordering an artillery strike on their position, resulting in their separation from the division. The "Double V" campaign—victory over fascism abroad and segregation at home—is illusive too, as a flashback to Camp Claiborne in Louisiana shows a scene in which Nazi prisoners, served ice cream in an establishment that refuses to serve the men of the Ninety-Second, are treated more hospitably by the local population than black soldiers training to fight overseas. In the Italian village, Negron reflects with Staff Sgt. Aubrey Stamps about the kinder treatment they find in Italy than back home. "All my tomorrows was based on America getting better," he says. "What if it doesn't?"

Ultimately Lee is unconvinced by the Spielberg-Hanks theme of ordinary men sacrificing to protect and preserve decency. A German assault on the village kills all of the men, save Negron. The white commanders of the Ninety-Second Division essentially leave the men to their fate. Negron survives only because of luck: a German soldier decides not to kill him, gives him a handgun, and encourages him to defend himself until US forces arrive in full. In a film reviewers otherwise found to be clumsy, Lee "is more interested in getting even than getting it right," according to critic Peter Travers.[58] In portraying the indecency of the white military command structure, Lee argues for a kind of equivalency for Nazism. He aims to shatter the myth of the fundamental decency of the white men portrayed in *Saving Private Ryan* and *The Longest Day*.

The soldiers' experience in Italy is set against a parallel narrative of Angelo, a little boy in the village who develops a close relationship with one member of the Ninety-Second, Private Samuel Train. Train finds Angelo injured in a collapsed building and insists on tending to him, despite the risks of dragging along an injured child in a war zone. To heal Angelo and to protect the stranded men, the simple, childlike Train has placed his faith in a statue head that he discovered and carries with him, believing it has magical powers. It is a ridiculous plotline, and it hinges on a portrayal of Train that hews uncomfortably close to the "magical Negro" stereotype; "a condescending extension of the Noble Savage," wrote *Washington Post* critic Ann Hornaday of Train, "the shamanistic gentle giant is a trope no less troubling for being so putatively benign."[59] The labeling here is particularly ironic, since the popularization of the criticism of the trope is often attributed originally to Lee.

Faith in the supernatural is Train's superpower in a world in which the white Americans commanding armies will not save the black soldiers trapped behind enemy lines. If the "magical Negro" is often a black character who exists to save a white protagonist, then in *Miracle at St. Anna* at least this power goes to rescue an Italian boy who, in contrast to his white American counterparts, "ain't studying how to keep a Negro down," in Stamps's words. And the boy will ultimately return the favor. The Italy scenes occur within a long flashback to 1944 from a contemporary moment in 1983, when Negron, working in a post office at the beginning of the film, shoots and kills a man, who the audience later discovers was an Italian partisan who proved to be a traitor responsible for the Nazi massacre of a local village. At the end of the film, Negron is tried and acquitted and then flown to the Bahamas by an anonymous wealthy figure, who turns out to be an adult Angelo, who now owns the statue head and repays Negron for his kindness by removing him from the country that never appreciated his and his fellow black soldiers' sacrifice. It is, again, ridiculous—the film was both a critical and a commercial bust—but it reaffirms Lee's counterargument to Spielberg that the war was never really about protecting and preserving decency.

"I Will Sacrifice Myself for My Brother": *Hacksaw Ridge*, *Unbroken*, and the Comic-Combat Hybrid

Mel Gibson's *Hacksaw Ridge* (2016) meets Basinger's test for combat films. It also meets the aesthetic-visual-violent standard that Spielberg-Hanks films have cemented as the way twenty-first-century combat movies should look. Shot in Australia, the film hired ex–Royal Australian Navy frogman Jon Iles to put the cast through "boot camp."[60] Cinematographer Simon Duggan desaturated the film during the three main combat sequences.[61] Although the nature of cliff-top fighting necessitated the use of a crane, Gibson and Duggan used Steadicam for close action shots, even using cameras "placed right under soldiers running through SFX bomb explosions."[62]

The central thematic element of the Spielberg-Hanks film, equating ordinariness with decency via positive links to women in stereotypical mother/wife roles, is also present. Desmond Doss is portrayed as having a loving mother, and having earned the romantic love of Dorothy, a hospital nurse, through his decency and goodness. When it comes time for him to leave Lynchburg, Virginia, Doss tucks a picture of Dorothy into his Bible.

Tom Doss, Desmond's father, is a Great War veteran so corrupted by the violence of war that he drinks to dull the pain. After Desmond declares he will serve, despite his Seventh-Day Adventism forbidding him from handling a weapon, Tom attempts to scare Desmond out of joining: "If by some, I don't know, miracle chance you survive, you won't be giving no thanks to God." Yet if Spielberg and Hanks argue that Americans of the period built up a wellspring of decency at home to fend off the corruption of war abroad, and Ayer argues that this decency at home is so worth fighting for that the GI had to sacrifice that very decency in order to preserve it, Gibson is arguing something else entirely. Everyone outside of Lynchburg is corrupt and indecent. One of Desmond's fellow soldiers, Smitty, seizes his Bible, makes crude remarks about Dorothy's picture, and attempts to goad Desmond into a fistfight. His company commander attempts to have him found psychologically unfit to serve. When this fails, the rest of his company cruelly attacks him at night. The army, a soulless bureaucracy devoted to the management of industrial-scale violence, begins proceedings to court-martial him for not touching a weapon. Gibson's argument is that what decency a GI possesses has nothing to with his being an ordinary American inside the continental United States.

After playing Spider-Man in two films, Andrew Garfield reprised his role as a superhero for *Hacksaw Ridge*. Burke notes that the comic-book-film protagonist was "a vigilante or outside character," an apt description of Doss. Burke also states that the protagonist was "engaged in a form of revenge narrative." Gibson's Doss emphasizes how personally he took the war. At his court-martial, he declares, "Why, I had a job in a defense plant and I could have taken a deferment, but that ain't right. It isn't right that other men should fight and die, that I would be sitting at home safe." Serving as a medic would fulfill his obligation as an American while honoring his creed.

The third part of Burke's definition, however, the heightened reality of the comic-book aesthetic, is where *Hacksaw* hits home. Doss's inner life, impossible to restrain, let alone conceal, makes him a superhero. His superpower is his decency. Peter Rainer memorably dismissed Andrew Garfield's Doss as "an anointed version of Forrest Gump," but this is incorrect. Doss is not mere witness to events. His upbringing and hometown filled him with decency. His treatment in the army placed it under pressure. Far from home, pressed up against the Shuri Line, it exploded and remade the extraordinary a little more ordinary.[63]

Scott Bukatman argues, "The central fascination of the superhero film is of the transforming body. . . . Much attention is given to the discovery of the body's own transformation, which explains why superhero films are even more obsessed with origin stories than the comics themselves."[64] *Hacksaw Ridge* is no different. In fact, Gibson gives Doss *two* origin stories. One shows Desmond as a boy, renouncing violence after nearly killing his brother. The other is the older story, the Greatest Story Ever Told, a companion piece, in a sense, to Gibson's *The Passion of the Christ* (2004). For Gibson, Doss's decency is part and parcel of his faith. The film opens with a combat sequence, Garfield's voice overlaid: as Doss goes about saving lives, Garfield recites the Book of Isaiah, chapter 40, verse 28. During the extended sequence later in the movie, Doss continually calls out to God to give him strength, to "help me get one more." In an interview with *Time* magazine, Garfield marveled at how Doss drew on his faith:

> I was so soothed spending time with Desmond because he managed to transcend or get underneath the pervading cultural attitudes through his faith and become a symbol of, "Do unto others as you would have them do unto you"; of, "I will sacrifice myself for my brother." The fact that he was able to say, in the face of men with guns, with the innocence of a child: "I can't do that." There's a part of me that wants to do *that* just to shut you up, to be accepted and loved by you, and to make you like me. But to suffer you not liking me, you not understanding me—to listen to this deeper thing, I'm pretty sure that's God speaking to me, whatever I understand God to be.[65]

Perhaps *Fury*'s sacrifice is redemptive, but Wardaddy does not claim to be the resurrection and the life; Norman comes to believe in him, but even Machine will not live forever. Nonetheless, Gibson's Doss literally and physically saves his fellow soldiers. In his so doing, his tormentors concede that they were wrong. In combat, Smitty apologizes for his conduct. After the fighting, Doss's company commander does the same, and in their own way, so do the company's survivors. As the captain tells Doss before they go into action for the last time, "Most of these men don't believe in the same way you do, but they believe so much in the way you believe." Spielberg and Hanks tell us that decency permits ordinary men to transcend the extraordinary circumstances of combat. Ayer tells us that combat creates extraordinary—indeed, extra-ordinary—men, by removing at least part of this decency. Gibson tells us that decency neither transcends combat, nor transforms into something else. Decency itself is transformative.

Desmond Doss was not the only "decent" real-life hero to get the Hollywood treatment in recent years. In 2014, director Angelina Jolie brought the story of Louis Zamperini to the big screen in *Unbroken*, based on the 2010 book by Laura Hillenbrand. Zamperini's real-life war story was as extraordinary as Doss's. Serving as a bombardier on a B-24 in the Pacific, his plane crashed into the ocean in May 1943. Zamperini survived forty-seven days floating in the sea until he was captured by the Japanese Navy. He then spent the rest of the war at several POW camps, including on mainland Japan. His story had bounced around Hollywood for decades, going back to the 1956 publication of his memoir, *Devil at My Heels*. The renewed interest in the graying "Greatest Generation" in the 1990s, spurred by *Saving Private Ryan*, generated another push to bring the story to Hollywood, and Hillenbrand's best-selling book got the attention of Jolie and producers.[66]

Zamperini's superpower is the film-negative inverse of Doss's decency: Zamperini is able to resist extraordinary indecency, almost Christ-like in his capacity for suffering the degradation of war. While imprisoned, as Jolie's film recounts in excruciating detail, he was tortured by a particularly sadistic Japanese officer, Mutsuhiro Watanabe, nicknamed "the Bird" by POWs. Zamperini's prewar life as a working-class kid and a long-distance runner (he competed in the 1936 Berlin Summer Olympics) prepared him for the physical ordeal of surviving the sea and the camps. But even by the standards of the harsh conditions of the war and POW camps in the Pacific, *Unbroken* argues that Zamperini's treatment was exceptional. Indeed, the implication of the film's title was that many men were broken by the experience of the war, but it was Zamperini's extraordinary individual spirit, linked to a vague Christian spirituality, that enabled him to overcome seemingly insurmountable challenges. Like *Captain America* and *Hacksaw Ridge*, *Unbroken* posits that the American war experience is best understood through stories of exceptional individuals proving their mettle rather than combat units of ordinary men working together in extraordinary circumstances.

Conclusion

Hacksaw Ridge's merging of the combat and comic-book genres may portend a new synthetic genre that will define the World War II films to come. As the Global War on Terror rounded out its second full decade with no end in sight, war emerged as one of the "fault lines" on which American society had fractured.[67] War stories no longer seemed a unifying force, as Spielberg believed them to be when he made *Saving Private Ryan*, or as the US government argued they were in the 1940s. Instead, the comic-book-filmization of war movies reflected a broader polarization of national political culture in the twenty-first century. "The year 2008 represents the tipping point in the genre," writes Tanine Allison, "when the reverent nostalgia for World War II transformed into the cynical echoing of contemporary wars."[68] To be sure, the combat film will persist, in part because Spielberg and Hanks will keep making and remaking it, driven as much by their own sentiment for the World War II generation as by consumer demand for what is now nostalgia not for the war itself but for the war representations Spielberg and Hanks made two decades ago. But outside of that nostalgia trap, it is difficult to imagine a World War II film reflecting a national political consensus in the century's third decade.

In the context of the twenty-first century's "forever wars," as critics dub them, Desmond Doss does not quite represent a unifying figure, a cultural icon to illustrate the fundamental decency of the ordinary men and women fighting US wars around the world. Instead, as the Pentagon's global commitments increasingly seem permanent—ordinary, even—the superhero Doss offers Americans the possibility that such people will be extraordinary, that they will save us from our own national indecency.

NOTES

1. "Medal of Honor Recipients: Statistics," US Army Center of Military History, history.army .mil/moh/mohstats.html (accessed February 12, 2019).

2. The biographical details in this paragraph are drawn from "Audie Murphy's Biography," US Army Military District of Washington, www.mdwhome.mdw.army.mil/mdw-sergeant-audie -murphy-club/audie-murphy%27s-biography (accessed February 12, 2019). Murphy told his own story in To Hell and Back (New York: Henry Holt, 1949).

3. This account is drawn from the citation for Murphy's Medal of Honor, posted at "Medal of Honor Recipients: World War II (M–S)," US Army Central of Military History, history.army.mil /moh/wwII-m-s.html#MURPHYAL (accessed February 12, 2019).

4. Jeanine Basinger, The World War II Combat Film: Anatomy of a Genre, rev. ed. (Middletown, CT: Wesleyan University Press, 2003).

5. Basinger, World War II Combat Film, 16, 56–57.

6. Liam Burke, The Comic Book Film Adaptation: Exploring Modern Hollywood's Leading Genre (Jackson: University Press of Mississippi), 106, 179 and following pages; Miller quote on 252.

7. The other films were The Thin Red Line, which was a remake of a 1964 film, and When Trumpets Fade, an HBO production easily overshadowed by the other two.

8. Janet Maslin, "Saving Private Ryan: Panoramic and Personal Views of War," New York Times, July 24, 1998, E1; Joe Morgenstern, "Battle Rages Ahead But Plot Limps Behind in 'Saving Private Ryan,'" Wall Street Journal, July 24, 1998, W1.

9. John Dower, *War Without Mercy: Race and Power in the Pacific War* (New York: W. W. Norton, 1986).

10. On superhero films and the Global War on Terror, see Andrew C. McKevitt, "'Watching War Made Us Immune': The Popular Culture of the Wars," in *Understanding the U.S. Wars in Iraq and Afghanistan,* ed. Beth Bailey and Richard H. Immerman (New York: New York University Press, 2015).

11. Qtd. in James Carney, "How to Sell an Invisible War," *Time,* September 29, 2001, content.time.com/time/nation/article/0,8599,176892,00.html (accessed February 27, 2019).

12. Mark Harris, *Five Came Back: A Story of Hollywood and the Second World War* (New York: Penguin, 2014), 280, 281–82.

13. Huston later cut another twenty minutes or so. This new cut was released in July 1945, to some public acclaim. Harris, *Five Came Back,* 332, 383–85.

14. Basinger, *World War II Combat Film,* 254; Basinger, "Translating War: The Combat Film Genre and *Saving Private Ryan,*" *Perspectives,* October 1998.

15. Basinger, *World War II Combat Film,* 256.

16. Tanine Allison, *Destructive Sublime: World War II in American Film and Media* (New Brunswick, NJ: Rutgers University Press, 2018), 133–35.

17. *War Stories: Mark Cousins Talks to Steven Spielberg,* dir. Nick Rossiter, BBC, 1998, www.youtube.com/watch?v=rFblqNrc814 (accessed February 16, 2019).

18. *War Stories,* 1998. This was also an homage to director George Stevens, who also served in the Signal Corps as a combat cameraman. John Meroney and Sean Coons, "The Man Who Brought War to Hollywood," *The Atlantic,* August 27, 2010, www.theatlantic.com/entertainment/archive/2010/08/the-man-who-brought-war-to-hollywood/62070/ (accessed October 20, 2018).

19. Meroney and Coons, "The Man Who Brought War to Hollywood."

20. Roger Ebert, "Private Spielberg," July 19, 1998, www.rogerebert.com/interviews/private-spielberg (accessed December 12, 2018).

21. Jean Oppenheimer, "Close Combat: HBO's Intense 10-Part Miniseries *Band of Brothers,*" *American Cinematographer* 82 (September 2001): 32–34.

22. Jennifer Mittelstadt, "Military Demographics," in *At War: The Military and American Culture in the Twentieth Century and Beyond,* ed. David Kiernan and Edwin A. Martini (New Brunswick, NJ: Rutgers University Press, 2018), 90.

23. William B. Foster et al., *Physical Standards in World War II* (Washington, DC: Office of the Surgeon General, Department of the Army, 1967), 19–24.

24. Adrian R. Lewis, *The American Culture of War: The History of U.S. Military Force from World War II to Operation Iraqi Freedom* (New York: Routledge, 2007), 62.

25. Richard Corliss, "Hollywood's Last Decent Man," *Time* 144 (July 11, 1994).

26. Basinger, *World War II Combat Film,* 152, 153.

27. *War Stories,* 1998.

28. Paul Bullock, "Saving Captain Miller: Spielberg, Private Ryan, and the Morality of War," fromdirectorstevenspielberg.com/2017/01/30/saving-captain-miller-spielberg-private-ryan-and-the-morality-of-war/ (accessed February 17, 2019).

29. "Apple Launches In-House Studio, Sets 'Band of Brothers' Follow Up Series," *Variety,* variety.com/2019/tv/news/apple-launches-in-house-studio-sets-band-of-brothers-follow-up-series-1203367345/ (accessed October 15, 2019).

30. David S. Cohen, "The Skinny on 'Captain,'" *Variety,* August 1, 2011, 3.

31. Qtd. in Jeff Jensen, "Captain America Reports for Duty," *Entertainment Weekly* 5 November 5, 2010.

32. Jensen, "Captain America Reports for Duty."

33. Daniel Mendelsohn, "When Jews Attack," *Newsweek,* August 24, 2009.

34. Jeffrey Goldberg, "Hollywood's Jewish Avenger," *The Atlantic,* September 2009, 74.

35. David Denby, "Americans in Paris," *New Yorker,* August 24, 2009.

36. Christopher Orr, "The Movie Review: Inglourious Basterds," *The Atlantic,* August 21, 2009.

37. Qtd. in Scott Foundas, "Kino Über Allies," *Film Comment,* July–August 2009, 33. See also Allison, *Destructive Sublime,* 202.

38. Steve Weintraub, "Director David Ayer Talks FURY, Shia LaBeouf, Reshoots, and More," *Collider,* collider.com/david-ayer-fury-interview/ (accessed October 27, 2018).

39. Michael Cieply, "The Brutal Truth," *New York Times,* August 3, 2014, AR10.

40. Steve Pond, "'Fury' Director David Ayer Reveals Why Brad Pitt and Shia LaBeouf Got Punched During Rehearsals," *The Wrap,* www.thewrap.com/fury-why-brad-pitt-and-shia-labeouf -got-punched-during-rehearsals-david-ayer/ (accessed October 20, 2018).

41. Michael Goldman, "Rolling Thunder: Roman Vasyanov, RGC, Films the Graphic World War II Tank Drama Fury the Hard Way for Director David Ayer," *American Cinematographer* 95 (December 2014): 69, 73.

42. Daniel Eagan, "Fury," *Film Journal International* 117 (November 2014).

43. "Exclusive Interview With *Fury* Director David Ayer," Historynet.com, www.historynet .com/exclusive-interview-with-fury-director-david-ayer.htm (accessed February 20, 2019).

44. Brian Crim, "'I Got No Problem Killing My Kin': *Fury* (2014) and the Evolution of the World War II Combat Film," *Film and History: An Interdisciplinary Journal* 48 (Summer 2018): 7.

45. Kofi Outlaw, "'Fury' Interview: Jon Bernthal Talks Savagery and Brotherhood," *Screen Rant,* October 19, 2014, screenrant.com/fury-movie-interview-jon-bernthal/ (accessed February 22, 2019).

46. J. Ryan Parker, "Fury's Director Explains the Film's Theology," *Relevant,* October 24, 2014, relevantmagazine.com/culture/film/furys-director-explains-films-theology (accessed February 22, 2019).

47. Sean P. Means, "Making 'Fury': Michael Peña on Driving a Tank, and Taking a Punch," *Salt Lake Tribune,* October 16, 2014, archive.sltrib.com/article.php?id=58525388&itype=cmsid (accessed February 22, 2019).

48. Rick Bentley, "Michael Peña Lured by the Writing in 'Fury,'" *Fresno Bee,* October 16, 2014, www.fresnobee.com/entertainment/movies-news-reviews/article19526193.html (accessed February 22, 2019).

49. "3rd Armored Division," World War II Divisional Combat Chronicles, US Army Center of Military History, history.army.mil/html/forcestruc/cbtchron/cc/003ad.htm (accessed February 22, 2019).

50. Belton Y. Cooper, *Death Traps: The Survival of an American Armored Division in World War II* (Novato, CA: Presidio Press, 1998), viii.

51. Shawn Woodford, "U.S. Tank Losses and Crew Casualties in World War II," *Mystics and Statistics,* www.dupuyinstitute.org/blog/2016/08/26/u-s-tank-losses-and-crew-casualties-in-world -war-ii/ (accessed February 22, 2019).

52. Crim, "I Got No Problem," 10–11.

53. Allison, *Destructive Sublime*, 204.

54. J. Ryan Parker, "Fury's Director Explains the Film's Theology," *Relevant*, October 24, 2014, relevantmagazine.com/culture/film/furys-director-explains-films-theology (accessed February 22, 2019).

55. Crim, "I Got No Problem," 10.

56. Crim, "I Got No Problem," 9.

57. Allison, *Destructive Sublime*, 198.

58. Peter Travers, "Miracle at St. Anna," *Rolling Stone*, September 26, 2008.

59. Ann Hornaday, "Spike Lee's Heavy Artillery Blasts 'St. Anna,'" *Washington Post*, September 26, 2008.

60. "Hacksaw Ridge Production Notes," Lionsgate Publicity, www.lionsgatepublicity.com/up loads/assets/HACKSAW%20RIDGE%20-%20Production%20Notes_2.pdf (accessed October 27, 2018). Iles's name is spelled "John" here, but his IMDB page lists him as the military advisor; see "Jon Iles (II)," Internet Movie Database, www.imdb.com/name/nm7485089/ (accessed October 27, 2018). See also "About Us," Live Action Training, www.liveactiontraining.org/about-us/ (accessed October 27, 2018).

61. Bill Desowitz, "How Mel Gibson's Cinematographer Captured the Horror of 'Hacksaw Ridge,'" IndieWire, www.indiewire.com/2016/11/mel-gibsons-cinematographer-hacksaw -ridge-1201742253/ (accessed October 27, 2018).

62. Garth Cecil, "AC MAGAZINE / Hacksaw Ridge," www.cinematographer.org.au/cms/page .asp?ID=22425 (accessed December 11, 2018).

63. Peter Rainer, "'Hacksaw Ridge' Often Has Bloodlust Pose as Religiosity," *Christian Science Monitor*, www.csmonitor.com/The-Culture/Movies/2016/1104/Hacksaw-Ridge-often-has-bloodlust -pose-as-religiosity (accessed October 28, 2018).

64. Scott Bukatman, "Why I Hate Superhero Movies," *Cinema Journal* 50 (Spring 2011): 121.

65. Sam Lansky, "Andrew Garfield on Faith, Politics, and the Making of Hacksaw Ridge," *Time*, November 3, 2016, time.com/4557018/andrew-garfield-hacksaw-ridge-interview/ (accessed October 28, 2018).

66. Jenelle Riley, "Cracking 'Unbroken,'" *Variety*, November 18, 2014.

67. Kevin M. Kruse and Julian E. Zelizer, *Fault Lines: A History of the United States since 1974* (New York: W. W. Norton, 2019), 254–70.

68. Allison, *Destructive Sublime*, 196.

The Forgotten War in American Film

The Evolving Portrayal of the Korean Conflict

DAVID KIERAN

On the cloudy Saturday morning of July 27, 2013, President Barack Obama stepped to a podium at the Korean War Veterans Memorial on the National Mall in Washington, DC. His audience included the secretaries of defense and veterans affairs; the Army and the Air Force secretaries; a delegation from South Korea that included General Paik Sun Yup, who had been the wartime chief of staff; and several US veterans of that conflict, some of whom were no doubt regretting their decision to dust off their old uniforms as they sat uncomfortably in the humid air that had blown in overnight.[1]

Standing before this group, Obama marked the sixtieth anniversary of the cessation of military conflict on the Korean Peninsula by noting the conflict's fraught position in US public memory and within debates about US militarism. "[A]sk these veterans here today and many will tell you, compared to other wars, theirs was a different kind of homecoming," he argued. "Unlike the Second World War, Korea did not galvanize our country. These veterans did not return to parades. Unlike Vietnam, Korea did not tear at our country. These veterans did not return to protests. Among many Americans, tired of war, there was, it seemed, a desire to forget, to move on." Despite this reception, he argued, the war mattered, and its veterans deserved recognition because "Americans faced down their fears and did their duty . . . in some of the most brutal combat in modern history," "because your lives hold lessons for us today," and, perhaps most significantly, "that war was no tie. Korea was a victory." The contrast between South Korea's standard of living and North Korea's misery, the president maintained, "[is] your legacy."[2]

Obama's determination to define the Korean War's significance, and how he did so, marked the latest effort in decades-long campaign to rehabilitate a conflict, as Kristin Ann Hass points out, "to which people in the U.S. have paid little attention since it ended." The very memorial at which he was speaking had itself opened in 1995, the result of what Hass describes as a process that sprang from "a fairly straightforward, not unreasonable desire for acknowledgement of service in the Korean War" but that became "explicitly and determinedly part of a struggle to rebuild American nationalism in the wake of the Vietnam War" through a focus on the sacrifices of US service members.[3] That in 2013 Obama made arguments essentially identical to those that had animated the debate over and dedication of the memorial two decades earlier, however, highlights the fraught position that Korea continues to occupy in American public memory.[4]

The Korean War's place in US film history has been no less fraught. As historian Melinda Pash points out, unlike the Second World War or Vietnam, it has not received substantial, consistent celluloid treatment. "Perhaps understandably, average Americans found themselves too busy to pay attention to the conflict raging thousands of miles away in Korea or to the soldiers trickling home," she writes, "but moviemakers, novelists, and even historians proved no better at acknowledging the sacrifices made by those American servicemen and women."[5] Indeed, with the potential exception of *Pork Chop Hill* (1959) and *M.A.S.H.* (1970)—which is better known as a TV series—most Americans would struggle to name a significant Korean War film; not even the fiftieth anniversary of the war's end prompted renewed cinematic attention.[6] For Pash, this failure makes sense. "With its dependency upon public interest for earnings," she argues, "one can readily appreciate Hollywood's reasons for paying such short shrift to the Korean War and its veterans."[7]

The absence of the Korean War from American cinema thus parallels a larger silence about the war in US culture. "Silence," the historian Jay Winter tells us, is a critical component of remembrance, "is always part of the framing of public understandings of war and violence." Often, he explains, "silence is chosen to suspend or truncate open conflict over meaning and/or justification of violence."[8] This seems to have been the case with the Korean conflict, a war that was both more violent and less satisfying in its conclusion than most Americans living in post–World War II US culture expected, and thus difficult to make sense of.[9] But that silence was never monolithic. Over the years a relatively small number of films about the war have appeared, some of which have received scholarly attention and public acclaim to shape Americans' perceptions and remembrances of the war. Remembrance is never static, of course, and the way the war has been represented has followed the broader contours of Korean War remembrance in US culture—an initial period in which the war appeared nonsensical and inscrutable was followed by a long period of silence that has culminated in a twenty-first-century recuperation linked to national efforts to recuperate exceptionalist narratives in the wake of the national trauma of Vietnam.[10]

The films I explore here contribute to both the construction of the Korean War as "forgotten" and to its rehabilitation as a necessary, valorous act in which Americans sacrificed themselves to ensure the democratic hopes of Asian people. The war was represented in its immediate aftermath in *Hold Back the Night* (1956). This portrayal of US Marines' combat experiences following the entrance of the Chinese troops into the war in 1950 facilitates the construction of the war as not only "forgotten" but "forgettable," a war about which Americans might best be silent, while anticipating the celebration of American soldiers' sacrifice and dedication that would later come to define the war. Korean orphans appear frequently in American films about the war, as seen in *War Hunt* (1962), the presence of these children challenging constructs of the US presence as benevolent and necessary and assertions that US intervention was warranted based on the ultimate emergence of a democratic South Korea. One of the few major twenty-first-century US films to deal explicitly with the conflict is the 2008 Clint Eastwood vehicle *Gran Torino*, which completes the celebratory narrative of the Korean War and its veterans by positioning them as cognizant of the terrible costs of war but willing to sacrifice themselves to protect Asian people from totalitarian aggression so that they can embrace American values and US-style democracy. Despite the paucity of cinematic attention that the conflict has received, film has played a critical role in the forgetting and the remembering of the Korean War.

"I Wonder What Our Kids Will Call This One": Constructing the Forgotten War in *Hold Back the Night*

Three years after the armistice, Alan Dwan's film *Hold Back the Night* appeared in theaters across the United States. Starring John Payne as Captain Sam McKenzie, and Chuck Connors—two years before his iconic role in *The Rifleman*—as his platoon sergeant, the film is set in the days after Chinese entry into the war and follows a company of Marines dispatched to provide security along a secondary access road while the main force retreats from the Chosin Reservoir.[11] Over the course of the film, the company dwindles in the face of incessant attacks from Chinese troops and struggles to care for its wounded as supplies run low and they become increasingly isolated from their command.

This portrayal of US service members determinedly completing such a dubious but dangerous mission places it firmly in the mainstream of early Korean War films. The first Korean War film, *Steel Helmet* (1951), Scott Laderman explains, "complicates Cold War representations of the United States as an indisputable force for good."[12] Likewise, as historian Andrew Huebner writes, the better-known and more critically acclaimed *Pork Chop Hill* (1959) "fit[s] squarely with the other Korean War pictures [because it] depicts powerless GIs victimized by the politicians and generals above them"; this film, he argues, emphasizes "the futility of warfare."[13] Coming five years after *Steel Helmet* and anticipating *Pork Chop Hill* by three years, *Hold Back the Night* exemplifies these themes. Portraying a shift from expectations of a quick victory to the bewildered awareness of a long, brutal, and seemingly pointless war that brutalizes civilians, the film captures American sentiments about the Korean War and contributes to its construction as "The Forgotten War."

In the aftermath of the decisive victory of the Second World War, the war in Korea was indeed incomprehensible to many Americans. As Melinda Pash explains, "Hastily pulled from civilian life or from the peacetime American military, the men and women stuck at ground level during the Korean War can be forgiven for not immediately understanding the reasons for their sacrifices or the forces that swept them to that remote corner of Asia." This difficulty emerges in part, she further argues, from what seemed to many Americans a shifting and often unclear mandate. At first, she explains, "it looked as though the war would go on forever and that sacrifices would never lead to victory or peace," but then with MacArthur's amphibious assault at Inchon, "the war without end gave way to almost certain victory."[14] That was until Chinese troops entered the war in November 1950. Despite Chinese warnings that they would send troops into North Korea, writes Odd Arne Westad, "The Americans seems to have been wholly unprepared," and in the initial Chinese invasion, "more than one thousand US soldiers were killed." Westad argues that "ordering an offensive against the Chinese troops whom he still believed were few in number" was Douglas MacArthur's "biggest miscalculation of the war," one that "gradually forced a UN retreat."[15] The result was "a deadly stalemate between Chinese volunteer and United Nations troops" that persisted until the 1953 cease-fire. With the Chinese intervention, Pash explains, "American troops had to pull back and try to find a line they could hold . . . [and] the enemy resisted even their retreat and men caught at the Chosin reservoir and elsewhere had to fight no matter which direction they went."[16] For Americans in the combat theater and at home, the movement from a protracted war to a near-victory and back again rendered the war difficult to comprehend.

Hold Back the Night captures this sentiment. Set in the moment of Chinese entry into the war, the film's opening scenes convey the Marines' shifting sense of the conflict. "Resistance had collapsed and the end of the war seemed certain," Captain Sam McKenzie explains in his opening voice-over, "The only problem was, could we capture the North Korean army before it escaped into China?"[17] With these remarks, the film captures the optimism that followed Inchon and MacArthur's decision to seek "full and unconditional North Korean capitulation" by capturing North Korean forces."[18] The next sentence of McKenzie's opening soliloquy, however, foreshadows the consequences of MacArthur's hubris: "or rather, that seemed to be the problem."

Indeed, the film's opening scenes alternate between the Marines' expectations of a quick victory and an imminent homecoming—what Pash describes as "Americans once again smell[ing] victory and the sweet aroma of Christmas dinner that would welcome them home before long"—and anxiety that the war will go on forever.[19] "With pressure relaxed, men's thoughts veered towards home," McKenzie explains, as the scene fades from an exterior shot of Easy Company's camp to the inside of a tent, where a Marine writes a letter to his wife while Eckland asks, "What are you writing her now? That we'll be home by Christmas?" "No, but soon after," the Marine replies. To the young Marine's visible surprise, Eckland cautions him, "We could be here a couple years more." Nonetheless, the younger Marine confesses, he has instructed his wife to buy a ranch because "a man has to make a start somewhere."

This thirty-second exchange captures much of what made Korea confusing for so many Americans. With his dreams of being home by Christmas and of enjoying the economic security that many white World War II veterans had gained—this was the era of the GI Bill and of a 1947 *Life Magazine* cover that proclaimed "The Homesteading Veteran" with a picture of a man and his young family gazing out over an open prairie—the young Marine captures the initial innocence with which the United States entered Korea. His surprise at Eckland's remark reflects the nation's bewilderment at the turn the war took.[20] As Pash explains, most Americans raised during the Depression and World War II were willing to carry the burden the nation asked of them. "When the Korean War rolled around," she argues, "they determined to pay their debt to America and become heroes in their own right."[21] This young Marine's surprise—and, of course, his inevitable death at the hands of Chinese communists—highlights how the war's incomprehensibly shifting goals betrayed that expectation.

So too does Eckland's own frustration. A veteran of the Second World War, he is cynical enough to be dubious of any celebration of wartime heroics. When McKenzie tells him that he's won the Silver Star, he responds, "I hope I don't get a chance to earn another." But when he's informed that he will not be promoted, his frustration at the military and the war seeps through. "Guess I was a dope, Captain. I had a real good job, but when this thing started I rushed back in. I didn't have to do it, but my girl and I decided there was a future for us in the Marines. I guess we were wrong." He rejoined, hoping to become an officer, he tells McKenzie, "but if I didn't make it, I could get out pretty quick. We thought it would be all over in a couple of months. But this thing could go on forever." Here, Hold Back the Night aligns with Pork Chop Hill's victimization narrative, which that Huebner notes.[22] However, it perhaps takes that victimization a step further: Eckland is a victim of both an unappreciative military bureaucracy and an inexplicably interminable war; he has sacrificed the prosperity that the Greatest Generation earned for a war that defied his expectations.

What Huebner terms "the betrayal of American troops by their superiors" that is central to Korean War film is likewise a key trope in Hold Back the Night. If in Pork Chop Hill "the futility of warfare" is captured in a portrayal of "men [dying] only so diplomats can save face at the negotiating table," in Hold Back the Night the mission is perhaps even more ludicrous. Easy Company's mission is to travel along a road flanking the main force so as to warn of any Chinese advance as it retreats south. The Marines—and even their commanders—recognize the mission's absurdity. After McKenzie's company repels a Chinese advance, and he informs one of his men that the "regiment's been getting it too, all up and down the line," the Marine asks whether they will "counterattack," to which McKenzie orders, "No, we're moving out in the morning. South." The insertion of dramatic music and the departure of McKenzie and his radioman as the bewildered, dejected Marine steps to center screen casts the retreat as absurd in the face of Americans' willingness to fight and the sacrifices already made.

This notion was captured earlier, when Lieutenant Colonel Toomey first gives McKenzie his orders. "If the Chinese have attacked in force anywhere, they'll attack everywhere," he tells McKenzie and Lieutenant Couzens. "We're next. The regiment will have to fight its way back south the sea." When an incredulous Couzens asks, "Retreat?" Toomey's response is initially a paragon of bureaucratic doublespeak: "No, Lieutenant. This is a fighting withdrawal. Back the way we came." But even a senior officer cannot maintain the charade that such an action is honorable. He quickly confesses that it "Still has the sound of a dirty word, doesn't it?" In these scenes, the film captures Americans' broader inability to understand the Korean War: how had what seemed at first a "certain" victory turned into "a fighting withdrawal," and how could that possibly be noble?

Easy Company's difficulties during the "fighting withdrawal" constitute the bulk of the film, and in doing so it, as Huebner writes of *Pork Chop Hill,* "invite[s] sympathy and gratitude for the colossal sacrifices American society asks of U.S. troops. Men behave heroically in the face of horrific battle conditions, incomprehensible orders from above, and an awareness of their own status as cannon fodder."[23] At the end of the film, the only victory is that the remaining members of the company are reunited with their regiment; there seems no greater purpose, victory, or rationale for their actions. Indeed, a recurrent trope of the film is McKenzie's inability to affirm a noble purpose for the war, or in fact to say anything meaningful about it at all. When he is presented with a Korean woman who accuses one of his men of sexual assault—a scene in which, it bears noting, McKenzie's dismissal of her complaint highlights a long history of Americans overlooking wartime sexual violence—he can hardly come up with an explanation of why such violence happens. "Tell this woman we're sorry," he tells his translator.[24] The best he can come up with is a halting "Tell her it's wartime and . . . Ah, tell her we're sorry about the whole thing."

McKenzie reiterates this sentiment later in the film, when Easy Company occupies a destroyed village only to encounter a Korean schoolteacher living among the rubble. Informed that "the Reds told them Americans would kill all Koreans," McKenzie surprisingly does not affirm communist duplicity so as to validate the US presence. He only responds, "Tell him we're sorry for the inconvenience we've caused him, but war's just plain inconvenient for everybody." Yet when the teacher describes the long history of imperial occupation in Korea and describes a country that "celebrates national humiliation day because they are not free," McKenzie gallantly tries to strike a hopeful note. In the scene, John Payne, who plays McKenzie, stands up somewhat straighter as he begins, "Tell him someday . . ." before struggling to find words, eventually settling on "Never mind. Tell him I am honored."

The importance of these scenes—the only ones in which Americans interact with the South Koreans they are putatively defending—lies in McKenzie's inability to explain why the war has occurred, why it is important, or how it will end; in fact, he can't even summon platitudes. Rather, the film reduces the Korean War to an inconvenience that defies explanation and defense but requires apology.

Indeed, the notion that the war will neither guarantee peace in Korea or elsewhere and that Americans will struggle to understand or even remember the conflict is suggested early in the film. When McKenzie reveals that he has been carrying a totemic bottle of Scotch in his rucksack since he left for Guadalcanal, Couzens marvels, "The last war, too?" McKenzie reflects, "My father used to talk about the last war. Only that was the war before the last war. Wonder what our kids will call this one." Eight minutes into the film, the lead character asserts that Korea would hardly, as Harry Truman had told the nation at the war's outset, "stand as a landmark in mankind's long search for a rule of law among nations."[25] Rather, McKenzie intimates, it will hardly prevent future conflicts and will have no clear place in the annals of American history.

In making this argument, *Hold Back The Night* thus departs from the better-known *Pork Chop Hill*. If in the latter, as Huebner points out, war is "futile," in the former it is entirely inexplicable. This construction likely resonated with its 1956 audience, members of a culture that had paid the Korean War little mind while it was happening, could not make sense of it in its aftermath, and seemed eager to move beyond it. Americans lost interest in the war quite quickly. "In October 1951," Pash explains, "*U.S. News and World Report* labeled Korea 'the forgotten war,' not surprising given that in a poll the same month 56 percent of Americans agreed that Korea was an 'utterly useless war.'" When the war ended, "a surprising number of Americans seemed apathetic about the conflict and about those who did their patriotic duty and served in it."[26] *Hold Back the Night* did little to assuage that apathy. Rather, the film stoked it through an acknowledgment of an indefensible and unheroic military strategy, an explicit contrast with the sense of purpose and the outcomes of the Second World War, and the acknowledgment that the war's purposes couldn't be articulated, much less defended. *Hold Back the Night* helped American audiences conclude what historian Odd Arne Westad would write more than a half-century later: "It had been a useless and terrible war for everyone involved."[27]

"If You Really Care about That Boy, You've Got to Tell Him the Truth": Korean Orphans and Ambivalence about the War

On December 16, 1950, a few days after the Chinese entered the Korean War, President Truman declared a national emergency. As part of the declaration, he explained that, "if the goal of communist imperialism were to be achieved, the people of this country would no longer enjoy the full and rich life they have with God's help built for themselves and their children."[28] This declaration is in a sense not surprising; it is the sort of language that frequently frames appeals for war around the defense of innocents. But it does foreshadow the centrality of children, and particularly orphans, to American remembrances of the Korean War. As Arissa Oh points out, "Korean orphans captured the American imagination from the moment the Korean War erupted." As Oh explains, the plight of children during the Korean War profoundly shaped the system of international adoption that we know today. And, just as Korean orphans frequently appeared in US newspapers and magazines during the war, they are frequent characters in films about the war. Media coverage "roused sympathy and loosed a flood of donations from Americans," and "there are countless stories about how servicemen encountered starving children in terrible conditions and banded together with voluntary agency workers and missionaries to provide food and shelter."[29]

And, as Christina Klein has shown, narratives about adoption were not simply feel-good stories—they were deeply tied to ideas about US foreign policy. "[A]doptive U.S.-Asian families," she explains, "met many of the ideological demands of the Cold War. They encouraged a sense of political obligation to a part of the world with which most Americans had limited ties," particularly because "they gave millions of Americans a sense of personal participation in the Cold War."[30] Such encouraging narratives are absent, however, from early films about the war. Films like *Steel Helmet* (1951) and more particularly *War Hunt* (1962) both feature Korean orphans as central characters, but in both cases their alignment with, and figurative adoption by, US troops is hardly beneficial.[31] In showcasing the devastating consequences of the war in general and these adoptions in particular on Korean children, these films further the critique of the war as brutal and meaningless.

Denis Sanders's 1962 film *War Hunt* has to stand out in the filmography as one of the bleakest takes on the Korean conflict. Set in the war's final days—it actually concludes the day after the cease-fire—the film also paints the war as inexplicable. "We got a funny kind of war of war here," the company commander tells a group of new recruits. "It's a war that we can't win because it's got to be settled around a conference table. In the meantime, we have to keep fighting and we have to keep dying." The reason for this, he explains, is, "The enemy has got to keep getting hurt. Every day he stalls at Panmunjom has got to be a day that hurts him good." As in other films, it is thus the bureaucrats who emerge as the true enemy, to the frustration of the soldiers on the ground. "We haven't lost a war yet," one veteran of both World War II and Korea tells Roy Loomis, the new recruit and antagonist played by Robert Redford, "but we sure are pussyfootin' around this one."

War Hunt's central drama however, revolves around the tension between Loomis and another soldier, Raymond Endore, who is deeply skilled at perpetrating solo attacks behind enemy lines but who has also clearly become unhinged in the process. More important than his martial exploits, however, is his relationship with the North Korean orphan Charlie. Early in the film, a soldier tells Loomis "one of the guys in the squad looks out for him. His people are dead." As Oh points out, such arrangements were not unfamiliar during the war. "Servicemen cared for Korean boys under a semi-formal 'mascot' system," she explains. "Servicemen fed, clothed, and even educated mascots, integrating them into their units, into military culture, and into American Culture." These arrangements had obvious benefits for these children—"'mascots' wearing of child-size army and marine uniforms," Oh explains, "marked their symbolic importance and their association with the rich and powerful Americans"— and they often did important and war-related work and served as "emotional outlets" for US troops. But these relationships were problematic as well. As Oh points out, "By entering into unwritten, uncertain contracts with servicemen, and providing emotional and physical services in exchange for material and other care, mascots operated in the same kind of economy as prostitutes." Nonetheless, media coverage in the United States celebrated mascots, who were frequently adopted by American families, and highlighted "how seamlessly these Korean boys traveled from Korea to their new American homes, not just physically but culturally."[32]

War Hunt rejects these narratives of a mutually beneficial relationship between soldiers and mascots and instead highlights only the exploitation, degradation, and uncertain futures that Korean children face as a result of the US presence. Charlie, it turns out, is not an orphan because of communist perfidy—

as Short Round is in *Steel Helmet*—but because the US military firebombed his family home, and his experience with the military has not led to his embrace of American values. Indeed, in one of his first scenes he nearly stabs another Korean boy, indicating that all he has learned from Endore is how to kill; later, we see Endore explicitly teaching him how to slit an enemy's throat. In between these scenes is another that illustrates how Korean orphans are both harmed and disregarded by the US military. Loomis attempts to teach Charlie how to throw a baseball, recalling an image from a wartime *Stars and Stripes* that Oh points out "demonstrate[ed] how a mascot . . . could cross from one world into another . . . emphasiz[ing] his suitability for adoption and potential for assimilation into American society."[33] Yet as Charlie does so with some success, Endore arrives to escort him away, and the company commander tells Loomis to "leave him alone. He belongs to Endore . . . [and] Endore's a valuable man." Here, the child is hardly a beneficiary of American attention, nor is he a future citizen; he is only a possession that must be managed to ensure the Army's effectiveness.

The central drama of the film thus surrounds what will happen to Charlie when the war ends. Endore, it turns out, has promised Charlie that they will run away together to the Korean mountains, a fantasy that Loomis rejects with a statement of realism. "If you really care about that boy, you've got to tell him the truth," he tells Endore. "He's got to go to an orphanage, right here. His clothes may not be anything special. The food they give him will probably be barely enough to keep him going. But there'll be other children there, and they'll play games. Children's games. And there'll be a teacher." This statement, as well as his subsequent threat that Charlie "needs to go where he belongs," suggests the impossibility of transnational adoption and a rejection of the narrative in which Korean children benefit from the US intervention. Even the film's voice of moral authority, in rejecting Endore's abuse, cannot imagine an American future—or, for that matter, a particularly positive one—for Charlie.

And indeed, the film's final moments bear this out. Upon learning that the war has ended, Endore and Charlie sneak away, across the demilitarized zone. When they are confronted by Loomis and Captain Pratt, the soldiers struggle and Pratt kills Endore. Charlie, however, runs away, towards the bleak North Korean future. When Pratt catches up with Loomis, who had been pursuing Charlie, and asks if he is OK, Loomis can only answer negatively. Although Charlie does not die, as *Steel Helmet*'s Short Round does, the film suggests, first, that he has been emotionally destroyed by his encounter with US troops and, second, that he has little desire to embrace US values. He is not abandoned; he rejects Americanization. Moreover, the film implies that his future will be one of misery. With this despairing ending, the film rejects dominant narratives about Korean adoption while furthering the construction of the war as brutal and bewildering. Like *Hold Back The Night*, *War Hunt* thus casts the war in Korea as inexplicable but brutal, a war at odds with post–Second World War narratives of American exceptionalism. In films like these, the war became one that Americans, including those who served, couldn't, and didn't care to, understand.

"It's a Vietnam Thing": Redeeming the Korean War and American Exceptionalism in Gran Torino

Gran Torino is not, strictly speaking, a Korean War film. It's set in Detroit in 2008. But in the person of Walt Kowalski, the elderly Korean War veteran who is the film's protagonist and who sacrifices himself to save his Hmong neighbors terrorized by a street gang, the Korean conflict, and indeed the larger politics of the Cold War, animate the film. Scholars who have written about this film have emphasized the centrality of narratives of atonement and multiculturalism. In this section, I build on—and, at times, challenge—that work in order to position *Gran Torino* within the larger filmography of the Korean War. In particular, the film seeks to recuperate the war from the narrative that casts it as incomprehensible, unsuccessful, and ultimately meaningless. As well, it seeks to recuperate exceptionalist narratives about American benevolence and the validity of military commitments in the aftermath of the Vietnam War. By casting the Korean War veteran as capable of saving his Asian neighbors precisely because of his wartime service, *Gran Torino* avows that Korea was a noble intervention and asserts the capacity of a militarized United States to fulfill its obligation to rescue oppressed others. The film is thus part of a much larger history of cinematographic efforts to recuperate from the inglorious Vietnam War. For many conservatives, the most pernicious legacy of the Vietnam War was the "Vietnam syndrome," which Melani McAlister identifies as a set of beliefs grouped around the sentiment that, "in the wake of its failure to use force properly, the nation was afflicted with a profound failure of nerve."[34] As Patrick Hagopian puts it, the syndrome's adherents held that the war had "ma[de] Americans apologetic about the nation's past and timid in the face of aggression."[35] As many historians of American film, most notably Susan

Jeffords, have shown, much post-1980s US cinema can be read as a response to this perceived crisis.[36]

Gran Torino should be read as another installment of the enduring celluloid effort to recuperate from the Vietnam syndrome, a mission in which Clint Eastwood has played no small part. As William Beard points out, then, *Gran Torino* is in a sense an updating of *Unforgiven*.[37] Indeed, Jeffords's assessment of his 1992 film *Unforgiven* applies equally well to *Gran Torino*: "no matter how secure one's own nation may seem in a post–Cold War period, the world outside the home . . . 'remains a dangerous and unpredictable place.' And who, in such a place, will protect the innocent?" Reagan-era films, she explains, supply a ready solution to this danger: "Get those hard-bodied men back into circulation." *Gran Torino* presents a similar narrative of the aging warrior who returns, "reviving American idealism and force of action, [and] invoking as well as the basis for his actions the family and the country's domestic future."[38] Fifty years after *Hold Back the Night* constructed the Korean War as an inscrutable enigma, *Gran Torino* returned the veteran to "action," thus not only recuperating that war but also valorizing and validating the United States' broader Cold War mission and, with it, narratives of American exceptionalism.

Indeed, as Beard points out, Walt Kowalski's "haunted recollections of violence are echoes of William Munny's in *Unforgiven*."[39] In this, Walt is not unlike most Korea veterans. According to Melinda Pash, the men and women who fought in Korea did not immediately embrace their veteran status. Rather, "tired of arguing that America hadn't 'lost' in Korea, and quieted by the country's apathy, many Korean War veterans . . . tr[ied] to put the war behind them and forget they were veterans at all."[40] That's how Walt Kowalski defines his postwar life. "I survived the war, got married, had a family," he tells Father Janovich, the Catholic priest sent to extract a confession at Walt's late wife's request, when he's asked to describe his life. And indeed, he appears to have kept his wartime experiences hidden even from his children and grandchildren. As his family gathers in his home after his wife's funeral, his grandsons find his footlocker in the basement, festooned with a First Infantry Division sticker and filled with mementoes of his time in Korea, including a photo that informs viewers that Walt served in "3rd Platoon, E Company," in 1952. In this younger generation's reaction, Korea appears very much a forgotten war: bewildered, one of his grandsons asks, "Where's Korea?"[41] Even the discovery of Walt's Silver Star—the military's third-highest valor award, which certifies him as a legitimate war hero—is met only with a shrug of vague interest.

In point of fact, however, Walt's identity as veteran structures the film. As Beard explains, "*Gran Torino* studies its hero's propensity to violence, and traces it fundamentally to his experience in the Korean War. That taught him how to use the M-1 rifle that he still brandishes, it taught him how to kill and how to survive and be strong under unimaginable pressures. Walt's anger, and also his extensive repertory of racial insults and his reflexive instinct to regard Asians as the other and the enemy, come directly from Korea." With its central drama revolving around a Korean war veteran and his Hmong neighbors, then, *Gran Torino*'s context is affirmatively the Cold War and its legacies. Critics including Maria Del Mar Azcona and Beard have emphasized Walt's guilt over his actions in Korea, with Beard in particular asserting that "Walt's honourable military service to his country, whose flag hangs in front of his house and all around town, is not something he can be proud of. Patriotic pride keeps turning to acid in his mouth because his glorious wartime violence keeps presenting itself to him as a crime against humanity." In this sense, Walt appears as something of an aging Sam McKenzie, still unable to assign any valor to his service a half-century on. Indeed, Beard goes as far as arguing that Walt's death at the end is an atonement for his actions in Korea.[42]

Yet while *Gran Torino* certainly embraces a nuanced account of Korean War veteran attitudes, the film in fact justifies Cold War militarism and recuperates an American exceptionalism rooted in militarism by positioning Korea as a worthwhile conflict whose veterans hold important lessons for a nation still disempowered by the Vietnam syndrome.[43] Indeed, a revisionist narrative of the United States' failure in Vietnam structures the film. In making Hmong refugees' struggles in working-class Detroit the central tension of the film, *Gran Torino* calls attention to the United States' history of abandoning its anti-communist allies in Asia.[44] After Walt first rescues Sue Lor from an African American street gang, he asks her, "Where the hell is Hmong"—mispronouncing it by voicing the "H"—and "How the hell did you end up in my neighborhood, then? Why didn't you just stay there." This display of cultural ignorance and insensitivity, in addition to being entirely in keeping with Walt's racism, provides an opening for Sue to rehearse the narrative of American abandonment after the war in Vietnam: "It's a Vietnam thing. We fought on your side. When the Americans quit, the communists started killing all the Hmong. So we came over here."[45]

Sue's comment is rooted in revisionist narratives of the Vietnam War in which the United States "quit" and abandoned its allies.[46] As Ma Vang has shown, however, such narratives about the Hmong are central to defenses of the war. "[I]t is precisely the naming of the Hmong veterans as the 'new friend'— one racialized as always already behind—that allows the United States to justify its involvement in Laos," she explains, adding that the Hmong exemplify "US militarism's rendering of certain bodies as crucial yet expendable subjects of empire" because they are a population that "requires military intervention to help it sustain and develop self-determination. This 'new friend' logic renders the violence of war as necessary and just, because it simultaneously functions as a rescue of the racial other, who can never be self-determined."[47] Indeed, the notion that the war was just and that the United States abandoned its allies when it withdrew are central to revisionist narratives of the Vietnam War and particularly those that embrace the notion of the "Vietnam syndrome." In his 1980 speech condemning the syndrome, Ronald Reagan argued that, because the United States lacked "the means and determination to prevail," the people it left behind had suffered and particularly singled out the Hmong. "The hill people of Laos know poison gas, not justice," he inveighed. And the lesson that Reagan famously offered was that, "If we are forced to fight, we must have the means and the determination to prevail or we will not have what it takes to secure the peace."[48]

Resolving the abandonment of the Hmong thus emerges as a critical component of recuperation from the national trauma of the Vietnam war. However, as Ma argues, this has been a fraught process; the Hmong figure as "rescued yet unassimilated refugees," and "the offer of citizenship" to them "is about the United States and its recuperation of a political relationship with the 'new friend'—signifying the incorporation of 'primitive' stateless people into modernity and nationhood."[49]

This vision of Hmong citizenship animates *Gran Torino*.[50] As Beard notes, the moment of the Vietnam syndrome is critical for *Gran Torino*: Walt's eponymous car, he explains, symbolically references "nostalgia for a more stable and comforting time," the last moments before the national decline of the 1970s, a period defined in part by defeat in Vietnam.[51] That was also what Reagan was seeking in his 1980 speech, and to do so he invoked Korea: "Korea also became our first no win war, a portent of much that has happened since," he admitted, before adding, "But reflect for a moment how . . . our will and our capacity to preserve the peace were unchallenged. There was no question about our credibility and our welcome throughout the world."[52] In spite of its ambiguous ending, for Reagan, Korea was a victory; it exemplified the sort of commitment the United States must again make in the contemporary world.

So it is in *Gran Torino*, where the hero is, somewhat surprisingly, not a veteran of the Vietnam War—that is, a Rambo figure who "gets to win this time"— but a veteran of an earlier, problematic Asian War. This choice is not insignificant. While it may well be that making Walt a Korea veteran was necessary to cast the then seventy-eight-year-old Eastwood in the part, it also establishes the experience of Korea as one that can resolve the Vietnam War's damage to exceptionalist narratives of national identity. Initially, Korea appears as something that Walt clings to, or which haunts him, but which has no contemporary relevance.[53] Early in the film, Janovich asks Walt what he knows about life and death, to which Walt replies, "I know a lot. I lived for almost three years in Korea with it. . . . We shot men, stabbed 'em with bayonets, hacked seventeen-year-olds to death with shovels, stuff I'll remember 'til the day I die. Horrible things. But things I'll live with."

Janovich initially views Walt's acknowledgment of the violence that he has perpetrated as further evidence of Walt's need to confess his sins and move beyond the war. Later, when he condemns Walt for chasing gang members off of his lawn with an M-1 rifle, Walt defends himself by telling the priest that, "when things go wrong, you've got to act quickly. When we were in Korea and a thousand screaming gooks came across our line, we didn't call the police. We reacted." Janovich responds by exclaiming, "We're not in Korea, Mr. Kowalski," and tells him again, "Things done during war are terrible: being ordered to kill, killing to save yourself, killing to save someone else. . . . I've seen a lot of men who have confessed their sins, admitted their guilt, and left their burdens behind them. Stronger men than you. Men at war who were ordered to do appalling things, and are now at peace." With this speech, Janovich evokes the ethos of the earlier films, implying that the violence was for no greater purpose—it was simply "terrible"—and that Korea was an inscrutable conflict with no larger purpose.

Yet the film argues that it is precisely *because* Walt served in Korea that he is able to save the Lor family from a brutal Hmong street gang that he increasingly understands as threatening their capacity for a peaceful existence. Walt's decision to confront the gang, and to sacrifice himself so that they can be arrested and prosecuted, retroactively validates that war by constructing Walt as understanding the need for confrontation and able to carry it out effectively despite the horrific violence and great sacrifice that it will require.[54]

The film makes this clear both through Janovich's change of heart and Walt's rhetoric and action. After a drive-by shooting in which Thao is injured and after Sue returns home having been gang-raped, Father Janovich sits in darkness in Walt's living room, paging through an album of photos of Walt in Korea and at his wedding, a symbolic assertion that the war abroad made possible tranquility at home. As he does so, Walt tells him, "You know, Thao and Sue are never going to find peace in this world as long as that gang's around. Until they go away, you know, forever."

Here, the Cold War context is again clear; with this comment, the gang takes the place of the communists who initially imperiled the Lor family. It echoes not only Reagan's comment about the Hmong after Vietnam but Truman's Korean War–era rhetoric. Consider, for example, the doctrine's assertion that "it must be the policy of the United States to support free peoples who are resisting attempted subjugation by armed minorities or by outside pressures" and that the United States "must assist free peoples to work out their own destinies in their own way."[55] More importantly, it echoes Truman's statements about the Korean War. Repeatedly, Truman cast the war as an effort to ensure the autonomy of peaceful South Koreans against communist aggression. On December 1, 1950, for example, he told Congress, "The attack of the North Korean communists on their peaceful fellow-countrymen . . . was an attack upon the security of peaceful nations everywhere. Their action, if unchecked, would have blasted all hope of a just and lasting peace."[56] Four months later, Truman used Walt's precise construction to describe the US effort, telling an audience in April 1951, "At the present time our Nation is engaged in a great effort to maintain justice and peace in the world" and servicemen in Korea were "fighting and suffering in an effort to prevent the tide of aggression from sweeping across the world."[57]

Crucially, in this conversation, Janovich shifts from dismissing Walt's experience—"We're not in Korea"—and encouraging repentance for his actions there to at least partially accepting Walt's perpetration of violence. "You know what [Thao] expects," he tells Walt, and to Walt's evident surprise he adds, "I know what I would do if I were you. Or at least what you think you should do." And when Walt asks him what he would do, Janovich responds, "I'd come over here and talk to you, I guess. . . . [T]his pisses me off, too." In this scene,

Janovich's transformation recalls an earlier moment in Korean War cinema in which religious objections to violence give way to an acceptance of the necessity of violence. Writing on *Steel Helmet*, Scott Laderman explains that the film defines that war as "an anti-imperialist crusade against a 'North Korean' enemy intent on furthering the international communist conspiracy. And ruthlessness was required in such a campaign. Even Pvt. Bronte (Robert Hutton), whose World War II conscientious objection was consistent with his priestly ambitions, eventually saw the light."[58]

Moreover, it is precisely Walt's status as a Korean War veteran that positions him as capable of addressing the threat posed by the gang. The morning after the shooting and rape, Thao appears in Walt's kitchen, demanding action. When Walt counsels patience, he tells him, "You know I'm the right man for this job." Ordinarily, it might not be evident why an elderly retired autoworker is the "right man" to confront a violent gang, but the film provides an answer in the form of Walt's lighter, which bears the First Infantry Division insignia and which Walt earlier explains he has been carrying since the war. Its presence here establishes that Walt's wartime experience renders him "the right man for this job."

The film further defines Walt's climatic decision to intervene with the gang on behalf of the Lor family as the inevitable result of his veteran status when he presents his Silver Star to Thao. Explaining that he was the sole survivor of an attack on a Chinese machine-gun emplacement, Walt tell him that he's giving him the medal "because we all knew the dangers that night, but we went anyway. That's the way it might be tonight. There's always a chance you don't come back." Much as Reagan does in his 1980 speech, this comment positions embracing the Korean War as the antidote the Vietnam syndrome. As Beard noted, Walt acknowledges that the war was horrible and scarring—moments later, Walt tells Thao that killing people is "goddamned awful" and "Not a day goes by that I don't think about it, and you don't want that on your soul"—but it was nonetheless a necessary sacrifice that Americans willingly accepted for the greater good, here defined as ensuring the future success of the Asian other.[59]

Walt's comments to Thao assert that, by virtue of his experience, he can resolve the crisis. As he leaves Thao locked in his basement, he tells him, "Look you've come a long way, and I'm proud to say that you're my friend. You've got your whole life ahead of you. But I finish things. That's what I do." Such a statement is consistent within conservative rhetoric about the Vietnam War—consider, for example, George H. W. Bush, prior to the 1991 Gulf War, answering American anxieties about "another Vietnam" by promising that "there will not be any murky ending."[60] Despite the Korean War's own murky ending, *Gran Torino* recuperates the war and, with it, the sacrifices inherent in interventionist militarism by emphasizing the certainty of the cause and the willingness of the soldier to bear the burden. And indeed, the film's climatic scene cements that Walt's capacity to secure justice and peace for the Lor family is directly tied to his Korean War service. The climactic scene further asserts the earlier implication, when Walt equates a street gang in his front yard to a "a thousand screaming gooks [coming] across our line," that the current threat is analogous to that faced in Korea; when Walt ends up facing a hail of gang gunfire, it is the equivalent of the Chinese machine gun. And here again, he "went anyway," cognizant of the risks. To make this point explicit, the film reveals after he is murdered that the item that he had taken from his pocket and which induced the shooting was his First Division lighter. Writing about this moment, Beard juxtaposes Walt's reaching for the lighter with earlier Eastwood characters' tendency to reach for a gun, noting that, "where there used to be power, and lethal violence, now there is emptiness, nothingness, only the emblem of a nostalgia more bitter than sweet."[61] Walt, however, doesn't drop the lighter, which might suggest that he has "let the war go"; rather, he holds it, avowing the enduring value of the lessons that he learned in Korea and that he has carried for half a century, however horrific the war may have been.

It is in this context that Beard's claim that Walt's death "is an act of personal surrender for the benefit of a young Asian boy like the one he shot in Korea" must be understood; it is less an act of atonement than a sacrifice of the sort Reagan-era conservatives posited Americans once willingly made and must become able to make again. If Vietnam was a war marked by a "murky ending" and sacrifices made "in a war our government is afraid to let them win," here the Korean War veteran explicitly is identified as one whose sacrifice unequivocally ensures the future comfort and prosperity of the Asian immigrant.[62] In the film, those very values—in fact, the very people—that defined that Korean War make the contemporary realization of American democracy possible.

Gran Torino thus revises earlier narratives of the Korean War's meaningless and inscrutability. The orphan others' success depends on Americans' continued willingness to deploy violence on their behalf. This same logic animates the film's embrace and extension of the orphan trope that animates earlier films. Ma Vang has argued that Hmong refugees are problematic figures in US culture, "rescued yet unassimilated" figures who are "racialized as always already behind."[63] The film captures this problematic position, and the Korean War veteran's resolution of it by extending the trope of Asian orphan familiar from earlier films.

Sue and Thao are themselves orphans, and in the first scene featuring the Lor household, family members wonder "How could [Thao] ever be a man?" As Azcona explains, the answer is of course Walt Kowalski's reluctant but wise mentorship. Walt, Azcona explains, becomes the father figure who guides him towards successful integration into US culture:

> In the montage sequence . . . we see the young Hmong-American doing all kinds of labour and manual work in all kinds of weather conditions. We also see Walt's more than satisfied look when he sees the smooth and unproblematic way in which Thao begins to embody what he regards as the old traditional "American" values of hard work, tenacity and discipline that he can no longer find in the young Anglo generations. The dissolves between the shots of Thao doing the sort of maintenance job, through which Walt has defined himself, and those of Walt looking at him visually, convey the merging process between these two identities that is about to start.

Walt's mentorship is admittedly problematic, suffused as it is with racist comments and toxic masculinity, but the film embraces a vision of a diverse, inclusive US culture. Azcona observes that "Thao does not simply become another 'American,' at least not an illustration of the melting pot mentality. His merging with Walt and integration in US society is inseparable from his preservation of his own distinct cultural identity."[64]

The film's multiculturalism likewise contributes to the retroactive defense of the Korean War, for Truman repeatedly articulated that the US intervention in Korea sought to produce a peaceful but diverse world. Speaking in February 1951, Truman cast US foreign policy as "giving all the people a chance at the right kind of life" and explained, "We are acting as one member of a whole community of nations dedicated to the concept of the rule of law in the world. As in all other communities, the members of this community of nations have many different ideas and interests and do not all speak with one voice."[65] Seven months later, speaking in San Francisco as the peace treaty with Japan was being negotiated, he said with regard to Asian countries, "We want to see them grow and prosper as equal partners in the community of independent nations of both East and West. . . . We wish to see these nations attain in dignity and freedom a better life for their peoples." "Immense opportunities lie ahead if these countries can pursue their national destinies in a partnership of peace, free from the fear of aggression." He cast peace in Korea as a crucial step toward that goal.[66]

This language matters in the context of understanding the place of the Korean War in *Gran Torino*. As Azcona argues, the film embraces a transnational vision of US culture. "Rather than Thao's assimilation—and, therefore, erasure and invisibility—into the dominant white culture," she explains, the film "suggests the need for the dominant culture to be filled by the transnational Other in order to give way to a newly formed identity: one marked by a transnational experience"; in the end, she explains, "Eastwood, the fixer, sets out, however unwillingly at the beginning, to remake a US identity that is ineffective and obsolete because it has failed to embrace the transnational."[67] As Beard puts it, somewhat more grimly, "All that can be done, says the movie in a very forthright way, is hand over the reins of power to whatever citizens show a true commitment to right values, even if they're the racial Other."[68] This, in a sense, is an analogue for what Truman argued Americans were pursuing in 1951. "We cannot always have our own way in this community," he told his audience in Philadelphia, "But we have a tremendous responsibility to lead and not to hang back." Condemning the isolationism of the 1920s, he explained, "We shirked our responsibility in the 1920's. We cannot shirk it now."[69]

The role augured by Truman is analogous to Walt's. Just as Truman posited that the United States must play a decisive leadership role because other countries—in this case, Asian countries—could not become part of the global community on their own, Walt becomes the mechanism through which Thao can gain economic, familial, and personal security. This argument is well captured in a scene in which Sue tells Walt that "it's kind of nice of you to look after him like this. He doesn't have any real role models," and then tells him, "You're a good man Wally." Comparing him to their father—and thus highlighting their status as orphans—she says "he was really hard on us, really traditional, and really old school. But you're an American." Here, the film casts American paternalism as a necessary step towards an inclusive and diverse society.

Gran Torino's multicultural vision celebrates in 2008 the vision that Truman articulated in defense of the Korean conflict fifty-seven years earlier. Indeed, in the film's final scenes we see two indications of the global community that Truman sought. First, when Walt is murdered, it is a Hmong police officer who informs Thao and Sue, and he does so in Hmong—a clear indication of

Azcona's claim that the Hmong have become part of the nation (in this case, a representative of the state) without sacrificing their ethnicity. Second, in the final scene, we see Tao driving Walt's Gran Torino, a scene which, Azcona explains, shows that Thao now "shares with Walt a set of values that, like the borderlands, cut across different nations, races and cultures"; as she concludes, "His sacrifice allows Thao a future and, at the same time, the continuation of the values represented by Walt."[70] In this manner, the film recalls the rescued orphan trope of earlier films by asserting again that American sacrifices enable others, here in the sense of forging a newly inclusive nation.[71]

The Korean War's filmography is not nearly as robust as that of its predecessor or successor conflicts. Yet the films that have emerged about this conflict play a key role in shaping ideas about US militarism and the United States' role in the world. Those narratives have evolved over time. In the first decade after the war, Americans wondering how the nation that had won the Second World War had ended up in a stalemate in Korea found little balm in films like *Hold Back the Night* and *War Hunt*. The former presented a brutal, bewildering conflict in which the violence had little purpose; the latter countered narratives that celebrated Korean adoption by casting Korean children as victimized by a brutal US military. By the twenty-first century, however, *Gran Torino* had restored the Korean War's prominence while giving voice to conservative discourses about the need to recover American exceptionalism through a renewed will to sacrifice. If films about the Korean War thus initially highlighted the perils of the United States' commitment to an interventionist foreign policy and challenged exceptionalist narratives of inclusion and global leadership, after Vietnam they came to embrace and defend those notions. Considering these films together, it becomes clear that, while the Korean War remains the United States' "Forgotten War," its films nonetheless play an important role in the construction of national identity, one that has evolved over the course of the twentieth and twenty-first centuries.

NOTES

1. Barack Obama, "Remarks by the President at 60th Anniversary of the Korean War Armistice," July 27, 2013, The White House, obamawhitehouse.archives.gov/the-press-office/2013/07/27/remarks-president-60th-anniversary-korean-war-armistice; Mark R. Franklin, "Biography: Paik Sun Yup," New Jersey Korean War Memorial, n.d., www.nj.gov/military/korea/biographies/yup.html; Ian Livingston, "D.C. Area Forecast: Humidity Returns Today, Turning Wetter Into Sunday," *Washington Post*, July 27, 2013.

2. Obama, "Remarks by the President at 60th Anniversary of the Korean War Armistice."

3. Kristin Ann Hass, *Sacrificing Soldiers on the National Mall* (Berkeley: University of California Press, 2013), 33, 32–33, 39.

4. To compare Obama's speech and Bill Clinton's 1995 speech, see Hass, *Sacrificing Soldiers,* 68–69.

5. Melinda L. Pash, *In the Shadow of the Greatest Generation: The Americans Who Fought the Korean War* (New York: New York University Press, 2012), 1.

6. My assessment of this history is based on two popular lists of Korean War films: "List of Korean War Films," Wikipedia, undated, en.wikipedia.org/wiki/List_of_Korean_War_films#United _States; ferreiracarlos1504, "Korea War in Films," Internet Movie Database, March 19, 2012, www .imdb.com/list/ls003730943/. See also Andrew J. Huebner, *The Warrior Image: Soldiers in American Culture from the Second World War to the Vietnam Era* (Chapel Hill: University of North Carolina Press, 2008), 135.

7. Pash, *In the Shadow of the Greatest Generation,* 2.

8. Jay Winter, "Thinking About Silence," in *Shadows of War: A Social History of Silence in the Twentieth Century,* ed. Efrat Ben-Ze'ev, Ruth Ginio, and Jay Winter (Cambridge, UK: Cambridge University Press, 2010), 4, 5.

9. Pash, *In the Shadow of the Greatest Generation,* 92.

10. Jay Winter, *Remembering War: The Great War Between Memory and History in the Twentieth Century* (New Haven, CT: Yale University Press, 2006), 3.

11. For useful brief histories of the war, see Odd Arne Westad, *The Cold War: A World History* (New York: Penguin, 2017), 159–82, and Arissa Oh, *To Save the Children of Korea: The Cold War Origins of Interracial Adoption* (Palo Alto, CA: Stanford University Press, 2015), 20–22.

12. Scott Laderman, "War and Film," in *At War: The Military and U.S. Culture in the Twentieth Century and Beyond,* ed. David Kieran and Edwin A. Martini (New Brunswick, NJ: Rutgers University Press, 2017), 315.

13. Huebner, *The Warrior Image,* 149–50.

14. Pash, *In the Shadow of the Greatest Generation,* 92, 95.

15. Westad, *The Cold War,* 174.

16. Pash, *In the Shadow of the Greatest Generation,* 96.

17. *Hold Back the Night,* dir. Alan Dwan, www.youtube.com/watch?v=mKFqKspgDFg.

18. Westad, *The Cold War,* 171.

19. Pash, *In the Shadow of the Greatest Generation,* 95.

20. That security, of course, was highly racialized. See Ira Katznelson, *When Affirmative Action Was White: An Untold Story of Racial Inequality in Twentieth Century America* (New York: W. W. Norton & Co., 2005), 113–41; the "Homesteading Veteran" is on the cover of the January 20, 1947, issue of *Life* magazine.

21. Pash, *In the Shadow of the Greatest Generation,* 11.

22. Huebner, *The Warrior Image,* 149.

23. Huebner, *The Warrior Image,* 153.

24. See, for example, Kara Dixon Vuic, *The Girls Next Door: Bringing the Home Front to the Front Lines* (Cambridge, MA: Harvard University Press, 2019), 227–28.

25. Harry S. Truman, "Radio and Television Address to the American People on the Situation in Korea," July 19, 1950, in *The American Presidency Project,* ed. Gerhard Peters and John T.

Woolley, www.presidency.ucsb.edu/documents/radio-and-television-address-the-american-people
-the-situation-korea.

26. Pash, *In the Shadow of the Greatest Generation*, 30, 185–86.

27. Westad, *The Cold War*, 182.

28. Harry S. Truman, "Proclamation 2914—Proclaiming the Existence of a National Emergency," December 16, 1950, *The American Presidency Project*, ed. Peters and Woolley, www.presidency.ucsb.edu/documents/proclamation-2914-proclaiming-the-existence-national-emergency.

29. Oh, *To Save the Children of Korea*, 22, 2–3, 24.

30. Christina Klein, *Cold War Orientalism: Asia in the Middlebrow Imagination, 1945–1969* (Berkeley: University of California Press, 2003), 189–90.

31. Laderman, "War in Film," 315.

32. Oh, *To Save the Children of Korea*, 19, 32–33, 35, 36–37.

33. Oh, *To Save the Children of Korea*, 36.

34. Melani McAlister, *Epic Encounters: Culture, Politics, and U.S. Interests in the Middle East, 1945–2000* (Berkeley: University of California Press, 2001), 186.

35. Patrick Hagopian, *The Vietnam War in American Memory: Veterans, Memorials, and the Politics of Healing* (Amherst: University of Massachusetts Press, 2011), 37.

36. Susan Jeffords, *The Remasculinization of America: Gender and the Vietnam War* (Bloomington: Indiana University Press, 1989); Jeffords, *Hard Bodies: Hollywood Masculinity in the Reagan Era* (New Brunswick, NJ: Rutgers University Press, 1994).

37. William Beard, "*Gran Torino*: Clint Eastwood as Fallen Saviour," *CineAction* 85 (2011): 38.

38. Jeffords, *Hard Bodies*, 182, 183, 185.

39. Beard, "*Gran Torino*," *38;* Jeffords, *Hard Bodies*, 180–81.

40. Pash, *In the Shadow of the Greatest Generation*, 219.

41. Beard, "*Gran Torino*," 40.

42. Beard, "*Gran Torino*," 38, 40, 42.

43. Of course, this is a familiar trope in post-Vietnam "hard body" films of the sort Eastwood is famous for; see Jeffords, *Hard Bodies*.

44. Maria De Mar Azcona, "The Boy Next Door: Transnational Masculinity in *Gran Torino*," *Transnational Cinemas* 4, no. 1 (2013): 34.

45. This scene is also recounted in Azcona, "The Boy Next Door," 30 and 34, and Beard, "Gran Torino," 41. For a concise history of the role of the Hmong in the Second Indochina War, see Ma Vang, "The Refugee Soldier: A Critique of Recognition and Citizenship in the Hmong Veterans' Naturalization Act of 1997," *Positions: Asia Critique* 20, no. 3 (2012): 687–88.

46. For one articulation of this view, see Mark Moyar, *Triumph Forsaken: The Vietnam War, 1954–1965* (Cambridge, UK: Cambridge University Press, 2006), 140.

47. Vang, "The Refugee Soldier," 695, 688–89.

48. Ronald Reagan, "Peace: Restoring the Margin of Safety," Address to the Veterans of Foreign Wars Convention, August 18, 1980, Ronald Reagan Presidential Library and Museum, www.reaganlibrary.gov/8–18–80.

49. Vang, "The Refugee Soldier," 687.

50. Here I agree with Azcona's argument in "The Boy Next Door," which I discuss in greater detail below.

51. Beard, "*Gran Torino*," 41; Azcona, "The Boy Next Door," 34–35.

52. Reagan, "Peace: Restoring the Margin of Safety."

53. Beard, "*Gran Torino*," 39.

54. Here I disagree with critics like Beard, who view the film as a renunciation of violent confrontation ("*Gran Torino*," 42).

55. Harry S. Truman, "Special Message to the Congress on Greece and Turkey: The Truman Doctrine," March 12, 1947, *The American Presidency Project*, ed. Peters and Wooley, www.presidency.ucsb.edu/documents/special-message-the-congress-greece-and-turkey-the-truman-doctrine.

56. Harry S. Truman, "Special Message to the Congress Requesting Additional Appropriations for Defense," December 1, 1950, *The American Presidency Project*, ed. Peters and Wooley, www.presidency.ucsb.edu/documents/special-message-the-congress-requesting-additional-appropriations-for-defense.

57. Harry S. Truman, "Address at the Cornerstone Laying of the New York Avenue Presbyterian Church," April 3, 1951, *The American Presidency Project,* ed. Peters and Wooley, www.presidency.ucsb.edu/documents/address-the-cornerstone-laying-the-new-york-avenue-presbyterian-church.

58. Laderman, "War in Film," 317.

59. Beard, "*Gran Torino*," 39.

60. George H. W. Bush, "The President's News Conference," November 30, 1990, *The American Presidency Project,* ed. Peters and Wooley, www.presidency.ucsb.edu/documents/the-presidents-news-conference-19. On Walt's role as a "fixer," see Azcona, "The Boy Next Door," 26.

61. Beard, "*Gran Torino*," 42.

62. Reagan, "Peace: Restoring the Margin of Safety"; Azcona, "The Boy Next Door," 38.

63. Vang, "The Refugee Soldier," 685, 695.

64. As Azcona argues, "in *Gran Torino* Walter is forced to fight and revise his racial prejudices through his reluctant contact with the Hmong family next door" ("The Boy Next Door," 29).

65. Harry S. Truman, "Address in Philadelphia at the Dedication of the Chapel of the Four Chaplains," February 3, 1951, *The American Presidency Project,* ed. Peters and Wooley, www.presidency.ucsb.edu/documents/address-philadelphia-the-dedication-the-chapel-the-four-chaplains.

66. Harry S. Truman, "Address in San Francisco at the Opening of the Conference on the Japanese Peace Treaty," September 4, 1951, *The American Presidency Project*, ed. Peters and Wooley, www.presidency.ucsb.edu/documents/address-san-francisco-the-opening-the-conference-the-japanese-peace-treaty.

67. Azcona, "The Boy Next Door," 32, 38.

68. Beard, "*Gran Torino*," 40.

69. Truman, "Address in Philadelphia at the Dedication of the Chapel of the Four Chaplains."

70. Azcona, "The Boy Next Door," 36, 38.

71. Azcona, "The Boy Next Door," 38; Beard, "*Gran Torino*," 41.

We Have Seen the Enemy and He Is Us

Hollywood, the Cold War, and Battling the Enemy Within

JESSICA M. CHAPMAN

n the opening decade of the Cold War, the United States waged battle against communism as vigorously at home as it did abroad. The two superpowers emerged from the Second World War as geopolitically hostile as they were ideologically irreconcilable. As the Iron Curtain descended across Europe, an apocalyptic nuclear arms race developed between the United States and the Soviet Union, fueled by an almost hysterical mutual suspicion rooted in opposing worldviews and cemented by historical experience. By 1950, the year Joseph McCarthy steered American anti-communism to paranoid new heights, the territorial bounds of the conflict spread from Europe to Asia with the "loss" of China to communism, followed shortly thereafter by the outbreak of war in Korea. Americans understood the conflict in Manichean terms as a battle of good versus evil, a struggle for the "soul of mankind," in which a nefarious communist conspiracy threatened to extinguish American ideals of freedom, democracy, capitalism, and their attendant virtues at home and across the globe.[1] Communists in the United States, longstanding targets of political repression who had enjoyed a brief respite during the Popular Front period in the 1930s, were recast in the postwar years as criminal conspirators, acting universally in service of the Kremlin, who were bent on destroying American society and bringing down its government.

The red scare that gripped the United States in the late 1940s and early 1950s originated in the halls of power, as President Harry Truman launched a federal loyalty and security program, while hyperbolizing the communist threat in his 1947 Truman Doctrine speech. His Republican opponents in Congress, aided by the FBI, led the charge against leftists by calling suspected communists and fellow travelers before the House Un-American Activities Committee (HUAC) in what amounted to a series of well-publicized show trials. The anti-communist fervor soon trickled down to state legislatures, school boards, and private organizations like the American Legion, all of which did their part to surveil their communities with the goal of identifying and eliminating communists in their midst. A liberal anti-communist consensus also emerged, as organizations like the American Civil Liberties Union (ACLU) and the National Association for the Advancement of Colored People (NAACP) policed their own memberships in keeping with Cold War verities, largely as a means of inoculating themselves against suspicion amidst a deepening witch hunt. In the early Cold War, anti-communism percolated throughout American society, shaping the nation's culture and society in myriad ways. Through browbeating and intimidation, anti-communist crusaders worked to forge a new—highly circumscribed—national identity that exalted the virtues of conformity, prosperity, and religious piety while vilifying communism as its antithesis.[2]

The excesses of the domestic anti-communist movement reached their peak from 1950 to 1954 with the irresponsible smear campaign of Joseph McCarthy, the junior senator from Wisconsin. McCarthy's anti-communism, a self-serving media blitz based on lies and half-truths, was never justified. Indeed, in hindsight his actions seem to render domestic anti-communism almost indefensible. But McCarthy did not create the red scare; he simply exploited the deep-seated fear of communism that already pervaded American society. Without question, the Communist Party of the United States (CPUSA) invited suspicion through its fealty to the Kremlin and by recruiting spies in the State Department and the Manhattan Project. Ellen Schrecker, perhaps the most fervent scholarly critic of McCarthyism, concedes that "it was on some level a rational response to what was then perceived to be a real threat to American security."[3] But the threat, while not a complete fantasy, was dramatically exaggerated. In her view, and that of most historians today, the gross violations of individual civil liberties carried out in the name of national security were a travesty of justice and a much greater violation of the American system than communism ever threatened. Yet the debate is not entirely settled. Historians Harvey Klehr and John Earl Haynes challenge the "revisionist" view that American communism was simply a benign, idealistic, homegrown movement targeted unfairly by hysterical anti-communists. Instead, they maintain, recently declassified Venona transcripts and Soviet documents released in the late 1990s make clear that the communist threat was real, and that measures to combat it within the United States were reasonable and justified.[4]

This historiographical debate over who constituted the real enemies in early Cold War America—communists or their persecutors—continues a conversation that has taken place in the United States, not least on on the silver screens of Hollywood, since the early 1950s. It boils down to a conflict between two competing versions of American national identity. One view holds that the United States is a heterodox and eminently mutable land of refuge, equality, and free expression, a country ripe for sweeping changes that could bring its imperfect practices closer into alignment with its lofty founding principles. Taken to the other extreme, it is a Christian, capitalist society, founded by heteronormative Anglo-Saxons, a model society to be defended not only against threats from outside its borders, but from outside of the social categories it represents. This conflict in American society between liberal progressivism and conservatism was not unique to the age of McCarthy; more unique was the extent to which anti-communists succeeded in leveraging the threat of communist infiltration to promote their brand of Americanism at the expense of all others.

In the early Cold War era, as Hollywood became a chief target of red baiters, the range of acceptable political expression on screen narrowed considerably. As historian John Sbardellati has demonstrated, the persecution of communists in Hollywood by HUAC and the FBI, followed by Hollywood's own embrace of a stifling blacklist, augured the death of the "social problem film."[5] Movies tackling nettlesome issues like class conflict, labor relations, and racial strife were branded communist propaganda and shut down. From the late 1940s on, films that took a political stand at all almost universally reflected, and promoted, the core tenets of domestic anti-communism. Communists in early Cold War films like *I Was a Communist for the FBI* (1951) were, without question, the enemies within, bent on destroying American society and bringing down the US government. By the late 1950s and early 1960s, the rigid Cold War consensus that had straitjacketed Hollywood began to slacken, making room for films that challenged some of its premises, while in some cases continuing to uphold others. McCarthyism emerged in a classic political thriller, *The Manchurian Candidate* (1962), as a force as malevolent as that which it claimed to thwart, but communists were far from vindicated in the process. Just two years later, a black satire, *Dr. Strangelove* (1964) presented a much more full-throated attack on the foundations of anti-communist logic and the military and cultural perversions it fostered.

More recent films about the red scare, produced years after the collapse of the Soviet Union and in the eclipse of the wave of American triumphalism that greeted it, coincide with the prevailing scholarly consensus that the red baiters themselves were the enemies within. Two historical dramas, *Good Night and Good Luck* (2005) and *Trumbo* (2015), present two key figures in the domestic Cold War—CBS newsman Edward R. Murrow, who helped take down Joseph McCarthy, and Dalton Trumbo, of Hollywood Ten fame—as noble American leftists who took on their anti-communist accusers. In these films it is those accusers who sacrificed the lofty values and individual freedoms for which the United States stands in pursuit of a witch hunt that was at best hysterical, and at worst cynically egomaniacal and xenophobic.

Years before the blacklist came into force, the seeds of Hollywood's Cold War were sown by FBI Director J. Edgar Hoover, the 1940s' most influential anti-communist. Under his leadership, the FBI sought to criminalize the Communist Party by prosecuting it under the 1940 Smith Act's provisions against teaching and advocating government overthrow by force and violence.[6] Unlike the flamboyant Senator McCarthy, who lent his name to the seedier aspects of the red scare, Hoover was more comfortable maneuvering behind the scenes, rarely offering up his views to the public. His March 26, 1947, testimony before HUAC, a public utterance as illuminating as it was rare, provides a window into his worldview, a worldview that did much to shape the popular consciousness of the era and pervaded the films that Hollywood produced for the ensuing decade. In no uncertain terms, he warned that the communist movement in the United States "stands for the destruction of our American form of government; it stands for the destruction of American democracy; it stands for the destruction of free enterprise; and it stands for the creation of a 'Soviet of the United States' and ultimate world revolution." The "greatest menace of communism," to Hoover, was its agents' ability to "infiltrate and corrupt various spheres of American life."

Hoover warned that fellow travelers and Communist Party sympathizers were even more dangerous than open, card-carrying members because of their capacity to operate in stealth, using the well-developed Soviet propaganda machine to co-opt and exploit liberal causes undetected. Even before the Second World War ended, Hoover and the FBI had trained their sights on Hollywood as one of the most dangerous hotbeds of communist activity. Communist propaganda, they held, could be projected ever so subtly on-screen, thereby poisoning the minds of millions of Americans. Since communist messaging was dangerous exactly because it was so hard to detect, the FBI, with the help of HUAC, sought to purge the industry of known or suspected communists and their sympathizers as a means of preventing them from spreading their insidious propaganda. This was consistent with Hoover's conviction that the best antidote to Communist subversion was "vigorous, intelligent, old-fashioned Americanism with eternal vigilance." He promised that victory would be assured "once Communists are identified and exposed, because the public will take the first step of quarantining them so they can do no harm."[7] The need for this vigilance extended far beyond the halls of government and the studios of Tinseltown. Communist teachers, labor organizers, civil rights activists, and even medical professionals could just as easily infect the minds of Americans with their political disease, calling for vigilance at all levels of society. Americans were called to police their neighbors, and their own behavior, to protect the nation from the enemy within.

After the notorious Hollywood Ten trials in 1947, which resulted in contempt-of-Congress charges and stints in jail for the accused, Hollywood instituted a blacklist to police itself. In the late 1940s and early 1950s, as hundreds of leftist writers, directors, actors, and producers were purged from the ranks of film-making, a number of studios produced blatantly anti-communist propaganda films that served both to spread the basic tenets of "Hooverism" and to fend off suspicion by demonstrating loyalty to the anti-communist cause. Agitprop films like Gordon Douglass's *I Was a Communist for the FBI* (1951) were clearly produced to appease red-baiting critics, but also to cash in on the anti-communist hysteria sweeping the country at the height of McCarthy's crusade.[8] The film was a highly embellished version of the true story of double-agent Matt Cvetic. In what Sbardellati calls a "ludicrous stretching of the category's boundaries," it received an Academy Award nomination for best documentary. Yet Hoover, repulsed by Cvetic's personal degeneracy and self-aggrandizing tendencies, refused FBI cooperation with the production and would not endorse the final product, despite how closely its message hewed to the core tenets of his anti-communist ideology.

The communists in *I Was a Communist for the FBI* are racketeers and thugs acting directly in service of the Kremlin. Cvetic declares on screen that the American Communist Party "is actually a vast spy system founded . . . by the Soviet . . . composed of American traitors whose only purpose is to deliver the people of the United States into the hands of Russia as a colony of slaves." Conjuring up images of a criminal underworld, lurking in dark shadows and sneaking around to avoid detection, the communists in this film embody the typically sinister filmic representations of the era.[9] Utterly devoid of ideological commitment, their cynical involvement with social causes like civil rights and labor organizing serves only to advance their nefarious scheme to stir up racial and class conflict in American society where, it is implied, none exists organically. As Tony Shaw writes in *Hollywood's Cold War,* "The Communist party did not stand *for* anything, only against sacred American principles such as God, motherhood, and true love."[10]

At a Communist Party meeting held to recruit African Americans, Cvetic voices over the following comment: "Pittsburgh was too quiet, too peaceful. So they cooked up a hell-brew of hate from a recipe written in the Kremlin. It was the same old line they'd used for years on all racial minorities to create unrest and confusion." He goes on to note, "There are more ways than one to sabotage the safety of a country. The one he used was as dangerous as blowing up defense plants. It was the old rule of divide and conquer." Avowedly, the goal of the meeting is to stir up racial violence that would result in blacks killing whites, thereby creating an opportunity for the Communist Party to gain propaganda points by coming to the former's defense. The film presents this as a longstanding communist strategy to manipulate putatively gullible African Americans, for whom the communists can barely conceal their distain, into serving the party's objective of creating divisions and disharmony in American life. In a subsequent conversation with his FBI handlers, Cvetic comments that this was the same strategy the communists had used to start race riots in Detroit in 1943. "Those poor fellows," he laments, "never knew their death warrants had been signed in Moscow."

The communists similarly stir the pot at a union meeting where, according to Cvetic, "The commies used the same plan of campaign that has put them in power time and again." They planned to plant "a small group of specialists"—a few on the executive board and a few on the meeting floor—to out-talk, outlast, and outmaneuver legitimate union members until they could force a strike. To garner sympathy for the cause, they arrange to have female party members show up at the picket lines, dressed as union members' wives. And they import party members from New York to pose as scabs, injecting a dose of violence into the strike in the form of metal pipes wrapped in Jewish newspapers. Every move they make is intended to generate ethnic, racial, and class divisions rooted in falsehoods. With the union chairman and three members of the board en route to the hospital, one of the party leaders concluded, "That's a pretty good day's work."

Just as civil rights groups and labor organizations are shown to be infiltrated by communist saboteurs in *I Was a Communist for the FBI,* so too are schools.

Lending credence to Hoover's conviction that schools served as breeding grounds for communism, Cvetic's son's teacher, Eve Merrick, turns out to be a red. An idealist drawn to communism's socially transformative ideals, she seeks to indoctrinate adolescent minds with party ideology. "And," she asks, "what better field could I find to work than in a high school?" Demonstrating the broad scope of the problem and the need for widespread vigilance in rooting out subversives, Eve claims to be one of thirty-one teachers in her party branch. In the cosmology of early Cold War America, communist influences in schools served not only to threaten children, but to undermine entire American families at a time when "the ideology of domesticity was not only reaffirmed but also linked to national security."[11]

As Elaine Tyler May has argued, good Americans were expected to abide by traditional gender roles, contained within nuclear families, through which they could raise patriotic Americans capable of defending the country against communists in their midst, while also preparing to survive an impending nuclear attack.[12] Eve's deviation from traditional femininity in the form of Communist Party membership therefore represents a threat to national security in concrete and symbolic ways. But her ultimate rejection of the party for its brutality, and for "making a mockery of freedom," serves as a tale of redemption. Though her character starts off as the embodiment of the red seductress, she becomes a symbol of the virtue associated with the 1950s American woman. Once she saw the Communist Party for what it really was, she was compelled to flee its evil grasp and embrace the Americanism that truly represented the freedoms she desired.

The role of religion as a cornerstone of that Americanism, the antithesis of "godless communism," also pervades I Was a Communist for the FBI. Although Cvetic's character suffers grave personal consequences for his known Communist Party membership, he jealously guards the secret of his FBI affiliation, for fear of compromising his patriotic mission. The one notable exception is that he freely discusses his FBI ties with his priest. "That Cvetic could trust his priest with such knowledge," writes Sbardellati, "but not his son, or even his mother (who dies before learning of her son's true patriotism), suggests the high esteem for the church as a most trusted American institution."[13] By contrast, to demonstrate the contempt with which communists approached religion and the American values it upheld, and to drive home their basic inhumanity, the film shows Cvetic's comrades openly mocking the church, even at his mother's funeral. In this and several other overtly anti-communist films of the era, communists were positioned as foreigners not only by extraction, but through their active rejection of a panoply of fundamental American values.

John Frankenheimer's 1962 political thriller, *The Manchurian Candidate,* based on Richard Condon's 1959 novel of the same name, deviates from the stark Manichean plotlines of earlier Cold War films like *I Was a Communist for the FBI* by locating the enemies of the American political system and its underlying values both within and outside of the body politic. As Matthew Frye Jacobson and Gaspar González write, it "appeared at a peculiar juncture in the nation's political life—that moment when McCarthy had been so thoroughly discredited that a sound satirical thrashing was possible, but yet when the communist threat and McCarthyite vocabulary retained enough salience that a communist plot to take over the White House could provide the stuff, not just for camp, but for a plausibly compelling political thriller."[14] The lead character, Raymond Shaw, returns from the Korean War brainwashed by Chinese and Soviet communist operatives, transformed into a killing machine designed to facilitate a plot to seize control of the presidency. By the film's denouement we come to learn that his handler was none other than his mother, Eleanor, the embodiment of political, cultural, and sexual perversion, and also the puppet master behind her McCarthy-esque husband, Johnny Iselin.

The true villain of the film, Eleanor had convinced the communist powers to use her compromised son to install her husband, through whom she would control the government, in the Oval Office. The message is clear: threats to American democracy abound in the form of deception and false prophets, whether they be homegrown demagogues or foreign conspirators. Democracy depends on truth and light, both of which had been obscured in the early years of the Cold War by the thought-control projects unleashed by communists and McCarthyites alike. *The Manchurian Candidate* represents not a plea to abandon the vigilance Hoover urged, but to broaden the scope of subversive forces Americans should stand vigilant against.

The film's focus on Raymond's tortured relationship with his mother speaks to a prominent current in the ideology of America's domestic Cold War. Many feared that moral decline and so-called degeneracy posed a direct threat to national security by weakening the foundations of American civilization and rendering it vulnerable to communist infiltration. Mothers were positioned at the vanguard of the nation's fight against such moral slippage. J. Edgar Hoover himself opined in a 1944 article entitled "Mothers . . . Our Only Hope" that women's "patriotic duty" was "on the home front!" He warned that "parental incompetence and neglect" were the primary causes of perversion and crime.[15] On one end of the spectrum, women who smothered their sons with excessive affection and overprotection could make them weak and passive, perhaps even homosexual. On the opposite extreme, represented by Raymond's mother, were women who forsook their roles as the backbones of that central Cold War institution, the nuclear family. Eleanor, emotionally cold, manipulative, and lacking even a shred of maternal instinct, cheats on her husband, sacrificing her marriage and neglecting her son on the altar of personal ambition.

Raymond's treatment at the hands of his mother renders him incapable of meaningful human connection. He seems to overcome this affliction, briefly, in his relationship with Josie, the daughter of Eleanor and Johnny's chief political enemy. But his mother quickly sabotages this bourgeoning love affair, leading Raymond to despair, "I have been even less lovable than I was, since." That moment, he claims, is when he began to hate her. "It's a terrible thing," he laments, "to hate your mother." Indeed, the film makes clear that his emotionally stunted nature, stemming from his mother's deviancy, is what rendered him the ideal subject for the communist thought-control project. As Matthew Dunne argues, societal concerns about a "troubling new softness in American men," supposedly wrought by maternal failures, fueled Americans' anxieties about their susceptibility to brainwashing.[16]

Eleanor's husband, Johnny, is a variation on the dangerously weak male figure, akin to Joseph McCarthy. Released eight years after McCarthy's downfall in the 1954 Army-McCarthy hearings, *The Manchurian Candidate* was one of the first robust satires of the junior senator from Wisconsin, and remains among the best. Iselin, the real Manchurian candidate of the film, controlled entirely by his malevolent wife, appears in only ten brief scenes. But those scenes paint a clear picture of a spineless, vapid political icon whose political pageantry is particularly suited to the medium of television. The film seems to suggest that television, which spread rapidly throughout the country just as McCarthy launched his anti-communist crusade, facilitated a form of mass brainwashing that differed from, but complemented, the project of direct mind control to which Raymond was subject.[17] This bears out Dunne's claim that, "by the end of the 1950s, brainwashing as no longer perceived as a uniquely Communist threat, but had emerged as an internal enemy linked to capitalism and a decadent America."[18]

In reserving its condemnation for McCarthy's clearly disingenuous motives and deceptive, ramrod tactics, *The Manchurian Candidate* lets the broader project of domestic anti-communism off the hook. The film does not quibble with the substance of Iselin's anti-communism; to the contrary, it indicts his brash televised tirades as lacking substance altogether. Through Iselin, *The Manchurian Candidate* makes clear that McCarthy used abhorrent tactics of deception of fear mongering to manipulate anti-communist sentiment in dangerous ways, but it leaves intact the notion that Chinese and Soviet communists aimed to subvert the American political system by infiltrating its key institutions. Anti-communism, divorced from McCarthyite tactics, escapes the film's critique.

If *The Manchurian Candidate* challenges some of the verities of the Cold War while upholding others, Stanley Kubrick's classic 1964 black satire, *Dr. Strangelove*, launches a full frontal assault on its very premises. Released in 1964, it reflected a fraying of the Cold War consensus and, as Margot Henriksen writes, "Encapsulated the spirit and the substance of dissent in the 1960s, . . . relying on black humor to expose the deadly and irrational realities of life with the bomb."[19] Produced on the heels of the 1961 Berlin Crisis and the 1962 Cuban Missile Crisis that brought the world dangerously close to the brink of nuclear war, it eviscerated the nuclear deterrence strategy that underpinned the fragile Soviet-American standoff. Kubrick joined a chorus of voices rejecting Cold War foreign policy and the stifling value systems and cultural constraints that it had imposed on the generation that came of age in the early 1960s. The film— alongside an up-and-coming generation of college students who had grown up culturally and sexually straitjacketed by domestic anti-communism, and under the looming shadow of civil defense messages that "domesticated war and made military preparedness a family affair"—denounced the conformity and militarization of everyday life.[20]

Dr. Strangelove depicts a series of unfortunate events resulting in the total annihilation of mankind, events that, the film implies, were a natural outgrowth of the defense systems set in place by both the United States and the Soviet Union in the name of Mutually Assured Destruction (MAD), or brinksmanship. The clearly insane US General Jack T. Ripper sets the events in motion through his resort to "Plan R," a "retaliatory safeguard" put in place to enable the United States to launch a nuclear attack in case the chain of command was disrupted, leaving the president incapacitated. The purpose of this, we come to learn, was to lend credibility to the threat of nuclear deterrence. Out-of-control nuclear arsenals, after all, serve no strategic purpose if your foes are not persuaded of your willingness and ability to use them.

Unable to obtain the code from Ripper needed to call off the attack, a War

Room full of generals, the congenial but impotent President Merkin Muffley, the Soviet ambassador, and the wheelchair-bound ex-Nazi mad scientist Dr. Strangelove work to find a solution to the dilemma. Muffley initially seems to find common ground, and a mutual desire to avert catastrophe, in his telephone conversations with Soviet Premier Dimitri Kissoff. That is, until it is revealed that the Soviets had just developed a Doomsday Machine. We are told that this machine, also designed to lend credibility to Soviet deterrent power, would automatically detonate in the event of a nuclear attack, shrouding the Earth in a cloud of radiation for ninety-three years. Ironically, the Doomsday Machine's existence was yet to be announced, rendering it moot as a deterrent force. With no way to override the Doomsday Machine, the only possibility to save the planet rests with Washington's ability to call off the attack, or to assist the Soviets in shooting down the incoming American aircraft. Soviets and Americans working together succeed in thirty-three of thirty-four cases, but the cowboy Major T. J. "King" Kong, whose plane was damaged but not destroyed by a Soviet missile, never receives the message canceling his mission. Determined to carry out his orders in the face of technical failures, he ends up riding a missile bareback to its target, ensuring the end of the world.

The very premises of MAD are the chief target of Kubrick's satire, but he also takes steady aim at the paranoid nature of anti-communism that underpinned America's approach to the Soviet Union. General Ripper serves as the central vehicle for this critique. Ripper's insanity is most evident through his obsession with a communist plot to steal Americans' "precious bodily fluids" and sap them of their "essence." Explaining his decision to launch the attack, Ripper announces, "I can no longer sit back and allow communist infiltration, communist indoctrination, communist subversion, and the international communist conspiracy to sap and impurify all of our precious bodily fluids." He assumes that fluoridation, supposedly a bodily form of infiltration and chemical brainwashing, is the vehicle by which the communists carry out this conspiracy. Through Ripper's irrational fear of communist infiltration, Kubrick clearly makes a mockery of the anti-communist hysteria—and the fear of brainwashing—that gripped American society in the late 1940s and 1950s.

The film further critiques both the Soviet-American rivalry and the arms race as having taken on lives of their own, defying even the thinnest veneer of morality or rationality. This is most explicit in the character of Dr. Strangelove, who reveals his fascist nature by spontaneously blurting out "Mein Führer" instead of "Mr. President," as if possessed. In a thinly veiled reference to the totalitarian potential of scientific and technological development unrestrained by reason and humanity, his mechanized right hand jolts into a Nazi salute against his will, and even tries to strangle him as he speaks. After Major Kong's bomb goes off, guaranteeing global annihilation, he proposes a ludicrous plan for survival in mine shafts. Poking fun at early Cold War norms of gender, family, and sexuality, this plan appeals to the men in the war room for its eugenic requirement that they abandon monogamy to procreate with women selected for their sexual appeal, in a purportedly selfless effort to repopulate the human race.

Ultimately, unable to abandon Cold War assumptions of inevitable Soviet-American hostility, Buck Turgidson quickly raises concerns that the Soviets might, in a hundred years when it was safe to emerge from the shelters, utilize some big bomb they had stored away to take over the United States and co-opt its mine-shaft space. Just before the film cuts to a montage of mushroom clouds, he intones, "Mr. President, we must not allow a mine shaft gap!" Clearly, Kubrick implies, there is no limit to the illogic of the Cold War arms race.

Fast-forward to the twenty-first century. Years after the fall of the Berlin Wall and the collapse of the Soviet Union, and once the triumphalism with which most Americans greeted their Cold War victory had tarnished considerably, Hollywood revisited the postwar red scare. Two emblematic films, *Good Night, and Good Luck* (2005) and *Trumbo* (2015), present the domestic anticommunist projects of Joseph McCarthy and HUAC, respectively, as baseless and repugnant threats to the American body politic. Both period pieces hew fairly closely to the historical record, editorializing not only about the toxicity and moral squalor of red baiters, but also about the valor of those who dared to stand up to them, at great personal risk.

George Clooney's *Good Night, and Good Luck* tells the tale of CBS newsman Edward R. Murrow's famed takedown of Joseph McCarthy on his show, *See It Now*. This took place in the lead-up to the 1954 Army-McCarthy hearings in which the senator was finally undone, an undoing that Murrow is often credited with starting. Focused narrowly on the events of the newsroom, the film paints a picture of CBS leadership and staff nervously united behind Murrow, knowing his crusade is righteous, but fearful of the consequences should McCarthy's ire blow back on them.

Clooney utilizes original footage from Murrow's broadcasts to bring to life the characters he used to launch his attack on McCarthy. McCarthy speaks for himself throughout the film. And we hear directly from Milo Radulovich, an ethnic Serbian Air Force Reserve officer whom McCarthy targets for maintaining close relationships with his left-leaning father and sister, a charge that leads the Army to identify him as a security risk and strip him of his commission. We also see Annie Lee Moss, an African American communications clerk in the US Army Signal Corps whom the senator has named as a card-carrying member of the Communist Party. Murrow uses these individuals as vehicles to condemn the senator's vile tactics of implying guilt by association and making reckless accusations of communist affiliation without compelling evidence. In real life, Murrow broadcasts went a long way toward discrediting McCarthy's charges and rehabilitating his victims. Radulovich was reinstated by the Army, and Moss kept her job at the Pentagon.

Recent scholarship, however, has complicated Murrow's narrative by pointing to evidence that Moss did, indeed, have communist ties. Andrea Friedman argues compellingly that Moss, in her appearances before HUAC and McCarthy's subcommittee, played strategically upon racialized and gendered stereotypes of the "poor old colored woman" that would not be capable of the type of witting subversion of which she was accused.[21] This is not to say that Moss was a saboteur, for one of the main lessons of the mid-twentieth-century red scare is that communist political leanings did not necessarily imply the treasonous intentions that anti-communists charged. But, as Friedman points out, it reframes how we view Murrow's efforts to defend her and, by extension, the limits of his condemnation of McCarthy. By presenting Moss as a poor, defenseless woman who lacked the wit and guile to be a communist, rather than defending her right to belong to the political party of her choosing, Murrow made clear that he was willing to take on McCarthy's seedy tactics and false accusations, but not to issue a more fulsome defense of free speech and association. The film hints at this through Murrow's boss, William Paley, who points out that, amidst a litany of factual corrections to McCarthy's on-screen screed, the newsman neglects to point out that Alger Hiss was convicted not of treason, but of perjury. Was this, Paley asks, because Murrow was afraid of seeming to support a communist?

Despite its tight focus on the CBS newsroom and the Murrow-McCarthy exchange, Clooney weaves into the film several hints of the tense atmosphere of American life at the height of McCarthyite hysteria that can help explain Murrow's caution. Shirley and Joe Wershba sneak around, keeping their relationship a secret because CBS policy forbids the employment of married couples. "Their clandestine meetings and subtle communications," writes movie reviewer Roger Ebert, "raise our suspicions and demonstrate in a way how Mc-

Carthyism worked."[22] In a more direct display of how McCarthyism seeped into people's personal lives, forcing them to perform a rigid set of gender and sexual roles for fear of inviting suspicion, Clooney includes footage of Murrow's interview with then-closeted entertainer Liberace. Murrow, clearly bored with the assignment, and seemingly aware of the ridiculous nature of his question, asks, "Have you given much thought to getting married and eventually settling down?" Liberace, carefully avoiding references to gender, answers, "I want to someday find the perfect mate and settle down to what I hope will be a marriage that will be blessed by faith and that will be a lasting union." He subtly reveals a hint of truth by noting that he had been reading about Princess Margaret, who is "looking for her dream man, too."

The most tragic example of the toll exacted by McCarthyism in the film is Don Hollenbeck, a former CBS employee who had been fired in 1950 following a spate of attacks in a Hearst-owned newspaper accusing him of being a communist, which led advertisers to pull their spots from CBS. This was, writes Thomas Doherty, one of the ways that advertising dollars reinforced the red scare on the small screen in this era.[23] Hollenbeck, who responded to Murrow's assault on McCarthy by claiming he had "never been prouder of CBS," soon thereafter committed suicide. The film implies that he was despondent over having lost his career, and subsequently his family, as the result of an anti-communist smear campaign.

Good Night, and Good Luck offers a clear indictment of McCarthy as a bully more interested in assassinating people's characters for political gain than in protecting the country. It valorizes Murrow's willingness to stand up to him, and implores future journalists to apply the same vigilance in their reporting. Jay Roach's *Trumbo* (2015) picks up the critique of domestic anti-communism where *Good Night, and Good Luck* left off, this time focusing on HUAC and the Hollywood blacklist that paved the way for McCarthy's rise. In 1947, the same year the Hollywood Ten were brought before HUAC, J. Edgar Hoover claimed that "Communism, in reality, is not a political party. It is a way of life—an evil and malignant way of life."[24] And those in Hollywood with the ability to brainwash the American masses through their subtle but nefarious manipulation of film content were, he insisted, among the most dangerous communists. *Trumbo* roundly refutes that premise, arguing instead that the Communist Party was no less compatible with the American system—and no more deserving of being outlawed—than the Democratic Party or any other, for that matter. In defense of the First Amendment and the importance of free political expression, the film posits that adherence to communist beliefs and faith in American democracy were, even at the height of the Cold War, entirely compatible. As the title character, Dalton Trumbo, an avowed communist, explains to his daughter, "I love our country, and it's a good government, but anything good could be better."

Trumbo and his fellow travelers in Hollywood are, according to this film, American patriots, motivated by an arguably naive but sincere commitment to social justice that led them to embrace communism well before the Cold War grew hot. Far from the treacherous agents of a foreign power that Cold War era films made them out to be, Trumbo and his associates come off as victims of a senseless domestic political purge. As such, they were slow to recognize the ferocity of the anti-communist witch hunt bearing down on them. In the lead-up to the Hollywood Ten's 1947 appearance before HUAC, confident that they had the Constitution on their side, Trumbo joked about distributing a pamphlet stating, "Congress Unaware of the First Amendment," to which one of his fellow accused responded, "Oh, they're aware of it. They just don't give a shit. All they care about is this nice new war of theirs. These guys love war and this is a great one, because its vague, its scary, and its expensive. Anyone for it's a hero and anyone against it's a traitor." This line reflects the film's overall condemnation of red baiters' insincerity and political opportunism, not to mention their knee-jerk militarism.

For his determination to stand up for the rights of free speech and association, Trumbo was punished with an undeserved stint in jail for contempt of Congress, a place on the blacklist, economic hardship, familial strife, and the inability to claim credit for his Academy Award–winning scripts. In demonstrating the strain of the anti-communist witch hunt on Trumbo's personal life, the film implicitly challenges Cold War assumptions about gender and family. In Trumbo's case, a strong nuclear family marked by functional relationships between husband and wife, parent and child, and a commitment to core American principles of democracy and fairness was nearly torn apart by HUAC and the Hollywood blacklist. In other words, the social fabric necessary to sustain national vigor was threatened not by communists or bad mothers, but by the very project of domestic anti-communism.

And that project was not born of genuine concern about the dangers posed by communists in our midst, but of racism and xenophobia, particularly anti-Semitism. The villains in this story were not the communists, but the bigots who persecuted them. One character says of the anti-communist Motion Picture Alliance for the Preservation of American Ideals, "They're Nazis. They're just too cheap to buy the uniforms." And Hollywood gossip columnist Hedda Hopper's character cements the Nazi comparison by forcing a powerful producer to comply with her anti-communist purge by threatening to name names, "real names," before rattling off a list of Jewish monikers belonging to some of the industry's leading lights who were known to the public by their Aryanized screen names.

According to *Trumbo*, the title character and and those brave enough to stand up with him against the forces of oppression were largely responsible for bringing an end to the Hollywood blacklist. In retrospect, Trumbo was given credit for the award-winning scripts that he was forced to write under a pseudonym, and received a Writers Guild of America Laurel Award for advancing the literature of motion pictures. In his on-screen acceptance speech, he says, "The blacklist was a time of evil and no one who survived it came through untouched by evil." Pointing to scores of lost homes, jobs, families, and even lives, he argues that people were sucked into a vacuum of fear that swept up everyone in its path. "When you look back upon that dark time," Trumbo exhorted, "as I think you should now and again, it will do you no good to search for heroes or villains. There weren't any. There were only victims."

Some of the film's reviewers, however, were not convinced. Indeed, for some, Trumbo remains a villain, and the the film's effort to rehabilitate his image represents a dangerous rejection of reality. Patrick Buchanan, in a review titled, "Dalton Trumbo Had It Coming," writes, "Trumbo was not what Lenin would call a 'useful idiot,' a liberal simpleton. He was the real deal, a Bolshevik who followed every twist and turn in the Moscow party line."[25] And Ron Capshaw, pointing to Trumbo's Popular Front politics and defense of the Soviet Union during and after World War II, argues that "the image of him as a New Deal liberal hero defending civil liberties against homegrown fascists crumbles when you look into what he said and did in the 1940s and 1950s."[26] Though the pendulum in Hollywood may have swung from staunch anti-communism in the 1950s to impassioned defense of its victims in the early twenty-first century, the meaning of the postwar red scare remains up for debate.

The films discussed here, and many others of and about the red scare, depict a country at war with itself, revealing an ongoing debate about who constitutes the real enemy of Americanism. Consistent with Cold War orthodoxy, the films of the early 1950s posit communists—godless, soulless hypocrites bent on infiltrating and subverting solid American institutions to incite conflict—as the undisputed villains. While they always rely on American dupes, the communist masterminds behind these plots are alien forces, foreigners bent on extinguishing American freedoms in service of a tyrannical foreign power. The lofty ideals of social justice used to sway naive Americans to the communist cause are mere smoke screens, as evidenced by the frequently referenced realities of life under the brutal Soviet dictatorship. It would be a mistake, these films argue, to think of communism as a legitimate political philosophy deserving of constitutional protection. On the contrary, it is the criminal vehicle of a hostile foreign invasion that must be rooted out and destroyed.

As the Cold War consensus began to unravel, films emerged to challenge these premises. And recent films have turned the early Cold War narrative entirely on its head. In keeping with the overwhelming scholarly consensus that the domestic anti-communist movement was an extreme, and often tragic, overreaction to a very limited and misconstrued threat, they present a very different image of the country at war with itself. It is not communists but hysterical anti-communists that threaten to unravel the American system. Communists and fellow travelers, in these films, are not agents of a hostile foreign power, but idealists who believe communism offers solutions to pressing social problems. Prominent red-baiting organizations like HUAC, the FBI, the Hollywood Blacklist, the American Legion, and others are shown to consistently violate the civil liberties of communists, their sympathizers, and a host of vulnerable populations including immigrants, minorities, and homosexuals in ways that moved the United States closer to the totalitarian system that it claimed to oppose, while doing little to enhance national security. Those who carried out this witch hunt—Joseph McCarthy, HUAC, Hedda Hopper, and the like—were not motivated by genuine fear, but by petty hatreds and personal ambitions. The heroes were those leftists like Edward R. Murrow and Dalton Trumbo who put their necks out to condemn red baiters' abuses and defend core American freedoms of speech and association. In short, these post–Cold War films exalt the liberal progressive vision of American national identity that McCarthyites tried to quash.

These competing views on the mid-twentieth-century red scare provide a frame for thinking about some of today's most pressing issues. Is the country threatened by foreign infiltrators in the form of President Donald J. Trump, Russian agent? Or is our real national emergency the violent hoards of foreign invaders marching forth to penetrate the southern border? Or Islamic terrorists bent on infiltrating our institutions, poisoning our minds, and blowing us up? Is the country being overtaken by amoral opportunists in government, and their spineless followers, seeking to prey upon popular prejudices to justify scrapping the constitution, the liberal world order, and the environment for personal gain? Of course, these are real problems, not mere relics of Cold War culture. But, treating past as prologue, many of us look to the lessons of the McCarthy era to decode them, as evidenced by frequent references to Trump as a "modern day McCarthy" and his rejoinder that he is the victim of a "witch hunt." Perhaps we can all agree, "We have seen the enemy and he is us." But which of us is he, exactly?

NOTES

The expression "We have seen the enemy and he is us" is a parody of a message sent in 1813 from US Navy Commodore Oliver Hazard Perry to Army General William Henry Harrison after a victory in the War of 1812. Cartoonist Walt Kelly initially referred to it in a 1953 publication, *The Pogo Papers*, in which he first attacked McCarthyism. The quote exactly as cited in the title appeared in a 1970 anti-pollution poster for Earth Day.

1. George H. W. Bush's characterization of the Cold War aptly constitutes the title of Melvyn P. Leffler, *For the Soul of Mankind: The United States, the Soviet Union, and the Cold War* (New York: Hill and Wang, 2007).

2. Stephen J. Whitfield, *The Culture of the Cold War,* 2nd ed. (Baltimore: Johns Hopkins University Press, 1996), 53–57.

3. Ellen Schrecker and Philip Deery, *The Age of McCarthyism: A Brief History with Documents,* 3rd ed. (New York: Bedford/St. Martins, 2016), 3.

4. John Earl Haynes and Harvey Klehr, *In Denial: Historians, Communism, and Espionage* (San Francisco: Encounter, 2003).

5. John Sbardellati, *J. Edgar Hoover Goes to the Movies: The FBI and the Origins of Hollywood's Cold War* (Ithaca, NY: Cornell University Press, 2013), 193–95.

6. Schrecker and Deery, *The Age of McCarthyism,* 100.

7. J. Edgar Hoover, testimony, House Committee on Un-American Activities, *Hearing on H.R. 1884 and H.R. 2122,* 80th Cong., 1st sess., March 26, 1947, rpt. in Schrecker and Deery, *The Age of McCarthyism,* 101–7.

8. Dan Leab, "I Was a Communist for the FBI: Dan Leab Looks at a Classic Cold War Movie and the Shadowy Figure Who Inspired It," *History Today* 46, no. 12 (December 1996): 42–47.

9. Sbardellati, *J. Edgar Hoover Goes to the Movies,* 168.

10. Tony Shaw, *Hollywood's Cold War* (Amherst: University of Massachusetts Press, 2007), 51.

11. Sbardellati, *J. Edgar Hoover Goes to the Movies,* 174.

12. Elaine Tyler May, *Homeward Bound: American Families in the Early Cold War Era* (New York: Basic Books, 1988).

13. Sbardellati, *J. Edgar Hoover Goes to the Movies,* 178–79.

14. Matthew Frye Jacobson and Gaspar González, *What Have They Built You to Do? The Manchurian Candidate and Cold War America* (Minneapolis: University of Minnesota Press, 2006), 83.

15. Quoted in Tyler May, *Homeward Bound,* 73.

16. Matthew W. Dunne, *A Cold War State of Mind: Brainwashing and Postwar American Society* (Boston: University of Massachusetts Press, 2016), 119.

17. Jacobson and González, *What Have They Built You to Do?* 85–86.

18. Dunne, *A Cold War State of Mind,* 5.

19. Margot A. Henriksen, *Dr. Strangelove's America: Society and Culture in the Atomic Age* (Berkeley: University of California Press, 1997), 309.

20. Laura McEnaney, *Civil Defense Begins at Home: Militarization Meets Everyday Life* (Princeton, NJ: Princeton University Press, 2000), 4.

21. Andrea Friedman, "The Strange Career of Annie Lee Moss: Rethinking Race, Gender, and McCarthyism," *Journal of American History,* September 2007, 446.

22. Roger Ebert, "Review of *Good Night, and Good Luck,*" RogerEbert.com, October 20, 2005.

23. Thomas Doherty, *Cold War, Cool Medium: Television, McCarthyism, and American Culture* (New York: Columbia University Press, 2003), 43.

24. J. Edgar Hoover, testimony, House Committee on Un-American Activities, *Hearing on H.R. 1884 and H.R. 2122,* 80th Cong., 1st sess., March 26, 1947, rpt. in Schrecker and Deery, *The Age of McCarthyism,* 107.

25. Patrick Buchanan, "Dalton Trumbo Had It Coming," www.realclearpolitics.com, November 6, 2015.

26. Ron Capshaw, "Film the Legend," www.lawliberty.org, November 30, 2015.

Survivors of Natural Disaster

American Identity in Vietnam War Films

MEREDITH H. LAIR

As anyone on the Eastern Seaboard will tell you, September 11, 2001, was a beautiful day. Temperatures were comfortably mild, humidity was low, and the skies above New York; Washington, DC; and Pennsylvania were clear and brilliant. The violence came without warning, obviously, but the day lacked even a forbidding overcast to set the tone. The terrorist attacks, and the forever war they initiated, came quite literally out of the blue. Or so we like to tell ourselves. As Marita Sturken argues in *Tourists of History*, Americans have a troubling tendency to imagine themselves as innocents, people whose lives are upended suddenly and without provocation. Sturken writes, "The narrative of innocence enabled the U.S. response [to 9/11] to avoid any discussion of what long histories of U.S. foreign policies had done to help foster a terrorist movement specifically aimed at the United States."[1] There is no need for thoughtful self-examination when violence erupts out of nowhere.

The same could be said of the Vietnam War, which likewise caught the American public unawares. Americans' surprise and confusion, by 1967, at being mired in a war that no one bothered to announce was partly due to the Johnson administration's deliberate efforts to obscure American escalation in South Vietnam. But Americans were (and remain) largely ignorant of how the great Arsenal of Democracy emboldened, buttressed, and finally replaced French imperial control in Indochina between 1940 and 1965. "And the war came" in Vietnam, to borrow a phrase from history.[2] But came from where? In his Second Inaugural Address, Lincoln uses elegantly succinct (and politically expedient) language—"and the war came"—to suggest that the Civil War was God's punishment toward North and South alike for practicing, perpetuating, and tolerating slavery. Contemporary Americans are uncomfortable with a biblical explanation for their suffering in Southeast Asia, and so colloquial explanations of the Vietnam War often imply that the war came not from God but from nature. In this formulation, Americans passively receive and endure war rather than create it. It is a neat rhetorical trick that avoids thorny questions of responsibility, guilt, and shame, galvanizing public audiences across time into communities of grief and outrage. They have nowhere to direct their fury except outward, at foreign enemies and the sky.

Hollywood likes a neat rhetorical trick, especially one that will not alienate a substantial market share. For over fifty years, Hollywood has depicted and engaged with the Vietnam War in dozens if not hundreds of films, with varying degrees of historical accuracy and artistic merit. These films do not so much demonstrate an evolution of thought on the Vietnam War as they suggest a persistent unwillingness to examine carefully American values, assumptions, and decisions that led to war in the first place. Taken chronologically, the canon is bracketed by two hawkish treatments, *The Green Berets* (1968) and *We Were Soldiers* (2002), that assert unapologetically the necessity and legitimacy of US intervention in South Vietnam. It concludes with an epilogue, *Rescue Dawn* (2006), that elides the war's politics and aftermath altogether. In between, a slew of famous, familiar, and often financially successful movies attempts to transport audiences back to the war zone for catharsis or thrill. The paradigmatic Vietnam War film tends to examine themes as old as war itself: violence as an essential component of manhood, violence as enduring trauma, and the unbridgeable divide between soldiers and civilians. Rarely do these films even hint at a complex political struggle or a clash between sophisticated and equally legitimate worldviews.

Where then, did the war in these films come from? Filmmakers' repeated failure to engage thoughtfully with the political and cultural underpinnings of the war's causes reduces the conflict to a natural disaster, rendering its violence an incomprehensible inevitability, like an earthquake or a hurricane. On film, Vietnam becomes a breeze that beckons to young adventurers, it looms like distant thunder for those hoping to avoid service, it lashes combatants, and it falls in a torrent over families navigating fear and loss. The characters must rise to the occasion or be swept away. Caught in a fight for survival, they do not have time to question how they came to be there, why their suffering is necessary, or how future suffering might be avoided. As a result, audiences learn little about the Vietnam War from film, except what we know of war itself: it is brutish, unfair, and seldom resolves anything.

Distant Thunder: Anticipating Vietnam in *Tigerland*

Though it takes place entirely at Fort Polk, Louisiana, in the fall of 1971, *Tigerland* (2000) is a Vietnam War film nonetheless. It follows a small group of recruits through the final weeks of Army training prior to deployment, culminating in a realistic, multiday exercise in Tigerland, which an officer describes as "the stateside province of Vietnam." In the film, the Vietnam War serves simultaneously as character, setting, and inciting incident. It is the reason for the recruits' military service: the war's violence draws racists and sociopaths who want to kill; its romanticism calls to the naive writer seeking to prove his masculinity; and the draft's cruel inequity ensnares blundering recruits who are not fit for duty. Vietnam serves as the film's moral landscape, and, via a mock Vietnamese village, it is the literal setting of the recruits' final training exercise. As a character, Vietnam lurks as the uncredited monster beyond the door, just as it was for millions of American men subject to the draft.

Tigerland focuses on three recruits whose opinions about the war and military service reflect conflicting strands of belief within the American public. The film's main protagonist is Roland Bozz, an intelligent, sensitive draftee from Texas whose cynical wit and anti-authoritarian streak render him a poor fit for the US Army. The audience recognizes Bozz's natural capacity for leadership early on, as he demonstrates competence but also compassion. Other soldiers respect and listen to him, yet his contempt for authority makes him reluctant to lead. Bozz befriends Jim Paxton, a Harvard-educated volunteer who joined the service in search of experiences to fill the pages of his Great American Novel. Bozz and Paxton's primary antagonist (besides the Army and the war) is Wilson, a sociopath so hollow and one-dimensional that the script does not even grant him a first name.

Taken as allegory, these characters embody Americans' conflicting perspectives on the Vietnam War as well as disparate representations of American identity. Bozz characterizes the war as killing women and children, and Paxton specifically (and critically) invokes the My Lai Massacre when a sergeant describes the war as brutal. When a training instructor demonstrates how to use a radio to torture prisoners during interrogation, Bozz walks away in disgust, asking, "Why would I ever want to do that to another human being?" No one in the film advances a political argument for the war's necessity, which thus positions the conflict as natural, inevitable, and ultimately pointless. But, when Bozz suggests Paxton jump off a railroad car "to break those legs and get out of this war," Paxton invokes a moral obligation to other Americans: "I enlisted, so there's a place for me. If I don't go, someone's going to take that place. If they die, they are dying for me." If Bozz and Paxton represent American decency and restraint, Wilson is the personification of American imperialism: he relishes violence and spews racism in the naked pursuit of power. During Tigerland's final war-games exercise, in which some of the men portray Vietnamese civilians, Wilson tears through the mock village just as Charlie Company tore through My Lai. Throughout the film, it repeatedly falls to Bozz to lead when Wilson fails to do so, and Bozz must repair the damage wrought by Wilson's ineptitude and rage.

The plot's central question is whether Bozz will fulfill his destiny as a born leader in the US Army, or whether he will flee responsibility by escaping to Mexico. Over the course of the film, Bozz consistently runs interference for vulnerable people, saving them from bullies, the Army, and themselves—a propensity for heroism that reflects the better angels of American nature but also the most generous interpretation of US intervention in Vietnam. For example, Bozz counsels two struggling draftees about their rights, enabling them to invoke Army regulations to get psychiatric and hardship discharges. And when Paxton starts to buckle psychologically, Bozz abandons his Mexico escape plan to spare his friend and the rest of the platoon from Wilson's toxic leadership. In the film's climactic moment, when Wilson (improbably) replaces the blanks in his rifle with live ammunition to murder Bozz, Bozz performs a final act of rescue. He discharges the muzzled weapon near Paxton's face, an intentional error that inflicts a million-dollar wound—an injury unlikely to be life-changing, but significant enough for medical discharge. Paxton's war is over before it even begins, while Bozz's war—against authority, incompetence, and cruelty—presumably continues. Paxton's final voice-over narration explains only that Bozz went to Vietnam, not what happened to him or whether he survived.

Like many Vietnam War films, *Tigerland* situates its central conflict between Americans, rather than between Americans and Vietnamese. The enemy is the Army's ruthless authoritarianism and Wilson's mindless infatuation with violence. The film does offer vague political commentary on the Vietnam War, in that the good characters regard the war as bad, and the bad characters regard the war as fun. But the hero goes off to war anyway—a war that is understood to be pointless, given that it is 1971, and the audience knows how and when the war will end. *Tigerland* leaves off there, never venturing to Vietnam and never determining Bozz's fate. It is an ambiguous, unsettling conclusion for a film, just as American withdrawal from Vietnam in 1973 was an ambiguous, unsettling conclusion for a war. In both cases—what the United States did for South Vietnam, and what Roland Bozz did for his fellow soldiers—the best that can be said is that some lives were spared and some troubles eased. The distant thunder quieted, and the storm moved on.

Swept Away: Survival and Recovery after Vietnam

Whereas *Tigerland* anticipates the Vietnam War from a distance, an entire sub-genre of Vietnam War films presents the war as an immediate and irresistible force that alters the trajectory of the characters' lives, sweeping them far from home and from themselves. If they survive and manage to return, it is to ruin, compelling them to make their lives anew. In these films, Vietnam is a calamity, the great flood after which nothing is the same. In *The Deer Hunter* (1978), *Born on the Fourth of July* (1989), and *Dead Presidents* (1995), the audience follows men from the home front into the war zone and then home again. The war wreaks havoc and inflicts wounds—physical, psychological, and moral—that veterans and their families spend years overcoming, if they overcome them at all. These narratives carry the audience from peace into perpetual violence, from order into perpetual chaos, and from health into perpetual infirmity. In these films, Americans are good soldiers who excel at making war but cannot win it, who surmount impossible physical obstacles but cannot overcome structural inequalities that undermine any hope of a good life. Americans often lose their strength, and they always lose their innocence, in film after film. These losses force audiences to consider, at least fictively, how Vietnam swept away the power, promise, and exceptionalism of post–World War II America.

As a foundational treatment of the Vietnam War, *The Deer Hunter* helped to establish this narrative arc, with a lengthy first act that establishes life before the war for a group of friends—Mike, Nick, and Steven—in Clairton, Pennsylvania, a fictional steel town where the sun never seems to shine. Theirs is an imperfect existence, full of poverty, violence, and uncertainty, but it is also thick with love, joy, and hope. Early scenes offer a visually arresting juxtaposition of grime and beauty, of affluence and disrepair. Stout bridesmaids in pink fabric confections walk down bleak, muddy streets. The bride emerges from her dingy house in full bridal kit but gets her dress stuck in the door. And Mike's car, a white 1959 Cadillac Coupe DeVille with fantastically enormous red-rocket tail fins, suggests the impractical tastes of a young man entering adulthood, but also nostalgia for a golden age of American manufacture that is clearly receding from memory.

The lavish wedding sequence in *The Deer Hunter* is the stuff of Hollywood legend, a budget-busting epic shot on location with hundreds of extras. As spectacle, the scene rivals the opening wedding in *The Godfather Part I*, but it also establishes key elements of the plot. Angela and Steven are young, fragile, and unprepared for married life. Nick and Linda are together, but Mike longs for her, and she is clearly torn between them. Vietnam intrudes, in the form of a Green Beret who enters the bar adjacent to the reception hall and refuses the boisterous invitations of three new recruits. "Sir! Sir!" they yell at him, announcing their plans to go to Vietnam. "I hope they send us where the bullets are flying!" says Nick arrogantly and, in retrospect, ominously. "Fuck it," is all the Green Beret mutters in reply. Most importantly, the wedding sequence establishes Clairton as a community with universally shared values. The wedding is so well attended, one imagines the whole town is there. Everyone shares in the happy couple's joy, and everyone endorses the soldier's path; there are no dissenters. When the band leader introduces the wedding party, he introduces Mike and Nick too, because they are going to Vietnam "to proudly serve their country." The band plays an accordion-heavy "Stars and Stripes Forever" as the crowd poses for pictures.

The pre-Vietnam sequences of *The Deer Hunter* portend the war-zone violence that shocked theater audiences, for life in Clairton was often lived close to the edge. The steel mill provides honest but dangerous work. When pretty Linda, radiant in her bridesmaid dress, tends to her ailing, alcoholic father, he punches her in the face. When Stan observes his date getting groped by another guy, he moves the guy along—and then punches the girl in the face. The boys career around Clairton in Michael's Cadillac with abandon. And on the hunt, an exercise in surgical violence, danger stalks Mike as Mike stalks his prey. In director Michael Cimino's America, young men take chances and court death, while young women take domestic violence in stride. As unlucky drops of wine fall on Angela's wedding dress, the audience wonders what the war has in store for these nice young people and whether their upbringing has prepared them to survive it.

From a literal, historical perspective, the Vietnam War sequence in *The Deer Hunter* is dreadful.[3] But from a literary perspective, it successfully establishes the war zone as a place of random brutality. The first American treatment of the war to be filmed in Southeast Asia (Thailand), *The Deer Hunter* presents the war in four parts: first, an improbable battlefield reunion between Mike, Nick, and Steven, who have not seen each other in years; second, the famous POW scene, in which sadistic Vietnamese guards force their American captives to play Russian roulette; third, escape from captivity; and fourth, Nick's arrested trauma recovery, in which he descends into Saigon's underground Russian roulette gambling dens.[4] These scenes offer a broad metaphor for the war's senseless violence, in which one's decency and competence have no impact on one's physical survival, yet inner strength and discipline can offer protection from psychological harm. Like *Apocalypse Now* (1979), which debuted about eight months later, *The Deer Hunter* imagines Americans sinking into the Vietnamese landscape, an existential quagmire from which they cannot extricate themselves physically, morally, or psychologically. Whereas Willard's crew drifts upriver and disappears into the jungle in *Apocalypse Now,* Mike, Nick, and Steven drift downstream, and Nick disappears into Saigon's underworld. Christopher Walken's transformation as Nick from virile and hopeful to viral and lost is particularly poignant, given concern he expressed earlier in the film about being abandoned in Vietnam.

Initially, only Mike makes it home. He is clearly reluctant to reengage with his community, but Linda slowly draws him back in. As a veteran proudly in uniform, Mike is welcomed with hugs, handshakes, and free beer, a direct inversion of the chilly welcome that caused many Vietnam veterans to put their uniforms away and slip back into civilian life unnoticed.[5] But the warm welcome is not enough, for Mike struggles with isolation, and he harbors resentment towards friends who did not go to Vietnam. Mike visits Steven, now a wheelchair-bound double-amputee, in a VA rehabilitation center. Though Steven claims everything is great, he is clearly reluctant to return to Clairton. Over his protestations, Mike takes Steven home, but it is not his home of the film's first hour. Steven's wife is catatonic, presumably in response to his injury, and he cannot navigate the world without assistance. The life he knew before Vietnam is gone.

The film's final act involves a second attempt at rescue, this time of Nick, who Mike discovers is still alive when Steven reports that money arrives monthly from Saigon. Mike returns to Vietnam in search of Nick on the eve of Saigon's fall, hustling past panicked civilians at the American embassy—images that forced *The Deer Hunter*'s original audience to revisit familiar scenes of American loss and betrayal just four years on. Mike finds Nick in the throes of drug addiction, playing Russian roulette for money. The only way Mike can talk to Nick, to reach him, is to buy his own way into the game. Mike says, "I love you" as he pulls the trigger, hoping that this profound act of sacrifice will cause Nick to emerge from his well of despair. There is a brief moment between them when invocations of mountains and trees, of deer hunting—"one shot"—rouse Nick to his senses. Then he smiles, grabs the gun, and shoots himself in the head. The final scenes depict Nick's funeral back in Clairton and breakfast afterward, where old friends exchange vacant looks but have little to say. They haltingly sing "God Bless America," which critics have alternately interpreted as a sincere invocation of patriotism or a savage indictment of it.

The start of the credits sequence is arguably one of the most powerful and important elements in the film. Just nine minutes elapse between Nick's death and the credits, which begin with a smiling, healthy Nick back in the old days. The physical transformation Christopher Walken makes over the course of the film is impressive (Walken won an Oscar for his performance), and the inclusion of live footage in the credits serves to drive that transformation home. The gentle guitar of "Cavatina"—which the film's original audience would have recognized as the instrumental version of the 1973 song "He Was Beautiful"—secures the exquisitely nostalgic tone. The final frame of the cast credits returns to the wedding, a group shot of all the leads and extras, everyone laughing before the scene freezes, as if to preserve forever the golden memory of a single perfect day. The credits sequence affirms the film's central point, that the Vietnam War was an inexorable force of destruction.

The Deer Hunter was controversial from its initial release, with criticism on a number of fronts. Most prominent was the complaint, from progressive activists and organizations, that the film is overtly racist in its depiction of Vietnamese people. In hindsight, this critique is one facet of a broader interpretation of the film as an inherently conservative, politically uncritical treatment of the Vietnam War. The film *is* overtly racist in its depiction of Vietnamese people, whose myriad political and social identities are pancaked into one defined by self-interest—ironic, given Vietnamese culture's profound emphasis on social obligation. The film depicts Vietnamese people as universally devoid of compassion, humanity, and intelligence. Lacking subtitles or Vietnamese characters who speak English, the film reduces Vietnamese speech to unintelligible nattering for English-only-speaking audiences. A Viet Cong/North Vietnamese[6] soldier mindlessly murders a cowering family, an invocation of indiscriminate violence more historically associated with the United States, given US forces' reliance on airstrikes, artillery, and napalm. Vietnamese civilians mindlessly clog the roads in perpetual evacuation, like animals who have escaped a pen. The Russian roulette scenes are particularly offensive, because Vietnamese men are reduced to greedy psychopaths, and Vietnamese women are reduced to prostitutes. Lacking grace, nuance, or realism, *The Deer Hunter*'s portrait of Vietnam neatly memorializes lingering American rage at Vietnamese people who, in the American mind, were improper allies, enemies, and victims.

The Deer Hunter's racism is only the most obvious example of the film's inherently conservative perspective on the Vietnam War. The scenes in Clairton before and after the town's sons go off to war offer glimpses of a working-class America in which ethnic identity and traditions—often policed by bigotry and xenophobia—are alive and well. And yet, the good people of Clairton also express national patriotism frequently and explicitly. Nick himself highlights this tension between ethnic and national identity when an Army doctor asks if his last name, Chevotarevich, is Russian: "No. It's American." *The Deer Hunter*'s portrait of a white, working-class community gamely offering up its sons to the national interest is a useful reminder of the war's support in the American South, rural areas, and the Rust Belt. Progressive audiences might interpret Nick as a victim of the war, but that is precisely the point: *The Deer Hunter* presents Nick as a victim of the *war*—and of wicked Vietnamese people—not a victim of the government and nation that sent him to fight it.

The film's most aggressively conservative element is its handling of Steven's experience in the VA hospital. In May 1970, *Life* magazine published a searing cover story called "Our Forgotten Wounded" that detailed shocking conditions in several VA hospitals around the country.[7] *Life*'s reporting was big news, and media and activist attention to health care for veterans continued throughout the 1970s. *The Deer Hunter*, in contrast, depicts a bright, clean, well-staffed VA hospital filled with Greatest Generation volunteers who pass out treats and help the patients play bingo. Given *The Deer Hunter*'s release in late 1978, the VA scene serves as a rebuke to activists complaining bitterly about their home-front treatment. By foregrounding voluntary, not compulsory, military service; by indicting Vietnamese people (not American officials or institutions) for American suffering; and by offering an affirming portrait of Vietnam veterans' problematic homecoming, *The Deer Hunter* can be read as a subtle exercise in national absolution. The film indeed argues that the Vietnam War was brutal and ruined lives, but it does not go so far as to suggest that Americans erred in fighting it.

In contrast, Oliver Stone's *Born on the Fourth of July* (1989) corrects for *The*

Deer Hunter's ambiguity by foregrounding antiwar sentiment and generous depictions of antiwar activists. (The film is dedicated in memoriam to activist Abbie Hoffman, who served as a consultant.) While *Born on the Fourth of July* follows *The Deer Hunter*'s path from an idealized hometown into Vietnam and home again, it deviates by rendering visually and explicitly what Great War poet Wilfred Owen called "the old lie": "*dulce et decorum est, pro patria mori,*" from Horace's *Odes,* which translates to "how sweet and proper, to die for one's country." Distilled to its purest essence, *Born on the Fourth of July* depicts Ron Kovic as a true believer in American greatness and martial power, who goes to war, is literally broken, comes home to a community unprepared to care for him, and finally realizes, then says out loud, to anyone who will listen, "This war is wrong, this society lied to me."

Kovic's story begins in Massapequa, New York, which brims with icons of Americana: baseball, parades, and a blonde high-school sweetheart. Unlike Clairton, Pennsylvania, which seems to exist in one long, gray autumn day, Massapequa is literally drenched in sunlight that glitters through the leafy trees. Home is perpetual summer, perpetual abundance, and relentless hope—for marriage, family, and enduring prosperity. Even so, there are hints in the opening sequences of *Born on the Fourth of July* that all is not what it seems. In the parade, smoke from firecrackers engulfs the streets, and a wheelchair-bound veteran winces as the pop-pop-pop takes him back to the battlefield. In Kovic's own life, his support system—a stable, overtly religious, middle-class family and an extended community of like-minded citizens—seems strong, but there are signs of fracture. While watching a newscast on Vietnam, Kovic's father expresses skepticism about the war and hope that the Marines will send Ron to Europe instead. But Kovic's mother endorses the nation's fight against communism and frames it as "God's will" that her son should go to Vietnam. In another room, Kovic's younger brother learns to play "The Times They Are A-Changin'" on guitar.

The film's brief Vietnam sequence takes place on the sandy banks of the Cua Viet River near the coast in northern South Vietnam. In a collage-like sequence saturated in hazy reds, oranges, and yellows, Kovic and his squad accidentally kill an entire Vietnamese family in their home. A baby's cries follow Kovic as the Marines retreat under heavy fire across the dunes to safety. Intense sunlight does not illuminate the battlefield, but obscures it. Unable to see clearly in the glare, and in the chaos of retreat, Kovic fires on a figure silhouetted against the sky. It turns out to be a fellow Marine, Wilson, whom Kovic had comforted earlier in the scene. Kovic admits responsibility for Wilson's death to his commanding officer, but the CO refuses to hear it. The brief sequence elegantly establishes that it is very hard to be a hero in this kind of war, that young Ron's ideals are slowly turning to ashes.

In the next scene, Kovic receives the injury that paralyzes him. Shot first in the heel, he continues to fire and advance across the sandy ground. Ever the stalwart Marine, Kovic ignores this minor injury, continuing to fire until his rifle jams. He takes three shots to the chest and falls backwards, confused and struggling to breathe. At the aid station, he mutters, "There's something wrong with me," but medical personnel tend only to other patients. The audience recognizes what Kovic does not: he has been left to die. The film then cuts to the Bronx VA hospital, which was one of those highlighted in the 1970 *Life* magazine exposé. Conditions in the hospital are more horrifying than the war, because they represent profound betrayal of the nation's soldiers: puddles of urine, enormous rats, patients with gaping bedsores, failing equipment, and overwhelmed, indifferent medical personnel. Initially, Kovic focuses on his recovery with the same intensity that he approached military service, but over time, subsequent injury and inadequate treatment weigh on him. Unkempt and completely dependent on others to manipulate his body, Kovic cries out, "All's I'm saying is, I want to be treated like a human being. I fought for my country. I am a Vietnam veteran"—as if that argument would resonate, given increasing American contempt for the war. The African American orderly replies, "You can take your Vietnam and shove it up your ass."

Born on the Fourth of July's nuanced portrait of the American home front includes favorable treatment of the antiwar movement, in which Kovic eventually becomes involved. The film's presentation of antiwar sentiment is complex, as individuals who express opposition vary in opinion and likeability. At one end of the spectrum is Kovic's boorish friend Stevie, who suggests Kovic is a chump for having believed the "bullshit lies" the US government told him. On the other end of the spectrum is Donna, Kovic's winsome high-school crush. When Kovic visits Donna at college, she is well informed and conscious of the trauma the war is inflicting on Vietnamese people. Donna encourages Kovic to participate in an antiwar event with her, because his presence would lend credibility to the cause. But when they arrive at the venue, Kovic's wheelchair bumps up against a formidable flight of stairs. Kovic demurs, and Donna's optimism and ableism blind her to the obvious realities of his infirmity. The film creates space for audiences to accept antiwar arguments while also disliking antiwar people, who are presented in various characters as self-interested and poorly informed, but also well-intentioned—if a little clueless.

Born on the Fourth of July's treatment of the home front also ventures into the white, working-class America of *The Deer Hunter*, when Kovic visits the family of the Marine he killed in Vietnam. Kovic meets Wilson's father, mother, widow, and young son, who share a little house in rural Georgia, where dogs and trash fill the yard. In their conversation, the father rattles off the names of other local boys killed in Vietnam, then a list of ancestors who died fighting the nation's wars. He expresses confusion at why the Vietnam War is necessary. As the camera falls upon the little boy playing with a toy rifle, the old man offers up his future descendants in blind allegiance: "Can't figure it out. But, we got a proud tradition here in this town. . . . I guess this family has fought in every war this country's ever had. And I reckon we're ready to do it again if we have to." When Kovic tells them that their son/husband died at his hand, and not the enemy's—an unheroic, unnecessary death—they are stunned and do not want to hear it. They can bear the loss of their son/husband in the war, but not the thought that he died for nothing.

Dying for nothing—this is the bitter reality of American deaths in Vietnam, according to the war's critics and director Oliver Stone, who conjured the scene with Wilson's family from his own imagination. Kovic's war story reflects the story of US military intervention writ large: a competent, dedicated, well-intentioned military professional makes a terrible mistake and kills the wrong people. Over the course of the film, Kovic comes to realize that his error is not his alone, but rather is shared with the American people and government that sent him to Vietnam in the first place. One night, in a drunken rage, he repudiates his entire belief system in a fight with his mother: "Vietnam is a can of shit, and I am a fucking dummy!" He tells her they shoot women and children in Vietnam, but she denies it. This scene positions Kovic's mother as a stand-in for the prowar American public: ignorant, faithful, and blinded by belief. She declares, "It's not my fault!" and throws her son out for offending her religious and patriotic sensibilities. Homeless in the most profound sense, Kovic must make his entire life anew. Political activism eventually provides a new sense of purpose, culminating in a triumphant speech at the 1976 Democratic National Convention. Kovic's military bearing and love of country remain intact right through the final frame, as "You're a Grand Old Flag" swells into the credits. *Born on the Fourth of July* manages to condemn the Vietnam War but not its warriors, offering an expansive vision of American patriotism that includes antiwar sentiment and political dissent. But its vision of the war itself is singular: a toxic blast that annihilates everything in its path, including foundational ideas about what it means to be an American.

The Hughes brothers' *Dead Presidents* (1995) tells this story, of hope extinguished by military service in Vietnam, yet again, but from an African American perspective. Based loosely on a true story about a black Vietnam veteran who attempted to steal bank currency that was slated for destruction ("dead presidents"),[8] the film follows three friends (Jose, Skip, and Anthony) from high-school graduation to the end of their lives—at the hands of the police, from a drug overdose, and fifteen-to-life in prison—with a lengthy detour through South Vietnam. *Dead Presidents* presents the Vietnam War as a destructive force, much like *The Deer Hunter* and *Born on the Fourth of July*, but the Hughes brothers also indict racism, poverty, and corrupt policing for ruining American lives. *Dead Presidents* lacks the craftsmanship of the other films, but its thoughtful attention to black perspectives on the war make it worthy of consideration.

As with *The Deer Hunter,* the film's early scenes establish the young men's enduring friendship, boyish antics, and future aspirations. After high school, Jose wants to work and Skip wants to go to college to avoid "the white man's war," but Anthony wants to travel and see the world. He enlists in the Marines and spends years in-country without ever returning home. The Hughes brothers render the 1960s Bronx in vivid detail, but their treatment of Vietnam is generic, even cartoonish. Tropical plants look like they have been positioned by a set dresser, a pagoda-like structure adds an Asian dimension to the battlefield, and the soldiers' uniforms, weapons, and vernacular suggest a good-enough approach to costumes, props, and script. The war-zone violence in *Dead Presidents* is extreme, as if the filmmakers took the folklore of the Vietnam War and rendered it not as metaphor but as poorly executed realism. For example, a soldier named D'ambrosio dies when he slips off to relieve himself and is captured by the enemy. A similar sequence factors into *Platoon*, which is arguably one of the most "realistic" films of the Vietnam War genre, and stories of unheroic deaths due to sharpshooters date back to the Civil War.[9] But in *Dead Presidents,* it is insufficient to comment on the senselessness of war deaths with a merely dead soldier who dies because he needed to poop. When D'ambrosio is found, he has been disemboweled but is still alive, but not so alive that he can spit out his penis, which has been stuffed into his mouth.

Anthony, Skip, and Jose all serve in and survive Vietnam, but the war ruins them just the same. Jose returns home psychologically altered and physically scarred. Skip is addicted to heroin and suffering from mysterious ailments that suggest Agent Orange exposure. Anthony comes back seemingly fine, yet he fails to readjust after four years away. He struggles to maintain relationships and employment, he has a hair-trigger temper and startle response, and he self-medicates with alcohol—all symptoms associated with Post-Traumatic Stress Disorder. Despondent, Anthony reconnects with Delilah, a childhood friend involved in the Black Power movement, who introduces him to political perspectives that normalize his frustration and radicalize him to action. The heist plan capitalizes on the skills and resentments of every character, but it goes poorly, resulting in the deaths of Jose, Delilah, and several security guards. Skip dies of a heroin overdose as the police close in, and Anthony tries to make a run for it. At Anthony's trial, his public defender pleads for leniency because Anthony is a decorated Vietnam veteran, but the white judge (an uncredited cameo by Martin Sheen) will not have it. The judge announces that he himself is a Marine Corps veteran, of World War II—"a real war," he adds contemptuously—and declares Anthony a disgrace to everyone who has worn the uniform. The film's final scene depicts the bus to prison, which is filled with shackled men of color.

Dead Presidents finds its surest footing when it offers specific commentary on the black experience in the Vietnam era, often through striking imagery. During the heist, Anthony and his conspirators paint their faces white with blackened eyes, an inversion of blackface that erases the characters' racial identities and reduces them to ghouls. When Anthony is captured by police, he runs down a long hallway with policemen coming from both directions. The final frame of the chase, shot from above, shows Anthony trapped like an animal, with literally dozens of white hands pointing guns at him. Perhaps the most damning and affecting detail in Dead Presidents is the composition of Anthony's family, which is strong and intact, with still-married, employed, caring parents. By providing Anthony with a stable upbringing, Dead Presidents locates his decline not in a broken home or an absent father, racist tropes that have long animated conservative opposition to social reform, but in the unequal structures of American society and the traumas of wartime military service. The film argues that American racism and inequality made black men's success difficult, but it was service in Vietnam that made it impossible.

In all three of these films, the Vietnam War annihilates American lives. It destroys soldiers' bodies, unmoors their beliefs, shatters their families, and leaves despair, addiction, and a thirst for violence in its wake. Most Vietnam

War films, boxed in by the historical realities of the war's conclusion, offer no victory to celebrate, no meaningful change wrought by the violence, to suggest that the cost was worth it.

Riding Out the Storm: Enduring Vietnam on Film

Twenty years on from the war, the Vietnam generation had matured into adulthood but also a market demographic to whom cathartic reminiscence could be sold. Hollywood produced a spate of Vietnam War films in the 1980s, with *Platoon* (1986) setting a high bar in terms of artistic merit and box-office success. Directed by Vietnam veteran Oliver Stone, *Platoon* was a literal blockbuster, with sold-out screenings around the country despite premiering the week before Christmas. It facilitated a national conversation about Vietnam that helped to greenlight or build anticipation for subsequent projects, including *Full Metal Jacket* (1987), *Good Morning, Vietnam* (1987), *Hamburger Hill* (1987), *Casualties of War* (1989), and Stone's sophomore Vietnam picture, *Born on the Fourth of July*, among others.[10]

Platoon was the first high-quality Vietnam War film since the late 1970s, and its marketing centered on the film's authenticity. The theatrical trailer was highly unusual for featuring biographical information about the director's own Vietnam tour of duty, and the tagline described the film as the first "real" movie about the war: "The first real casualty of war is innocence. The first real movie about the war in Vietnam is *Platoon*." By the 1980s, American audiences seemed ready, even eager, for faithful renderings of Vietnam, suggesting a willingness to confront the war's dark energy. And yet, films like *Platoon*, *Hamburger Hill*, *Casualties of War*, and the more recent *Rescue Dawn* frame the war narrowly. They excise its causes, they invoke rather than depict the American home front, and they eliminate the war's aftermath altogether. These films take place almost exclusively in the war zone,[11] focusing on how Americans weathered the war's myriad challenges: racial tensions, lack of home-front support, friendly fire, Vietnamese combatants, and especially the physical environment of Vietnam itself. The war in these films is a hurricane, and all the American characters can do is ride it out until they are allowed to go home.

Though *Platoon* is credited with being among the most authentic treatments of the Vietnam War, its realism lay not in its allegorical plot, but rather in Stone's careful attention to detail. A spider's web across a tunnel entrance, the irritating whine of mosquitoes at night, red mud, dappled light through the jungle canopy, burnout latrines, the casual intimacy of combat troops, a DEROS (Date Estimated Return from Overseas) calendar in a soldier's wallet, the slang, the weapons, and insignia: it is all very, very good. *Platoon* transported many veterans back to the battlefields of their youth. The plot, on the other hand—a coming-of-age tale about a young man "born of . . . two fathers" who wrestle "for possession of [his] soul"—advances steadily toward the ridiculous as it unfolds. In contrast, the plots of *Casualties of War* and *Hamburger Hill* make up in realism what the props and settings lack in authentic detail. *Hamburger Hill* depicts the spectacularly bloody and pointless assaults to take Hill 937 during a larger operation to sever North Vietnamese infiltration routes through A Shau Valley in May 1969. Whereas *Hamburger Hill* tells the story of men in battle, *Casualties of War* depicts the moral dilemma of a single person, Max Eriksson, who witnesses a war crime: the kidnap, gang rape, and murder of a Vietnamese woman by American soldiers.[12] Compared to the painterly cinematography and exquisite detail of *Platoon, Casualties of War* looks like it was filmed on a soundstage, while *Hamburger Hill* tries mightily to deploy the right slang and set pieces, but the banter and bunkers always seem not quite right. Nonetheless, and setting aside their artistic liabilities and inauthentic details, all three films have something to tell us about Hollywood's understanding of Vietnam's challenges.

Racial tensions animate these films to varying degrees, dividing soldiers who should be united in common struggle. In *Platoon*, racial harmony/discord is more depicted than discussed, with a smattering of comments about race from black characters. The white protagonist, Chris Taylor, analyzes the platoon's demographics, but he fixates on poverty, not race, as the operative variable that drew his fellow soldiers into the Army: "They come from the end of the line, most of them, small towns you never heard of. . . . Two years' high school's about it. Maybe if they're lucky, a job waiting for them back in a factory. But most of 'em got nothing. They're poor. They're the unwanted. . . . They're the bottom of the barrel, and they know it." While race is not often discussed in *Platoon*, there is a strong racial dimension to divisions within the platoon that reflect Taylor's divided allegiances. The "heads" hang out in a candlelit bunker filled with music and mirth, while the rest of the platoon—who eschew pot for beer, listen to country music, and make anti-Semitic jokes—congregate in a barracks decorated with the Confederate flag.

In contrast, *Hamburger Hill* foregrounds racial tension and discourse in conversations within the platoon, which includes several black members. The film is especially on point for its prominent use of the dap, a system of elaborate handshakes between black servicemembers that conveyed unit, rank, city of origin, even information about the war—but most importantly that dap participants are not white. The dap represented black men's deliberate rejection of a typical (white) handshake but also the Army's salute, an assertion of racial identity as more important than other systems of belonging. The racial commentary in *Hamburger Hill* is persistent and overt, but racial conflicts are always resolved conveniently and to the benefit of social order. For example, when Doc, the platoon's black medic, is dying from his wounds, he extends brotherhood to the white soldiers comforting him by pointing to their shared plight as forgotten members of the American tribe: "We're all no good dumb n*****s on this hill." *Hamburger Hill*'s attention to race is admirable, but clumsy. Ultimately, Doc's race comments do not promote greater equality or alter white soldiers' perceptions. Rather, Doc and other black soldiers make rhetorical concessions at every turn, even when a white soldier uses the N-word. The film thus leverages Doc's views on race to establish the marginalization of *all* soldiers in Vietnam, even the white ones. Race and racism are challenges for black and white soldiers alike, the film implies, but they are not insurmountable challenges.

Home-front indifference and hostility pose additional threats to American soldiers in *Hamburger Hill,* which punctuates combat sequences with two lengthy monologues that offer a complicated view of stateside life. In the first, a soldier listens to a tape recording from his girlfriend, Claire, in front of his peers, who fall silent as she offers news of his family and expresses pride in her boyfriend's service. She also identifies one of the greatest hardships for deployed soldiers: that life for most Americans, 98 percent of whom did not serve in Vietnam, goes on without them. "I just don't think it's fair that everybody is back here acting like nothing is going on. Their lives are the same," she says. "It's just not fair." Claire closes by confessing her love for her boyfriend and dismissing criticism of the war. "I don't believe what they say about you. Anyhow. I don't care, because I love all of you." Claire and her affirming views of the soldiery were common in hometowns like Clairton and Massapequa, where a reckoning with the war's aftermath had not yet taken place.

Hamburger Hill's second home-front monologue offers an oblique critique of 1960s social movements and a devastating indictment of the antiwar movement in particular. Sergeant Worcester quietly describes getting pelted with dogshit at the airport when he arrived home to recuperate from wounds in a previous tour, finding his wife shacked up with a "hairhead," and a friend receiving harassing phone calls from "college kids saying how glad they was that his boy was killed in Vietnam." Worcester discourages a fellow soldier from believing that life will be great if only he can make it home: "You're right about everybody loving everybody back there. They tattoo it to their foreheads, and they wear 'love' buttons on their flowered shirts, you know? Yeah, they love everybody back there. Cats, dogs, n*****s, spics, kikes, wops, micks, greaseballs. And they're real fond of Luke the Gook back home, if y'all can believe that. They got a button for him too. Yeah. They love everybody but you." The final line—"They love everybody but you"—lands as a devastating betrayal of all soldiers, positioning Vietnam veterans as a social group defined not by race or ethnicity but by military service. Some of what Worcester cites is historically true. Soldiers' personal relationships were strained by distance. Telephone harassment of military families was a real and cruel (but rare) phenomenon.[13] The chant "Hey hey, Ho Chi Minh, NLF is gonna win!" did ring out at antiwar rallies. And people with antiwar views did express contempt towards soldiers in uniform, not necessarily by spitting on them (let alone pelting them with feces) but rather by assaulting them verbally and holding individuals to account for the execution of US foreign policy. While some soldiers took heart in the antiwar movement's efforts to bring them home, others found antiwar expressions deeply painful, compounding the difficulty of their time in Vietnam.

The soldiers in these films frequently look homeward, toward the United States, but their obvious preoccupation is with the enemy close at hand. And yet, the enemy in Vietnam War films is often less the People's Army of Vietnam or the National Liberation Front/Viet Cong than it is other Americans. In *Casualties of War,* Eriksson's principle antagonists are his sergeant and fellow squadmates, who force him to witness a heinous act, threaten to kill him if he intercedes, and attempt to kill him to ensure his silence. In *Platoon,* rival factions regard each other warily, they often fight each other, Barnes murders Elias, and Taylor expresses his final maturation by killing Barnes. If *Platoon's* ham-fisted allegory eludes the audience, Taylor's final narration makes American solipsism explicit: "I think now, looking back, we did not fight the enemy; we fought ourselves. And the enemy was in us." American duplicity, in-fighting, and betrayal also appear in *Apocalypse Now* (1979), *First Blood* (1982), *Missing in Action* (1984), *Rambo: First Blood Part II* (1985), *Bat-21* (1988), *Full Metal Jacket* (1987), *The Walking Dead* (1995), *Tigerland,* and *We Were Soldiers.* The frequency with which filmmakers invoke abandonment and betrayal of one group of Americans by another suggests an audience comfortable with narratives that disparage military authorities, civilian political leaders, and people with opposing political points of view.

To be sure, Vietnam War films do depict the Vietnamese enemy, but Vietnamese characters are often poorly rendered. In fact, "character" is usually too strong a word; "prop" is more descriptive. *Platoon* and *Casualties of War* include extended scenes in which Vietnamese civilians are brutalized, but we learn nothing of their beliefs, priorities, or desires. Though it fixates on the suffering a Vietnamese girl, *Casualties of War* also contains disturbing images of Vietnamese combatants as subhuman and duplicitous. In the film's opening combat sequence, Eriksson is nearly killed by a bloodthirsty insurgent with a knife in his teeth, who crawls through a tunnel on his belly like an animal, even though the tunnel is large enough for him to walk on two legs. Vietnamese soldiers and insurgents in *Platoon* are often shadowy and faceless, which makes them terrifying but not human or complex. They are also numerous, arriving in wave after wave, as if a natural resource in endless supply. The same is true of *Hamburger Hill,* in which North Vietnamese bunkers perpetually brim with soldiers raining fire on Americans below. In these and other Vietnam films, narrative tension flows from the perception that there are simply too many Vietnamese people for American protagonists to kill. American audiences like to root for the underdog, and at times North Vietnamese or Viet Cong fighters were able to create advantage out of darkness, surprise, sabotage, and occasionally greater numbers. More often, though, American access to high-tech weaponry and air support proved an insurmountable advantage. Vietnamese people on all sides suffered catastrophic casualties, with 8 percent of the total population perishing in the fighting and millions more suffering serious injury and/or homelessness. (Just .0003 percent of the US population died in Vietnam, and an additional .00075 percent were wounded.) These facts are uncomfortable and inconvenient in American narratives of the Vietnam War, hence Hollywood's focus on other threats to the American soldiery.

According to Hollywood, the final and perhaps ultimate enemy that American troops faced in Vietnam was Vietnam itself—the imposing natural environment of the war. In *Hamburger Hill,* the hill is as much the enemy as its North Vietnamese defenders, driving American soldiers down down down, again and again. Vietnam's heat, humidity, and parasites factor heavily into *Platoon,* with Taylor passing out from heat stroke on his first hump through the boonies. Whereas natural perils exacerbate Vietnam service in *Hamburger Hill* and *Pla-*

toon, they dominate *Rescue Dawn,* to the exclusion of almost every other kind of threat. Based on a true story, as well as director Werner Herzog's 1997 documentary *Little Dieter Needs to Fly, Rescue Dawn* depicts the captivity and escape of Dieter Dengler, a German American US Navy pilot who was shot down over Laos and captured by the Pathet Lao, then imprisoned by the Viet Cong. In the POW camp, Dengler and the other prisoners are poorly fed, due to the guards' cruelty but also because food is scarce. Their suffering is acute, and the physical transformations the actors made to depict starvation are astounding. The last to arrive at the camp, Dengler immediately develops a plan to escape, which the prisoners eventually execute together.[14] Dengler and American prisoner Duane Martin set off through the jungle in hopes of finding the Mekong River and floating downstream to freedom. Their path is obscured by insane vegetation— what American troops called "wait-a-minute vines," because one literally cannot pass without cutting through them. Dengler and Martin are barefoot and poorly clothed, they quickly run out of food, and they are constantly exposed to rain, snakes, insects, and leeches. Martin is eventually killed by villagers during an attempt to steal food. Dengler survives weeks longer and is finally rescued by an American helicopter patrolling a riverbed.

Rescue Dawn is an intimate portrait of men's response to physical hardship, not unlike a nature documentary in which the subjects crash-land onto a mountaintop or get lost hiking in a wilderness. Herzog's film maintains a strange, detached air, never telling the audience much about the war, the captives, the captors, or even Dengler himself. Besides his love of flying, attention to detail, and ability to eat anything, Dengler is a cipher with no family, no articulated memories of home, and no beliefs of any kind. When Dengler finally makes it back to his ship, the master of ceremonies at the welcome event asks, "Was it your faith in God and country?" Dengler is silent. "Come on," the MC coaxes, "You gotta believe in something." This is Dengler's—and Herzog's— chance to offer political comment in one direction or another about America, the Vietnam War, or war itself, but Dengler says only, "I believe I need a steak." Herzog presents Dengler not as a dedicated airman keeping up the fight via his own against-all-odds survival, but as a man confronting natural forces who wills his way through. The Vietnam War of *Rescue Dawn* is cruel and inevitable, like a predator without politics or an unrelenting gale—like nature itself. In their elision of causes and aftermaths, all four films present the Vietnam War as a natural disaster, a force to be endured and overcome. Americans in such stories have no choice but to ride out the storm, because they are powerless to prevent its occurrence, diminish its strength, or alter its trajectory. These films, *Rescue Dawn* especially, cast American military personnel as determined, even ennobled survivors, but they are not the agents of their fate.

The Prescribed Burn: Harnessing Destruction in Vietnam

Wildfires have two causes: natural ignition (heat, lightning, or volcano) and people. Fires that start as the result of accident or malice are arson, while fires deliberately set to prevent more fires are an important part of natural resource management. A prescribed burn represents the literal fighting of fire with fire, to turn the beast or deny it access to fuel. Prescribed burns represent the skillful manipulation of a natural force for rational ends, not unlike armies skillfully producing violence for political purposes. But sometimes even the most carefully set backfire can backfire, leading to an uncontrolled burn. If previous films imagine the Vietnam War as a natural disaster, a destructive force without cause or conscience, then *We Were Soldiers* conjures the prescribed burn— a deliberate attempt by professionals to harness destruction in order to prevent more of it. That is, the United States fought the Vietnam War to prevent a wider, more costly one, as predicted by the "Domino Theory." Like *The Green Berets* decades before, *We Were Soldiers* is a feel-good Vietnam War movie, because it affirms that violence is the key to national security. Because the film is set in 1965, before the Vietnam War expanded and devolved—before the prescribed burn grew into an unmanageable conflagration—audiences can imagine that the effort was successful, that the prescribed burn worked, that there was a path to American victory in Vietnam after all.

We Were Soldiers is an outlier structurally, because it toggles back and forth between the home front and the war, and thematically, because it examines the war's underlying causes and declares them legitimate. Based on the book *We Were Soldiers Once . . . and Young,* the film examines the war's first battle between American forces and North Vietnamese regulars.[15] Historically speaking, the Battle of the Ia Drang Valley was a meeting engagement—an unexpected battle but not quite an ambush—between a battalion of the First Air Cavalry Division and a division of the People's Army of Vietnam (the North Vietnamese Army). Both sides consisted of well-trained, well-equipped, conventional forces (that is, not lightly armed guerrillas) led by competent officers. The battle did not take place in a populated region of South Vietnam, but rather in a remote mountain valley near the Cambodian border—meaning, there were no civilians around to create ethical complexities or collateral damage. The battle took place early in the war, November 1965, when American soldiers were still largely volunteers. The film depicts only professional soldiers who chose military service, were properly trained, and had high morale. Gone from the film, then, are the troubling ethics of young men forced to become killers against their will. Gone are impoverished, unarmed peasants caught up in Vietnam's civil war. Gone is the "credibility gap" between what Johnson administration officials said and what the public later learned to be true. Gone, too, is the antiwar movement, which in late 1965 still operated largely on the fringes of American political discourse.

What is left in *We Were Soldiers*, then, is a World War II–style epic of competent, well-equipped soldiers sustained by strong belief in their cause who fight other competent, well-equipped soldiers who also have strong belief in their cause (except their cause is wrong). The film presents the morality of the war in absolute terms (communism = bad) and with strong religious overtones. Hal Moore is a devout Catholic who seeks and discerns God's blessing on his actions. When Moore prays, he asks for intervention: "Oh, yes, and one more thing, dear Lord, about our enemies. Ignore their heathen prayers, and help us blow those little bastards straight to Hell. Amen." The line is delivered mostly for laughs, though, because *We Were Soldiers* also considers decency and honor to be universal values.

In this film, the American soldier's adversary is not Vietnam's formidable natural environment or other Americans, but rather the actual North Vietnamese soldier who opposes him in combat. But, thematically speaking, the American soldier's *enemy* is those who do not fight—in particular, venal officials within the US government. Bad are civilian intelligence officials who seek to withdraw Moore from the battlefield prematurely to obscure public knowledge of what looks like a rout. Worse still are US military officials who fail to anticipate heavy losses and thus do not have a compassionate, orderly process in place for casualty notification. Back at Fort Benning, Georgia, families receive news of dead husbands and fathers via telegrams delivered by civilian taxi drivers. There is honor in toting a gun if one can use it rationally, the film suggests, but there is ignominy in failing to support those who do.

We Were Soldiers frequently takes pains to "other" the Vietnamese, comparing them repeatedly to Native Americans by way of allusions to the 1876 Battle of the Greasy Grass, better known as Custer's Last Stand. (The American units engaged in the Battle of the Ia Drang Valley have their historical antecedents in Custer's Seventh Cavalry.) On the other hand, *We Were Soldiers* does a better job of humanizing the enemy than any other American Vietnam War film. The film draws clear comparisons between Moore's own father-like leadership and that of the North Vietnamese commander, Nguyen Huu An, a historical figure identified by name who likewise comforts his men, commands their respect, and prays over their bodies. (Presumably Moore's prayer has rendered An's invalid.) An individual North Vietnamese soldier writes in his journal with a picture of his sweetheart clipped to the page. The film presents her not merely as a humanizing detail objectified in a photograph, but as a living, breathing woman, depicted by an actress in the film's epilogue sequence. When her young Vietnamese soldier sprints inside American lines to kill Moore, his run is so heroically shot and inspirationally scored that the audience almost hopes he succeeds. Most of the Vietnamese dialogue in *We Were Soldiers* is treated with subtitles, which frames the Vietnamese characters' words as the expression of thought rather than unintelligible sounds. And most importantly, Vietnamese bodies are rendered fully on screen, not in terms of character development but literally. Other Vietnam War films create suspense by depicting Vietnamese combatants as shadowy, incomplete figures—arms extending menacingly through the bushes (*Platoon*) or heads popping up like prairie dogs from holes in the ground (*Casualties of War*)—which diminishes their humanity and erases their politics, culture, and agency. In *We Were Soldiers*, Vietnamese characters have arms, legs, and heads, but also names, words, and beliefs.

We Were Soldiers' other distinctive feature is its handling of the American home front, which offers an affirming vision of American social progress. The film offers extended treatment of soldiers' waiting wives, who faced raising children and heading households alone, often in isolation and far from the support of their families. The progressive attitude that informs *We Were Soldiers'* thoughtful inclusion of women also informs its depiction American ethnic and racial diversity, but the result is naive and (unintentionally) uncomfortable. Prior to heading off to war, Moore gives an inspirational speech that foregrounds diversity as both a fighting strength and an essential component of American national identity:

> Look around you. In the 7th cavalry, we've got a captain from the Ukraine; another from Puerto Rico. We've got Japanese, Chinese, Blacks, Hispanics, Cherokee Indians. Jews and Gentiles. All Americans. Now here in the States, some of you in this unit may have experienced discrimination be-

cause of race or creed. But for you and me now, all that is gone. We're moving into the Valley of the Shadow of Death, where you will watch the back of the man next to you, as he will watch yours. And you won't care what color he is, or by what name he calls God.

All of that is probably true, historically speaking, because the US Army of 1965 was one of the most diverse institutions in American life. However, the discrimination Moore briefly acknowledges still infused Army policy and practice, just as it did civilian life. Moore asks his men to overlook structural inequality, and in combat that makes a certain amount of sense. But, troublingly, the film doubles down on this idea of racism as mere inconvenience in its handling of stateside segregation.

During a coffee hour, the wives trade information about life at Fort Benning. When a whites-only, off-post laundromat comes up in conversation, everyone turns to look in horror at the one black wife. She gamely assuages their momentary concern about structural racism with a sassy speech: "I know what my husband's fighting for, and that's why I can smile. . . . My husband would never ask for respect, and he'll give respect to no man who hasn't earned it. . . . And anybody who doesn't respect that can keep his goddamn washing machine, 'cause my babies are gonna be clean anyway." Snap! Racism solved! Vietnam in this iteration is not a "white man's war," as characters in *Born on the Fourth of July, Dead Presidents,* and *Hamburger Hill* assert, because black men are at liberty to deny deference to those who disrespect them, even in a rigid, authoritarian setting like the US Army. Racism does exist, *We Were Soldiers* contends, but it is black people's responsibility to overlook it and to reassure white people that it does not matter anyway.

We Were Soldiers is chock full of action-movie spectacle, sarcastic zingers, and heartfelt dying words ("Tell my wife I love her," "Tell my wife I love her, and my baby," and "I'm glad I could die for my country") that affirm traditional family structures, patriotism, and the Vietnam War itself. But *We Were Soldiers* is defined less by what it includes than by what it leaves out. When Hal Moore comes home from Vietnam, he is unchanged by the war. He has not lost his innocence, because he was not innocent to begin with. Moore was already a combat veteran (Korea), and he was prepared for what was asked of him. He suffers no moral injury, because he believes fully in the cause. There are no war crimes—no Russian roulette, no rape, no civilian deaths of any kind—and no senseless American deaths. Because the violence is surgical and meaningful, there is nothing for an antiwar movement to protest. Americans in *We Were Soldiers* are empowered and impassioned; they do not ride out the storm so much as they create it. It is a comforting thought, a fantasy even—that there was a Vietnam War fought by well-armed professionals who enjoyed the un-flagging support of the folks back home, who pointed their guns at all the right targets, and who skillfully prescribed violence in pursuit of a rational, worthy objective. Despite the film's relentless explosions, spurting blood packs, and gruesome napalm burns, *We Were Soldiers* is ultimately a feel-good movie. Because no one, who is not supposed to, gets hurt.

The Vietnam War as a "Natural" Disaster

The Vietnam War has long challenged filmmakers to depict its specific culture, events, and environment productively on screen, because the truth of the war cannot necessarily be rendered in the truth of the details. Tim O'Brien wrote an entire novel about this problem, *The Things They Carried*, which invokes the same dappled sunlight as *Platoon,* the same pointless battlefield deaths as *Born on the Fourth of July* and *Dead Presidents,* and the same devouring tropical land-scape as *Apocalypse Now.* O'Brien arguably does it better, because he does not suggest that American soldiers lost themselves in Vietnam's jungles, but rather that an American civilian did: a pretty, all-American girl named Mary Anne, "The Sweetheart of the Song Tra Bong," who is brought to the war zone by her boyfriend. Mary Anne gets a taste for blood when she helps some injured soldiers; then she slowly evolves, learning to kill and accessorizing her cute sweater set with a necklace of human ears. She eventually disappears into mist. O'Brien inserts lots of strange elements into his war zone, which he explicitly defends in "How to Tell a True War Story." "A thing may happen and be a to-tal lie," O'Brien writes. "Another thing may not happen and be truer than the truth."[16] So what does it matter if a Vietnam War movie uses the wrong kind of helicopter? Directors like Francis Ford Coppola (*Apocalypse Now*), Michael Cimino (*The Deer Hunter*), and even the Hughes brothers (*Dead Presidents*) rely on this imprecise calculus to account for their failure to bring the reality of the Vietnam war zone to life. Perhaps the violence, mayhem, and human toll of the Vietnam War defy telling after all.

The complicated politics and unsettling ending of the Vietnam War only ex-acerbate this problem of adequately explaining just what happened to so many good people in that strange, far-off war. Fifty-eight-thousand Americans died, and American objectives went unrealized, yet very little changed geopolitically for the United States. The dominoes stopped falling to communism well short of American shores, and the Cold War turned out pretty well after all. On the other side, the Democratic Republic of Vietnam achieved its goal of reunifying Vietnam under communist leadership, but at a shattering cost. The Vietnamese side of the war is divided into many constituencies: two governments, three armed forces, a political insurgency, and civilians on all sides calibrating their allegiances to survive. The American side is similarly complex: Cold War warriors, antiwarriors, reluctant draftees, and families struggling to remain intact amid the intersecting challenges of war, poverty, and social injustice. All of these people—these potential film characters, Vietnamese and American alike—have complex public and inner lives that are profoundly difficult to render on screen.

The easiest way to address these intricacies in film is to ignore them altogether. That is why so many Vietnam War films present American soldiers' antagonists not as fully developed human beings, but as wave after wave of lethal objects or, frequently, as other Americans—a plot device that nullifies Vietnamese agency altogether. Vietnam War films also tend to ignore the conflict as a political struggle, presenting it as allegory instead: good versus evil, man versus nature. These films may lay claim to being "apolitical," but "apolitical" cultural renderings usually have a latent agenda: shaming those who object. This is why Vietnam War films tend not to have an antiwar movement or, if they do, it is pathologized. (*Born on the Fourth of July* is the exception.) Hence, depictions of the Vietnam War as a struggle against the Vietnamese environment: no one protests a hurricane, which can be predicted but not prevented or deterred. Like an epochal storm, these films suggest, the Vietnam War killed millions, destroying American innocence in the process, and there was nothing anyone could have done about that.

It is true, Vietnam killed millions, though the phrasing gives the war agency it does not deserve. More accurately, millions died in the Vietnam War, killed by soldiers and machines deployed in pursuit of national political objectives. War comes, but not from nowhere. It is made by people—resisted by some, facilitated by others, and fought by soldiers on their behalf. Collectively, Vietnam War films grimly celebrate American survival against long odds, an inversion of historical reality that yields an American identity defined not by what we create, but by what we can endure. Strong, unyielding, blessed, but ultimately not responsible: these are the qualities of a storm's survivors. With rare exception, the filmography of the Vietnam War is in convenient concurrence on this point: that Americans are the battered survivors of a colossal disaster. But there was nothing natural about it.

NOTES

1. Marita Sturken, *Tourists of History: Memory, Kitsch, and Consumerism from Oklahoma City to Ground Zero* (Durham, NC: Duke University Press, 2007), 16.

2. Abraham Lincoln's Second Inaugural Address, delivered March 4, 1865, in Washington, DC.

3. Cimino depicts the war's violence as isolated and random rather than the managed product of professional, institutional processes. Several critical plot points rest laughably on the idea that American helicopters in South Vietnam were in short supply and that radio communication between them did not exist.

4. Historically speaking, this is not a thing.

5. Linda Mathews, "Homecoming for Viet Vets: Apathy, Hostility," *Los Angeles Times*, October 20, 1968, 1–3.

6. The film fails to distinguish Vietnamese people regionally or politically.

7. Charles Childs and Co Rentmeester, "Our Forgotten Wounded: From Vietnam to a VA Hospital: Assignment to Neglect," *Life* 68, no. 19 (May 22, 1970): 24–33.

8. Wallace Terry, *Bloods: Black Veterans of the Vietnam War: An Oral History* (New York: Random House, 1984), 89–108; Kim Masters, "'Dead Presidents' Precedent: The Heist Is Only Half of the Story, Says the Man Who Pulled It Off," *Washington Post*, October 15, 1995, G1.

9. Gerald Linderman, *Embattled Courage: The Experience of Combat in the American Civil War* (New York: Free Press, 1987), 146–48.

10. Richard Corliss, "*Platoon*: Viet Nam the Way It Really Was, on Film," *Time* 129, no. 4 (January 26, 1987): 54–64.

11. *Casualties of War* allocates about four and a half minutes to a thin stateside frame story in which the main character sees a Vietnamese woman on a train, triggering a flashback to his 1966 tour of duty in Vietnam.

12. Max Eriksson is based on Sven Eriksson, subject of a 1969 *New Yorker* story, which is a pseudonym for Robert Storeby, who witnessed, tried to prevent, and reported the death of Phan Thi Mao. See Daniel Lang, "Casualties of War: An Atrocity in Vietnam," *New Yorker*, October 10, 1969; Frederick L. Borch III, *Judge Advocates in Vietnam: Army Lawyers in Southeast Asia, 1959–1975* (Fort Leavenworth, KS: US Army Command and General Staff College Press, 2003), 71.

13. "Navy Wives Are Threatened, *New York Times*, December 8, 1965, 49.

14. The film depicts Dengler's version of events, but another survivor, Phisit Intharathat, has publicly challenged Dengler's story. At issue is whether Dengler planned and led the escape, as depicted in Herzog's films, or whether he arrived at the camp after the plan was already in motion. Intharathat also challenged the film's depiction of prisoner Gene DeBruin as a madman who undermined the escape plan. Intharathat claims that DeBruin was in control of his faculties, taught

English to other prisoners, and heroically elected to stay behind with a Chinese prisoner suffering from illness (www.rescuedawnthetruth.com/ [accessed January 4, 2020]).

15. Lt. Gen. Harold G. Moore (Ret.) and Joseph L. Galloway, *We Were Soldiers Once . . . And Young: Ia Drang: The Battle That Changed the War in Vietnam* (New York: Random House, 1992).

16. Tim O'Brien, *The Things They Carried* (New York: Houghton Mifflin, 1990), 85–110, 80.

Virtually There

The War on Terror

CALVIN FAGAN

Unlike films about the previous wars discussed in this volume, cinematic representations of the most recent conflicts in Iraq and Afghanistan—as well as the nebulous drone wars in Pakistan, Yemen, Somalia and Syria (among others)—have had only a short time frame in which to percolate in collective memory. The vast majority of these films were produced between 2005 and 2011, loosely corresponding to the actual period of the US military occupation of Iraq. The relative novelty of this situation has been highlighted by several historians of the war genre. Robert Eberwein, for instance, notes that it is the "first time a number of . . . films have been made about an ongoing unpopular war."[1] Although a few high-profile films have continued to appear in recent years—such as Ang Lee's *Billy Lynn's Long Halftime Walk* (2016) or Clint Eastwood's *The 15:17 to Paris* (2018)—there has nonetheless been a distinct decline in the quantity of Hollywood's War on Terror cinema over the last few years, and many of the more recent depictions largely conform to the formal and ideological templates established during the initial proliferation.

The contemporaneity of the films and the wars they depict has in many cases clearly muted any overt political stance, due either to a calculated attempt by studios not to alienate factions of their potential audience or, as Martin Barker, to a set of guidelines implicitly governing productions of the time which preclude anything "political" or "policy oriented" in favor of "human experience."[2] This widespread decontextualization of the politics of the conflicts has not, of course, resulted in truly apolitical films, but rather a heightened focus on the individual, sensory, and experiential aspects of combat whereby the "crisis over America's role in Iraq is being played out, more than anything, through cracks in the image of the 'American soldier.'"[3] As such, the forms of spectatorial American identity delineated by these films are not always easily mapped onto the preexisting political discourse of these conflicts, but constitute a rather more complex nexus around the notion of embodied witnessing, which is implicitly politicized in relation to the twin poles of trauma and enjoyment.

This is not to imply, however, that the War on Terror films appear entirely sui generis. Their aesthetics—and in particular, the relationship between embodied and technological forms of mediation—can indeed be seen as a particular reaction to the trends and modes of cinematic representation which characterized the Gulf War and Vietnam. In this introduction, then, I will briefly trace some of the pertinent issues around these two previous conflicts which reemerge and recombine in contemporary war cinema in quite distinctive ways. Broadly, the return to subjective, embodied, and experiential representations of combat which Barker identifies can be posited as a reaction to the Gulf War's perceived erasure of the body in favor of technological distancing and simulation. Infamously claimed not to have "taken place" by Jean Baudrillard, even more moderate characterizations highlight the overarching high-tech spectacle serving to control "public opinion by distancing, distracting and disengaging the citizen from the realities of war," and emphasize the incommensurability of this "farewell to both the subjective eye behind the camera as well as to the human subjects in front of the camera" with a cinematic aesthetic grounded in an embodied first-person point of view.[4] This return of the body is fueled by various sociopolitical factors of the conflicts themselves, not least of which is the decision to embed journalists with ground-level troops, particularly during the invasion of Iraq, and I will examine how this has generated a trend of embodied heroism epitomized by Kathryn Bigelow's award-winning and somewhat controversial *The Hurt Locker* (2008).

The foregrounding of embodied experience in contemporary war cinema is not, however, to the complete exclusion of technological mediation. Indeed, the advent of Unmanned Aerial Vehicles (UAVs) or drones can be posited as an intensification of Gulf War trends toward technological distancing, with the drone operator waging warfare from the safety of a compound thousands of miles removed from the combat zone itself. Yet the peculiar phenomena of Post-Traumatic Stress Disorder (PTSD) among drone operators indicates that the Gulf War–era discourse of technologically mediated combat as disembodied and virtualizing is perhaps no longer tenable. Rather, by carefully attending to the theorization of the drone assemblage and the operator's experience in recent studies, it becomes evident that the remote and virtual witnessing of combat via the drone interface is actually rather intimate and affective in a startlingly new way. The second section of this essay will explore representations of drone-mediated conflict in War on Terror films. This necessitates a degree of loosening in the generic delineation of war cinema, but one that is essential in order to properly register the changes taking place in the broader definitions of warfare itself. Specifically, CIA thrillers such as *Body of Lies* (2008) and *Syriana* (2005) mirror the wider political shift whereby drone warfare is administered by the CIA and JSOC (Joint Special Operations Command) rather than through conventional military channels. Although in the previous section I frame *The Hurt Locker* as essentially representative of the wider trend described, the methodology shifts a little for this second group of films. Since no single film comprehensively epitomizes the issues introduced above, I will therefore offer brief, though highly interconnected, analyses of *Body of Lies*, *Syriana*, and *Good Kill* (2014).

The third and final section of the essay will address the theme of homecoming soldiers as portrayed in films such as *In the Valley of Elah* (2007) and *Stop-Loss* (2008). This strand of the genre was largely elided in films dealing with the Gulf War, broadly due to the lack of opportunities for face-to-face combat during the highly restricted military operations, leading to a craving for "action" in, say, *Jarhead* (2005) and *Three Kings* (1999) which is almost diametrically opposed to the genre's typically reflective portraits of the psychological after-effects of combat. Contemporary instances of this subgenre thus draw more substantially upon the legacy of World War II and Vietnam homecoming films. However, where these films tended to posit the subjective trauma of combat experience as enacting a fundamental rift between military and civilian populations, a novel and perhaps quite radical transformation of this theme has taken place in War on Terror cinema, and particularly in *In the Valley of Elah* (2007). Through an analysis of the film's remediation of military video diaries and their relation to PTSD, I contend that digital mediation is framed as enabling an unfettered flow of this previously circumscribed sense of trauma into the civilian experience of war. This is concomitant with the new hypervisibility of contemporary warfare acknowledged throughout this essay: from embedded reportage through drone optics to the advent of military video diaries, the cultural legacy of the War on Terror can be fundamentally characterized by the emergence of digital modes granting the public new ways in which to engage remotely yet intimately with the visceral details of warfare.

Embodied Heroism: *The Hurt Locker*

In a notorious blog post, Slavoj Žižek attacked *The Hurt Locker*'s embodied and experiential aesthetic for obscuring the political context of the Iraq War in favor of a complicit form of spectatorial identification with its bomb-disposal heroes: "The film largely ignores the debate about US military intervention in Iraq, and instead focuses on the daily ordeals, on and off duty, of ordinary soldiers forced to deal with death and destruction. . . . In its very invisibility, ideology is here, more than ever: we are there, with our boys, identifying with their fear and anguish instead of questioning what they are doing there."[5]

For Žižek, then, the foregrounding of soldiers' embodied experience and "daily ordeals" is essentially opposed to any elucidation or analysis of the wider political context. This is evidently quite a widespread concern in contemporary war cinema and may apply to a significant portion of the War on Terror corpus. For instance, there has been a spate of Iraq and Afghanistan war films featuring a small group of Navy Seals (or similarly small but specialized unit) placed in a precarious position behind enemy lines. This trend is perhaps best exemplified by *Act of Valor* (2012) and *Lone Survivor* (2013), two films which quite unambiguously eschew any "questioning of what they are doing there" in favor of a simplistic and violent form of patriotic identity organized around the vicarious enjoyment of putting one's body at risk for one's country (often via the microcosm of the "brotherly" unit, though these films don't lack for more overt staging of patriotism). Similarly, though perhaps more surprisingly, the realm of documentary is equally implicated in this critique. A predilection for intimate, subjective portraits of the experience of soldiering can be also found in, for example, *Restrepo* (2010), *Armadillo* (2010), and *Gunner Palace* (2004). Patricia Aufderheide, in a scathing critique of these "grunt films," contends that they offer little more than "entertainment" for "war buffs," with the supposedly apolitical figure of the "grunt" (a trope deriving from Vietnam War cinema) serving to obscure any "public policy issue about the legitimacy or purpose of the war" since, in merely following orders, they "can't tell you whether we should be there."[6]

Certainly, there are a variety of wider contextual factors to which this embodied, experiential turn can be attributed. Particularly when compared with the previous Gulf War, the most recent conflicts in Iraq and Afghanistan undoubtedly entailed a greater degree of face-to-face combat, while journalists were afforded an opportunity for a far more intimate experience of ground-level conflict via the inauguration of media "embedding" during the invasion of Iraq. Indeed, the influence of embedded reportage on Iraq and Afghanistan war cinema is apparent even from a cursory overview of the films' sources. To cite just a few examples, Mark Boal's experiences of embedding in Iraq in 2004 led directly to the screenplays for *The Hurt Locker* and *In the Valley of Elah*. Likewise, Rajiv Chandrasekaran's *Imperial Life in the Emerald City*, based upon his embedded assignment in Baghdad, formed the basis for the Paul Greengrass film *Green Zone* (2010), while *Restrepo* is based on Sebastian Junger's *War*, his account of accompanying an army unit in Afghanistan's Korengal Valley over the course of a year.

Yet there is clearly more at stake here than a simple mirroring of these particular contextual factors. Framed in relation to the perceived disembodied spectacle of the Gulf War, the embodied aesthetic has been posited as a restoration of the reality of conflict[7] in arguments that are perhaps most revealing of the cultural valuation of embodied presence as a more privileged form of witnessing than technological mediation, with the latter often figured as virtualizing and distancing, particularly in this context. However, since this post–Gulf War context is no less characterized by a fundamental technological asymmetry, the relentless emphasis on the body at risk is perhaps less of an issue of verisimilitude than a reflection of a collective desire to remember the conflict in this perhaps nostalgic manner; in other words, as one in which the heroism of putting one's body on the line still makes a significant difference, rather than a war whose outcome is all but predetermined by the massive technological and economic imbalance which allows the United States to wage war increasingly remotely.

To further explore this question, I will now turn to an extended reading of *The Hurt Locker*, attending specifically to the relationship between the body and technological mediation as well as the form of spectatorial pleasure delimited by this mode of representing the war. The first of these issues is initially thematized through the contrast established between the Explosive Ordnance Disposal (EOD) squad's initial sergeant, Matthew Thompson (Guy Pearce), and the subsequent introduction of his replacement, William James (Jeremy Renner). In the film's opening sequence, the first point of view rendered is that of the robotic device employed by the unit to investigate a potential roadside IED (Improvised Explosive Device). The image is marked by digital static, a narrow focus, and a shallow depth of field. The robotic device's progress toward the IED is intercut with a depiction of escalating panic in the area as Iraqis flee the scene and US military vehicles arrive. This is immersively rendered with quick cutting between multiple, undefined points of view which break the classical 180-degree rule of editing, creating a paranoia-inducing instantiation of what Amy Taubin refers to as a "fully three-dimensional theatre of war."[8] This kinetic style is fundamental to the film's creation of an embodied sense of presence, yet here it is contrasted with the coolly distanced observation of protagonists Thompson, Sanborn, and Eldridge as they assess the explosive device through the remote interface of the robotic camera and casually make phallic jokes about the investigative robotic prosthesis. The technological mediation of the robotic device is implicitly linked to a detached sense of mastery as Thompson, preparing to remotely detonate the IED, precisely forecasts the intended blast radius.

Once the "bot" breaks down, however, and Thompson is required to put on the protective suit and approach the IED himself, there is a fundamental shift from the detachment of technological mediation to a distinctly embodied sense of danger. Aesthetically, this is conveyed by a noticeable intensification in Bigelow's use of embodied first-person perspectives. These include, on the periphery of the scene, rifle sightings of observers from Sanborn's point of view, but are primarily organized around Thompson's perspective from the interior of the bomb suit. Its physical restrictiveness lends his movement something of the ethereal quality of a slow-motion dolly, while the soundtrack amplifies the experiential sense of subjectivity through the prominence of his breathing patterns echoing in the helmet. The gradual emergence of a suspenseful electronic drone on the soundtrack heightens the sense of threat while Thompson, now in the "kill zone," lays the charge, and Eldridge sees a man with a mobile phone appear from a nearby butcher's shop. Furious crosscutting between these perspectives culminates in the highly aestheticized explosion of the IED, with extreme slow-motion and high-resolution imagery employed to highlight the details of the scattering debris.

Following Thompson's death, James's first mission as the new team leader clearly establishes his alternative approach to ordnance disposal, recklessly premised on individual and embodied pleasure. The sequence is introduced through a dynamic construction of three-dimensional space, similar to that of the film's opening, with Bigelow cutting between interior shots from the EOD unit's vehicle and various undefined points from which they are apparently observed. The absence of any specifically identifiable grounding to these diverse views on the action again generates an edgy, paranoid sensation of being under panoptic surveillance. As the unit emerges into this scene, the film also utilizes first-person points of view as a mode of embodied grounding, with the camera movements mimicking their scanning of the empty, littered street for signs of the IED as well as tracking across the overhead balconies to assess the gathering observers.

Having identified the location of the IED, James immediately dismisses Sanborn's assumption that they will use the "bot" to investigate, putting on the bomb suit instead and grinning with pleasure in defiance of warnings that it is "kind of tight down here." Approaching the IED, James deploys a smoke bomb to visually isolate himself from the support of Sanborn and Eldridge and largely ignores their communications, as though his evident pleasure in the job is heightened by disconnecting himself from the wider military network and individualizing the experience. It is at this point that the first-person point of view becomes more intensely engaged, with the rhythms of James's breath inside the helmet serving as a particularly embodied evocation of his subjective, experiential sensation.

The mission is then brusquely interrupted by a peculiar scene in which an Iraqi taxi driver breaks through the military barricade set up around James. A tense confrontation ensues as the driver implacably and motionlessly stares back at James despite the plethora of guns aimed at him. James's warning shots eventually convince him to begin reversing away from the scene, at which point he is detained. The total ambiguity of the driver's motives is matched by the sheer redundancy of this scene in terms of narrative causality. As a somewhat enigmatic interlude, then, it serves only to amplify the scene's tension and perhaps to provide some degree of face-to-face contact (if not quite combat per se) in contrast to the technological anonymity of IEDs. I will return to this point, and more generally to the film's characterization of Iraqis, just below.

As James returns to the procedure of disarming the IED, Bigelow reinstates the primacy of the first-person point of view. In visual terms, this is not strictly a sustained first-person view; although some shots heighten the sense of subjectivity by incorporating the edges of his visor as a frame within the frame, the scene also incorporates frequent cuts to perspectives that are just slightly askew from James's embodied position. Nonetheless, a sustained quality of embodied subjectivity is maintained throughout the entire sequence through the persistent use of the interiorized sound of his breathing. It is also worth noting the manner in which James seems to anthropomorphize the explosive by gently, almost sensuously brushing away the rubble which concealed it and intoning, "Hello, baby." After swiftly, almost anticlimactically disarming the

IED, James discovers a larger "secondary" explosive, the emergence of which is accompanied by a brief drone on the soundtrack, echoing that of the film's opening sequence. James's work on this second device is intercut with the point of view of an Iraqi on one of the balconies above. The significance of this observational perspective is subtly suggested by an initial match cut from inside James's helmet to a shot which frames him from above and uses the ovoid ornamental railing of the balcony to frame him in a graphically similar form. Although the technical details of the disarmament remain somewhat opaque, the viewer can nonetheless read this confrontation as a duel in which James is attempting to remove the detonator before the antagonist can trigger the IED, due to the cinematic grammar employed: specifically, an accelerating series of crosscuts which culminates in a face-to-face, shot/reverse-shot confrontation.

It is this characterization of James's working methods—particularly in contrast with the purportedly precise, technologically enhanced modeling of Thompson—that initially serves to frame the body at risk as the key mediator of the film's "fully three dimensional theatre of war."[9] For war-film scholar Robert Burgoyne, this serves to create a radical rupture between individual embodied experience and any overarching political framework: "Framing combat as an addictive pleasure, an ongoing, private and collective need, the film departs radically from genre convention, disdaining the formulas of older war films—the pathos formulas of sacrifice and loss—for a mode of address that emphasizes the adrenalized experience of risk. . . . The Hurt Locker foregrounds the idea of private experience and pleasure in war, rendering war as a somatic engagement that takes place outside any larger meta-narrative of nation or history."[10] This view of the film is apparently shared by Steven Shaviro, whose account of Bigelow's proceduralism posits that the intensive focus on "operational techniques" in both The Hurt Locker and Zero Dark Thirty drains these works of any ideals or overarching rationale.[11] However, as with Patricia Aufderheide's critique of the "grunt doc," one should be wary of the presentation of individual embodied experience as inherently apolitical.

Yet Burgoyne also notes, perhaps more pertinently, an equivalent dichotomy in the film between embodied and technologically enhanced mediation: "By underscoring the body at risk, The Hurt Locker also presents an implicit critique of the distance—moral and physical—of remote targeting and weaponry. The reality of war as embodied activity and embodied violence asserts itself here in a visceral way."[12] This argument more directly addresses the contrast between Thompson and James, as the procedure for dealing with IEDs shifts from the detached precision of robotic mediation to the viscerally embodied risk of James's approach. James's association of embodied pleasure with a lack of technological mediation and isolation from the wider military network becomes even more pronounced after the initial mission, as he subsequently begins to work without the bomb suit and jettisons his radio.

It may be possible, developing Burgoyne's line of argument, to read this shift from Thompson's technologically aided insularity to James's riskier engagement as a metaphor for the degeneration of asymmetrical warfare with minimal casualties into a drawn-out counterinsurgency program throughout which the death toll escalated alarmingly. However, while I concur with the suggestion that *The Hurt Locker* frames embodied experience and technological mediation as a key binary opposition, the claim that embodiment "presents a critique" of technological distancing does not quite, I believe, satisfactorily address the significance of James's reckless endangerment as a willingly self-imposed form of pleasure. Furthermore, the film does not seem to posit either embodied or technologically mediated modes of warfare as the ontologically privileged "reality of war"; indeed, both are depicted as potentially lethal, and if the film ultimately focuses on the embodied form to a greater degree, it is primarily in order to explore this aspect of James's combat addiction.

This body/technology dialectic may appear somewhat disjunctive for a war film in which "combat" is primarily constituted by the body–versus–anonymous-technology scenario of a soldier attempting to disarm IEDs, though Bigelow does just about manage to sustain this notion by consistently incorporating human antagonists, such as the taxi driver or, more frequently, a combatant who lingers on the margins of the scene waiting for an opportune moment to trigger the explosion. As this implies, the film's characterization of Iraqis is particularly reductive. In the majority of cases, they simply represent an undefined threat. No attempt is made to contextualize the reasons for insurrection against the US occupation of Baghdad, and the closest the film comes to ascribing an equivalent sense of subjective motivation is the vague implication that the taxi driver in the above-described sequence may be mirroring James's enjoyment of embodied danger. Even the most prominent Iraqi character in the film—a young boy nicknamed "Beckham" for whom James develops some paternal sympathy—appears to be defined solely through his relation to James. Beckham, however superficially, holds a flattering mirror to James's recklessness by praising EOD work as "fun, it's cool, it's gangster, yeah?" which contrasts markedly with the suspicions and fears emanating from Eldridge and Sanborn.

The implied infantilism of James's self-image that emerges here is but one element of critique which suggests that James's position as the film's purveyor of embodied, experiential pleasure in war is perhaps not to be taken at face value, thus problematizing a model of American identity which would derive enjoyment (whether as individual pleasure or patriotic glory) from the visceral experience of placing one's body at risk. While his actions throughout approximately the first half of the film may be read as eccentric yet heroic, a degree of distancing is introduced during a sequence in which Sanborn and Eldridge consider fragging him,[13] with the audience seriously invited to consider whether this action is justifiable as a means of self-protection for the unit. In the latter half of the film, James's escalating paranoia becomes increasingly difficult to identify with, and supplants his heroic self-image with delusions of persecution.

The first substantial evidence of this occurs during the sequence in which the unit finds a "body bomb," with James mistakenly identifying the victim as Beckham.[14] In stark contrast to the pleasure derived from earlier sequences of ordnance disposal, James is in this instance visibly disturbed and subsequently embarks upon a bizarre and clearly misguided nocturnal attempt to find the perpetrators. When he later discovers Beckham selling DVDs inside the military compound, James simply ignores him as though refusing to acknowledge the fantastical grounding of this escapade. The motivating factor behind this shift in James's character seems to be rooted in the very notion of a body-bomb, which perhaps enacts a radically disconcerting literalization of his anthropomorphizing of IEDs, although it is worth noting that the circumstances, in contrast to earlier ordnance disposal procedures, do not provide any identifiable human antagonist nor anyone to rescue, thus thwarting any opportunity to fulfil his perceived heroic role.

Structurally, this sequence plays a significant role in beginning to erode the degree of audience identification with James. The combination of his charisma and unconventional success with the use of a first-person, experiential aesthetic designed to induce audience identification may have precluded any critical reading of his character up to this point, yet Bigelow here begins to establish a degree of distance whereby one cannot simply identify with the delusional grounds of his decision-making. This is further developed during the following mission in which the unit is called in to assess an oil tanker explosion. Surveying the chaos of the aftermath, James refuses the straightforward terms of the mission. Invoking a paranoid vision of "guys watching us right now and laughing at this" to justify chasing his "adrenaline fix" (as identified by Eldridge), James leads the unit into a reckless pursuit of unseen perpetrators through unknown back alleys, which results in Eldridge's brief capture and injury. Once again, the conjunction of arriving too late for any heroics and the absence of an identifiable antagonist seems to induce this paranoid delusion.

This notion of James as a victim of military circumstance is ultimately compounded by the film's conclusion. During his brief sojourn at home, prior to reenlisting, he explains his singular motivation to his infant son: "You love everything, don't you? But you know what, buddy? As you get older, some of the things you love might not seem so special. Like your jack-in-the-box. Maybe you realize it's just a piece of tin and a stuffed animal. And the older you get, the fewer things you really love. By the time you get to my age maybe it's only one or two things. With me, I think it's one."

Read in conjunction with the film's opening quotation from Chris Hedges— "The rush of battle is a potent and lethal addiction, for war is a drug"—this clearly posits James's unrelenting compulsion to put his body "on the line" as an addiction.[15] Žižek's critique of the film is equally skeptical of this construction as it is of the experiential aesthetic, arguing that this "focus on the perpetrator's traumatic experience enables us to obliterate the entire ethico-political background of the conflict."[16] Certainly, the general notion of victimization in this context does appear to coincide with genre tendencies to circumvent politics by internalizing and psychologizing the soldiers' experience, as shown by Guy Westwell's analyses of the Vietnam veteran figure.[17] Additionally, *The Hurt Locker*'s diegetic restriction to James's experiences does preclude any engagement with the "ethico-political background of the conflict." Žižek's contention that "we are there, with our boys, identifying with their fear and anguish instead of questioning what they are doing there" is justified, then, in the sense that the experiential rendition of disarming IEDs does not directly open up to questioning the political basis for the war, nor, to reiterate Aufderheide's critique of the "grunt docs," does the film address its audience as a voting public.[18] This flattening of the distinctions between wars is certainly a valid critique of *The Hurt Locker*, since political context presumably has no bearing on James's addiction to bodily risk, and evokes a rather harrowing vision of American spectatorial identity whereby the cause, context, and politics of conflict are displaced entirely by the solely material pleasure of embodied yet anonymized combat.

Despite these pertinent criticisms of the film, I would nonetheless maintain that Bigelow's use of the experiential mode is rather more sophisticated than that of many similar films since the positing of combat addiction does suggest, albeit on an individual-subjective level, some sense of "questioning what they are doing there." By manifesting James's enjoyment of combat through a highly subjective aesthetic which invites audience identification, subsequently establishing a greater degree of distancing through his escalating paranoia, and finally reframing the opening construction as an addiction, the film ultimately seems to imply a kind of auto-critique of the war film's experiential mode. In other words, *The Hurt Locker* lavishly and artfully revels in this embodied form of enjoyment of the body at risk and its concomitant heroism, but also *problematizes* it through the eventual emergence of this reflexive framework which recasts the former as a debilitating addiction. The film can thus be read as linking this conceptualization of conflict as a distinctly embodied form of entertainment with James's condition, implying that the American spectatorial relationship to war within this particular discursive regime leads inexorably toward an encompassing state of disillusionment and compulsive repetition. This reading of the film may be somewhat against the grain given Bigelow's apparent predilection for this particular style of visceral action. Yet this almost paradoxical structure, whereby the subjective enjoyment of combat is both manifested and critiqued, does leave the film open to diverse and potentially contradictory readings which may account for both its wide audience appeal at a time when war films were proving largely unpopular and for the ensuing polarizing critical debate over the film's politics.

Drone Wars: Syriana (2005), Body of Lies (2008), Good Kill (2014)

In terms of technological innovations, the War on Terror era is likely to be remembered above all for the advent of Unmanned Aerial Vehicles (UAVs), or drones as they are more commonly termed. Effecting controversial shifts in military doctrine through their use in countries with which the United States is not technically at war and their administration by the CIA and JSOC (Joint Special Operations Command), an anti-terror unit that Medea Benjamin describes as "even more cloaked in secrecy and less subject to accountability than the intelligence agency," they have further generated deeply troubling questions over the ethics of remote killing. Policies such as "signature strikes," allowing for the targeting of "groups of men who bear certain signatures, or defining characteristics associated with terrorist activities, but whose identities are not known," and "double tap" strikes, in which a first missile is shortly followed by a second aimed at the same location (often resulting in deaths of civilians attempting to aid the initial casualties), have been widely condemned.[19] Many critics have also specifically denounced the inequality of drone warfare, with the body of the operator safely located thousands of miles from the combat zone, as reducing warfare to the level of gaming. This is exemplified by Akbar Ahmed and Lawrence Wilkerson's 2013 *Guardian* article "Dealing remote-control death, the US has lost its moral compass," which explicitly denounces "armchair warriors" as perpetuating a "dishonorable" mode of combat by "making warfare more like a video game and giving technicians the dissociated power of life and death for the figures on the screen before them."[20] In such accounts, the analogies drawn with gaming tend to bolster an argument focused primarily on the geographical and ethical distancing apparently inaugurated (or at least pushed to a new extreme) by drones' particular form of screen-mediated remote combat.

However, this conceptualization of drone warfare as concomitant with a virtualizing panoptic regime has been challenged by several studies which more closely examine the drone assemblage and the operators' experience.[21] These works by Derek Gregory, Caroline Holmqvist, and Alison Williams reframe drone mediation as comprising a distinctive rupture from the military lineage of aerial abstraction or distancing, arguing instead that drones effect a highly sensory and intimate engagement with combat spaces and bodies.[22] For instance, Derek Gregory explicitly refutes "critics who claim that these operations reduce war to a video game in which the killing space appears remote and distant," suggesting instead that the "new visibilities" enabled by drone mediation produce a highly distinctive mode of "intimacy."[23] This distinction is expanded upon in a subsequent essay by Gregory, foregrounding as central to this shift the high-resolution imagery of ground-level events now instantaneously transmitted back to the pilot by drone video feeds and the networked reconfiguration of subjectivity that takes place with the instantiation of the digitally connected kill chain:

> But the flight crews repeatedly insist that real-time video feeds bring them right into the combat zone: that they are not 7,000 miles away but just 18 inches, the distance from eye to screen. Insofar as this is a "videogame war" then it shares in the extraordinary immersive capacity of the most advanced videogames. This is significantly different from the detachment— the "distance and blindness"—experienced by bomber crews over Germany and Vietnam. And yet the reality-effect this produces may be sufficiently

powerful where remotely piloted aircraft are providing armed overwatch or close air support to convert proximity not distance, visibility not blindness, into a serious problem. . . . [Operators] interact regularly with troops on the ground through live video feeds and online communications, and the intimacy created by these new forms of military-social networking can predispose them to interpret the actions of others in the vicinity as a threat to their comrades and precipitate lethal action.[24]

Caroline Holmqvist's study of drones similarly claims that analogies with gaming can be made only on the level of their "*immersive* quality." Expanding on Gregory's account of how the drone video feed induces a sense of intimacy, Holmqvist explores how the unique "hyper-vision of drone optics" exposes one to "high-resolution images of killing including the details of casualties and body parts that would never be possible to capture with the human eye," which, combined with a networked sense of "*proximity* to ground troops" is the probable source of the perhaps startlingly high number of incidences of PTSD among drone pilots.[25] Alison Williams concurs that drone mediation can be characterized as a distinctly "sensory engagement with the combat spaces," thus fracturing the body/technology dichotomy inherent in accounts of drone virtualization to suggest instead a distinctive fusion of affective embodiment and technological mediation.[26]

Beyond the issue of verisimilitude, these starkly divergent accounts of drone warfare have significant implications for the construction of spectatorial identity. Those which emphasize distancing via analogies with gaming tend to suggest that both actual drone operators and spectators of the footage (via YouTube, for instance) are able to derive enjoyment of the spectacle without any concomitant risk to themselves in a particularly callous instantiation of American military identity, while the alternative theorizations of drones by Gregory, Holmqvist and Williams punctures this veneer of insulating distance and suggests that drone optics are more likely to lead to particularly traumatic new forms of witnessing.

The stark disparities between these early theories of drones are reflected in the varying configurations of drone mediation in War on Terror cinema. They first began to appear in the subgenre or cycle of CIA thrillers around 2005 to 2008, exemplified by *Syriana* and *Body of Lies*. Stephen Gaghan's *Syriana*, from 2005, is loosely based on *See No Evil: The True Story of a Ground Soldier in the CIA's War Against Terrorism*, a memoir by former CIA agent Robert Baer. The film's multiple, intersecting and globe-spanning narrative threads deal predominantly with the struggle for control of oil reserves in an unspecified Middle Eastern emirate, focalizing this geopolitical conflict through the perspectives of Prince Nasir (the unnamed country's foreign minister), a CIA agent assigned to assassinate Nasir, an energy analyst from Switzerland, two Pakistani migrant workers, and numerous US lawyers and lobbyists. Ridley Scott's 2008 film *Body of Lies* employs a similarly globe-spanning narrative structure, cutting fluidly between Iraq, Jordan, Syria, United Arab Emirates as well as the United States, United Kingdom, Turkey, and the Netherlands to track the pursuit of terrorist Al-Saleem by CIA agent Roger Ferris. Video feeds from all these locations are relayed, via satellites and drones, to the CIA control room run by Russell Crowe's character, Ed Hoffman.

With their aesthetics and narrative modes recalling 1990s surveillance/spy films such as *Enemy of the State* (1998) as much as what is more conventionally considered war cinema, *Syriana* and *Body of Lies* pose an ontological dilemma for definitions of the "war film" itself in the digital era. Garrett Stewart refers to them as "the new Hollywood plots of surveillance paranoia, in overseas and homeland settings alike," in contrast to the "traditional war (or anti-war) film," but does acknowledge that there is increasingly a "dubious overlap" between these two "intersecting spheres" of Iraq War–era conflict films.[27] The veneer of fiction cast over *Syriana* and *Body of Lies* also serves to detach them from any specific conflict—via the coy refusal to specify the key oil-rich location in *Syriana,* and the pursuit of an individual terrorist without reference to any particular war between nation-states in *Body of Lies*—in a manner curiously out of synch with the framing of more conventional war cinema. Yet, while these aspects create a degree of ambiguity in defining the corpus here, they simultaneously evoke a shift in US military doctrine inextricably related to the advent of drone warfare. Specifically, the films' global, panoptic reach, fluid border-crossings, and focus on individual assassinations carried out by the CIA mirror the actual context of drones' use as part of the War on Terror more closely than the embodied/experiential conventions of the "traditional" war film might allow. Thus, I think the representations of drones in these films should be taken seriously as a burgeoning branch of contemporary war cinema reflecting a shift in military doctrine from full-scale combat to counterinsurgency operations, rather than treated as distinct from the war genre per se and aligned with spy or action films.

The very narrative structures of these two films are also complicit with the digitization of military technologies. Stewart suggests a sense of this through his claim that "Screen narratives such as *Syriana* . . . are not political first of all in regard to the inferred content of their ideological stance and its typifying dialogue. They are political in the very form of their narrative mapping. In this way, they can almost unconsciously mirror what they might intermittently resist or critique."[28]

While the employment of multiple interconnected storylines predates the digital as both a literary and cinematic technique, the particular engagement of parallel editing in *Syriana* and *Body of Lies* does suggest a distinctly panoptic instance of this device through the suggestion (occasionally explicit, but largely inferred) that the films' global scope is activated by and fundamentally reliant upon the CIA's surveillance network. It may even be said to evoke the "time-space compression . . . [which] has brought all those in the network much closer to the killing space" that Gregory posits as a crucial characteristic of the digitally connected drone kill chain.[29] However, since the films do not overtly distinguish a "drone aesthetic" from the wider range of surveillance technologies—particularly satellites—this narrative structure seems to connote a more generalized panoptic model of digital imaging.

This lack of distinction between drone and satellite footage is particularly apparent in *Body of Lies*. While the ground-level agent (Roger Ferris) does intermittently make reference to his ability to spot the distinctive gleam of a drone in the skies above, they are otherwise figured as a mere extension of CIA chief Ed Hoffman's panoptic vision, with a complete absence of any sequences depicting drone piloting per se or an employment of their armed capacities. Instead, drones are represented as an interchangeable element in a uniform digital surveillance aesthetic. This is demonstrated most clearly in the montage sequences that bookend the film. The closing sequence, for instance, begins with a drone-mediated shot of Ferris, overlaid with annotations of coordinates as well as a tag specifically marking the feed as "UAV" followed by a string of numbers. The drone camera then begins to zoom out, and, without any legible cuts, seamlessly transitions into an extreme long-shot satellite image of the city (annotated once again, in this case as "SAT KH11–12"). This satellite feed then begins to fragment, ultimately splitting the screen into four juxtaposed panels. The upper-left segment here appears to be the same satellite image as in the previous shot, while the lower-left retains the drone annotations seen in the initial shot of Ferris; the specific source of the two segments on the right, however, remain unclear. Ultimately, this split-screen surveillance image begins to flicker and degrade, marking the close of the film with a haze of digital static.[30]

Garrett Stewart's reading of this sequence posits "cancelled voyeurism" as "the closest thing to narrative resolution," elaborating on the perceived equivalence between the film's diegesis and the panoptic model of surveillance evoked by the above montage:

> There's nothing left to see if the technopticon has lost interest. . . . To compensate for any lack of satisfying climax, at least we've supposedly been privy to some top-secret CIA feeds, allowing us for once to see the world the way the secret service does. And not, of course, just visually. For at a certain level of geopolitical oversight—to whose plotting our hero (any hero) is no longer instrumental—all monitored enemy activity, whether or not we foment or even fabricate it, can be made to serve our militarist purposes. A film doesn't have to be even half good to be fleetingly brilliant, which is not to say popular, when it lets American imperialist logic declare itself so nakedly.[31]

The way this "technopticon" is distinctly invoked at the opening and closing of the film, with the digital noise serving as a kind of transition, does seem to imply that the film's diegesis is accessed by hacking into "some top-secret CIA feeds" as Stewart suggests. However, this notion also sits somewhat awkwardly with the film's relentlessly technophobic moralizing, which is perhaps the clearest instance of the tendency for a kind of "high-tech technophobia" that Stewart elsewhere identifies as characterizing this group of films.[32] I think there is another, perhaps paradoxical, reading to be made of this closing sequence. The reductive collapsing of drone and satellite imaging, coupled with the destabilizing eruption of this exaggeratedly digitized static, may also be viewed as a kind of "othering" of digital surveillance, as aesthetically and ontologically distinct from the realm of the cinematic—which is almost exclusively aligned, in this case, with the mediating point of view of the ground-level agent and his dangerous and embodied heroics.

Body of Lies contrasts the methods of Hoffman and Ferris throughout, with a repeated privileging of Ferris's embodied presence and capacity for adapting to the complexity of localized situations against the cruel, Machiavellian scheming of Hoffman, which is implicitly aligned with his panoptic power. This overt and somewhat facile character-centric critique seems to enforce a rather rigid distinction between the cinematic heroism of ground-level agency and the moral vacuum of the digitally enhanced aerial view. I hesitate to label the film's rendition of drone imaging as disembodied since it is quite neatly aligned with Hoffman's perspective, yet this binary opposition that the film establishes does seem to imply that drone-mediated space differs ontologically from the properly cinematic diegesis, and in doing so perhaps ascribes to drones (via their indistinction from satellites) the values of virtualizing distancing and the effacement of embodied experience that are highlighted by critics who equate drone operation with gaming.

In summary, then, the use of drones in *Body of Lies* seems to offer little more than the opportunity of zooming from an extreme-long-shot satellite image to the medium-long-shot of the drone, thus ultimately comprising little more than a slight tweak of cinematic grammar and a slight increase in the detail of panoptic imagery. By neglecting to engage with the contemporary assemblage of armed drones—in other words, the material context of their application including the subjective experience of piloting and the intersubjective network of the so-called kill chain—this representation fails to demonstrate any real difference between contemporary uses of armed drones and their use for unmanned aerial observation throughout the late twentieth century. Ultimately, the film does attempt to critique this panoptic military power as complicit in an increasingly distanced, insulated, and callous American form of waging war, but doing so via the use of a somewhat anachronistic divorce between aerial and ground-level perspectives seems to substantially underestimate the true scope of how drones have transfigured contemporary warfare.

Syriana, on the other hand, does feature at least one key sequence which forcefully emphasizes the armed capacity underlying the drone interface, although it simultaneously enacts a similarly problematic split between ground-level and aerial perspectives. The sequence occurs towards the end of the film, with the CIA attempting to assassinate Prince Nasir and his convoy while, at ground level, a CIA agent (Barnes) opposed to the mission races to intercept the convoy and warn them of the impending strike. Gaghan composes this sequence from these two distinct points of view: the screen of the CIA control room, on which the drone video feed is blown up to gigantic proportions for the assembled observers, and the ground-level perspective of Barnes. In the process, *Syriana* demonstrates a similar kind of aesthetic and ontological split between drone-mediated space and embodied perspectives to that seen in *Body of Lies.*

Although the drone image is in color, and unburdened by the clutter of annotations or overlays, it remains an extreme long shot with a distinct lack of resolution which, significantly, does not enable the identification of the individuals on the ground. The film therefore relies exclusively on the ground-level element of its parallel editing schema to depict the ensuing action with any narrative clarity. This aesthetic strategy purports to privilege ground-level complexity against aerial abstraction or virtualization in the same manner as *Body of Lies;* and indeed, the film's sympathies are quite explicitly aligned with rogue agent Barnes, whose ethics remain untainted by the military-industrial machinations in which his superiors are enmeshed. The fact that Barnes remains unidentified, and thus that the film's most recognizable star (George Clooney) is killed as collateral damage in the strike is seemingly intended to emotively flag the wanton destruction unleashed by this mode of aerial warfare.

Nonetheless, it is rather problematic to perpetuate the notion that drone operators cannot necessarily verify the identity of their targets. Numerous studies of drones have emphasized the unparalleled detail that their high-resolution video feeds afford, which renders the verisimilitude of *Syriana*'s drone imagery somewhat questionable. Yet this becomes more significantly problematic when considered in relation to the infamously loose rules of engagement for actual US drone strikes, whereby any adult male of military age within a pre-authorized target area may be deemed a legitimate target. In this wider political context, *Syriana*'s drone-strike sequence risks corroborating this procedure (in contradiction to the film's ostensible political sympathies) through the technological justification of low-resolution imagery.

Andrew Nichols's *Good Kill* is significantly differentiated from *Syriana* and *Body of Lies* by the simple fact that it is set in Las Vegas. As such, the film contains no ground-level perspective on combat to complement the drone's aerial imagery, and thus the ontological split between the aerial and the ground level perpetuated by the above films is not replicated here. This serves to embed *Good Kill* more firmly within the notion of remote warfare and engenders a more substantial degree of reflection upon how warfare is altered when mediated exclusively via the drone interface.

Although released in 2014, Nichols's film is set in 2010, offering a slight historical distance on this period characterized by the peak of US drone strikes in Pakistan. This context is acknowledged by the film's opening titles, which declare 2010 as the year of "the greatest escalation of targeted killings." It is also narratively significant in situating the film amidst a boom in the recruitment of gamers as drone personnel—an issue addressed most explicitly via an admonitory speech to the recruits which simultaneously acknowledges that war has become a "first-person-shooter" while warning them that the consequences are real "flesh" and "blood"—and amidst a burgeoning of CIA-run drone missions, which are operated by the film's Air Force drone crew.

The opening sequence of *Good Kill* immediately establishes an intimate, immersive conceptualization of drone imagery that is closer to the accounts of Gregory and Holmqvist than to the disembodied, virtualizing panoptic regime of *Body of Lies*. Forgoing establishing shots entirely, the film opens with a full-screen remediation of the drone interface, the drone camera thereby established as synonymous with the film camera. While the drone crew's presence is conveyed via the soundtrack, with their radio communications played as voice-over, they are introduced in a visually striking manner that reinforces the sense of immersion suggested by the drone/film-camera equivalence. Nichols gradually begins to cut away from the drone interface, establishing a shot/reverse pattern between the operators and the drone screen. Yet these reverse shots are uniformly extreme close-ups with a particularly shallow depth of field—first of an eye, then a mouth, a hand operating a joystick, and finally a foot pressing down on a pedal—that offer a highly fragmented sense of the operators and their location. The way the drone operators' awareness of self and space here is wholly subsumed by their absorption in the drone point of view clearly evokes the immersive "reality-effect" of the drone feed, described by Gregory as the sensation of being "not 7,000 miles away but just 18 inches, the distance from eye to screen."[33]

This immersion effect is implicitly ascribed as a point of equivalence between the drone screen and the film screen. The detail of the imagery—later described by *Good Kill*'s protagonist as "so beautifully clear . . . it couldn't be clearer if I was there; you can see everything, the looks on their faces, everything"—contrasts unambiguously with the soft, grainy appearance of the drone feed in *Syriana*. In a further contrast with the CIA films, the drone feed is here permitted to exclusively fulfil the role of combat mediation. Rather than employing a "cinematic" ground-level perspective to complement aerial abstraction, *Good Kill* posits the drone feed itself as inherently cinematic, immersively transporting both operators and viewers into the film's combat spaces. As the posters taped to the operators' cabin doors claim, then, on entering the realm of drone mediation, "You are now leaving the U.S. of A."

Alongside this evocation of immersion, the fragmentation of the operators' bodies in this opening sequence simultaneously renders them less as individual, distinct subjects than as a disjointed collection of organs and motor functions intertwined with the drone apparatus. In doing so, Nichols presents drones as akin to what Alison Williams terms an "assemblage, composed of both human and machine elements." Williams's study of the drone assemblage goes on to suggest that this kind of bodily fragmentation leads to a fundamental "interchangeability" of the human element as bodies begin to "perform more like machine components."[34] While this is consistent with the particular vision of the assemblage presented by the opening sequence, the majority of the film does however balance this fragmented, distributed sense of subjectivity with a dramatization of the injurious psychological effects of drone piloting and a reflection on the ethics of remote warfare which are quite heavily dependent upon more conventional models of subjective agency.

Indeed, protagonist Major Thomas Egan's sense of individual guilt and ethical resistance to drone operation is established quite early in the film. A former pilot made redundant by the Air Force's increasing prioritization of drone operations over piloted missions, Egan reluctantly works as a drone operator but still idealizes the embodied "risk" of flight above the "cowardly" mode of remote combat in which he is now implicated. This contrast between piloting and drone operation is suggestive of the binary relationship between embodied combat and the virtualizing abstraction of drones that runs through *Body of Lies* and *Syriana*—or perhaps more accurately, the relationship between embodiment and technological mediation proposed by *The Hurt Locker*—albeit with a notable concession to conceptualizing drones through a more cinematic aesthetic. It remains somewhat ambiguous whether the film treats this distinction seriously, or simply employs it as a signification of Egan's fantasy of escape from the drudgery of drone assassinations and surveillance, though it clearly also contributes to his tendency to assume *individual* responsibility for the killings carried out by his crew despite his colonel's repeated invocations of *networked* responsibility through such lines as "we all pulled the trigger in that box."

In addition to this individualized sense of guilt, the film also posits an inability to adapt to drone warfare's blurring of military and civilian realms as central to Egan's descent into alcoholism, depression, and marital discord. Initially, this facet of remote warfare is presented somewhat comically, with Egan baffling the sales assistant in a local shop with the declaration that he "blew away six Taliban in Pakistan just today; now I'm going home to barbecue." However, this ironic approach quickly cedes to a more troubled incarnation of blurred boundaries, with the film drawing visual parallels between Vegas suburbia and Waziristan via aerial shots of the landscape and highlighting Egan's increasing detachment from family life as he repeatedly gazes absently up to the skies. He is warned to "keep compartmentalizing," but evinces a nostalgia not only for flight itself, but also the clean lines demarcating military and nonmilitary space, or war and peace, which have been fractured by drone mediation's elision of distance.

At this point, Egan's unit is selected to run secret drone missions for the CIA, and the film's distinctions between embodied and remote combat gradually give way to more precise ethical distinctions among the procedural applications of drone strikes. This is neatly glossed in an introductory speech by Colonel Johns, who notes that the CIA has "progressed" (a hint of irony in the intonation of this word) beyond personality strikes (that is, targeting known individuals), operating under alternate rules of engagement which permit "signature strikes" on unidentified individuals—or even groups—based on "patterns of behavior." Even more controversial than signature strikes, however, is the newly introduced practice of the "follow up" or "double tap" strike. During the unit's first mission for the CIA, Egan and sensor operator Vera Suarez are apparently shocked by the instruction to carry out a second strike. The rich visual detail of the drone feed is particularly relevant here, allowing the viewer a window on the scene which is clearly populated by rescuers with spades rather than armed combatants. Although they reluctantly carry out the order, Suarez nonetheless rebukes the officers with the question, "Was that a war crime, sir?"

The CIA are villainously figured in the film as a disembodied voice over the intercom, addressed only as "Langley." Although obviously connected to the same network—such that "we see what you see"—there is clearly something of a disjunction between the tightly knit drone crew and the near-anonymous CIA which is reinforced by the increasingly manifest differences in procedure and ethical decision-making. For instance, in response to the drone crew's cautioning over likely civilian casualties, the CIA's response is typically aloof and dogmatic: "In our assessment, the combatants we are targeting pose a grave enough threat to the United States to justify potential civilian casualties; not to mention that this pre-emptive self-defense is approved and ordered by the administration. Please engage." Such callous applications of drone warfare ultimately emerge as the prime target of the film's critique, especially as they are increasingly contrasted with the more idealistic aspect of "overwatch." A sequence in which Egan willingly puts in overtime to watch over a ground patrol in Afghanistan as they sleep is framed as a somewhat redemptive release from the CIA missions, as he returns home content that he "did something good today."

While this critique of ethical standards in the administering of drone strikes is more precise and insightful than the woolly distinction between piloting and remote warfare that preceded it, the way the film ultimately resolves Egan's internal ethical conflict is perhaps the most deeply problematic element of *Good Kill*. Having been downgraded to surveillance duty after deliberately sabotaging one of the CIA double-tap strikes, Egan finds himself once again watching the house of a supposed Taliban commander, a locale in which the crew had earlier witnessed the rape of the housekeeper by an unknown visitor. Recognizing the return of the same man, Egan persuades the rest of his crew to exit the cabin for a break and assassinates the rapist with a Hellfire missile.[35]

The procedural details of this sequence mirror that of the CIA strikes, particularly Egan's disengagement of the drone apparatus's recording function, in a manner that might suggest a subversive parallel between Egan's assumption of a position of omnipotent and vengeful moral judgment and the CIA's dogmatic standards. However, as he triumphantly exits the cabin and drives off into the horizon, the film seems to frame this concluding act as one of liberation and catharsis for Egan, as though it were another "good deed" to counterbalance his guilt over the civilian casualties inflicted during the CIA operations. This rather disturbing catharsis risks undermining the film's critique of the indiscriminate use of drones under the CIA. Although the rapist is undeniably guilty, Egan's vengeful judgment of him ultimately seems to advocate an *extension* of drone assassinations to any subject deemed guilty by the moral conscience of the individual drone pilot, rather than a restriction of their use solely for personality strikes without risk of civilian casualties.

If by this point *Good Kill* has substituted a somewhat retrogressive and problematic model of individual subjective agency for the more distributed, networked evocation of subjectivity articulated in the opening sequence, the film does nonetheless present a more substantial interrogation of drone warfare than any of the above CIA films. Rather than enforcing a binary distinction between the embodied, ground-level realm of cinematic space and the virtualizing distancing of drone/satellite surveillance, *Good Kill* does quite successfully demonstrate a more thorough integration of drone and cinematic aesthetics. The film also represents the material context of drones' use, ranging from the drudgery of reconnaissance to the varying frameworks for strikes, with a precision unparalleled in contemporary war cinema and, despite the troubling resolution, is undeniably valuable for inviting its audience to reflect on the ethical considerations involved in their application.

Although all three films discussed in this section are ostensibly critical of drone warfare, *Body of Lies* and *Syriana* offered something of a way out of the Machiavellian panopticon via identification with the ground-level agents (Ferris and Barnes) who are better able to appreciate the nuances of various international contexts, thus retaining the possibility of a more conventionally heroic form of American military identity. Yet this is strikingly absent in *Good Kill*, which not only realizes more forcefully the intimate and traumatic consequences of remote warfare, but also offers no escape from the networked responsibility for drone killings, thus burdening both drone operator and viewer with a more overtly guilty sense of moral responsibility.

Video Diaries, Homecoming, and PTSD: *In the Valley of Elah*

The third and final theme serving as a key marker in the cultural memory of the War on Terror is the advent of the soldier's video diary. This may not ostensibly seem quite on a par with drones in terms of technological novelty, since war cinema has mimicked the video diary format at least as far back as *84 Charlie Mopic* (1989), a Vietnam-set simulation of a found-footage video diary, as subsequently emulated in films such as *Man Bites Dog* (1992) and *The Blair Witch Project* (1999). Nonetheless, the most recent conflicts in Iraq and Afghanistan were the first in which soldiers could publicly and instantaneously share video diary footage via YouTube (or similar online video platforms). This innovation can be situated alongside the introduction of journalistic embedding in the sense that it contributes to the proliferation of intimate and experiential (self-)portraits of combat, possibly at the expense of wider context. Yet it may also be consistent with the technological trends highlighted in the previous section in enabling a new and remote hypervisibility whereby the intimate and traumatic details of combat are brought home in unparalleled detail and volume.

The video diary is remediated in a range of contemporary war films, the most prominent including *Redacted*, *Battle for Haditha*, *Stop-Loss*, and *In the Valley of Elah*. A further grouping could pair *Redacted* with *Haditha*—as films principally exploring the consequences of abuses of power by US soldiers in Iraq captured on amateur video diaries—and *Stop-Loss* with *Elah* as films set in a post-combat, homecoming context and focusing on PTSD. In *Elah*, the military video diary in fact becomes the film's exclusive mode of mediating combat, which is set alongside various other authenticating devices such as the opening claim to be "inspired by real events" and the remediation of actual television news footage from Iraq, and serves to bind the film's diegetic world as closely as possible to the real war. It also indicates the culturally determined value of authenticity increasingly ascribed to the amateur immediacy of digital media, perhaps even in opposition to a more polished cinematic restaging.

The video diaries in *Stop-Loss* are collaboratively shot on a handheld camera that is passed around the unit and subsequently screened (post-homecoming) only for the soldiers involved in its production, thus serving to materialize a collective identity very specifically confined to its military network. In *Elah*, however, the author of the diaries (Mike Deerfield) is missing from the very start of the film—and soon to be found dead—so that the diegetic spectatorship of the diary takes place within more of a civilian context. Structurally, Haggis's film is composed around two interlocking investigations: that of a local police officer (Emily Sanders) into Mike's death, and Hank Deerfield's parallel investigation of his son's video diaries, which initially seem to proffer an explanation for his disappearance and ultimately serve to reveal the behavioral transformation of Mike from a naive and idealistic young recruit into the sadistic "Doc," thus nicknamed for his propensity to torturously probe the wounds of Iraqi captives.

Due to Mike's phone being "seriously fried" by the "intense heat" of Iraq, the video diaries unfold serially throughout the film as a technician emails the unscrambled fragments to Hank. This aspect of the film is the focus of a study by Nicholas Chare, who argues for "a greater recognition of the materiality of the digital and an acknowledgement of its indexical properties," primarily by detailing the film's emphasis on Mike's phone as an essentially material and fragile container of the videos.[36] Certainly, the film does place a greater than usual emphasis upon the evidential materiality of both the phone and its videos and photographs, with the latter particularly conveyed through a sequence in which Hank prints an enlarged still and runs his thumb over it, highlighting simultaneously the tangibility of the image and the significance of what is later revealed to be a child's dead body in the street. Chare further proposes that the film's "episodic" remediations of the video diary form a valuable corrective to the unassimilable "glut of images . . . [that] overwhelmed any capacity of spectators to filter them or to engage critically with specific representations," which he defines as the characteristic feature of television news coverage of the Iraq War. Specifically, he locates this possibility of critical contextualization in the remediated video diaries' fragmentation, noting that instances in which the image freezes "'open a space for thinking' by 'inviting reflection on what surrounds them.'"[37] Although this fragmentation is essential to the film's mystery/investigation structure, I would suggest that the close readings of the diary content that the film invites are rather a consequence of cinematically narrativizing them in this way, especially in contrast to the way that such videos would appear to the YouTube viewer. Though it remains unclear whether the videos unspool chronologically (according to their time codes), their presentation within *Elah* outlines a clear arc from a buoyant optimism to an increasingly desensitized nihilism, and ultimately sadism. This trajectory can be productively situated in relation to actual YouTube videos from Iraq, as outlined by Christian Christensen's article "Uploading Dissonance: *YouTube* and the US Occupation of Iraq," which encompasses the full range of the medium from amateur atrocity footage to the official/propagandistic output of the MNFIRAQ ("Multi-National Force—Iraq") channel.[38] I will also examine the further ways in which Haggis juxtaposes the diaries with remediated television news excerpts from the Iraq War, and with the parallel, present-tense investigation of Mike's death, for the allusive links that are thereby created regarding the state of the nation and the blurring of military and civilian realms.

The first video depicts Mike and his unit casually throwing a football before a raucous audience of Iraqi children, with Mike charitably offering the children their "first time" playing with a "real American football." This innocuous content clearly echoes what Christensen terms the "good deeds" genre among the MNFIRAQ videos, particularly "Troops Give Gifts to Iraqi Children," designed to "create the impression that the US military has a good rapport with Iraqi civilians."[39] However, in this case the video ends with Mike berating the children as they steal the ball and run away, presaging the diaries' subsequent darker turn. As befits the film's investigative structure, then, the videos begin by presenting the public face of the Iraq War, with just a sparing hint at the frustration and anger soon to be unleashed. This tone is also echoed in the fragments of television news remediated during the opening section of the film, which capture a distinctly optimistic post-invasion period characterized by Bush's proclamations that "freedom is on the march, and we are safer because of it," or "because we have done the hard work, we are entering the season of hope."

The second video, heavily marred by glitchy transitions that leap from day to night, and across discontinuous scenes, begins with a literal window on the escalating destruction in Iraq, showing an iconographic urban roadside littered with exploded vehicles. It abruptly cuts to a low-angle on Mike driving in a convoy, distressed by something in the road ahead. As the passengers fearfully bark orders for him to "speed up," there follows a distinctly audible thump as the vehicle fails to avoid the collision. This is by far the most ambiguous of the diary entries, and the as-yet-unsolved mystery at its core drives Hank's continued investigation. It is subsequently reframed as the central crisis which irrevocably alters Mike's character, when in a later interview a soldier from his unit reveals that they ran over a child.

The remaining diary installments are unabashedly graphic in their violent content, diverging starkly from the "sanitized" and superficially "victimless" violence that Christensen identifies in the MNFIRAQ videos. They begin to segue instead into the realm of "unofficial," amateur footage which Christensen describes as frequently "disturbing" not only in terms of their content, but also for the directorial pleasure evinced, such as "British Troops Beating Young Iraqis on Camera," in which the soldier filming the incident "can be heard laughing violently and encouraging his fellow troops . . . even mak[ing] moaning noises suggesting a pleasure that borders on the sexual."[40] A diary sequence in which Mike's unit clears a bombed-out building, for instance, shows Mike voyeuristically scanning a charred corpse, noting with dispassionate wonder how the clothes remained untouched, and finally, callously, placing a fireball sticker on the head of the victim. This scene immediately follows the discovery of Mike's burned body, in an explicit parallel apparently intended to convey how such violence cannot be constrained to the realm of war and inevitably permeates the soldiers' civilian behavior. The final diary sequence represents Mike's ultimate descent into sadism as, gleefully encouraged by his unit, he asks a hooded captive "where it hurts" and proceeds to stick his fingers into the open wound, thus earning his "Doc" sobriquet.

The latter videos are juxtaposed with remediations of television news which evince a clear undermining of Bush's earlier declarations of victory through a shift to counterinsurgency rhetoric (particularly with reference to Fallujah), thus allusively mapping Mike's moral and psychological deterioration onto the wider contextual degeneration from the ostensibly successful invasion to the escalating chaos in occupied Iraq. The climax of this theme is a didactic final sequence in which Hank hoists an inverted US flag as an "international distress signal." The final unveiling of Mike's evolution into "Doc" is also paralleled by the conclusion of the investigation into his death, with Penning's confession providing a further frame through which to read the diaries. A sense of the two characters' equivalence is sketched through Penning's observation that the "Doc" scenario was "pretty funny" and simply Mike's "way to cope," and further reinforced by his claim that "on another night it would have been Mike with the knife and me in the field." The murder is narrated passively, as if acting on uncontrollable instinct, through the line "I look down and I'm stabbing him." More than a simple avoidance of moral responsibility, this hints at the notion of military "desubjectification" highlighted in Patricia Pisters's reading of the film, linking these "recurring flashbacks, undeletable memories," to what she describes as a "state of desubjectification necessary in combat," which may later manifest as symptoms of PTSD since it is "not a simple on/off switch but has lasting, de-realising consequences on the mind."[41] This is implicitly framed as the source of further incidents of domestic violence among the community of returning soldiers. The sense that the violence cannot be constrained to the war zone also has significant ethical implications regarding the viewing of the later diary videos, subverting the sadistic pleasure taken in the pain of the Other by ultimately turning it back upon the initial perpetrator.

The theme of spectatorship is further developed through the film's distinctive rendering of the way Hank engages with his son's video diaries, which clearly evince a concern with the idea of transsubjective memory. In a few cases, this scenario is very straightforwardly represented with Hank, in his hotel room at night, receiving an email and opening the next video file. Yet Haggis soon begins to elide this preface to the videos, cutting rather abruptly into full-frame remediations of the diary, and immediately following them with a shot of Hank waking in the morning, as if to suggest that they are slipping into the more imaginative realm of fantasy or nightmare. This lingering aura of fantasy reaches its climactic fulfilment in a remarkable sequence in which Hank imaginatively reconstructs the incident in which Mike's convoy ran over the child. A part of this sequence is composed of the ambiguous video diary footage that Hank has already seen, yet in this fluid reconstruction, the diary material is supplemented by a series of diegetically unmotivated camera angles, and further augmented by cutaways to Hank sitting at the wheel of his car to clarify the internal status of the sequence.

As such, *Elah* seems to posit the diaries as enacting a mediatized form of the transmission of memory, which in this case transcends the military realm to enter the civilian. A comparison with *Stop-Loss* is again quite illuminating in this regard. Although Kimberley Peirce's film similarly associates the diaries with traumatic memory and PTSD, in what Garrett Stewart perceptively terms "flashback as digital playback," these effects are circumscribed to the network of military personnel who were actually present at the original scene. In *Elah,* however, the digital transmission of trauma is enacted across the military-civilian divide (albeit via a veteran of Vietnam), radically eliding the necessity of an embodied witnessing of the original event. This implies the complicity of even the civilian viewer in the sadistic spectacle of the video diaries, collapsing the "us and them" distance inherent in viewing war footage through the intimacy and imaginative interactivity of digital connectivity, as further elaborated by Stewart's reading of the film: "You don't have to have been there. You only have to be willing to envision it, to internalise the optic record as your own inherited flashback. . . . The whiplash exchange between then and now, us and them, is the immediate political charge of this climactic montage. Digital surveillance via optical data mining, here on a one-to-one basis, breaking as it does with the system of suture, has brought the trauma into focus from another space and time."[42]

One might even compare this model of spectatorial subjectivity with the experience of the drone operator. There remains, of course, a clear distinction in moral culpability as defined by the difference between this imaginative, spectatorial interactivity and the actual, lethal effects of the drone operator's weaponized interactivity. Nonetheless, the notion of digital connectivity as instantiating a peculiarly intimate form of viewing at a distance, akin to a kind of virtual presence, does unite the subjective experience of the drone operator with the model of spectatorial subjectivity established by *Elah.*

War cinema of this era can thus be credited with dispelling the notion of digital technologies as fundamentally virtualizing or distancing. Rather than enacting an erasure of the body in its departure to a virtual realm of algorithmic targeting, digital mediation is shown in this group of films as broadly consistent with the immediacy of the war film's embodied aesthetic legacy, offering new ways of remotely imaging war in unparalleled intimacy and detail. This radically ruptures any insulated sense of an American identity forged in relation to digitally mediated killing, leaving in its place a legacy marked predominantly by intimate and traumatic new visibilities and a sense of collective or networked complicity.

NOTES

1. Robert Eberwein, *The Hollywood War Film* (Chichester, UK: Wiley-Blackwell, 2010), 134.
2. These "guidelines" are drawn from Barker's analysis of the production context of the (un-

released) film *No True Glory,* an adaptation of the memoirs of a Marine who served in Iraq. See Martin Baker, *A "Toxic Genre": The Iraq War Films* (London: Pluto Press, 2011).

3. Barker, *A "Toxic Genre,"* 33.

4. Roger Stahl, *Militainment, Inc.: War, Media, and Popular Culture* (Abingdon, UK: Routledge, 2010), 3; Patricia Pisters, "Logistics of Perception 2.0: Multiple Screen Aesthetics in Iraq War Films," *Film Philosophy* 14, no. 1 (2010): 236.

5. Slavoj Žižek, "Green Berets with a Human Face," *London Review of Books,* online blog.

6. Patricia Aufderheide, "Your, My Country: How Films About the Iraq War Construct Publics," *Framework* 48, no. 2 (2007): 61.

7. See, for instance, Robert Burgoyne's claim that *The Hurt Locker* "presents an implicit critique of the distance—moral and physical—of remote targeting and weaponry" by showing the "reality of war as embodied activity." Robert Burgoyne, "Embodiment in the War Film: *Paradise Now* and *The Hurt Locker," Journal of War and Cultural Studies* 5, no. 1 (2012): 12.

8. See Amy Taubin, "Hard Wired," *Film Comment,* May–June 2009.

9. Taubin, "Hard Wired."

10. Burgoyne, "Embodiment in the War Film," 13.

11. Steven Shaviro, "Kathryn Bigelow," *The Pinocchio Theory* (blog), March 2010; Shaviro, "A Brief Remark on *Zero Dark Thirty," The Pinocchio Theory* (blog), January 2013.

12. Burgoyne, "Embodiment in the War Film," 12.

13. Specifically, Sanborn and Eldridge ponder detonating the ordnance that the unit is assigned to dispose of before James can retreat to a safe distance. The term "fragging" derives more generally from the Vietnam-era practice of soldiers killing their own officers with hand grenades.

14. This sequence has been the source of some confusion among viewers and critics. Robert Burgoyne, for instance, assumes that the body-bomb is Beckham's corpse, and neglects to discuss his reappearance. However, given the evident paranoia displayed by James from this point onward in the film, and the comparative clarity of identifying Beckham in his subsequent reappearance in contrast to the distorted, bloodied corpse, I believe this reading has a greater justification. The commentary by Kathryn Bigelow and Mark Boal on the US Summit Entertainment DVD release confirms that this was the authorial intention. See Burgoyne, "Embodiment in the War Film," 16.

15. See Chris Hedges, *War Is a Force That Gives Us Meaning* (New York: PublicAffairs, 2002).

16. Žižek, "Green Berets."

17. See Guy Westwell, *War Cinema: Hollywood on the Front Lines* (London: Wallflower, 2006), 64.

18. Žižek, "Green Berets."

19. Medea Benjamin, *Drone Warfare: Killing by Remote Control* (London: Verso, 2013), 62, 131.

20. See Akbar Ahmed and Lawrence Wilkerson, "Dealing remote-control death, the US has lost its moral compass," *The Guardian,* May 4, 2013.

21. I am aware that this discussion of PTSD among drone pilots could be misconstrued as advocating a misguided empathy for the drone operator at the expense of his/her victims, and it not my intention at all to minimize the suffering of civilians (or even combatants) in the countries (primarily Pakistan, Afghanistan, Yemen, Somalia, and Syria) forced to endure this illegal and unethical bombardment. Yet, in the context of cinematic representations, I maintain that a questioning of our spectatorial and ethical subject positions (relative to the diegetically constructed subjectivity of the drone operator) is valid and perhaps even necessary if we are to take seriously

cinema's role in shaping public understanding of the ways in which warfare is transformed by the advent of such technologies.

22. See Derek Gregory, "From a View to a Kill: Drones and Late Modern War," *Theory, Culture and Society* 28, nos. 7–8 (December 2011); Derek Gregory, "Lines of Descent" in *From Above: War, Violence and Verticality,* ed. Peter Adey, Mark Whitehead, Alison J. Williams (London: C. Hurst & Co., 2013); Caroline Holmqvist, "Undoing War: War Ontologies and the Materiality of Drone Warfare," *Millennium—Journal of International Studies* 41, no. 3 (June 2013); Allison Williams, "Enabling persistent presence? Performing the embodied geopolitics of the Unmanned Aerial Vehicle assemblage," *Political Geography* 30 (2011).

23. Gregory, "From a View to a Kill," 193.

24. Gregory, "Lines of Descent," 62.

25. Holmqvist, "Undoing War," 541, 545, 542 (emphasis in original).

26. Williams, "Enabling persistent presence," 385.

27. Garrett Stewart, *Closed Circuits: Screening Narrative Surveillance* (Chicago: University of Chicago Press, 2015), 173.

28. Stewart, *Closed Circuits,* 34.

29. Gregory, "From a View to a Kill," 196.

30. This effect is mirrored by a sequence in Robert Greenwald's documentary *UnManned: America's Drone Wars* (2013). In the absence of any actual drone footage, Greenwald's dramatic recreation begins with an aerial shot of the Waziristan landscape, then begins the transition to a "drone" aesthetic by bleaching all color from the shot, overlaying the landscape with operational gridlines, and eventually destabilizing the image itself with the embellishment of digital static. In a similar manner to *Body of Lies,* this fetishistic exaggeration of the drone interface seems to ascribe a deeply sinister, almost otherworldly ontology to it, one that is equally alienated and detached from the main body of the film's diegesis.

31. Stewart, *Closed Circuits,* 177. Stewart's account of "fabrication" here refers to a narrative thread in which the CIA creates a fake terrorist cell (replete with digital traces), which claims responsibility for a staged bombing of a Turkish air base in order to draw out the real terrorist, the egoistic and competitive Al-Saleem.

32. Stewart, *Closed Circuits,* 173.

33. Gregory, "Lines of Descent," 62.

34. Williams, "Enabling Persistent," 381, 387.

35. Hellfire missiles are the principal munition with which Predator drones are armed and are used for so-called precision strikes of targeted individuals.

36. Nicholas Chare, "Warring Pixels: Cultural Memory, Digital Testimony, and the Conflict in Iraq," *Convergence* 15.3 (2009): 334.

37. Chare, "Warring Pixels," 335, 342.

38. See Christian Christensen, "Uploading dissonance: *YouTube* and the US occupation of Iraq," *Media, War and Conflict* 1, no. 2 (August 2008).

39. Christensen, "Uploading Dissonance," 166.

40. Christensen, "Uploading Dissonance," 163–65, 168.

41. Pisters, "Logistics of Perception," 245–46.

42. Stewart, *Closed Circuits,* 179, 182.

CONTRIBUTORS

Essayists have been asked to choose which character from a film featured in his or her respective essay they would sit next to on a transatlantic flight.

Jessica M. Chapman is a professor of history at Williams College. She is currently working on an international history of Kenyan running. She would love to spend a transatlantic flight chatting with Gen. Jack D. Ripper (*Dr. Strangelove*) because it would be great to hear him expound upon his conspiracy theories, knowing that he was unarmed.

Liz Clarke teaches film studies at Brock University. Her book, *The American Girl Goes to War: Women and National Identity in US Film, 1908–1918*, is under contract. She would most like to sit next to Diana (*Wonder Woman*) to hear stories about life with the Amazon warriors.

Calvin Fagan completed a PhD in film studies at Queen Mary, University of London, in 2017, focusing on digital technologies and modes of subjectivity in contemporary war cinema. Other publications include "Hypermediacy, Embodiment and Spectatorship in Brian De Palma's *Redacted*" for *Screening the Tortured Body: The Cinema as Scaffold*. There are no characters in any of the War on Terror films that he would want anywhere near his flight.

Andrew R. Graybill directs the Clements Center for Southwest Studies at Southern Methodist University. With Ari Kelman, he is writing a book about the Indian Wars for the American West as part of the "Very Short Introductions" series for Oxford University Press. He would ask Capt. Joe Blocker (from *Hostiles*) just when he decided to board that train at the end.

Richard N. Grippaldi teaches American military history at Rutgers University in New Brunswick, New Jersey. His non-film interests include officership and enlisted service in the Jacksonian army. Given the chance to talk to Peggy Carter (*Captain America*), he would ask whether she fell in love with a super-hero, or a GI.

Kylie A. Hulbert teaches at Hampden-Sydney College. A historian of early America, her book project exploring the experiences and legacy of privateers during the American Revolution is under advance contract. Hulbert would sit next to John Adams (*1776*) on a transatlantic flight, despite his claim of being "obnoxious and disliked." The conversation could always turn toward his "dear-est friend," Abigail.

Matthew Christopher Hulbert teaches American history at Hampden-Sydney College in Virginia. He is the author or editor of three books, including *The Ghosts of Guerrilla Memory: How Civil War Bushwhackers Became Gunslingers in the American West* (2016), which won the 2017 Wiley-Silver Book Prize. He would choose to sit beside Tom Dobb (*Revolution*)—because Dobb couldn't possibly be worse in person than he was in the film!

Brian Matthew Jordan teaches Civil War history at Sam Houston State University in Huntsville, Texas. His next book is *Enduring Civil War: Life, Death, and Survival in a Union Regiment* (2021). He would sit next to Newton Knight (*Free State of Jones*), another rebel from rebeldom.

David Kieran is assistant professor of history at Washington and Jefferson College. His most recent book is *Signature Wounds: The Untold Story of the Military's Mental Health Crisis* (2019), and he would happily sit next to Sam McKenzie (*Hold Back the Night*), provided he's finally willing to crack into that bottle of single malt.

Meredith H. Lair is an associate professor of history at George Mason University, where she teaches courses on war and American society. She is the author of *Armed with Abundance: Consumerism and Soldiering in the Vietnam War*. The character she would choose to sit next to is Elias (*Platoon*), because he would let her have the armrest.

Andrew C. McKevitt is an associate professor of history at Louisiana Tech University. He is the author of *Consuming Japan* (2017) and is currently writing a book about the intersections of US gun violence and foreign relations. He would be curious to hear Lieutenant Aldo Raine's (*Inglorious Basterds*) thoughts on fascism in the twenty-first century.

Jason Phillips teaches nineteenth-century American history at West Virginia University. His most recent book is *Looming Civil War: How Nineteenth-Century Americans Imagined the Future* (2018). He would sit beside Dr. King Schultz (*Django Unchained*), because he's a brilliant conversationalist and, at five foot, seven inches, no competitor for elbow or leg room.

Matthew E. Stanley is associate professor of history at Albany State University. He is the author of *The Loyal West: Civil War and Reunion in Middle America* (2017). He would choose to sit next to Colonel Kurtz (*Apocalypse Now*) because he's lived all over the Ohio River Valley but never once heard of a "gardenia plantation."

James Hill "Trae" Welborn III of Georgia College and State University studies the emotional dimensions of virtue, vice, and the role of violence in shaping these concepts during the American Civil War era. His book *Dueling Cultures: Manly Virtue, Vice, and Violence in the Civil War Era-South* is under contract. A flight with William B. Travis (*The Alamo*) would promise an ideal case study along these lines.

INDEX

15:17 to Paris, The, (2018), 261

1776 (1972), 7; Benjamin Franklin, 32–33, 42; Broadway roots, 24, 30, 33; George Washington, 31–32, 33, 44; John Adams, 24, 31, 42; John Dickinson, 31–33; representation of Founders, 23, 32–33, 41

49th Parallel (1941), 1

7th Heaven (1927), 148

84 Charlie Mopic (1989), 284

Act of Valor (2012), 264

Adefarasin, Remi, 166

Alamo, The (1960), 106, 107, 136; characterization of Mexicans, 116; Davy Crockett, 115; manhood, 112–113; post-WWII values, 108; slavery, 108, 114

Alamo, The (2004), 9, 106, 107, 136; conflicted lead characters, 110; Davy Crockett, 111; Jim Bowie, 111; manhood, 113, 114; nonwhite characters, 114–115, 116–118; slavery, 108, 114; War on Terror connections, 110, 114; William Travis, 111–112

Aldrich, Robert, 96

All Quiet on the Western Front (1930), 9, 155; antiwar message, 151–153, 157; causes of WWI, 151; German protagonists, 144–145

Amistad (1997), 47; abolitionism, 55, 56, 61; academic background, 48; black resistance vs. white savior themes, 54–55, 58; legal proceedings, 58, 60; Middle Passage, 57–58

Anderson, John, 90

Androsky, Carole, 92

Apocalypse Now (1979), 13, 239, 250, 257

Apostle, The (1997), 55

Arlen, Richard, 149

Armadillo (2010), 264

Ayer, David, 175

Baer, Robert, 274

Baldwin, Adam, 39

Bale, Christian, 97

Balsam, Martin, 93

Band of Brothers (2001), 166, 169, 171

Barry, John, 94

Basilone, John, 170

Bataan (1943), 161

Battle Cry of Peace, The (1915), 146

Battle for Haditha (2007), 284

Battle Hymn (1936), 51–52, 63n9

Battle of San Pietro, The, (1945), 165

Beach, Adam, 97

Beguiled, The (2017), 8; anti-Lost Cause, 78; antipatriarchal, 77–78; contemporary meanings, 73; gendered meaning of Civil War, 78–79. *See also* Coppola, Sofia

Behind the Door (1919), 147

Bellini, Cal, 93

Benet, Stephen Vincent, 50

Bergen, Candice, 89

Bernard, Raymond, 9

Bernthal, Jon, 176

Best Years of Our Lives, The (1946), 1

Better 'Ole, The (1926), 148

Big Parade, The (1925), 147, 156

Bigelow, Kathryn, 262, 266–272

Billy Lynn's Long Halftime Walk (2016), 261

Birth of a Nation, The (1915), 65

Birth of a Nation, The (2016), 8, 47, 58; black agency, 54–55, 60; connection to American Revolution, 61; distortion of identity, 59; gothic setting, 64n22; negative impact of slavery on southern whites, 55; religious war against slavery, 55, 56; revolt triggered by protection of women, 57. *See also* Parker, Nate

Blackboard Jungle (1955), 54

Blackton, J. Stuart, 146

Body of Lies (2008), 263, 280; CIA thriller genre, 274; drone war, 276, 278, 281, 284, 291n30; global narrative, 275, 279; ground-level presentation, 279; as war film, 275

Bond, Ward, 1

Born on the Fourth of July (1989), 10, 13, 247; anti-"Good War," 241–242; civilian deaths, 242; depiction of antiwar Leftists, 243–244, 258; friendly fire, 242–243; idealized home front, 242, 243; Vietnam as calamity, 237, 245, 257; white cast, 256

Bow, Clara, 149

Broken Arrow (1950), 94

Bronson, Charles, 1

Broussard, Stephen, 172

Brown, John, 8, 47; abolitionism, 49, 53, 58, 59, 60; box office appeal, 54, 55; family, 53; Harpers Ferry raid, 126; historical representations, 50–51; insanity, 48, 49–50; political icon, 51–52; pop culture, 50–51; religion, 55. *See also Battle Hymn* (1936)

Burt the Turtle, 10

Bush, George H. W., 206

Bush, George W., 164, 231n1, 286, 287

Camp, David, 97

Captain America: The First Avenger (2011), 9; comic-book movie genre, 162, 163; pop culture background, 161; transition to superhero protagonists, 171–172

Carey, Harry, Jr., 88

Casablanca (1942), 1

Casualties of War (1989), 247, 259n11; American infighting, 250; combat realism, 248;

depictions of Vietnamese, 251, 255. *See also* Stone, Oliver

Chandrasekaran, Rajiv, 265

Cheyenne Autumn (1964), 94

Cimino, Michael, 238, 257, 259n3

Civil War, The (1990), 67

Civilization (1915), 145–146,

"civilianization," 1, 18n2

Clooney, George, 225, 226–227, 279

Cochrane, Rory, 97

Condon, Richard, 221

Connors, Chuck, 191

Cooper, Chris, 40

Cooper, Gary, 57, 60, 150, 153, 155, 157

Cooper, Scott, 96

Copperhead (2013), 73, 81n19

Coppola, Francis Ford, 257

Coppola, Sofia, 77–79

Corporal Kate (1928), 148

Costner, Kevin, 94, 101n16

Cullum, John, 31

Curry, John Steuart, 51

Curtiz, Michael, 53, 63n11

Da Silva, Howard, 31

Dances With Wolves (1990), 8; interactions with Indians, 95, 96; within western genre, 94, 100. *See also* Costner, Kevin

Daves, Delmer, 94

David, Thayer, 93

Dead Presidents (1995): African American perspective, 245, 246, 256; graphic violence, 245; Vietnam as calamity, 237, 257

Deer Hunter, The (1978), 10, 257; controversies, 240–241; as genre foundation, 237; graphic violence, 238–239; home front, 237, 244, 245; postwar issues, 239–240; Vietnam as calamity, 237

de Havilland, Olivia, 85, 86

DeMille, Cecil B., 84

Dengler, Dieter, 252, 259n14

Destination Tokyo (1943), 1

Devil's Disciple, The (1959): American masculinity, 24, 28, 29–30, 367; criticism of,

23; depictions of British, 28–29; theatrical roots, 28. *See also* "Rambo turn"

DiCaprio, Leonardo, 56

Dixon, Thomas, 48

Django Unchained (2012), 8, 47, 55; Americanism, 61; disguised identities, 59–60; gender biases, 64n23; Gothic setting, 64n22; religion, 63n16; resistance to slavery, 54–55, 56–57; as western, 58

Douglas, Kirk, 28,

Douglass, Gordon, 218

Dr. Strangelove (1964), 10; Cold War satire, 216, 223; critique of Soviet-American rivalry, 224–225; MAD, 223–224

Duell, William, 31

Duggan, Simon, 181

Dunaway, Faye, 93

Dwan, Alan, 191

Dye, Dale, 166

Eastwood, Clint: as director, 10, 83n30, 94, 191, 201, 212n43, 26; as Walt Kowalski, 204, 207, 209. See also *Gran Torino* (2008)

Edelman, Randy, 70

Emmerich, Roland, 37

Enemy of the State (1998), 275

Evans, Chris, 171

Fall of the Nation (1916), 146

Farrow, John, 96

Fletcher, Dexter, 34

Flynn, Errol, 52, 60, 85

Fonda, Henry, 1, 167

Ford, John, 1, 51, 87, 89, 94

Foreign Correspondent (1940), 1

Fort Apache (1948), 7, 87

Foster, Ben, 98

Foxx, Jamie, 57, 60

Frankenheimer, John, 221

Free State of Jones (2016), 8; anti-Lost Cause, 77; Civil War memory in modern America, 73, 77; historical reception, 75–76. *See also* Ross, Gary

Freeman, Morgan, 56, 61

Full Metal Jacket (1987), 13, 247, 250

Fury (2014), 9; aesthetic, 175–176; extraordinary protagonists, 163, 175, 176–177; Wardaddy, 178–179

Gable, Clark, 1

Gadot, Gal, 142

Gaghan, Stephen, 274, 278

Garfield, Andrew, 182–183

George, Chief Dan, 92

Gettysburg (1993), 69–71

Gibson, Mel, 27, 34, 41, 163, 181, 182–183

Glory (1989), 74; black-white relations, 69; combat scenes, 67. *See also* Zwick, Edward

Gods and Generals (2003), 79

Gold, Mike, 51, 63n10

Gone with the Wind (1939), 52, 85

Good Kill (2014), 11, 263; remote warfare, 279, 280, 283, 284

Good Morning, Vietnam (1987), 247

Good Night and Good Luck (2005), 10; anti-McCarthyism, 227; domestic Cold War, 217, 225

Gorman, Patrick, 70

Gran Torino (2008), 10, 191, 204, 207; as war film, 200–201; Cold War context, 202, 210; Hmong representations, 203, 207, 209, 213n64

Green Berets, The (1968), 12, 234, 253,

Green Zone (2010), 265

Greene, Graham, 95, 101n17

Greengrass, Paul, 265

Grey Zone, The (2001), 3

Griffith, D. W., 65–66, 84

Gunner Palace (2004), 264

Hacksaw Ridge (2016), 9, 181; superhero protagonist, 163, 182–183, 184–185

Hamburger Hill (1987), 13; depictions of Vietnamese, 251–252; home front issues, 249–250; racial issues, 248–249; realism, 248, 256; Vietnam genre, 247

Hanks, Tom, 163; Spielberg collaborations, 165–167, 169–171, 174, 175, 177, 179, 180–183, 185. *See also* Spielberg, Steven

Hanoi Hilton, The, (1987), 12

Harriet (2019), 62

Hearts and Minds (1974), 17

Heston, Charlton, 1

Hillenbrand, Lauren, 184

Hines, Patrick, 32

Hobsbawm, Eric, 4, 14

Hoffman, Dustin, 92

Hold Back the Night (1956), 10, 200, 201; forgotten war, 191, 192, 210; pointlessness of conflict, 193, 194, 196

Hollywood Ten, The, 217, 218, 227, 228. *See also* Trumbo, Dalton

Hombre (1967), 94

Hondo (1953), 96

Hoover, J. Edgar, 217–218, 220–221, 227

Hopkins, Anthony, 61

Hopper, Hedda, 10, 230

Horsechief, Xavier, 99

Hostiles (2017), 8, 96; western genre, 100, 102n19; white-Indian relations, 96–98

Hounsou, Djimon, 56

Howard, Ken, 31

HUAC, 15, 214, 216, 217, 225, 226, 227, 228, 230. *See also* McCarthy, Joseph

Hudson, Hugh, 33, 34, 35, 37

Hughes, Albert, 245, 257

Hughes, Allen, 245, 257

Hunter, Jeffrey, 49, 60, 88

Hurt Locker, The (2008), 262, 265; depiction of war, 268, 271, 272, 290n7; drone war, 263, 268, 269, 281

Huston, Danny, 157

Huston, John, 165

Hutton, Robert, 206

Iles, John, 181, 188n60

In the Valley of Elah (2007), 11, 263, 265; digital trauma, 289; video diary, 284–285, 286, 288. *See also* Post-Traumatic Stress Disorder (PTSD)

Inglourious Basterds (2009), 163, 174–175; as comic-book film, 173; reception, 173–174

Isaacs, Jason, 38

I Was a Communist for the FBI (1951), 10; depictions of communists, 215, 218, 219–220; government propaganda, 218; religion, 220–221

Jarhead (2005), 263

Joan the Woman (1916), 146

Johnny Got His Gun (1971), 9, 13, 155–156

Johnston, Joe, 171, 172

Jolie, Angelina, 163, 183–184

Jordan, Dorothy, 88

Junger, Sebastian, 265

Karyo, Tcheky, 40

Kennedy, Arthur, 85

King, Aja Naomi, 57

Kubrick, Stanley, 223–225

LaBeouf, Shia, 176

Lancaster, Burt, 28

Lang, Stephen, 70, 97

Leckie, Robert, 170

Ledger, Heath, 37

Lee, Ang, 261

Lee, Spike, 163, 179

LeMay, Alan, 87

Lemmons, Kasi, 62

Leslie, Joan, 154

Lincoln (2012), 73–74; dark war, 77; historical responses, 75

Lincoln, Abraham, 51–52, 68, 100n1, 126, 233

Little Bighorn, 85–86, 92–93, 100n2

Little Big Man (1970), 8, 95; criticism of US military, 93–94; depictions of Indians, 92–93; influence on western genre, 100; reception, 92, 102n17

Little Dieter Needs to Fly (1997), 252

Lone Survivor (2013), 264

Longest Day, The (1962), 7, 9, 179, 180

Lost Battalion, The (1918), 147

Madden, Donald, 31

Malcolm, Robyn, 98

Malcolm X (1992), 55

Mallon, Brian, 70

Manchurian Candidate, The (1962), 10, 216, 221; satire of McCarthyism, 222–223. *See also* McCarthy, Joseph

Marvin, Lee, 1

M.A.S.H. (1970), 7, 13, 190

Massey, Raymond, 50–51

Masters of the Air, 171

Matrix, The (1999), 162

Maxwell, Ronald F.: *Copperhead*, 81n19; *Gettysburg*, 69, 70, 71; *Gods and Generals*, 79

McCarthy, Joseph, 10, 216, 225, 231; anticommunist paranoia, 214, 215; feud with Edward R. Murrow, 217, 225–226, 227; satire of, 218, 222–223. *See also* Trumbo, Dalton

McConaughey, Matthew, 61

McCullough, David, 22, 67

McDaniel, Hattie, 85

McDonnell, Mary, 95

Miles, Vera, 87

Milota, Eric, 35

Miracle at St. Anna, The (2008): focus on black soldiers, 179–181; supernatural heroes, 163

Missing in Action (1984), 4, 250

Mission, The (1986), 55

Moreno, Ruben, 92

Mr. Death (1999), 3

Mulligan, Richard, 93

Murphy, Audie, 160–161, 169

Murrow, Edward R., 217, 225–226, 230

My Lai Massacre, 91, 101n12, 101n14, 235–236,

Nation's Peril, The (1915), 146

Nelson, Ralph, 89

"New Hollywood," 36, 46n8

Newman, Paul, 1

Nichols, Andrew, 279

Norris, Chuck, 4

Obama, Barack, 189–190, 211n4

O'Brien, Tim, 257

Office of Strategic Services, 1

Old California (1910), 84

Olivier, Laurence, 28

Owen, Sid, 34

Pabst, G. W., 9

Pacific, The (2010), 166, 169–170

Pacino, Al, 24, 33

Paget, Debra, 49

Parker, Nate, 55, 61

Passion of the Christ, The (2006), 55, 183

Pastorelli, Robert, 95

Patria (1917), 146

Patriot, The (2000), 7, 37–38; American identity, 24, 40–41, 43–44; George Washington, 44; reception, 44. *See also* "Rambo turn"

Patton (1970), 7, 16

Payne, John, 191, 195

Pearce, Guy, 265

Pearl of the Army (1916), 146

Peña, Michael, 177

Penn, Arthur, 92

Pierce, Tony, 96

Pike, Rosamund, 96

Pine, Chris, 142, 157

Pitt, Brad, 173

Platoon (1986), 166, 257; American infighting, 250; depictions of Vietnamese, 251, 255; graphic violence, 101n11; racial issues, 248; realism, 245, 247–248; reception, 247

Plemons, Jesse, 98

Pork Chop Hill (1959), 190, 196; forgotten GIs, 194, 195; reception, 192

Post-Traumatic Stress Disorder (PTSD), 98, 102n19, 246, 262, 289, 290n21

Predator (1987), 4

Prine, Andrew, 70

Quinn, Anthony, 86

Rambo: First Blood (1982), 250

Rambo: First Blood, Part II (1985), 250

"Rambo turn," 35, 36, 38, 41, 46n8

Ravenous (1990), 9; distorted memory, 106, 136; violent manhood, 125; western setting, 120

Reagan, Ronald, 128, 134, 203–4, 205, 206, 207

Rebel Without a Cause (1955), 54

Redacted (2007), 284

Redford, Robert, 81n19, 198

Renner, Jeremy, 265

Rescue Dawn (2006), 234, 247, 252–253

Restrepo (2010), 264–265

Revolution (1985), 7, 33; frontiersman-turned-rebel, 24, 36, 41 45n6; George Washington, 44; reception, 43. *See also* "Rambo turn"

Ridge, Stanley, 85

Rio Grande (1950), 87

Rippy, Leon, 39

Ritt, Martin, 94

Rivero, Jorge, 90

Roach, Jay, 227

Robe, The (1953), 55

Rocketeer, The (1991), 172

Rogers, Charles, 149

Romero, George A., 4

Ross, Gary, 75, 78

Sahara (1943), 1

Sand Creek Massacre, 91, 101n12

Sanders, Denis, 197

Sanders, George, 25

Sands of Iwo Jima (1949), 167

Santa Fe Trail (1940), 47, 51; antiradical message, 52, 60, 63n11; depictions of John Brown, 49, 50, 53, 54, 55, 59; western setting, 58

Saving Private Ryan (1998), 142, 165; effect on WWII cinema, 3, 161, 162, 166; "Good War" narrative, 9, 184; representation of GIs, 163, 175, 180. *See also* Spielberg, Steven

Scarlet Coat, The (1955), 7, 25–26; American identity, 24, 30, 36; depictions of enemy, 34

Schindler's List (1993), 3

Schwarzenegger, Arnold, 4, 45n6

Scott, George C., 4, 16

Scott, Ridley, 275

Searchers, The (1956), 8, 87–88, 89; racial politics, 99; referenced by other films, 96, 99

Sergeant York (1941), 143, 153, 154, 155, 174

Seven Angry Men (1955), 47; antiabolition, 49, 55; civil rights movement, 54; John Brown, 50, 53, 59–60; western setting, 58

Shaara, Michael, 69

Shaw, George Bernard, 28

She Wore a Yellow Ribbon (1949), 7, 87, 102n19

Sheen, Charlie, 101n11

Sheen, Martin, 246

Shutter Island (2010), 3

Siegel, Don, 77

Simms, William Gilmore, 104–5, 135, 138n4, 138n5

Skarsgård, Stellan, 56

Sledge, Eugene, 170

Smith, Gregory, 38

Soldier Blue (1970), 8; revisionist western, 92, 94, 100; Sand Creek influence, 91; source of title, 90; Vietnam influence, 89, 101n11

Sophie's Choice (1982), 3

Souls at Sea (1937), 8, 47, 57–60

Spartacus (1960), 64n19

Spielberg, Steven: *Band of Brothers*, 166, 169; collaboration with Hanks, 174–175, 177, 179, 180, 181–183, 185; *Lincoln*, 73–74, 75; *Masters of the Air*, 170–171; *The Pacific*, 166, 169, 170; *Saving Private Ryan*, 161–164, 165–166, 167–168, 176, 184. *See also* Hanks, Tom

Squaw Man (1914), 84

Stagecoach (1939), 87

Stallings, Laurence, 147

Stallone, Sylvester, 4, 45n6

Steel Helmet (1951), 7, 192, 197, 199, 206

Stevens, George, 186n18

Stewart, Jimmy, 1

Stone, Oliver, 166, 241, 244, 247

Stop-Loss (2008), 11, 263, 284–285, 288

Storeby, Robert, 259n12

Strauss, Peter, 89, 90

Stuart, Patrick, 70
Studi, Wes, 95, 97
Sullivans, The (1944), 1
Sutherland, Donald, 34
Syriana (2005), 11, 284; CIA thriller genre, 263, 280; drone war, 274–276, 278, 279, 281. See also *Body of Lies* (2008)

Tarantino, Quentin, 163, 173–174
Ten Commandments, The (1956), 55
Thewlis, David, 142, 157
They Died with Their Boots On (1941), 8, 85–87, 95, 99
Thin Red Line, The (1964), 185n7
Thin Red Line, The (1998), 185n7
Thornton, Billy Bob, 107
Three Kings (1999), 263
Tigerland (2000), 10, 235–237, 250
To Hell and Back (1955), 160, 185n2
Triumph of the Spirit (1989), 3
Truman, Harry, 196; Korean War, 197, 205, 208–9; Truman Doctrine, 214
Trumbo (2015), 10, 217, 225, 227, 229
Trumbo, Dalton, 217, 229, 230. See also *Trumbo* (2015)
Turner, Frederick Jackson, 9, 135–136

Ulzana's Raid (1972), 96
Unbeliever, The (1917), 147
Unbroken (2014), 9, 163, 183–184
Unforgiven (1992), 94, 201

Vance, Kevin, 175
Vasyanov, Roman, 176

Walken, Christopher, 239, 240
Walker (1987), 9, 106, 129–134, 136

Walker, William, 127, 128
Walsh, Raoul, 85, 86, 87
Waltz, Christoph, 57, 60, 173
War Hunt (1961), 10, 191, 197–198, 200, 210
Warner, Jack L., 30
Warren, Robert Penn, 8, 66
Washington, Kerry, 57
Wayne, John, 1, 49, 107, 167, 179. *See also* Ford, John
We Were Soldiers (2002), 10, 250; American home front, 255–256; depictions of Vietnamese, 254–255; pro-intervention, 234, 253, 257–257; racism, 256
Werner, Herzog, 252
Westerman, Floyd Red Crow, 96
What Price Glory? (1926), 147
When Trumpets Fade (1998), 185n7
Wild Bunch, The (1969), 13
Wild One, The, (1953), 54
Wilde, Cornel, 25
Wilding, Michael, 25
Wilkinson, Tom, 39
Williams, Daniel, 24, 30
Wilson, Scott, 98
Wilson, Woodrow, 11
Wings (1927), 149–150
Winter Soldier (1972), 17
Womanhood, The Glory of the Nation (1917), 146
Wonder Woman (2017), 9; antiwar message, 142, 143, 158; WWI in popular memory, 144–145, 156–158
Wood, Natalie, 87

Zamperini, Louis, 183–184
Zero Dark Thirty (2012), 268
Zwick, Edward, 67, 74, 81n9

CPSIA information can be obtained
at www.ICGtesting.com
Printed in the USA
LVHW042336161020
669015LV00004B/246